DUEL

=OF=

EAGLES

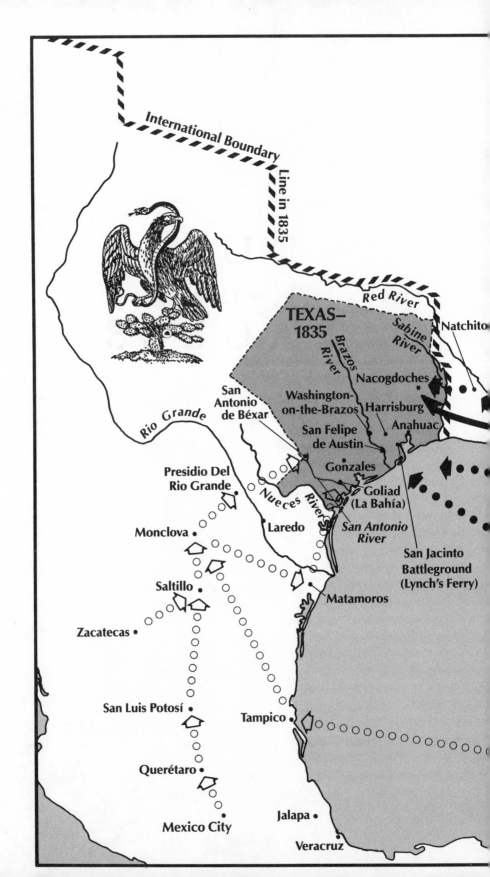

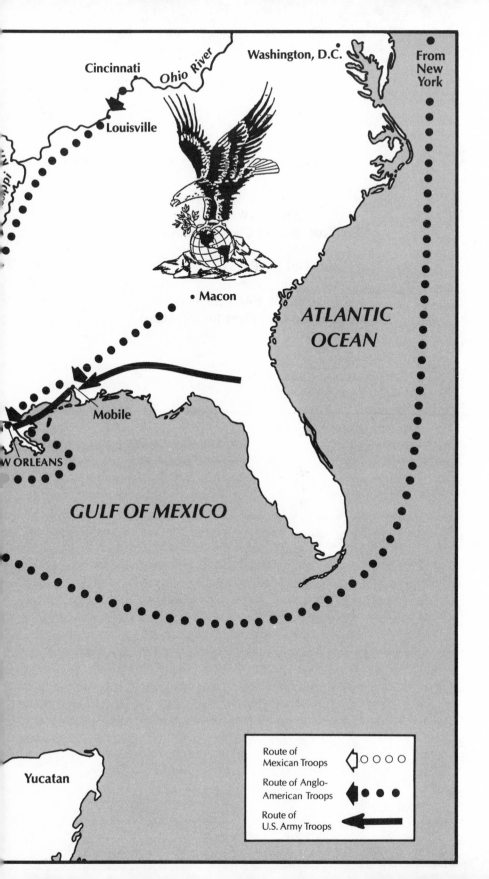

Cincinnati

Ohio River

Washington, D.C.

From
New
York

Louisville

• Macon

**ATLANTIC
OCEAN**

Mobile

W ORLEANS

GULF OF MEXICO

Yucatan

	Route of Mexican Troops	◁ ○ ○ ○ ○
	Route of Anglo-American Troops	◀ ● ● ●
	Route of U.S. Army Troops	⬅

Books by Jeff Long

OUTLAW
The True Story of Claude Dallas

ANGELS OF LIGHT

DUEL OF EAGLES
The Mexican and U.S. Fight for the Alamo

D U E L
=OF=
E A G L E S

The Mexican and U.S. Fight
for the Alamo

JEFF LONG

Quill
William Morrow
New York

to Helena and Andy,
who brought me in upon the
bright Texas gulf

The Library of Congress has cataloged the hardcover as follows:

Long, Jeff.
    Duel of eagles : the Mexican and U.S. fight for the Alamo / Jeff
Long.
        p.   c.m.
    ISBN 0-688-10967-5 (pbk.)
    1. Alamo (San Antonio, Texas)—Siege, 1836. I. Title.
F390.L63   1990
976.4′03—dc20   90-30787
                                                                 CIP

Printed in the United States of America

First Quill Edition

1   2   3   4   5   6   7   8   9   10

BOOK DESIGN BY WILLIAM McCARTHY

MAPS DESIGN BY ARLENE GOLDBERG

ACKNOWLEDGMENTS

Old books become "foxed" when their printing ink spreads in a stain throughout the book, discoloring pages, sometimes obliterating text. Similarly, myths of the Alamo and Texas Revolution have foxed American history. I wish to acknowledge the following people for helping interpret many of the stains and blotches during my passage across the ink of Texas history.

I am indebted to two people in particular at the Daughters of the Republic of Texas History Research Library: librarian and archivist Bernice Strong, and former director Sharon R. Crutchfield. Each guided me to material and issues with the patience of archangels. Thanks also to Martha Utterback, who magically located pictures that seemed lost, and to the rest of the staff for ideas, translation, and hospitality: Jeannette Phinney, Sandra Hood, Charline Pavliska, Diane Gonzalez, and Leticia Nava. I owe several ideas to Steve Beck, curator at the Alamo Museum, and to Edwin Gearke, the assistant curator. The curator emeritus at the Alamo Museum, Charles J. Long, provided both information and inspiration. Waynne Cox and Anne A. Fox of the Center for Archaeological Research, University of Texas at San Antonio, shared insights about their digs at the Alamo; Dora Guerra, the special collections librarian at UTSA, led me to several obscure works; Gilberto M. Hinojosa and Felix D. Almarez, Jr., both of the UTSA history department, helped set my compass. William E. Green, the former capitol historian of the state of Texas, spent hours going over material and discussing theories. John Leal, the Bexar County archivist, graciously shared some of his many finds. Thanks also to Jean Carefoot at the Texas State Library in Austin; Wanda Turnley and Anne H. Jordan at the Nettie Lee Benson Latin American Collection at UT/Austin; John Slate at the Eugene C. Barker Texas Center at UT/Austin; Diane Cooke at the National Portrait Gallery; Cynthia Ott at the Archives of American Art; and Tom Shelton and Diane Bruce at the UT Institute of Texan Cultures.

Special thanks to John Collins, director at the Presidio La Bahía, for his ideas and encouragement. And Kevin R. Young, then chief of interpretation at the Presidio La Bahía, now with IMAX Theater in San Antonio, made 1836 Texas come alive. It was he, and Norman Power, a Goliad rancher and living-history buff, who first taught me how to shoot a flintlock: May my words be more accurate than my bullets. Robert Thonhoff, a teacher and military historian, devoted hours explaining the little-appreciated 1812–1813 filibuster expedition. John Davis was especially selfless in sharing his unpublished day-by-day account of the Texas Revolution, along with providing Texas maps pinpointing battle sites and army routes. Tom Jones, a Victoria artist, literally injected color into past events. Adolph Herrera, whose roots in San Antonio go two centuries deep, gave me invaluable context on a tour of his family cemetery and property. Mary Ann Noonan Guerra, who has written numerous works on San Antonio history, was especially helpful in leading me to research material. No sooner did I ask about the Bowie knife, than historical researcher Etna Scott shared her extensive work on it.

In Mexico City, Enrique Franco Torrijos, his wife, Barbara, and daughter, Stephanie, accelerated my quest with their keen perspectives and warm hospitality. Captain Paulino Candelaria Serafin, chief of security, went to great lengths to accommodate my inquiries at the Chapultepec Museum of History in Mexico City. Guadalupe Aguirre Perez Ortega and Luis Cuervo Martinez and their splendid family threw open their home in Jalapa and spent days guiding me through the birthplace of Santa Anna. And throughout, Leslie Brown provided patient and invaluable interpretation of both the language and the culture. Christie Northrup too provided translation and insights.

To Barbara, who was there, I am grateful.

For their candlelight in the dark days, thanks to authors David Roberts and Pamela Novotny, and to Jenny Shaddock and Diane Botticelli. I also owe thanks to my research assistants, Gretchen Sibley and Jeanne Bessette. I owe special gratitude to David Hays, who tutored me on Jacksonian America, encouraged heresy, and overloaded my bibliography throughout these last four years. Similarly, Elizabeth Crook challenged my ideas with true Texas fire and selflessly shared research for her own books on Houston and the revolution. Finally, I wish to thank Gwen Edelman, my agent, for her persistence and support, Jim Landis for his faith, and Jeanne Bernkopf, my editor, who saved me from silence.

DUEL
=OF=
EAGLES

$$= 1 =$$

T HE EARTH FROZE tight that People's day—March 4, 1829—when Old Hickory took the oath. Frontiersmen, slaves, war vets, office seekers and just plain curious folk, maybe twenty thousand of them, gathered in the cold mist wrapping the Capitol building to watch Andrew Jackson take power. The assemblage reminded one Washingtonian of "the inundation of northern barbarians into Rome. . . . Strange faces filled every public place, and every face seemed to bear defiance on its brow."[1]

Jackson spoke the inaugural words, each syllable a burst of frost. He kissed the Bible. And then they mobbed him.

He mounted a horse and rode the Avenue. They followed. Through doors and windows, they invaded the White House, thronging the rooms. Noses got bloodied, crystal glasses and china broke. Clodhoppers with muddy boots stood on chairs each worth more than a 120-acre plot of public land. Frightened by the chaos, congressmen fled with their wives through the windows. "I never saw such a mixture," groused one Supreme Court justice. "The reign of King Mob seemed triumphant."[2]

They were a generation of muscular Christians, children of a religious movement called the Second Great Awakening. Their parents had trained them to be aggressive and self-assured and righteous, to push hard and take plenty. When the rosy-cheeked congressman from Tennessee, David Crockett, pronounced, "Be sure you are right, then Go Ahead," they heard more than a motto. They heard a prayer. "Go Ahead" made spiritual sense to them. In a single lifetime their nation of thirteen colonies had swallowed the best part of an entire continent. Before that lifetime was out, they would Go Ahead and bear-hug it all, coast to coast.[3]

All through the shapeless West, particularly in that part now called the South, poor people like Crockett were spreading out, dubbing each new territory the final Eden. But no sooner did one region fill than the next beckoned. Kentucky fever cooled in time for Ohio fever, which gave

11

way to Missouri fever and Illinois fever. And then the greatest heat of all swept the South—Texas fever.[4]

Texas seemed to open her prehistoric arms to Old Hickory, to Crockett, Houston, Bowie, and tens of thousands of other Anglo-Americans. She seemed to await their powerful hand, their radical voice, their ax and gun. To await their seed . . . cotton and otherwise. Texas offered herself as the last Eden, a soil in need of industry, an idea in need of consecration. The Americans visualized Texas in their own image.

The strange thing was not how they needed Texas but how—they testified—Texas needed them. Even those who had never seen the land, and most had not, were transfixed by the thought of saving it. To those pilgrims who actually crossed the Sabine River or sailed down from New Orleans, Texas sang like a flock of naked angels. Texas bewitched and seduced them.

Texas had the fabric of a dream, here dangerous, there the stuff of ecstasy. As they followed the old semivisible Spanish trace grandly labeled El Camino Real (the Royal Highway), one day they thirsted, the next they swam. At night they had to prepare against centipedes, rattlesnakes, and quarter-pound tarantulas. Deadly Comanches monopolized the prairies. There were blue northers, those cold instantaneous storms from the far north. In the bayous mosquitoes swarmed so thick that tunnels could be punched through their clouds. Gadflies bathed the horses with sheaths of blood. Mysterious swamp gases knocked whole parties of men flat with malaria or ague.

But there were the Texas treasures. Almost before their eyes, meadows ignited with bluebonnets, Indian paintbrush, other wildflowers, and butterflies. Along the rivers wild turkeys crowded the oaks. Bears fattened on fallen acorns and longhorns feasted on mesquite pods. Flocks of pelicans or ducks or wild geese blotted out the sun. At night, not even the smallest star could hide in the crystalline sky. River frogs as large as a man's head gave rhythm to the constellations, and fireflies competed with the meteor showers. The song of screech owls wove with those of wolves and coyotes. A thousand white cranes would suddenly erupt into the moonlight. Immense buffalo herds stampeded upon the infinite distances. Prairie grass grew saddle high, and in eastern Texas the dense canebrake towered two and three times the height of a man on horseback.

Best of all, along the river bottoms lay rich black soil that grew cotton in abundance. The Gulf crescent presented itself to the Southern eye as a whole new paradise, a cotton empire waiting to happen.

There was only one problem. Texas did not belong to the United States.

But an Anglo-Saxon, most especially a Scotch-Irish frontiersman, knew that you didn't just settle a frontier. You lusted for it and preyed upon it. You cracked its bones and sucked its marrow. You fed upon it or it fed upon you. For these tall, bony-faced Americans with butcher knives in their belts and muzzle-loaders in their hands, frontiering was more than an art. It was confirmation that they had a place on this earth.[5]

And in 1829 the fiercest Anglo-Saxon of them all became president.

"I was born for a storm," the warrior-king Andrew Jackson warned at the beginning of his term. "Calm does not suit me."

The Old Chieftain . . . Old Hero . . . Old Hickory was an odd savior, a gaunt wand of a superman. At sixty-one years of age, six feet one inch and 140 pounds, his emaciated body read like a warning against Southern frontier life. His blue eyes were sunk into his long head, and his skin was tinged yellow with the jaundice of semitropical fevers and illnesses. Malaria wracked him, along with chronic amoebic dysentery, cramps, and the ache of old war wounds. He had carried a saber scar across his head and one arm from age thirteen, when he had refused to clean a British officer's boots. Two lead balls rode in his thin body, one near his heart, from a duelist Jackson had coldly gutshot over a racetrack dispute. Even simple respiration was a battle for him. He suffered extreme shortness of breath, and when he coughed he bled from pleuritis and pulmonary abscesses. His legs swelled, for his kidneys were failing. He had headaches and distorted vision. Worse than his ailments was his cure, for he treated himself orally with liberal doses of lead.[6]

From childhood on, Jackson had been fighting the world. Now he combatted his own body. The force of will—nothing else—kept him standing. Andrew Jackson was a self-educated lawyer—the type they called a cornstalk lawyer, or quack—who didn't bother to study law, history, or political science and probably never finished reading more than one secular book in his lifetime. John Quincy Adams called him "a barbarian who could not write a sentence of grammar and hardly could spell his own name."[7]

The old Tennesseean was an utterly self-confident man, a fatalist brimming with Old Testament wrath and righteousness, a fighter of violent temper. Besides killing one man in a duel, the ambitious general had threatened to kill two others for daring to call him ambitious, and he had made noises about killing a secretary of war for linking him, accurately, with Aaron Burr. Near death, Jackson disarmingly confessed that his two greatest regrets were that he hadn't hanged one political foe and shot another. Not surprisingly, Jackson's political saint was the military dictator Napoleon Bonaparte.[8]

The General inspired enormous loyalty, but also enormous loathing. Among his most devoted enemies stood fellow Tennesseean David Crockett. In casting off Jackson's patronage, which had helped install him in political office in the first place, Congressman Crockett denounced Old Hickory as "the driver at my heels, with his whip in hand, commanding me to ge-ho-haw, just at his pleasure."[9] Jackson did not try to placate his enemies, especially not traitors like Crockett. Instead he simply terminated them.

Jackson's political machine carefully fostered the image that the General was an honest commoner. In fact he was a wealthy plantation owner who had gained his wealth through corrupt land dealings and owned over two hundred slaves by the time of his death.[10] He was a machine boss who built power through an elaborate spoils system. As a military chieftain, he was willful and predatory. He was the ultimate Go Ahead man. And he wanted Texas.

Despite contemporary history, treaties and maps to the contrary, Jackson persisted in thinking Texas belonged to the United States, not to Mexico. He was not the first President to believe it, just the most fervent. What slender ambiguity lay beneath Jackson's conviction had come with the Louisiana Purchase (which Napoleon had grandly announced from his bathtub[11]). French negotiators had coyly hinted that the Louisiana territory extended all the way west to the Rio Grande, a claim without any title whatsoever. The United States had informally accepted that either the Sabine River or the nearby Nueces River marked the division between American real estate and Mexico. But some Americans went right on insisting that the Purchase was meant to include all the watersheds of the Mississippi River, and that that automatically incorporated all land west to the Rio Grande. Not a single map showed rivers in present-day Texas—least of all the Rio Grande—draining into the Mississippi. But men like Jackson were crusaders, and crusaders fed on faith, not facts.

As early as 1805 the U.S. government (under Jefferson) had contemplated an invasion of Texas, which at the time belonged to Spain. The plan had called for sending the U.S. Army across the Sabine River, dismantling Spanish fortifications, spiking their cannons, and scattering their troops. Following this naked act of war, the army would then retire across the U.S. border. The aggression was meant to knock some sense into Spain and force a quick cession of Texas. Working behind the scenes, Secretary of State Madison had killed this muscular approach. But for American expansionists, some of whom declared the United States had a "natural" border extending to the Isthmus of Panama, the Mexico border issue remained hazy.

Thirteen years later, in 1818, Gen. Andrew Jackson invaded another Spanish holding, East Florida. Claiming hot pursuit of renegade Indians, he crossed the border, seized Pensacola, Gadsden, and St. Marks, destroyed their artillery, and executed two British subjects. Though he was severely criticized for provoking war with both Spain and Britain, and for acting without direct authority from Washington, D.C., Jackson nevertheless had supporters in the Monroe administration. The most influential was Secretary of State John Adams, who justified the invasion as "a defensive act of hostility." Fortunately, Spain backed down. She recognized that both East and West Florida were beyond her control; moreover, she needed her troops to fight revolutionaries in Mexico. In 1819, the Floridas were ceded to the United States in exchange for formal U.S. recognition that Texas was part of Mexico.

The admission that Texas belonged to Mexico outraged Jackson. Like many Westerners, he believed to the bottom of his soul that Spain had duped the United States into giving away Texas.[12] And as he put it later, the way to obtain a territory was first to occupy it, then treat for it, the way the United States had after his invasion of East Florida.[13]

Before there was a Republic of Mexico, long before there was a United States, these continental neighbors had thought they knew all there was to know about each other. For hundreds of years, the sole contact between Mexicans and Anglo-Saxons had been English pirate raids along the coast and upon the high seas. Every Hispanic came to understand that Anglo-Saxons were godless marauders who plundered quiet villages, desecrated Catholic images, raped pious women, and were born with an unholy appetite for gold and silver. Mothers warned naughty children to behave or the Drake (Sir Francis) would get them. Nineteenth-century reports of buckskinned Americans padding silently west through the woods were instantly familiar.

"Nothing disconcerts [the frontiersman]," reported a Mexican newspaper, "he is always astute and agile: his penetrating observation never deserts him, and he is quick to seize any occurrence and turn it to his advantage. Moreover, he has a thousand ways of acquiring his necessities. He will even use his teeth to round off another bullet from an already spent rifle shell."[14]

Likewise, Americans instinctively reached for their own precolonial folklore in dealing with Hispanics. They believed every Spaniard was a dusky, lazy, priest-ridden, bloodthirsty idolater, an archetype left over from Europe's imperial wars. The conquistadores were demons who raped, mutilated, tortured, and killed millions of innocent natives.[15] When Henry Clay spoke in Congress of "despotism and slaves" and "the vile domination of the inquisition and superstition," every American knew he meant their satanic southern neighbor.[16]

For 250 years Hispanics and Anglo-Saxons had been living upon the North American land mass, never mixing, rarely meeting.[17] For the most part, Americans and Mexicans viewed each other the way their feuding ancestors had, with hatred and fear and jealousy.

No sooner did Spain gain clear title to Texas on February 21, 1821, than she forfeited it. Exactly two days after the ratifications, Mexican revolutionaries declared independence, and Spain soon lost not only Texas, but all of Mexico.

Next to cotton, revolution was one of the United States' chief exports in the early 1800s. The revolutions rocking Spanish America drew heart from both the French and American precedents. Even though the United States refused to aid Mexico's bloody, decade-long independence struggle (in which a tenth of her population, mostly young men, died), Mexicans joyously embraced the principles of democracy, modeling major portions of their government after the American system and borrowing language from the Declaration of Independence and Constitution for their own. In the beginning, anyway, they felt an almost spiritual affinity for their northern brother. So it was with great pride and friendship that Mexico anticipated her first diplomatic contact with the United States.

President Adams's first choice for minister to Mexico was none other than Andrew Jackson. But Jackson, recognizing that this was Adams's way of removing him from the political picture, declined. In his place went one of the era's most talented men, Joel Poinsett.

When Poinsett presented his credentials to the Mexican government, the chambers were, in his words, "crowded to suffocation with senators, members of Congress and respectable inhabitants of the city."[18] They welcomed him as a brother in freedom. He treated them like a pack of stunted children.

To Mexico's shock, Poinsett announced the United States wished to purchase Texas for an unspectacular $1 million.[19] But Mexico was learning to appreciate her northeastern territory in a way Spain never had. In 1828 a group of scientists, led by a remarkable renaissance-soldier named General Manuel de Mier y Terán, traversed Texas overland from one side to the other and discovered a lost land with a disinherited people.

From the moment they crossed the Rio Grande ("like a silver thread upon the immense plain," said one member) and passed through a collapsed forest of petrified trees, Texas—or *Tejas*: the word was a native term for "friend" or "ally"[20]—enunciated to them a poetry all its own. The profusion of animals and vegetation startled the Mexican scientists and their guardian soldiers. Even more startling was the very idea of profusion.

Ever since the cross-and-sword *entradas* of sixteenth-century Spaniards had returned without gold, Texas had been anchored in the Mexican imagination as a netherworld, a place at once amorphous, gigantic, and barbarian. North to them had always been the direction of abandon and nomadic violence. North lay wolves, Comanches, and the cold. During revolutions, clever Mexican generals found it useful to tell enemy troops that their commanders meant to ship them north to Texas, which invariably caused desertions. Colonies of convicts, roped and chained together, had been planted in this limbo province, but no sooner were their experimental towns denoted on maps than they became nonexistent, their inhabitants having defected back toward the center.[21] As late as 1833 Mexicans in neighboring Coahuila bleakly dismissed Texas as "out of the world."[22]

In all Texas, only three towns had managed to emerge from the Spanish colonial era: San Antonio de Béxar, La Bahía del Espiritu Santo (renamed Goliad in 1829), and Nacogdoches, each more decadent and wracked with poverty than the others.[23] By the late 1820s, the Hispanic settlements in Texas struck Mexican visitors like Terán's expedition as disgraceful, impoverished, and lazy.

"The character of the people is care-free," observed José Sánchez, one of Terán's urbane expeditionaries. "They are enthusiastic dancers, very fond of luxury, and the worst punishment that can be inflicted on them is work."[24] Even their Spanish language was in ruins, filled with anachronisms and ear-bending slang.

More than simple exploration had brought Terán north. He had come to analyze the extent and influence of Mexico's continental neighbor upon the Tejano settlements. Terán's small expedition found unimagined fertility and untapped resources, a cornucopia potentially able to dump its harvest into Mexico's tight belly. But they also found Anglo-Saxons.

Their first view of the norteamericanos was of skulls and bones scattered upon the sandy flats south of San Antonio. These were the remains of hundreds of *filibusteros* (from the Dutch *vrijbuiter* or "freebooter") who had fallen before the Spanish sword in 1813. The farther east Terán's crew rode, the more Anglo-Americans they encountered. Some thirty-five hundred Americans had established themselves as legitimate colonists under the patronage of the Mexican government, roughly the same number of Hispanos living in Texas. At least as many more Americans had come and simply squatted. All told, Terán estimated with some alarm, the Anglo-Americans outnumbered the Hispanos ten to one.[25] In fact the ratio was closer to two to one, but even that was far beyond expectations.[26]

"How strange are these people from the North!" José Sánchez decided as he rode among them. In San Felipe de Austin, the crown jewel of colonist-agent Stephen Austin's land grant, Téran's expedition found fifty wooden houses scattered along the Brazos River in "an irregular and desultory manner." Of the two hundred people living there, only ten were Hispanic. Two stores provided the populace with essentials. One sold only rice, flour, lard and cheap cloth, the other only whiskey, rum, sugar, and coffee. Sánchez considered the settlement more pitiful than exotic. "The Americans from the North . . . eat only salted meat, bread made by themselves out of corn meal, coffee, and home-made cheeses. To these the greater part of those who live in the village add strong liquor, for they are in general, in my opinion, lazy people of vicious character."[27]

Very few Anglo-Americans had migrated to "Spanish country" in western Texas, where most of the Tejano population clustered, for it promised no cotton or sugar crops and Anglo-Americans tended to stay out. But wherever the two cultures intersected, Hispanics quickly developed an image of Anglo-Americans as smugglers, livestock rustlers, and land thieves.[28]

Beware the Anglo-American, one prominent Tejano warned. They follow no laws "unless they find it convenient to what they want anyway." The *ayuntamiento* (town council) of La Bahía agreed. "Let us be honest with ourselves, Sir, the foreign *empresarios* [Anglo-American land agents] are nothing more than money-changing speculators caring for their own well being and hesitating not in their unbecoming methods."[29]

Drunkenness, poverty, and indolence aside, what most shocked Terán and his refined Catholic scientists about the Anglo-American settlers was their appalling use of chattel slaves, their arrogance, and their immorality. In Nacogdoches they were horrified to find a number of the Anglo-Americans selling their wives for sex to Mexican troops stationed in the local presidio (fort).[30] In that grotesque mongrel of a town, with its Anglo-American log cabins vigorously crowding Spanish architecture in ruins, Terán found the Mexican presence in embarrassing decay. The few ignorant, poor, and grasping Hispanics still remaining had been thoroughly corrupted by Anglo-American ways. Terán gamely conceded that if his sole contact were with these debased Nacogdocheans, he too might look down on Mexicans.

Over the next few years, various Mexican bureaucrats and soldiers weighed and evaluated their holdings in faraway Texas.[31] One and all, they pronounced that Texas was golden. This made Mexico all the more unwilling to sell Texas. But the North Americans seemed deaf to the word no.

Following his inauguration, Andrew Jackson raised the offer for Texas to $5 million, cautioning his minister Poinsett that Mexico should accept in order to prevent "collisions" with the United States. Poinsett was a polished cosmopolitan, fluent in five languages, trained in medicine, military science, and law, a former congressman, and an amateur botanist (he discovered the beautiful red plant, the poinsettia). But he was also a Southerner, a racist and patrician, filled with the Anglo-Saxon mission. He recommended a patronizing tone when trying to reason with Mexicans. "One must not judge the Spaniards of the New World too severely," he said. "When the Revolution caught them, they were still living in the sixteenth century. . . . I have often found that idea useful in my dealings. I have often asked myself what sixteenth-century men would have done in such circumstances and what they would have thought. Answering those questions enabled me with near certainty to foretell the future."[32]

Besides antagonizing Mexicans with his real estate bids, Poinsett began dabbling in local politics. Masonic lodges of the Scottish rite had been serving better-heeled Mexican conservatives as a political machine for years. Poinsett took it upon himself to establish rival lodges for Mexican liberals.[33]

After enduring four years of Poinsett's odd, byzantine capers, the Mexicans finally demanded his recall. As if to punish Mexico, Jackson replaced Poinsett with a South Carolinian (until 1844 every U.S. minister to Mexico was from a Southern state) named Anthony Butler. In addition to being twice as brazen as Poinsett, Butler was hopelessly vulgar, corrupt, and insolent. Sam Houston would later call him a swindler, cheat, and gambler. Butler's task now was somehow to relieve Mexico of Texas, but he managed to sabotage his mission even before arriving in Mexico City. All the way across Texas, Butler bragged about his upcoming offer of $5 million for Texas. The Mexican newspaper *El Sol* obligingly printed his remarks, and so even before Butler could present his offer, the Mexican government quashed it, calling it a disgrace.[34] The U.S. minister to Mexico promptly began looking for officials to bribe.

Jackson was clever enough to distance himself from the sordid business of corrupting a foreign government. When his minister detailed some of his handiwork, Jackson replied with a curious letter that condemned bribery, but also expressed "astonishment . . . astonishment that you would entrust such a letter, without being in cypher, to the mail. . . ."[35] When the information became public, Jackson vilified Butler as a scamp and a liar. But Butler would go to his grave insisting that Jackson had authorized half a million dollars for the purpose of corrupting Mexican officials, of which two hundred thousand was earmarked for one Mexican in particular: General Santa Anna.[35]

Despairing at the Mexicans' reluctance to sell, Butler decided to prod them with a rebellion. He wrote two anonymous letters (signed "O.P.Q.") to Anglo-Americans in Texas, inciting them to revolt. Surely, he reckoned, the Mexicans would opt to sell the troubled region. However, his O.P.Q. letters were promptly handed over to Mexican authorities and he failed to revolutionize Texas.

Butler's end came abruptly, after he publicly insulted Mexico's secretary of war, José María Tornel, and threatened to whip or cane him upon next encounter. By Southern U.S. standards there was nothing extraordinary about his threatened mayhem.[36] But in Mexico, among the sensitive and refined elite, that kind of behavior held little attraction. As with the first U.S. minister, Mexico demanded the recall of this second minister.

But Jackson was not finished yet. He was playing for Texas at every level.

"I have but little doubt but there will be an insurrection in Texas . . ." he wrote in 1832. "A revolution is intended, and people are emigrating to that country with a view to this thing, and it will be attempted shortly."[37] Once Texas revolted, he added, the United States would need to immediately annex it to defend itself against border Indians. It had happened before in West Florida. It was destined to happen again.

For Jackson destiny was a wild horse. You broke it to your will or else you stayed out of its way. In those days before Mexican *vaqueros* had shown them the art of the lasso, frontier Southerners had a method of capturing wild horses called "creasing." It was blunt and simple. You simply drew a bead and shot a lead ball into the horse's neck. With luck and good placement, the creasing nicked the animal's spine and stunned it long enough to be roped. Bad shots fed the buzzards and crows.[38]

With Texas, Jackson shot destiny in the neck and hoped for the best. Twice he shot wide of the mark—once with Poinsett, once with Butler. He had another shot left, though, and he took quiet aim.

This final player went by different names: the Raven, Big Drunk, Governor, General, the Wanderer. He was an undisciplined, bright-eyed giant, practically a son of the sticklike President. Sam Houston would be Jackson's last wild bid for Texas.

=2=

HEY TOLD OF a horseman lost on the Texas prairies who ended up following his own tracks for days in a giant circle. Texas was crawling with similar men, circling in their own pasts without any firm direction. They were fringe dwellers who had lost their vision or never had any, Go Ahead men who just kept going. More and more Texas was filling with these shadowy men who had left behind them the peculiar obituary "GTT." Gone to Texas. Creditors, lawmen, wives—all found the ephemeral notation scrawled on doors, declared in letters, posted without flair. Clerks closed out unpaid loan accounts with the three letters.[1]

Among these refugees pouring into Texas were a hard core of utopians who called themselves the War Party. They fancied themselves rebels . . . even founding fathers of a new republic. But other settlers pictured them as grasping troublemakers and called them War Dogs, or worse, Craze-orians. In the beginning there was only a handful of them, mostly lawyers and speculators who understood that a "free" Texas would be a lucrative Texas, especially for them. Before they could trigger the profits, however, they needed to trigger a revolution, something explosive enough to nudge Texas out of the Mexican orbit.

With dirt under their fingernails, lice in their hair, they took the high ground of revolutionaries, stainless and sure of themselves, inviting martyrdom. They shouted liberty, shed blood, and risked chaos. They conspired with festooned eloquence and brute horse-slaughter slang, with the purity of heretics and the stink of ignorant, trigger-pulling white trash. They spoke like revolutionaries. They complained like revolutionaries. Like revolutionaries they cocked one boot upon the disputed soil.

There weren't many of these War Dogs, but they had an idea. They looked around them in that land owned by the exhausted progeny of conquistadores and saw in their fellow Anglo-American wanderers a whole new set of conquistadores. They saw their army.

Sam Houston was very nearly the last of them. Before him, men like William Travis and James Bowie, and lesser names like Patrick Jack, Mosely Baker, Robert "Three-Legged Willie" Williamson, and the Wharton brothers, had kicked the ribs of Texas. But Houston's coming illuminated their cause. He dreamed their dream of theft and he spoke their language of glory. He knitted his path with theirs and together they called their conspiracies destiny. Before it was all over he would ride a great white horse at the head of their army.

No one who ever saw Sam Houston forgot him. He guaranteed it. Standing two to four inches above six feet, he had shoulders the size of ox yokes and brilliant gray eyes. And he clothed himself in jaw-dropping fashions of his own genius, audacious combinations of everything from Indian and Mexican dress to Arab and European styles. Sometimes he swept about in a Turkish sultan's silk robe.[2] A Frenchman once spotted him in a velvet vest coat with gold embroidery worth twelve hundred francs.[3] In later years he delighted in sporting a Mexican sombrero and poncho, and he did not shy from strapping on a waist-trimming corset or girdle.[4]

Stumping for the governor's seat in 1828, he looked like Beau Brummel in a ruffled shirt, black satin vest, "shining" black trousers, silk socks, pumps with silver buckles, and a bell-crowned black beaver hat . . . to which he added a "gorgeous" Indian hunting shirt and beaded red sash.

The wife of Jefferson Davis (later the Confederate president) remembered that Houston "rejoiced in a catamount [wildcat] skin waistcoat; it was very long waisted, and his coat was left ostentatiously open to show it. Another waistcoat, which he alternated with the catamount, was of a glowing scarlet cloth."[5]

Sometimes he combed his hair forward upon his temples for the popular Caesarean or Napoleonic look, sometimes he slicked his hair with bear grease or powdered it "in a grotesque way of his own invention."[6] Once he dressed as George Washington and donned a wig. He wore rings on his fingers and gold, silver, and iron earrings.

"He acquired the bizarre taste in dress from the Indians with whom he lived for years," a French diplomat decided.[7] But even his adoptive Cherokees found Houston ludicrous and once created a "living" cartoon by painting a black slave in extravagant colors and seating him at Houston's place in the local council house.[8] When someone asked Andrew

Jackson about "this freak of Houston," the old man replied, "Thank God there is one man who was made by the Almighty and not by a tailor."[9]

Everything Houston did was larger than life. Men got a restrained "Howdy do" and a handshake. But women got to marvel at an overblown ritual that looked more like a mating dance. "When he met a lady," recalled Mrs. Jefferson Davis, "he took a step forward, then bowed very low, and in a deep voice said, 'Lady, I salute you.' It was an embarrassing kind of thing, and it was performed with the several motions of a fencing lesson."

He met pomposity with greater pomposity. Once he confronted a small Frenchman who fancied himself to resemble Napoleon and carried a chestful of honorary medals. Houston did not miss a beat. Sweeping away the Indian blanket he was wearing, he exposed his bare chest laced with old war scars. "Monsieur," he declared, thumping at his naked rib cage, "an humble republican soldier, who wears his decorations here, salutes you."[10]

When Congress tried Houston for beating a political foe with a hickory cane, he delivered freewheeling oratory about honor. He received not only acquittal, but a thunderous round of applause and a bouquet of flowers thrown by a woman in the galleries.[11] He survived scandals and war wounds that would have buried ordinary men, and he seemed to find reality every bit as peculiar and unreal as people found him.

Part of his teenage years were spent living with Cherokees, less to learn their ways than to protest his job as a village store clerk: "I preferred measuring deer tracks to tape."[12] There in the Cherokee forests he dedicated himself to memorizing Pope's translation of the *Iliad*, imbibing Indian lore, and frolicking with Indian girls.

Then, in 1813, he joined the army to fight Great Britain in the War of 1812. As the southern front developed, that meant fighting Creek Red Sticks (named for their symbolic crimson war club). It was a dirty war marked by atrocity, retaliation, and unrelenting hunger. One man who chronicled it most honestly was a twenty-seven-year-old squatter who participated in a massacre at the Creek village of Tallussahatchee, Alabama. His name was David Crockett.

In a chapter that would echo in the history of the West, several hundred frontier volunteers stormed the village filled with women, children, and warriors on November 3, 1813. "Most of them wanted us to take them prisoners," Crockett remembered with dark humor. "Their squaws all would run and take hold of any of us they could, and give themselves up. I saw seven squaws have hold of one man, which made me think of Scriptures. So I hollered out the Scriptures was fulfilling; that there was seven women holding to one man's coattail. But I believe it was a hunting-shirt all the time.''

Yelling, firing, killing, the avenging volunteers overwhelmed the village, at last trapping forty-six warriors in a log house. A lone Creek woman propped herself in a doorway, set her feet on a bow, drew an arrow, and neatly feathered one of the volunteers ("... the first man I ever saw killed with a bow and arrow"). Instantly, twenty musket balls were "blown through" the backwoods Amazon. With that the massacre began in earnest.

"We now shot them like dogs," said Crockett, whose grandparents had been killed by Creeks in 1777. The volunteers torched the log house filled with men. The heat grew intense. A wounded twelve-year-old Creek boy tried to crawl away and "the grease was stewing out of him."

Next day the volunteers scoured the smoking town, "hungry as wolves." The gruesome corpses "looked very horrible, for the burning had not entirely consumed them, but given them a terrible appearance, at least what remained of them." Beneath the torched cabin, they discovered a potato cellar. "We found a fine chance of potatoes in it, and hunger led us to eat them, though I had a little rather not, if I could have helped it, for the oil of the Indians we had burned up on the day before had run down on them, and they looked like they had been stewed with fat meat."[13]

Crockett got fed up with military life and returned home. He hired a substitute to finish his tour of duty and missed the closing battle of Horseshoe Bend a few months later.

But Houston was there, a twenty-one-year-old kamikaze in search of fame and glory. Sword fanning the air, he led a charge on foot and all alone vaulted across a Creek breastwork to capture the point. By the time his men could join him, Houston was reeling and bloody—but triumphant. A barbed arrow jutted from one thigh. Houston ordered an officer—at sword point—to yank it out. A few hours later General Jackson came riding by, paused by the wounded giant, and ordered Houston to stay out of further combat. Recognizing a rare opportunity, Houston promptly leapt into the most visible fighting he could find. Attempting to repeat his charge of the day before, he ran toward a final Creek position. Five yards from the breastwork, the Creeks opened up on him. Musket balls broke his right arm and shoulder and nearly killed him. His charge failed, and the Americans ended up burning the position out. But Jackson never forgot Houston's glorious moment.

After an extended and painful recuperation, which left him with a ghastly, suppurating wound for the rest of his life, Houston quit the army. He studied law for a few months, then set up practice in Nashville. Within a year he was elected district attorney. Two terms in Congress followed, and after that he gained the Tennessee governor's seat with Jackson's help. One of his first acts as governor was to marry a wealthy blonde and blue-eyed plantation belle named Eliza Allen in a picture-book wedding in the state mansion. Step by step, he assembled the profile of a future President.

Then the young lion threw it all away. Four months after the wedding, Eliza mysteriously fled to her parents' home. The event exploded into a major scandal. Some said Eliza had another lover. Others hinted that Houston had abused his teenage wife or that his unhealed war wound had repulsed her. An effigy of Houston was burned in the streets.

Houston spent a night burning private letters. Then, maintaining an obstinate and gallant silence about the scandal, Houston quit office. He hopped the next packet out.

"I was in an agony of despair and strongly tempted to leap overboard and end my worthless life," he wrote. "At that moment, however, an eagle swooped down near my head, and then, soaring aloft with wildest screams, was lost in the rays of the setting sun."

Throughout his adult life, Houston claimed the eagle was his true totem. In his memoirs eagles repeatedly appear to him at critical moments. Standing upon the steamer's deck, Houston watched the bird turn into sunlight. "I knew then," he said, "that a great destiny waited for me in the West."[14]

Houston exiled himself to liquor and his Cherokee family. Floating upriver on a flatboat, he chanced to meet up with James Bowie. The famed duelist had just returned from San Antonio de Béxar and was brimming with tales of potential fortune in Texas. There were lost Spanish gold mines and sloe-eyed señoritas in loose blouses. In Texas there was no law, just plenty of sanctuary out there for men wanting a fresh start. Above all, there was land, millions of acres of it. Some of it came in the form of river bottoms with prime cotton soil the color of chocolate. Some of it came timbered or flush with prairie grass. All of it was good for speculation. It was cheap, a tenth the cost of public lands in the United States (then selling at a minimum $1.25 per acre), and the Mexican government didn't grant it in the miserly 80-acre lots the United States did. They set a man right with up to a league (4,428 acres) and more at a time. All one had to do was become a Mexican.

Houston listened, and the idea seated in his well-pickled imagination. He trumpeted how he meant to seat himself as an emperor in Texas or deeper Mexico and be worth $2 million in two years.[15]

But Houston wasn't ready for real action. He had to cross into his dream time for a while. That was his way. He shook Bowie's hand good-bye and drifted on, taking refuge with his beloved Cherokees, jug in hand.

Over the next few years Houston sank into depression, disease, and serious alcoholism. He was not alone in his inebriation. Drunkenness was a national institution at this period. In 1830 the annual per capita consumption of pure alcohol was a staggering ten gallons.[16] Whiskey fueled every type of social event, from contract signings to quilting bees. One Kentucky politician stated that "the way to men's hearts is *down their throats.*" The U.S. surgeon general discouraged any recruiting or reenlistment that excluded alcoholics because the army might disintegrate.[17] In short, the nation was drunk on its feet.

Even so, Houston was conspicuous for his debauchery. The Indians gave him a new name, "Oo-tse-tee Ar-dee-tah-skee"—Big Drunk.[18] On top of his alcoholism, Houston also chewed opium, possibly a carryover from his painful recuperation from the Creek wars.

Somehow Houston made his way to Texas for a firsthand reconnaissance. As he entered San Antonio, he realized this was his destiny. There was an eagle overhead.

He stayed footloose for the next few years, residing on both sides of the international border, speculating in land, practicing a spot of law, and remaining, in one roommate's words, "of excellent heart but dissipated, eccentric, and vain." During visits east to Washington, he solicited money from the U.S. government, and when that failed, solicited the support of Texas-land speculation companies in New York, Baltimore, and Philadelphia. When that, too, produced no results, Houston prevailed upon Jackson, who gave him five hundred dollars and supplied him with official powers and a confidential mission to Texas under a U.S. passport.[19]

After a while Houston became a Mexican. He took the Mexican oath of citizenship, swore to abide by Mexican law, and promptly cheated the Mexican government to squeeze out a little extra land for himself. Houston took a married man's grant of one league of land in Stephen Austin's colony, then skipped over to David Burnet and Lorenzo de Zavala's colony and took an unmarried man's grant.[20]

Land was everything in Texas. Yet there was so much of it that people found it hard to take very seriously. One Anglo-American swapped a dog for thousands of acres. Even the Mexicans were cheating on land deals, especially the Coahuila y Tejas state legislature, and governor, which couldn't seem to dump huge tracts fast enough.[21] James Bowie landed the position of ''special land commissioner'' and in a single month (September 1835) signed away a staggering half million acres (outraging even Anglo-American colonists). Houston was hardly alone, then, when he dabbled in both land speculation and land fraud.

In December 1834, an Englishman named G. K. Featherstonhaugh passed through Washington, Arkansas, near the Texas border. He found the town thick with conspirators who offered ''the pretence of purchasing government lands, but whose real object was to encourage the settlers of Texas to throw off their allegiance to the Mexican government.''

Chief among the schemers was Jackson's protégé.

''General Houston was here,'' Featherstonhaugh said, ''leading a mysterious sort of life, shut up in a small tavern. . . . I had been in communication with too many persons of late, and had seen too much passing before my eyes, to be ignorant that this little place was the rendezvous where a much deeper game than faro or rouge-et-noir was playing.''[22]

Spawned in shadow, wary of the light, James Bowie was a similar creature. By nature crafty and acquisitive, he was a man who saw the world as his bastard slave.

Bowie was six when his parents moved from Georgia to Louisiana. One of his early memories was of his father being jailed after killing one of several squatters in a land dispute, and of his mother and an armed slave breaking their breadwinner free.[23] Bowie led a wild childhood, full of roping wild deer, trapping bear, breaking mustangs, even riding alligators. By the time he hit his majority, Bowie carried 180 pounds of meat on his six-foot frame. He was able with frontier weaponry, including firearms and the ubiquitous butcher knife, fearless, and he was full of the Go Ahead. One of the first places he went was Texas, joining a filibuster army under James Long, the American doctor who ''conquered'' a virtually barren Nacogdoches and was consequently routed, captured, and executed in Mexico City in 1822.

Brothers frequently formed teams to get a financial leg up on life. So it was with James, John, and Rezin Jr. The hard-charging Bowie brothers took as their role model a slightly older set of brothers, the entrepreneurial Laffites, Jean and Pierre.

In those days the Louisiana bays and backcountry swarmed with brutal smugglers, privateers, slave runners, and cutthroats in need of a bridge between their darkness and the legitimate world. They needed middlemen who could convert their illegitimate merchandise into money. Early on, the Laffite brothers learned to fence contraband and stolen goods. They excelled and soon parlayed their "agency" into a gang numbering four hundred or more men. Their smuggling and piracy kept New Orleans flush with cheap goods: The finest wines sold for a peso per gallon, Irish linen cloths for six dollars apiece.[24] Jean reveled in his romantic notoriety, mixing freely with New Orleans society. Following the Battle of New Orleans, he counted among his admirers Andrew Jackson and called his own the keys to the city.

Among the Laffites' clients between 1812 and 1819 were various waves of Anglo-American and assorted filibusters heading for doomed attempts to take Texas. The Laffites provided the filibusters with weapons, supplies, transportation, sanctuary, and fighting men.[25]

Around 1818 the Laffite crime syndicate discovered a fabulous new commodity: African slaves. For a decade the foreign slave trade had been outlawed in the United States. One could buy and sell Negroes, but only those Negroes already within the U.S. border. Prices rose, and businessmen like the Laffites soon recognized that one could turn a breathtaking profit by smuggling in Negroes from Africa or from transit stations like Cuba. The Laffites then required middlemen to turn their goods. The ambitious Bowie brothers obliged. They were in their early twenties, eager, physical, and quick to learn.

As the arrangement developed, the Laffites would sell the Bowies raw, half-dead African Negroes at a dollar per pound (the average unit weighed 140 pounds upon delivery). Then the Bowies would herd their caravan through the semitropical wetlands and forests of eastern Texas across the U.S. border into Louisiana. It was a long, brutal drive, demanding vigilance and strength. (James once lost thirty slaves to a mass escape, when they vanished across the Colorado River into deeper Mexico.[26])

Once across the border, the Bowies would promptly turn themselves in to the authorities. The punishment for slave running was confiscation of the slaves, which were then sold upon the auction block. The Bowies always bid highest on their own confiscated property, for their reward for turning a slave runner (themselves) in to the customs officer was half of the slaves' purchase price. That meant that no matter how much they bid, the Bowies only paid half the market price. Moreover, by buying back their own slaves, they received legal title to them. That freed them to turn around and immediately sell off these slaves on the legal market, fetching on average a thousand dollars per person. The brothers realized a small fortune—sixty-five thousand dollars—at this game before turning to other schemes.[27]

In 1828, at the age of thirty-two, James Bowie relocated to Texas. Instinctively drawn to the bigger money, he bypassed eastern Texas, where the majority of Anglo-Americans were settling, and chose San Antonio de Béxar for his next theater of operations. He rode into a town that looked, from a distance, "like a city of white marble."[28] Closer, the white marble turned to adobe and rubble rock walls coated with lime, and the feudal splendor diminished into tight straits. Far away from the world, San Antonio had a style and folk culture all its own. Time found its measure in the braiding of day and season, the blossoming of flowers, the weather patterns, and the elaborate calendar of saints' days. Up and down the river, ranchers raised cattle, and farms grew corn, beans, chiles, and sugarcane for sweet *piloncillas*.[29] With markets so far away in the Mexican interior, few bothered to raise agricultural surpluses, though some enterprising ranchers drove longhorns east to Louisiana and the American table. Except for the occasional Comanche raid, life was easy in San Antonio. Compared to the malarial wetlands of the American South, it positively abounded with health. People grew to such old ages there, it was said they finally just withered up and blew off with the wind.[30] One proverb warned people who wanted to die not to go to San Antonio.[31]

For Bowie, the prospects in San Antonio were a ripe fruit. He immediately cultivated a friendship with the upper crust of Tejano society, especially with the next vice governor of Texas, Don Juan Martín de Veramendi. Bowie exercised his charm and skillfully leveraged his Stateside reputation as a gentleman. He confided that his assets were vast, though not, at present, liquid. His fortune, he said, included sixty thousand arpents of Arkansas land (a fiction he had used in an earlier land fraud scheme[32]) plus other chattels, lands, and contracts. In sum, he represented that he was worth $222,000. The gullible Veramendi and his wife, a daughter of the important Navarro family of San Antonio, were suitably awed. They went so far as to sponsor the American gentleman at his baptism into the Catholic faith.

Shortly after his baptism, Bowie rode horseback east to the States for business purposes. It was at this point that he met the heartbroken ex-governor Sam Houston floating aimlessly in his cups and took time to recommend Texas to the besotted gentleman. It was a momentary connection, one of the many matrices that eventually brought the War Dogs into power.

In 1831, back in San Antonio, Bowie courted and married Ursula Veramendi, the beautiful teenage daughter of Governor Veramendi.[33] He also took full Mexican citizenship, but his motives were less romantic than fiscal. The Veramendis were the wealthiest and most stellar of Tejano families and there were vast amounts of land involved. By gaining full citizenship (through a specially arranged act of the Coahuila y Tejas legislature), Bowie qualified to buy eleven leagues (48,712 acres) of public land at roughly a nickel per acre. He then persuaded a number of Governor Veramendi's Mexican acquaintances to apply for their eleven-league grants also, and to sell the titles to him. In quick order, the groom accumulated 750,000 acres of Texas.

At the age of thirty-five—he presented himself to the Mexicans as thirty—Bowie acquired more prestige, power, and wealth than most Go Ahead men ever conceived of. He turned nothing (part of the dowry guaranteed to Ursula was his nonexistent sixty thousand arpents of Arkansas land) into something and acquired what few frontier shadow creatures ever could: legitimacy. The day he stood among the smoking wax candles of San Fernando Church in San Antonio and exchanged marriage vows, James Bowie thought that he had finally entered the light.

The first thing Bowie did was borrow money from his in-laws ($750 from Ursula's grandmother, $1,879 from the governor) and take his beautiful Mexican bride to New Orleans and Natchez for a honeymoon. A few months later he was back in Texas with his brother Rezin, plus seven Americans and two slaves.[34] Using his in-laws' house as a well-appointed base camp, the jobless Bowie spent the next year and a half hunting in Mexico for Spanish gold or silver or making business trips to Louisiana and Mississippi. He had no money of his own, but he always managed to appear a man of means. Ursula's father apparently furnished the restless treasure hunter with a handsome allowance. Bowie's gratitude toward his Mexican family may be summed up by the will he drew up in Natchez in October 1833. He left them—including his beloved wife—nothing.

Bowie's neglect didn't matter. For one thing his lifetime of fraud and hoaxes amounted to only seventy-seven dollars in the end: a two-dollar

trunk of clothes plus a few sawmill tools. As it turned out, the Veramendis left Bowie nothing either, as he soon enough discovered.

The cholera epidemic was slowly clawing its way through Mexico
between 1832 and 1834. In Mexico City twelve hundred victims were
buried in a single day. In Goliad, Texas, bodies were buried while still
warm. Cistern water for drinking was filtered through burned bread.
Houses were fumigated with gunpowder smoke. In Brazoria, eighty
Anglo-American settlers died and Velasco was depopulated. Bodies lay
unburied on distant plantations. German doctors prescribed the use of a
copper amulet worn around the neck. Mexican doctors treated patients
with tea made of peyote or opium, massages with whiskey and salt, and
hot bricks applied to the feet.[35]

The Veramendis were in their summer residence in Monclova,
Coahuila, when the cholera arrived. Bowie was in Mississippi drawing up
his will. Ursula and her father and mother died within three days of one
another. The Bowie fairy tale states that he and Ursula had two cherished
children, both of whom succumbed to the plague. According to stock
legend, the grief-stricken husband fell into desperate alcoholism and
never fully revived until the Texas Revolution. In fact, there were no
Bowie children.[36]

Whatever grief Bowie suffered was remarkably thin. Within the year
he was suing the Veramendi estate for property "placed in the hands of
his late wife."[37] He was suing to get back his dowry of the fictitious sixty
thousand arpents of Arkansas land. He didn't want it in Arkansas title,
however. He wanted it in Texas real estate or in Mexican coin.

Nothing ever came of this scheme. But that didn't stop Bowie. There
was still all of Texas to gain, if only the War Dogs could trigger a
rebellion and gain the land. But they had a problem.

Nobody was buying their patriotic rhetoric. Established colonists with
clear title to their huge Mexican estates didn't want to risk losing everything for another spasm of grandiose filibusters. And squatters, who had
no title at all, harbored a natural suspicion of land speculators eager to
convert them into cannon fodder. Frustrated, the War Party redoubled its
agitations to swing opinion its way.

It was not that the Anglo-Americans didn't understand rebellion.
They were the children and grandchildren of the American Revolution.
They had grown up listening to their uncles and elders weave common
war straw into a gleaming peacock tapestry of battlefields and great men.
As late as the 1830s venerable old troopers still hobbled along dirt roads,
their hair worn in Revolutionary War–style cues down the middle of their

wrinkled necks. For them, independence verged upon being a revealed religion, and the Constitution was its temple.

The War Dogs posed as high priests of liberty, but year after year they acted like clowns and bullies. The ultimate War Dog, the man who would have to decide the fate of the Alamo, was not an important man, not even a leader of men, though he desperately yearned to be. He was not the deadly James Bowie, who had his hands full squeezing loans from gullible Tejanos and galloping around in search of gold mines. Nor was he ex-governor Sam Houston, who was, despite his slovenly binges, too fundamentally dignified to indulge in gutter pranks and high jinks.

Rather the quintessential Craze-orian was a good-looking, if shallow, Southern boy-lawyer named William Barret Travis, or Buck. He was a tall, high-minded frontier playboy, who used ointment on his red hair and wore bergamont and lavender perfumes and stockings and pumps—not boots—to fandangoes and hoedowns. Addicted to romantic novels, he would come to write some of the most enduring propaganda in American history.

Aptly enough, the young rebel was born in Pandemonium (Home of the Devils), a nickname bestowed on Edgefield County, South Carolina, by religious revivalists.[38] In 1818 the Travises removed along the Federal Road to the woods of Alabama, a region cleared of "bad" Indians by Gen. Andrew Jackson, Sam Houston, David Crockett, and others only three years before.

For a time, until the men could clear land and erect a proper home, the family lived in a hovel made of saplings with their wagon canvas for a roof. It was a hard, raggedy, barefoot start that was echoing up and down the undulating frontier line. Families would carve a scanty hut from the forest, throw down some corn among the trees, lay in some meat, and call the surrounding acreage home. The Southern ideal was to plant a cash crop; in the 1820s that meant cotton. With time, every settler hoped to expand his house and acreage, buy some slaves, raise some livestock. But Buck Travis wanted wealth and prestige that very few farmers could obtain.

After learning the basics, plus a smattering of Latin and Greek, at his uncle Alex's Sparta Academy, Travis became a schoolteacher in nearby Claiborne. He began reading law under a local judge and before his twentieth birthday was practicing law. He married one of his pupils, a thin, flinty-jawed girl named Rosanna, and they set up house in what today would barely pass for a sharecropper's shack.

Sights set upon civic respectability, Travis entered the local Masonic lodge and got himself commissioned an adjutant of the hometown militia. On the side, he published a small newspaper, the *Claiborne Herald*, with the motto Thou Shalt Not Muzzle the Ox That Treadeth the Corn.

Then, abruptly, in his twenty-second year, Travis went to Texas. Rosanna was in her fifth month of pregnancy with their second child and their first was barely a toddler. But just as Sam Houston never relieved the mystery of his broken marriage, Travis offered no explanations. He just stormed west to Texas, traveling by wagon to Nacogdoches in 1831. He left behind rumors of Rosanna's infidelity, and of his preposterous outrage at some yokel cutting off his horse's tail and mane. The darkest rumor had him killing a man, supposedly his wife's lover, and pinning the murder upon an innocent slave.[39] One thing was certain. To Travis, his past was dead. When he took his Mexican oath as a colonist, he listed himself as a widower (*"de Estado viudo"*).[40]

Texas was spinning with men like Travis. So many fugitives circulated in Texas that it was commonplace for strangers to be asked what they'd done to make them leave home. The assumption was of criminality, the general attitude was nonchalance. The line between fact and fiction was exquisitely thin. Texas was a place where a man could not only escape, but completely reinvent himself.[41] In crossing the international line, Travis stepped into the world of his vivid imagination. He became his own creation: a womanizer, a gambler, a gallant gentleman, and a martyr-rebel.

There were ten or more men for every woman in Texas. Yet somehow, by the age of twenty-four, Travis had slept with over fifty frontier belles, slave girls, and prostitutes. The dashing Don Juan wore a white hat and rode a black Spanish mare, and he bore gifts of cinnamon, cologne, or spare change. To his immense discomfort, he also carried a bad case of venereal disease. He kept meticulous count of his conquests in his diary. At the end of daily entries, he documented his affairs in crude, slang Spanish.

On Thursday, September 26, 1833, for example, he remarked that he felt unwell. He listed the day's legal transactions and noted his loss of nine dollars at a faro game. Then he wrote, *"Chingaba una mujer que es cincuenta y seis en mi vida"* ("I fucked the fifty-sixth woman in my life).[42] *Chingaba* was coarse and brutal slang for lovemaking, and in Mexico it implied degradation.[43]

His 1833–34 diary was not a confession or a brag, it was a mirror. Travis wanted to remember even the bad moments, even the trivial detail.

His diary told of buying himself a watermelon or a bushel of corn. It documented—to the penny—how much pocket change he gave little children. It stated that he paid a woman fifty cents for a roll in the hay. He wrote of the persistent venereal disease (*"Venerao mala"*—"venereal bad"), which he unwittingly transmitted to his fiancée, Rebecca Cummings.[44]

He and his paramours were by no means alone in their suffering. The West was jammed with frontiersmen in one or another stage of venereal disease. The treatment for syphilis and gonorrhea in those days was the so-called "Sampson of the Drug Stores," liquid mercury, taken in the form of calomel (mercurous chloride), Blue Pill, or a blue ointment. The cure was arguably worse than the affliction. The effects of mercury poisoning ranged from abdominal pain, kidney failure, tremors, cramping, and bloody diarrhea to derangement and death. The neurological symptoms included confusion, hallucinations, increased irritability, sleep disturbances, memory loss, emotional instability, reduced self-confidence, and a narrowing of sensory perceptions.[45] "Mad as a hatter" referred to insanity caused by the fumes of mercury used in processing beaver pelts into the felt hats so popular at the time. And Travis was drinking the toxic element.

Certifiably a lover, Travis was certifiably not a fighter. Following the tradition of other petulant Southern gentlemen, Travis lost his temper one day in midtrial, pulled a Bowie knife upon another lawyer, and demanded satisfaction. His opponent, Ephraim Roddy, considered the proposition and reached into one pocket for his weapon: a small broken penknife used to trim goose quill pens. While Travis towered in a rage with his foot-long butcher knife, Roddy turned to the judge. "Your Honor," he quipped, "owing to the discrepancy of our weapons I cannot do opposing counsel much bodily harm, but if he insists upon it I will try." To peals of laughter, a chagrined Travis sheathed his knife and shelved his anger.[46]

Travis was young, vain, ambitious, and stuffed full of heroic nonsense. His most unique talent was for shaping and wielding propaganda, but he never seemed to grasp that his soaring patriotism masked soaring ambitions and that his heroism had been hatched in popular novels.

Much of the blame lay with an English novelist named Sir Walter Scott. It is hard to underestimate the influence this best-selling author had upon not only Travis but whole generations of Southerners. Starting with *Waverly*—the story of a young English lord swept up in a Scottish revolt called the Jacobite Rebellion—Scott asserted principles dear to the South with her semifeudal agriculture and slavocracy.[47] Brutally independent from the start, Southern frontier life gained from Scott clearly written codes of chivalry, dueling, and female worship, of honor, hierarchy, romantic oratory, hospitality, and the dignity of arms. It bestowed beauty upon their order. It gained the glorious Great Heart. One other thing made Scott appealing to the South. His novels spoke nostalgically about separatism. While Scott built fictions about once-free Scotland, Southerners were daring to construct their nascent Confederacy.[48]

Southerners avidly appropriated bits of Scott's archaic language: "Southron" for Southern, "aristocratical" for aristocratic. Travis called his military superiors in Texas "chieftains" as if they were a tribe of Highlanders on the heath.

Like threads sewing together his narrative, Travis's diary mentioned three things over and over: sex, money, and the purchase of candles. Days were reserved for business—in less than a year's time, 1,001 cases with names of five hundred people. His work included recovery of a stolen chamber pot, prevention of the sale of a blind horse, the drawing up of wills, deeds, and titles, the collection of bad debts and execution of bills of sale. Days he worked. But nights he read.

One dripping candle at a time lit his readings. It was the flame of a candle, night after night, that linked Travis with his Great Heart. It was these readings that ultimately made him such a marvelous propagandist.

It was through James Kirke Paulding's *Westward Ho!* that Travis first met with David Crockett, or at least a prose version of him. Three years before shaking hands with the famous congressman among the adobes of San Antonio—only a few weeks before the Alamo was stormed—Travis huddled by his candlelight and read about a frontier captain who claimed to be "half horse, half alligator." A second Crockett character in the novel was an old Indian-fighting backwoodsman who roamed far ahead of white civilization and ultimately died west of the Mississippi "sitting upright against a tree, his rifle between his legs, and resting on his shoulder."[49]

Whether he wore buckskin or Arthurian armor, Travis's heroes all carried the Great Heart. They were equally ready with rapier, lance, or long rifle, or with a pointed Latin snippet or pungent American slang, to defend their honor, meaning their nation, their race, and their opinion.[50]

Like every politician, the War Dogs—nearly all of whom were young Southern lawyers like Travis—needed an issue. On April 6, 1830, the Mexican government manufactured one for them. It was called the April 6 Law for short, and it came as a direct result of General Terán's expedition through Texas. Passing through the Anglo-American colonies in east Texas, Terán had seen how Mexican colonization policy was being abused and ignored by a swelling population of foreigners.

"These measures involve the safety of the nation, and the integrity of our territory," Mier y Terán warned his government. "Indeed, there is no choice of measures in this matter. Either the government occupies Texas *now,* or it is lost forever. . . ."[51]

Mexican officials listened with alarm and accumulated Terán's recommendations into a new blueprint for Texas.[52] The April 6 Law meant to imprint Mexico's control over the region. It was an entirely reasonable goal since Texas was a Mexican department; even President Jackson's administration had confirmed that fact by treaty.

The Mexican plan had numerous articles, but essentially one thrust: to treat Texas as a state instead of a drifting purgatory. There was to be military occupation of the region, the opening of Texan coastal trade, countercolonization (the introduction of Europeans and Mexicans), and finally, against Terán's advice, a blanket prohibition of further Anglo-American immigration. Terán preferred a more diplomatic balancing of the races in Texas, proposing a ratio of one American immigrant to every three Mexicans or Europeans.[53]

The Anglo-American colonists in Texas realized that their free lunch was over. Many of them were essentially economic refugees, fleeing bad debts, financial discomfort, land speculators, and other difficulties. In Texas they had found not only huge tracts of inexpensive land but sanctuary from U.S. tariffs, unrestricted passage back and forth across the border, and a virtually law-free vacuum. Now the new law forbade the passage of foreigners across the border for any reason unless they carried a passport and Mexican visa and it forbade the importation of any further slaves.

The Mexican government had promised colonists a seven-year window free of duties on imported goods. Now the seven years were nearly expired and enforcement loomed like a hangover.

Since the U.S.-Texas border was porous, continued immigration was not a real issue. A nonstop flood of what could be called American "wetbacks" made the visa requirement a joke, not an issue. Nor did the law affect Southerners' bringing their slaves into Texas; before reaching the border, they simply had their ignorant Negroes sign themselves into an outrageous ninety-nine-year indenture.

But the payment of tariffs rankled even the most law-abiding immigrant. Anglo-Americans had gotten so used to paying no tariffs at all that they regarded the absence of tariffs as a right. And the War Dogs cooked up other complaints: that the seat of state government and justice lay hundreds of miles away in Coahuila, that legislative business was conducted in a foreign tongue, that the Mexicans had never established schools for them, that there was no trial by jury.

Just the same, these were relatively trivial issues to most Anglo-Americans coming to Texas. The distance to Coahuila was more a blessing than a hindrance, for it meant the Mexican government was far removed from their daily activities. Besides that, Tennesseeans of the period faced a similar legal geography, having to trek a hundred miles across poor roads to Supreme Court sittings to find themselves saddled with incompetent, legally illiterate magistrates and with "trifling errors" that cost them dearly. At least one Anglo-American settler found the Mexican judicial system a step up: "I . . . beleave [sic] the laws here are as well administered as they are in Arkansas and perhaps better, and equally as well as they were when I first went to Missouri."[54]

The truth was that very few Anglo-Americans troubled themselves with Mexican government or law.[55] As for education, it was up to the various towns to build their own schools and hire their own teachers.[56] But education happened to be at an extremely low premium among Americans of the period—in fact they downright distrusted it—and in Texas they simply didn't want to pay for it.

As for trial by jury, that instrument so sacred to English law, it was granted to Texas in 1834. Mexico introduced it on an experimental basis and appointed an Anglo-American judge to practice it. But by then, the War Dogs had prevailed and it was too late.

By far the War Party's most valuable issue was the presence of the troops sent to enforce customs laws, which threatened to choke off an enormous, flourishing smuggling trade. By focusing on the tariffs issue, the War Dogs successfully identified the April 6 Law with the odious Stamp Act, which had preceded the American Revolution, and also connected the Mexican garrison commander with the British arch-villain of Revolutionary Boston, General Gage.

This much maligned Mexican officer, Col. Juan Davis Bradburn, was no more Mexican than the colonists he was sent to police. Before joining the Mexican army, the native Kentuckian had been a filibuster, a slave trader, and an escaped convict—in short a character with whom the Anglo-Americans could easily identify. General Terán had cautioned the colonel to be circumspect in his dealings with the volatile locals, instructing him to employ Anglo-Americans to erect the barracks and to assure them that their interests were safe in his hands.

For a time Bradburn succeeded in blending in as a regular guy, going hunting with the local men in and around Anahuac, a semitropical slum that was a hotbed of discontent. Among the locals he labored to reassure was a twenty-two-year-old lawyer who soon dedicated himself to making Bradburn's life pure misery: Buck Travis.

One day some trappers snared a small, thirty-inch alligator in the river and brought it to town. For some reason, Colonel Bradburn kept a bear tied to a tree near the barracks. One of the trappers got the idea of staging an old-fashioned bearbaiting, and a crowd quickly developed. The alligator was brought close to the bear. It snapped and hissed. With a calflike bleat, the bear took fright and climbed the tree. Travis seemed to find the event portentous.

Before long the War Dogs were baiting more than Bradburn's bear. Branding the official a renegade, a contemptible tyrant, and "a damn rascal," they began compiling a litany of atrocities worth fighting against. Ignoring the fact that many of the Americans arriving daily were wanted for everything from bank and land fraud to murder and bigamy, the locals railed against the convict-soldiers sent up from Mexico. The most notorious of the convict-soldiers was an old man who had allegedly murdered "not less" than eleven people; one morning the dangerous old desperado fell facedown in a puddle and drowned.

When three of the convict-soldiers decided they'd had their fill of Texas and tried to desert, an Anglo-American helpfully volunteered to fetch them back . . . but only upon terms of taking them dead or alive. Tracking them on horseback, he caught the trio fashioning a raft on the bank of Turtle Bayou. He promptly issued warning shots into one deserter's back and another's face. Upon delivering up the survivors, he announced to Bradburn, "Colonel, I have sunk one of your men and brought home the rest."[57]

Several of these miserable soldiers were accused of outraging an Anglo-American or slave woman. Accusing enemy troops of assaulting one's womenfolk is one of the most potent and classic methods of wartime propaganda. If there was a rape by Mexican soldiers in the Anglo-American community, it was certainly an isolated crime, for General Terán had cautioned his command to treat the colonists with sensitivity. Being from the South himself, Colonel Bradburn knew well the adoration of the Southern female.

Another potent rumor circulating the Galveston Bay held that Bradburn's Mexican soldiers were inciting the slaves to rebel against their white masters. The possibility of a slave insurrection was a constant nightmare for Southerners.[58]

At the center of the rumor was "a young & very bad Negro man, known as Big Jim," who knew Spanish and had "a vindictive & brutal Nature." Big Jim supposedly ran off, conspired with Mexican authorities, and returned to his plantation with the "fiendish work" of insurrection in mind. Then, the story went, a War Dog named Pleasant D. McNeel wrestled Big Jim to the ground and tied him up, but the next afternoon the slave escaped. "P D McNeel seized his Rifle & ordered Him to halt, but he was at that time over 100 yards away & on the edge of the woods. He defiantly turned & said 'Shoot, God Damn you.' In a Moment the Gun was raised & a clear report rang out on the still air & Jim fell to the ground mortally wounded. When he knew he was to die he gave the details of a Hellish plot to Massacre the old women & children, and to burn every dwelling. The younger women were to be taken as captives to the Mexican camp . . . "[59]

The absurd story gained a degree of credibility when Colonel Bradburn sheltered two fugitive slaves from Louisiana. Their owner, William Logan, showed up to reclaim his property. Bradburn demanded proof of ownership and authority from the governor of Louisiana. Days later, when Logan returned with the paperwork, Bradburn informed him that the three slaves had become citizens and were now serving in the Mexican army.

Slave owner Logan contracted a local lawyer to retrieve his property. The lawyer, once again, was young Travis. After he failed to pry the slaves loose from Bradburn, Travis baited the Mexican colonel.

One rainy night in May 1832, a tall man wrapped in a big cloak approached the Anahuac fort with a letter. Then the stranger vanished into the darkness and raindrops. The letter, signed only "Billew," confided that an American magistrate had assembled a company of one hundred men and was going to cross into Texas and descend upon Anahuac to take back the three slaves. For the following week the garrison was kept on alert as scouts searched in vain for the advance of this small army.

Bradburn finally realized he'd been duped, and in questioning the rainy-night sentinel, deduced that the stranger had been Travis. A day or so later, thirteen soldiers showed up at the lawyer's office door and arrested both Travis and his partner, Patrick C. Jack. To move his two prisoners to a more secure brick kiln by the riverside fort, Bradburn took the precaution of escorting them with his entire garrison plus cavalry. As the two were conducted down the path, colonists and drifters stood upon fence posts and wept.

P. C. Jack's brother, *Alcalde* (judge) William H. Jack, raised a troop of men and threatened to rush the fort. Colonel Bradburn had his two prisoners shackled to the floor of the brick kiln and threatened to shoot them if the Anglo-Americans charged. Travis was prepared. Chained to his dungeon, Travis orgiastically called out for his supporters to fire away, he would "rather die a thousand deaths than permit this oppressor to remain unpunished."[60]

In short order Bradburn arrested more War Dogs, sweeping up a total of seventeen. Rumors flew that the men were being mistreated and that Bradburn had threatened to send them to the old Spanish dungeon fortress of San Juan Ulloa in Veracruz Bay where they faced certain execution. Few colonists supported Travis and his radical friends, but none was willing to stand by while a white man got executed by a bunch of dusky Indians in uniform. William Jack's little band grew into an army of 160 men. They sent for cannons to be brought in by boat, then clustered to await their artillery at Turtle Bayou. Their call to arms attracted more and more men toting muzzle-loaders and gourds of gunpowder. The Anglo-Americans finally numbered two hundred to three hundred strong.

While they waited, a few of the leaders had second thoughts. Skirmishing with a few dozen convict-soldiers was quite different from taking on a national army. How much wiser, they argued, to mask this "disturbance" as a unique and necessary occasion. The conquistadores of early colonial Mexico had often hidden their insubordination to the faraway king behind a clever saying—*"obedezco pero no cumplo,"* meaning "I obey but do not comply." The neo-conquistadores gathered at Turtle Bayou then issued the same message. We support Mexican rule, their Turtle Bayou Resolutions declared, but reject its representatives. They repudiated the current Bustamente presidency. Instead, they renewed their loyalty to the liberal Constitution of 1824 and expressed their full support for an up-and-coming Mexican strongman, none other than the "firm and manly" General Santa Anna.

Near the mouth of the Brazos River, an army of rebels was returning by boat to Turtle Bayou with three cannons. On June 26, Domingo de Ugartechea, the Mexican colonel in command of the riverside fort at Velasco, tried to halt their schooner with his artillery. The Anglo-Americans aboard the ship stacked bales of cotton to form a protective wall (just as Andrew Jackson had at the Battle of New Orleans) and then hove to off the riverbank and fired their cannons at the fort. As the eleven-hour firefight commenced, snipers at the rear of the fort took their bite of the Mexican troops.[61]

This was the first real battle of the so-called Texas Revolution, and it resulted in ten Anglo-Americans dead, eleven wounded, and five Mexicans dead, sixteen wounded. The Mexican soldiers finally ran out of ammunition and were forced to surrender and leave Texas.

In the meantime a third Mexican colonel, José de las Piedras, had arrived from Nacogdoches with a small troop of soldiers. Piedras was a clever and perceptive man who recognized a no-win situation when he saw one. The Anglo-Americans far outnumbered his tiny command. They were heavily armed and eager to fight. This was no time to be standing upon the authority of the Mexican eagle, and so Piedras sagely and courteously negotiated with the rebels. He listened to their complaints about Bradburn's tyranny, the imprisonment of Travis and the War Dogs, and various other grievances. Then he released the prisoners, stripped Bradburn of his command, and completely erased the Mexican government's presence in Anglo-American Texas. The Anahuac garrison of Mexican soldiers declared for Santa Anna and sailed off to Mexico, overjoyed to be done with Texas.

The Anglo-Americans—ill-prepared as they were—were nearly ready for what would have been a disastrous confrontation with the Mexican government. Luckily for them a different disaster struck at that moment. Without warning, the cholera epidemic suddenly arrived from New Orleans, floods swept down, and a fierce season of malaria followed. Velasco lost much of its population. Eighty settlers died at Brazoria, a War Party hotbed.

The graveyards were busy enough without a full-scale revolt, and the hotheads knew it. The War Dogs quieted their barking.

For the next several years the Anglo-Americans enjoyed eastern Texas as in the old days. Between 1832 and 1835 there was no Mexican authority east of the Spanish country: no troops, no practicing customs agents, no challenge to their smuggling, immigration, and settlement. For three full years they wallowed in freedom like hogs in mud. They thought it would go on forever.

= 3 =

Because he was the bastard son of José María Morelos, one of the greatest revolutionaries ever to live, and because he had been a revolutionary himself, Col. Juan Nepomuceno Almonte knew revolutionaries. But as he inspected Texas in the early summer of 1834, the polished, square-shouldered Mexican with the pleasant smile saw the Anglo-Americans for what they were, nothing more than pretenders.

Colonel Almonte had lived and been educated in the United States and was familiar with American pride in their Revolutionary War. But for most Americans, the event was a memory, while for Mexicans revolution was a reality: They were still living among their war's ruins.

For three centuries—not the few years or few months these Anglo-American "revolutionaries" had been fluttering about in Texas—Mexicans had been accumulating their grievances against Spanish tyranny. Spain had sweated the wealth from Mexico. Gold and silver flowed directly from Mexico's veins into galleons bound overseas, there to pay for imperial wars in Europe. The Spanish empire had formed an elaborate and comfortable palace that Mexico was allowed to share. But it was not Mexico's palace, and in 1810 Mexico had finally revolted.

The struggle had begun almost accidentally on September 16, 1810, when an aging parish priest named Miguel Hidalgo y Costilla issued a *grito* (a cry) to his Indian parishioners.[1] In it he declared vivas for Catholicism and America (that is, Mexico) and death to bad government. He called his revolt a *reconquista,* a reversal of Cortés's conquest of Mexico in 1521, an echo of the centuries-long *Reconquista* in the Middle Ages over the Moors. Hidalgo was not a good military leader, but he was charismatic and had a keen mind.[2] He was helped along by the fact that Mexico had suffered terrible droughts for two years, followed by two years of famine. Like the French Revolution, the Mexican war broke out at the apogee of sky-high food prices.[3]

Armed with machetes, bows and arrows, clubs, lances, axes, slings, and a few muskets, Hidalgo's small army swelled to twenty thousand as

43

it passed through town after town toward Mexico City. It marched behind a banner of the powerful, dark-skinned "Mexican" Virgin of Guadalupe, who had been invented by some early priests to replace a popular Aztec goddess (also a virgin and little mother). The royalists countered with images of the Virgin of the Remedies, the virgin imported by the conquistadores and called *La Conquistadora* (the Conqueress). Over the next ten years of fighting, captured images of the enemy's virgin were summarily shot.[4]

Under Hidalgo the revolution turned into a race war, and soon each side was matching atrocities with greater atrocities. After six bloody months, Hidalgo's phase of the revolution crumbled in the face of a royalist army that was "as terrible as a lobster."[5] Hidalgo fled toward Texas and sanctuary in the United States, but he was betrayed along the way and captured in the northern deserts. The civil authorities handed Hidalgo over to the Inquisition, which defrocked him and then gave him back to the authorities. In July 1811, he was shot by a firing squad. His head was cut off and for the next ten years it grimly hung in a cage at the site of his first atrocity.[6]

Shortly before his capture, Hidalgo had handed off command of the southern Mexican war theater to José Morelos, Colonel Almonte's father. Morelos, like Hidalgo, was a discontented parish priest who fathered illegitimate children. He too had the dark skin of a mestizo and he cared deeply for his destitute Indian parishioners. But once Morelos went into action, the resemblance ended.

Morelos waged a crafty guerrilla war that largely controlled southern Mexico. His army was disciplined, relatively small, and highly mobile. He avoided the excesses of Hidalgo's mob by resorting to the use of untrained Indians as soldiers only as a last measure.[7] Morelos tried to limit his army's destruction of property and worked to show that he was fighting for Mexico and social equality, not because of racial hatred. *"La Patria"* (the Homeland) became his watchword. He organized a Congress which issued a declaration of independence in 1813 and endorsed his program of reforms. His reforms included the abolition of slavery, *fueros* or extralegal privileges for the Church and military, and the ending of all class distinctions. In those times, one qualified for advancement in the government, clergy, and military by demonstrating *limpieza de sangre* (purity of blood), a pedigree so precious it became necessary for those of mixed heritage to purchase proof of their purity. By eliminating the intricate caste system——there were over fifty recognized combina tions of races—Morelos sought to revolutionize all of Mexican society. The *criollos* (pure-blooded, Spanish-born Mexicans) recognized that as a threat to their stations in society and shunned Morelos. Ultimately their skepticism cost Morelos his cause and his life.

Morelos was captured in November 1815 while fighting to give his revolutionary Congress time to escape. The Inquisition panel declared him a heretic and ordered him to attend a special mass dressed as a penitent and bearing a green candle symbolizing his sin. His property was confiscated, his illegitimate children (including Juan Almonte) were branded infamous, and any children they bore were to suffer legal disabilities too.

The civil court ordered that Morelos be executed, that his head be severed and displayed in an iron cage in the plaza of Mexico City, and that his right hand be amputated and shown in an iron cage in Oaxaca.[8] A last-minute reprieve saved him from the mutilation. On December 22, the shackled priest made his confession. His arms were tied with gun slings. He knelt and just before the firing squad shot him, he lifted his head and said, "Lord, thou knowest if I have done well; if ill, I implore thy infinite mercy." The first volley of lead balls left him still moving. A second volley finished him.[9]

Before it was all over, Mexico's War of Independence cost 600,000 lives out of a population of six million. By comparison, the American Revolution had cost between 15,000 and 20,000 American lives of a population of two and a half million.[10]

The Mexican population was literally decimated. One in ten perished, most of them young men. Mining production collapsed to less than 25 percent, agriculture to 50 percent, industry to 30 percent.[11]

Independence arrived in 1821, but Mexico went on suffering and bleeding. The struggle for national subsistence, to say nothing of growth, dragged on and on. What Anglo-Saxons had dreamed of as a fabulously wealthy kingdom proved to be bankrupt almost from the birth of the Mexican Republic.

Rebels and royalists alike had spent ten years tossing precious mining machinery down shafts, cannibalizing the shoring for wood, and generally jugulating the industry. Untended, the mines flooded with water, and even if ore could be drawn out, there was no mercury with which to process it.

The attempt to impose a federal income tax—amounting to three days' pay per year—produced only thirty-five thousand pesos in thirteen months and was abandoned to individual states to pursue.[12] The government floated—barely—atop its customhouse money, which amounted to 60 percent of the national income.

But smuggling emptied that income before it could even be collected. The sales tax on tobacco, for instance, supported a third to a half of certain regions' budgets. But in the off-season or when their farms failed, Anglo-Americans would casually run mule trains loaded with American tobacco through Texas and across the Rio Grande.

The greatest drain on the Mexican budget was the War Department, which soaked up 10 million pesos annually, or 75 percent of the budget. Yet predatory foreign nations—like Spain, France, and especially the United States—made the military absolutely vital.

In the mid-1820s Mexico and the United States were roughly equal in land area.[13] While the two countries had been equal in population—six million—at the turn of the century, by 1825 the United States had nearly doubled that number, and Mexico's population had remained dormant.[14] By the mid-nineteenth century, the United States would number over 23 million, an almost 400 percent increase; Mexico would number only 8 million, an increase of just 33 percent.[15] By then the United States would have taken half of Mexico's territory by force. Prophesying the loss of patrimony to the United States, Gen. Mier y Terán despaired and took his own life.

Colonel Almonte entered Texas the way Terán had entered six years earlier, not quite certain of what he would find. Like Terán, he squinted hard at this astounding and beautiful crescent of the Mexican patrimony. Unlike Terán, he did not despair. It was not too late to hold Texas, he believed. He still saw hope.

It was the April 6 Law—that set of rules so detested by Anglo-Americans in Texas—that first set Almonte in motion. Article 3 required the government to send inspectors to the colonies of the Texan frontier and monitor immigration and settlement. Following the violence in Galveston Bay in 1832, Mexican troops had been pulled out from the Anglo-American sector of Texas. For two years, the area was left alone, unpoliced, untaxed, essentially a cloud of undefined, but dangerous gases. In 1834, Mexico sent in Almonte to assess the damage. He was an inspired choice to infiltrate the suspicious colonies.

As a little boy, Almonte had been sent into safekeeping in the United States by his father.[16] He had been schooled in the United States and was fluent in English. He was a brilliant student, grinding science, politics, economics, and diplomatic manners into an unblinking, focused lens.

Like his father before him, Almonte saw Mexico as a single nation, not just a set of competing races and interests.

Upon returning to Mexico in his teens, Almonte joined the guerrilla general Vicente Ramón Guerrero.[17] After Independence, when he was only twenty-one years old, he was sent to England to negotiate Mexico's first commercial treaty with a major foreign power. While serving in the national Congress and editing the newspaper *El Atleta,* he accused President Bustamente of allowing foreigners to manipulate Mexican affairs. His paper was fined into bankruptcy and Almonte had to hide from government persecution. By 1834, when he inspected Texas, Almonte had lived a remarkably dramatic and cosmopolitan life, ranging from hot guerrilla battlefields to the chambers of Mexico's Congress to the most elegant drawing rooms in Europe. He was thirty-one years old.

The government encouraged Almonte to be imaginative in his dealings with the Anglo-Americans in Texas. "Sr. Almonte shall attempt by as many means as be at his disposal to paralyze the movements of the colonists," his instructions read, "with the view of gaining time so that the supreme government, unburdened by the care with which it today finds itself surrounded, may be able to dedicate all of its endeavors to the conservation of the integrity of the territory of the republic."

Each side was hiding behind empty words and stalling for time. Mexico meant to assert control over Texas, but pretended to be sympathetic to colonists' demands. The Anglo-Americans meant to Americanize Texas, but pretended loyalty to Mexico. Even the Peace Party, headed by Stephen Austin, had a Texas breakaway in mind. They differed from the War Dogs only in their opinion of when the moment would ripen.

"A gentle breeze shakes off a ripe peach," Austin said, trying to muzzle the War Dogs for a while longer. "Can it be supposed that the violent political convulsions of Mexico will not shake off Texas so soon as it is ripe enough to fall. All that is now wanting is a great immigration of good and efficient families this fall and winter [1835]. [Then] . . . the peach will be ripe."[18]

Almonte rode into a labyrinth of disguised intentions, well disguised himself. The Anglo-Americans were not sure what to make of him and his journey, but they knew he was not to be trusted. Later, when the Alamo lay in rubble and Almonte was a prisoner of war in Anglo-American hands, the *Gazette of Louisville* described him much the way he was viewed in 1834.

"Colonel Almonte is of a copper complexion (such as Indians have)," the paper said, ". . . his face is round, and he has a jolly phiz [physiognomy] telling you upon first approach that he is 'a good fellow and true' but upon closer examination there is an expression of his eye, which tells you that he is a 'real single cat' i.e. worse than he looks to be. He speaks English as fluently and as correctly as any American and while here, laughed and talked with different persons quite unconcernedly."[19]

This "real single cat" was indeed an artful dodger, extending every fiction his government could dream up, and then some. He had come, Almonte claimed, to listen to the Anglo-American complaints and channel them to the central government. He had come to conduct a head count, to determine if the region qualified for statehood separate from Coahuila. Texas would soon become a territory, he told them, then a state.

On the issue of manumission, Almonte was free to tell slaves already in Texas that they could gain their liberty by invoking the protection of the April 6 Law. But he was expressly forbidden from spreading that fact to slaves in the United States, lest an international incident result.

So long as he lulled the rebellious settlers, Almonte had carte blanche to say whatever he wished.[20] In fact most of the suspicious Anglo-Americans mistook him for an ordinary border commissioner and paid little attention to the friendly and charming man. Later, when their rebellion was complete and they had Almonte chained to a tree, the Anglo-Americans would remember him less kindly. One colonist bitterly declared, "I consider him a greater villain than Santa-Anna, because, like a serpent, he only embraces to sting—whereas you can read deceit and indifference in Santa-Anna's countenance, and you know what to expect."[21]

Almonte, on his part, found the settlers to be crude and inferior to other Americans. They were after all Southerners, he pointed out, considered in the United States to be "the least advanced in civilization."[22] In a private letter, he portrayed them as being "influenced by self-interest and not by patriotism."[23] The Texas situation was both worse and better than he had expected.

In his statistical analysis of Texas, Almonte noted that there were 20,700 Anglo-Americans (plus 600 to 700 of their slaves), and 4,000 Hispanics: a five to one ratio.[24] By 1836 that ratio would have widened to 10 Anglo-Americans for each Hispanic in Texas. Something like one thousand settlers were arriving each month via the Brazos River, a number that did not include the hundreds more coming overland through Nacogdoches.[25] There was not the money, the will, or the troops to stem the flow.[26]

As Almonte crossed Texas he found a number of wealthy Tejanos *opposed* to constricting the Anglo-American advance. Francisco Ruiz of San Antonio—who would soon be cremating tons of Anglo-American corpses at the Alamo and throwing the Mexican dead into the river—went so far as to say, "I cannot help seeing advantages which, to my way of thinking, would result if we admitted honest, hard-working people, regardless of what country they came from . . . even hell itself."[27]

This skewed loyalty flowed from the fact that the Tejanos' economic ties were to the Anglo-Americans and the United States rather than to mother Mexico. They sold cattle and horses to eastern markets, and they enjoyed goods smuggled in from across the border.[28]

Almonte estimated that annual exports from Texas, mainly cotton (seven thousand bales by 1834) and animal skins, came to $500,000, but that imports equaled $630,000. The resulting trade deficit left Texas almost barren of currency. "Money is very scarce," said Almonte, "and one may say with certainty that out of every hundred transactions made not ten involve specie."[29]

Smuggling was a nationwide disease, but nowhere so debilitating as in the northern states with their long, unguarded coastlines. A staggering portion of the nation's trade went into smugglers' pockets, the estimates ranging from one third to three quarters of the annual total.[30] Entire shiploads of slaves from Africa or Cuba were landed without challenge, and with the complicity of entire communities. Smuggling was not merely a pastime, it was a full-blown industry, freighting contraband both in and out of the Mexican interior.

One American traveler in 1831 saw a fifty- or sixty-animal mule train arrive from a half-year trip deep into Mexico. "They were loaded with different articles to such a degree that I was astonished at their being able to travel. . . . The owners of the caravan, with several hired Mexican attendants, rode their mustangs. . . . Overseen and directed by such an escort, and bowing under the burthen [*sic*] of three hundred and sixty pounds without including the panniers, which were bound on so tight as almost to stop their breath, the poor mules formed a sorrowful line."[31]

More than the smuggling concerned Almonte. As he made his way across Texas, he began gathering some of the O.P.Q. letters written with poor anonymity by Anthony Butler. Initially Almonte refused to believe that the American minister to Mexico might be guilty of penning such crude and inflammatory letters. Butler described Mexicans as "this ignorant, fanatical and arrogant race" and "cowards." He warned his fellow Anglo-Americans in Texas that Almonte meant to lull them until

Mexico could overwhelm the settlers and turn them into slaves, a potent charge to a Southerner. He recommended giving Almonte twenty-four hours to vacate Texas or be hanged.[32]

Almonte knew how dangerous these Anglo-Americans were to Mexico. They had killed and run off officials of the Mexican government, refused to pay duties, scorned Mexican law, destroyed fortifications, organized themselves into militias, and collected artillery and ammunition. Their hunger for Texas was naked and Almonte was not the only one to see it. Other travelers through Texas saw through the land greed and attributed it to slavocracy.

"However lightly these people [Anglo-Americans in Texas in 1835] may hold the Mexicans whose superiors they undoubtedly are in industry and enterprise, yet the Mexicans stand at a proud moral distance from them in regard to slavery, which is abolished in their republic," said an English tourist. "What can be more abominable than the hypocritical cant with which these people intrude into a country which does not belong to them? To believe them, they have no motive but to establish 'free institutions, civil and religious.' Yet in defiance of human freedom, just laws and true religion, they proceed *to consummate their real purpose, which is to people the country with slaves in order to cover it with cotton crops.*"[33]

Almonte happened to meet an American named Benjamin Lundy on the road and as the two rode side by side on horseback they discussed ways of ending slavery. In the 1820s and 1830s, the United States was pregnant with crusaders against slavery, alcohol, and other social evils, and Lundy was possibly the most prominent abolitionist alive. He had an idea. Rather than send freed slaves back to Africa, an experiment that was already proving too expensive, Lundy proposed settling distant regions with them. He had already visited Haiti and Cuba with this vision in mind, then fastened his high hopes upon Texas. In all he made three exploratory trips to Texas.[34] Possibly as a result of this chance encounter with Almonte on a Texas trail, the Mexican government warmed to Lundy's grand plan.

It was very plain to Almonte that some other group had to be introduced to Texas to countercolonize the region. While he did not mention using freed slaves as Lundy had proposed, he did recommend that friendly Indians be settled in Texas as a buffer against the Anglo-Americans. Certain tribes, like the Chacta, Cherokee, Choni, Kickapoo, Creek, and others were good warriors, superb marksmen, and agriculturists. Mexico could count on their loyalty, Almonte insisted, because the United States had treated them so badly. In exchange for land, ammunition, and cheap gifts, Mexico would secure a quick, natural barrier against the Anglo-American flood.[35]

But countercolonization alone—whether with Indian refugees, freed slaves, or Europeans—was not going to save Texas, and Almonte knew it. Texas was being radicalized by men who stood to gain fortunes if they could cut it loose of the Mexican republic.[36]

In order to keep Texas, Almonte declared, Mexico needed to send troops. He recommended that warships land two of Mexico's very finest battalions in eastern Texas.[36] Delay, he warned, and we lose all of Texas.

=4=

WHILE THE ALLIGATORS roared and ambushed thirsty dogs, while herds of buffalo connected vast circles in the prairie grass, the Go Ahead men went nowhere, not for a while.

The men clustered about to talk war and work one another into a fury. They whittled curlicues off pine sticks and knocked down liquid corn and hectored their demons of liberty. They spit brown juice, watched the cotton spring loose under yellow sunbeams, and practiced their attitudes on one another. In July, they gathered beneath pecan trees or under the "dog runs" connecting one cabin to another. In January, while northers bruised the horizon cobalt blue and cold perforated the log walls, they grouped around big fires and tied fierce words to embers pouring up the mud-and-stick chimneys. On summer nights, the War Dogs among them fanned at clouds of fireflies and barked at the moon. They called conventions—a widespread Southern habit in the early 1830s—elected delegates, adopted resolutions, and formed Revolutionary War–style "committees of safety" or "vigilance."[1] They even sent an ambassador to Mexico City bearing their demands. This unfortunate soul was Stephen Austin.

The spare, chaste bachelor, wrinkled and worn far beyond his years, was renowned—and also reviled—as an apostle of conciliation and peace. Back in 1821, he and his father, Moses, who once colonized land in Spanish Missouri, had been stipulated the first legal Anglo-American colonists in Spanish Texas. When Mexico gained independence, the new Mexican government granted Austin the same rights to colonize.

As an *empresario* (agent), Austin was responsible for settling three hundred families, each of whom was given one *labor* (177 acres) if they intended to farm, or one *sitio* or league (4,428 acres) if they intended to ranch. Naturally, most of the Southern planters applying for grants enjoyed an instant conversion to ranching, at least until they left the office with title in hand. In return for settling a tract, Austin earned twenty-two *sitios* (97,416 acres). Like many other leaders of frontier settlements, Austin took local law and order upon himself. Through persuasion, sometimes by force, he exercised his will upon the colony. But then there were other willful men to contend with, and they won. They undermined his policy of compromise and camouflage, then hammered together a plan and elected Austin to present it in the Mexican capital.

A dozen years earlier, Austin had gone to Mexico City disguised as a beggar to protect himself from bandits. This time he arrived with a document demanding separate statehood for Texas. Presented in the form of a state constitution the Anglo-Americans had decided was suitable for themselves, this haughty demand struck the Mexicans as an outright *pronunciamiento*, a paving stone for revolutions. But Austin seemed oblivious of the dry gunpowder he was toting in his saddlebags.

Like most of the Anglo-Americans reaching Texas, Austin despised Mexicans. During his first visit to Mexico City in 1822–23 he had written, ". . . the people are bigoted and superstitious to an extreem [*sic*], and indolence appears to be the general order of the day. To be candid the majority of the people of the whole nation as far as I have seen want nothing but tails to be more brutes than the apes."[2]

Feeling that he was getting nowhere in the capital, Austin lost patience and wrote a letter to the San Antonio *ayuntamiento* (combination town council and county commission) in Texas. He recommended that Texas take steps toward self-government and separate from Coahuila. This was seditious language, highly uncharacteristic of him. He had barely posted the letter, when events suddenly turned around.

After five months of finagling, Austin was finally given an audience with the prime mover and shaker: President Santa Anna. Santa Anna heard him out, but balked at the demands. The Mexican constitution clearly stated that a region needed a population of eighty thousand before it qualified for statehood, and Texas had less than half that many. Statehood was out. But Santa Anna thought something might come of some of the lesser demands. A few weeks later, the government granted most of the requests as one more tactic for holding off a rebellion in Texas. Trial by jury, revision of the tariff, and repeal of the anti-immigration law were all approved.

Well satisfied that his mission was accomplished, Austin saddled up and rode north into the desert. But his letter to the San Antonio *ayuntamiento* had fallen into the hands of Mexican officials, and before he got to the Texas border, Austin was arrested. He was returned to

Mexico City and placed in solitary confinement for three months. For the next eighteen months, he was held in a physical limbo while he watched the cholera arrive in Mexico City and decimate the population.

Back in Texas, little occurred in Austin's absence for another year. Then a chain of events dropped rebellion upon the Anglo-Americans.

For some time now, the state legislature in Saltillo, Coahuila, had been sinking into a cesspool of corruption and land speculation, with the governor and legislators handing out thousands of leagues of Texas land. These were sold off to hundreds of unwanted Anglo-Americans at such a scandalous rate that even Anglo-American colonists were appalled by the giveaway. Santa Anna sent his brother-in-law, Gen. Mártin Perfecto de Cós, to Saltillo to put a stop to the wholesale corruption and waste of public lands. In early June 1835, Cós arrested the governor and suspended civil government. He also snared several of the Anglo-American land speculators including the aging filibuster Ben Milam.

Cós didn't manage to net all of the speculators, however. James Bowie was one of a number who escaped arrest and took refuge in Texas. They wasted no time in trying to alarm their countrymen into taking up arms and marching on Cós. They spread the fiction that the governor's arrest meant martial law for the whole state. On the Fourth of July, War Dog "Three-Legged Willie" Williamson stood upon his wooden leg and orated at length: "Let us no longer sleep in our posts; let us resolve to prepare for War—and resolve to defend our country against the danger that threatens it. . . . Liberty or Death should be our determination and let us one and all unite to protect our country from all invasion—and not down our arms so long as a soldier is seen in our limits."[3]

For the time being, Anglo-American colonists saw through the propaganda, realizing that the speculators were out to protect the potential fortunes they would realize if their lands were confiscated. By attacking Cós, the speculators stood to gain everything. The settlers stood to lose their lives. The settlers didn't budge.

As Cós took control of Saltillo, word arrived that the Anglo-American sector was causing trouble for a new set of customs officers in Anahuac and Velasco. The government officials were being mocked, tricked, and fired upon as the colonists and squatters continued their smuggling. Cós dispatched a messenger east to the captain of the Anahuac garrison, Don Antonio Tenorio, with a private message and a circular for public consumption. The circular assured the Anglo-Americans that order was restored and all was well. This conciliatory propaganda was delivered to, among others, the town of San Felipe. Unfortunately an excited crowd there seized the messenger's saddlebags and found Cós's private letter to Captain Tenorio, which excited them even more. In it, Cós counseled the captain to be patient, for heavy reinforcements—some of them battle-hardened by a recent suppression of rebels in the mining district of Zacatecas—were on the way. "In a very short time, the affairs of Texas will be definitely settled," Cós's second in command, Colonel Ugartechea, wrote to Tenorio. "Nothing is heard but God damn St. Anna [*sic*], God damn Ugartechea. These Revolutionists will be ground down, and it appears to me that we shall very soon see each other, since the Government takes their matters in hand."[4]

At last the dance of the chameleons was nearly over. The illusion of conciliation evaporated. Each side stood in the full glare of the summer sun with its true colors exposed. Now all that was needed for the fight to begin was a single spark.

Buck Travis stepped forward and offered himself as the flint to strike the spark.

In a perfect miming of Sir Walter Scott's *Waverly*, Travis rounded up a couple of dozen well-liquored fighters excited by talk of tariffs and foreign government.[5] They chartered the sloop *Ohio* and carried on board a small iron six-pounder cannon, and floated across the bay to ignite their grand revolution.

Almost from the start, their "battle" was a comedy of errors. The ship sailed all night long, preceded by a yawl. Early next morning the combatants arrived in the Anglo-American town of Lynchburg, where the citizens treated them coolly as troublemakers. At a second landing, they threw a small party for themselves and Travis got himself elected captain of the rebels.

As the *Ohio* approached Anahuac and the rebels readied for battle, the sloop grounded a mile short of their target, sticking fast in the shore mud. Probably to punctuate his frustration as much as to alert Anahuac, Captain Travis ordered up a warning cannon shot. Nothing could have been more ridiculous than that sloopful of tigers stuck fast in the mud, blowing off a harmless fist of gunpowder.

Luckily, a few friendly yawls came alongside and rescued the mired revolutionaries. Bristling with muskets and shotguns, Captain Travis and sixteen stalwarts headed for shore. A curious crowd lined the shore and the Mexican garrison marched back and forth in front of their *cuartel*. Treated as a curiosity, not a threat, Travis and his men landed, put their dismantled cannon back on its wheels and prepared themselves to go and let some blood. Just then a messenger handed Travis a letter from the local *alcalde,* William Duncan, who politely insisted that they not disturb the peace.

Travis shot back a demand that Captain Tenorio surrender his garrison with all its arms and ammunition. By then the sun had sunk and Travis was getting nervous lest all momentum be lost. Before Tenorio could parley, indeed almost the moment the messenger departed with the rebels' demand, Travis formed his little army into battle lines and advanced upon the *cuartel* at their meanest double time. Their cannon was loaded, their firearms were primed. But the *cuartel* was empty.

Seeking to avoid bloodshed, Captain Tenorio had pulled his garrison back into the woods. Travis ordered the little six-pounder fired off again, this time into the motionless forest.

Eventually the forest disgorged two messengers, both Anglo-American, bearing a request from Tenorio to parley down by the riverbank. Travis took the occasion to declare his general distrust of Mexicans, and ordered a trio of riflemen to hide along the shadowy riverbank, where they could snipe at Tenorio if he made any false moves.

Moonlight glittered upon the river as Travis strode toward the rendezvous. But Tenorio had even less trust in Anglo-American honor than Travis did in Mexican honor and refused to show himself. Travis finally stepped out of the moonlight into the trees. There the two captains discussed terms.

Travis repeated his demand that Tenorio surrender. Tenorio requested till dawn to answer. "Fifteen minutes is all we will allow you," Travis told him. "If you do not surrender in that time every man will be put to the sword."

Tenorio was no fool. He was deep in the Anglo-American sector, and his garrison was a token presence unequipped for full-scale combat. He took a face-saving hour, then surrendered.

As per the terms, Tenorio turned over sixty-four muskets with bayonets, twenty-one cartridge boxes, and miscellaneous supplies to the rebel "army." The Mexicans were permitted to retain twelve muskets as a defense against Indians during their overland evacuation from Texas. Travis hauled Captain Tenorio and his soldiers "bag and baggage" via the *Ohio* to Harrisburg, where on July 4 the whole region had gathered for the annual celebration.

There, to Travis's astonishment, he was snubbed and shunned by the Anglo-American settlers. Worse yet, his captive Captain Tenorio strolled about, perfectly at ease with the crowd, shaking hands, "and acting as if he was the hero of the occasion." His soldiers made themselves comfortable, smoking cigarettes and playing cards. The following evening, Tenorio waltzed and chatted in French with one of the colonists' wives.

It was no different in San Felipe. Travis had grossly miscalculated the local sentiments. All through the area settlers condemned Travis's Battle of Anahuac, and his mandate to touch off a war became an embarrassment for the young lawyer. Not only he, but the whole War Party fell into disfavor.[6]

For a man of Travis's fiery, fanatical temperament, the whole affair became a nightmare. His letter to Colonel Ugartechea was characteristically vain but also contained a renunciation of his attack upon Tenorio. "I am confident that I have acted from pure motives, which through mistaken impressions have given rise to false rumors which at the time were all manifestly untrue." He closed, "I beg you to excuse me for not writing in Spanish, but I do not know how to express myself in this language."

General Cós determined to make an example of the delinquents. He ordered the arrests of Travis and his close friend, "Three-Legged Willie" Williamson, who, because his right leg was permanently bent back at the knee, wore a third leg made of wood. With them were five other men, including a Mexican liberal and land speculator named Lorenzo de Zavala, who later became the first vice president of Texas.

Overnight the Anglo-American wind changed direction. A widely circulated rumor that the prisoners were to be court-martialed and shot chilled the Anglo-American community. That would never do. Never. By the end of August, Travis was gratified to see Harrisburgers—who had welcomed Captain Tenorio as a hero on July 4—praising the War Dogs' liberty and war platform.[7]

Almost miraculously the War Party resurrected itself and took a step, only to find itself sprinting. Preparation for hostilities began in earnest. From New Orleans men, money, and arms were starting to come in. Five cannons, a hundred kegs of gunpowder, and lead and shot arrived by boat.

"The people call now loudly for a convention in which their voices shall be heard," Travis wrote to an Anahuac neighbor and merchant, Andrew Briscoe. "They have become almost completely unified. And now let *Tories, submission men* [sic], and Spanish invaders look out. . . . We wish to beat them in their stronghold, and I have no doubt we shall do so. But I wish to see them overwhelmed. I have seen your publication," Travis said, referring to a letter Briscoe had written to the editor of the *Texas Republican*. "It does you credit. You have shown yourself the real white man and uncompromising patriotism. Stick to the text and Texas is saved.''[8]

In late September rebellion broke out. This time it wasn't one of Travis's pranks or gang fights, but a bona fide, grass roots conquest. At the heart of it, the rebellion was just another filibustering grab for the pie. Some of the settlers had lived on Texas land for as long as fifteen years, marginally qualifying them to demand revolutionary changes in the government. But very few of these colonists wanted war, for they stood to lose everything they had invested, every stick of property, every shadow in their dreams. Rather it was the young turks with their land schemes, and the squatters lacking titles, and the Go Ahead driftwood from the other side of the border who wanted a fight, men who had little but wanted much, newcomers and opportunists, white trash and outlaws whose roots in Texas were no deeper than their boot prints. In September, there were enough of them to seize the day. This time the rebellion caught fire. This time it worked.

September was the prime month to start a war. Those with crops had finished their harvest. There was plenty of corn to eat and the cattle were fat. The summer heat had broken, and winter was still two or three months away. It was a relatively dry season, meaning rivers were easily fordable, roads and trails solid, and men could sleep on the ground without a shelter.

In September, when General Cós landed at Copano Bay in Texas at the head of four hundred soldiers, rumors flew: Thousands more soldiers were on their way; Anglo-American women would be raped; their men would be marched to the Mexican interior hobbled with eight hundred pairs of iron shackles Cós had brought for the purpose.

And September was the month Stephen Austin returned from Mexican imprisonment. The exhausted man had been freed as part of a general amnesty of criminals and political prisoners, meaning his release carried neither a pardon nor the stamp of a completed sentence. Pale and hampered by coughing, he arrived by boat, but only after being fired upon by an English privateer commissioned by the Mexican government to patrol the coast for smugglers. It was a changed man who stepped onto the Texan dock. For fifteen years he had taken the Spanish motto *Dios Castiga el Escándalo más que el Crimen* (God punishes the exposure more than the crime) as his guiding principle, carefully clothing every move to please or deceive the Mexican eye. No more. Two excruciating years in Mexican hands had stripped away Austin's patience. He saw no reason to pretend anymore. ''The fact is,'' he declared for the first time, "we must, and ought to become a part of the United States. . . . Texas must be slave country. It is no longer a matter of doubt," the weary leader wrote. "A large immigration will prepare us, give us strength, resources, everything."

But he was no longer talking about a wave of peaceful farmers bearing cottonseed. He envisioned a specific kind of man, one who shared a certain conviction. Austin wanted Southerners. He wanted filibusters.

"A great immigration from Kentucky, Tennesse [sic] etc, each man with his rifle or musket, would be of great use to us—very great indeed," he outlined to his cousin. "If they go by sea, they must take passport from the Mexican Consul, comply with all the requisites of the law, and get legally into the country, so long as the door is legally open. Should it be closed it will then be time enough to force it open—if necessary. Prudence, and an observation of appearances must therefore be strictly attended to for the present."[9]

Austin electrified the Anglo-American sector. This was not just any man, not just any leader. By throwing Austin into prison the Mexicans had created a martyr. By granting him a passport to return to Texas, they had made a mistake. For Austin had become a frail, quiet messiah.

This metamorphosed Austin differed from the eager young turks galloping around in eastern Texas. His suffering in Mexican jails had given the sickly little bachelor enormous substance. His sobriety and gravity made each of his words all the wilder and more terrible. Even the fact that he quit signing papers with his Hispanicized *"Estevan"* declared the spirit. Like no other man, Austin was able to stand still in the sunshine and pronounce the Anglo-Americans ready.

In the third week of September, Austin declared war.

"Every man in Texas is called upon to take up arms in defence [sic] of his country and his rights. . . . It is expected that each man will supply himself with provision arms and ammunition to march with."[10]

Several days west of San Felipe de Austin, Colonel Ugartechea determined to cut any potential bloodletting by rounding up weapons loaned out to the Anglo-Americans. The citizens of Gonzales, midway between San Antonio and San Felipe, had been given a six-pounder almost identical to the one Travis had fired at Anahuac. Shorter than a man's arm and weighing less than seventy pounds, it wasn't much of a cannon to begin with. It had trundled behind an earlier band of filibusters (Magee's outfit in 1812–13) until the Spanish army, including young Lieutenant Santa Anna, overran the adventurers. At that point the little cannon had been spiked with a piece of metal driven into the touchhole. In later unplugging it, the blacksmith had gouged a touchhole the size of a man's thumb, badly compromising the ballistic force of the cannon. Consequently it had considerably more bark than bite. This sorry, worn-out tube of iron was the ordnance Colonel Ugartechea attempted to retrieve in late September.

When the settlers at Gonzales received Ugartechea's order, they secretly buried the cannon in a peach orchard and plowed it over. The women and children were sent to hide in the river bottoms. A handful of Mexican soldiers who had been sent to fetch the cannon were captured, but one escaped to alert his superiors in San Antonio. A call to arms fired through the colonies. "Freemen of Texas," screamed one broadside. "TO ARMS!!! TO ARMS!!! Now's the day, and Now's the hour."

The Gonzales "boys" began rigging for a fight. Boats beached on the west side of the Guadalupe River were rowed and poled across to the east side, beyond Mexican recall. Several souls applied themselves to making a flag for their minuteman army. Daubing black paint upon a six-foot section of white cotton cloth, they painted a crude black cannon tube with a lone star above it and the words "Come and Take It" beneath.[11]

Then they waited. Within days, an exotic menagerie of Anglo-Americans came pouring in to the "seat of war," weapons in hand.

"Words are inadequate to convey an impression of the appearance of the first Texas army as it formed in marching order," wrote one of the members of that army, a blacksmith named Noah Smithwick. "Nothing short of ocular demonstration could do it justice. It certainly bore little resemblance to the army of my childhood dreams. Buckskin breeches were the nearest approach to uniform, and there was wide diversity even there, some being new and soft and yellow, while others, from long familiarity with rain and grease and dirt, had become hard and black and shiny. . . . Boots being an unknown quantity, some wore shoes and some moccasins. Here a broad-brimmed sombrero overshadowed the military cap at its side; there a tall 'beegum' rode familiarly beside a coonskin cap, with the tail hanging down behind, as all well regulated tails should do. Here a big American horse loomed up above the nimble Spanish pony ranged beside him; there a half-broke mustang pranced beside a sober methodical mule. Here a bulky roll of bed quilts jostled a pair of 'store' blankets; there the shaggy brown buffalo robe contrasted with a gaily checkered counterpane. . . . In lieu of a canteen, each man carried a Spanish gourd, a curious specimen of the gourd family, having two round bowls, each holding near a quart, connected by a short neck, apparently designed for adjusting a strap about. A fantastic military array to a casual observer, but the one great purpose animating every heart clothed us in a uniform more perfect in our eyes than was ever donned by regulars on dress parade." [12]

A preacher whipped this strange-looking crew into a frenzy with a recitation of the wrongs the Mexicans had visited upon them. Among the most vocal and agitated fighters, one savage man stood out, Martin Palmer, the so-called Panther. A huge Virginian and chronic frontiersman, Palmer had earned his nickname while serving in the Missouri legislature and thrashing fellow members in a free-for-all fistfight. He looked, dressed, and acted more like the already-famous Davy Crockett than Crockett himself. His skin was burned bronze and his hair hung long and braided Indian-style. He wore a buckskin hunting shirt and leather pants, and parked a panther-skin cap on his head. He came well mounted and armed, and people who knew him knew he'd come for a fight. In his own words, he was "just itching and clawing for a scrap with the cowardly greasers." [13]

Next to such greasy-haired, barrel-chested warriors, young lawyer Buck Travis was nondescript. Practically invisible, he milled among the army of a hundred or so men and boys, a mere recruit with no rank at all. Among the group's leaders was a Georgia slave trader named James Walker Fannin, probably the most formally trained Anglo-American soldier in all Texas. In his midteens, Fannin had spent seventeen months at West Point. A few days later another salty War Dog showed up. This was Ben Milam, freshly escaped from Mexican custody in Coahuila. Having shredded his clothes in the desert, he had confiscated pieces of a Mexican uniform and arrived in Gonzales with sleeves and cuffs six inches too short.

The men were put to various tasks, from cutting chain and iron bars into grapeshot and crude cannonballs to carving down cane from the riverside brake and lashing on hammered, sharpened files to make lances. Some dug the cannon out from the peach orchard and mounted it on a primitive truck with wheels made of a cottonwood tree trunk cross-sectioned and fitted with axles. Except for a few rifled barrels, the rebels' technology was no different from that employed by their ancestors in the Revolutionary War and War of 1812. For most, the Bowie knife or Arkansas toothpick, a butcher knife with a handle guard, represented innovation, and nearly all came equipped with one.

Many of the men pulling together at Gonzales had little or no idea why they were fighting. "I cannot remember that there was any distinct understanding as to the position we were to assume toward Mexico," said Smithwick. "Some were for independence; some for the constitution of

1824; and some for anything, just so it was a row. But we were all ready to fight.''[14]

On the last day of the month, a unit of one hundred Mexican cavalry appeared on the west bank of the Guadalupe, but then withdrew to a more defensible point seven miles upriver to await further instructions from San Antonio. Their retreat spurred the Anglo-Americans into a concerted pursuit.

In darkness, the rebels stalked the Mexican cavalry. Their cannon, dwarfed by its shrieking, smoking log wheels and timber axles and towed by two yokes of longhorn steers, was under the command of a Gonzales blacksmith named Almeron Dickinson, who patiently nursed along the "flying artillery," as the contraption was christened.

More than 160 volunteers had thrown in together by this time, two thirds of them on foot. Raging for a fight, they waited out the darkness, only to face a solid bank of river fog at dawn. The fog hung just above knee level, so they could see some distance by peering underneath it. Forming up in a line on either side of their makeshift Come and Take It flag, the rebel army pressed forward through the fog to within 350 yards of the Mexican unit. Dickinson touched off a blast of their flying artillery. The Mexican cavalry instantly retreated and requested a parley.

The commander from each side met upon horseback in the center of a cornfield to confer. The Mexican captain wanted to know why the Anglo-Americans were attacking him. The Anglo-American colonel gave a high-handed lecture about constitutional rights and liberty and invited the Mexicans to join the revolution. The Mexican captain explained that he had his orders, which were to demand the cannon, and if refused to encamp somewhere in the vicinity until further orders arrived. The Anglo-American colonel told him either to surrender or fight. The Mexican captain repeated that he had his orders. Each returned to his side of the cornfield.

The American colonel wheeled on his horse and raced back to his army. As he drew close he shouted, "Charge 'em, boys, and give 'em hell."[15]

Once again Dickinson fired off his cannon. The rebels double-timed across the field while the cannon played into the Mexican ranks, killing or wounding several of the enemy soldiers.

The Mexicans fled, abandoning their baggage and making off for San Antonio. The victorious rebels were back in Gonzales shortly after noon, their sole casualty a bloody nose. The locals staged a huge celebration with corn bread and barbecued beef and all-night dancing in the open air.[16]

Within a week the undermanned presidio at nearby Goliad fell to the Anglo-Americans, providing them with ten thousand dollars in military stores, including two hundred muskets and carbines, six saddles, a hundred four-pounder balls, four dozen lance heads, and one to two hundred bayonets. Equally important, the capture of Goliad gave the Anglo-Americans further momentum. Even without looking at a map of Texas, every man knew what lay next. San Antonio glistened in their minds.

= 5 =

"THE VOLUNTEERS FROM the States!"

A muscular frontiersman raised his sparkling goblet in toast to the fifty mercenaries who had just arrived on foot from the other side of the Sabine River. "The Greys!"

An unearthly sight met the New Orleans Greys. It was, in the classical sense, grotesque . . . a fanciful marriage of nature and man.

There in the center of a 150-foot-long plank table set with white china and polished crystal—but lacking a single fork or knife—lay an entire black bear, "hide and bones, meat and claws." For some reason, this giant carcass had been christened "Mr. Petz." Locked between Mr. Petz's fangs hung the red, white, and green flag of the Mexican Republic with the legend "1824." That particular year had produced a version of the Mexican constitution most favorable to colonists, therefore they were now claiming allegiance to it. Actually the 1824 Constitution clearly established religious *in*tolerance—one had to be Catholic to settle Texas lands. It prohibited the slave trade the colonists engaged in and authorized the President to arrest any person when the safety of the nation was threatened, which was exactly why Travis and other War Dogs had been ordered imprisoned. But the colonists could comfortably bind themselves to the 1824 Constitution because the Mexican Congress under Santa Anna had just revoked it. By supporting a usurped constitution, the Anglo-Americans could go about pretending their good faith had been abused and they had been duped by evil tyrants.

Besides the grisly black bear, the table was heavy with raccoons, squirrels, turkeys, and the hindquarters and backbone of a roasted ox. To the youngest Grey, a seventeen-year-old German boy named Herman Ehrenberg, the table presented a weird, incongruous solar system with "foaming champagne and sparkling Rhine" orbiting the scarcely dead wild animals.[1]

Most if not all of the Greys had come to Texas equipped with Bowie knives, and so they set to the meat with relish. "Toast was drunk on

64

toast," young Ehrenberg remembered. "Political speeches were made; the causes of the war were discussed; inflammatory appeals resounded; thought was also taken of the squatter women [who had cooked] as they sat at their hearths, and it was already very late when the feast was over."

This was the way they'd envisioned the revolution, a gallant lark through wild, exotic terrain, with beautiful women presenting hand-stitched silk flags and citizens gladly offering up their fruits of the land. In San Augustine, the local militia marched out to greet them, and a gray-haired planter advised the boys to make every shot count the way he had at the Battle of New Orleans. A second company of New Orleans Greys were greeted by cannon salutes and handkerchief-waving crowds. In Brazoria little girls cast flowers in their path and the Mother of Texas, Mrs. Jane Long, "the queenly and patriotic widow of General Long," spread before them the finest fare Texas had to offer. Not one man or boy among the Greys could have imagined that just a few months later—on Palm Sunday—they would be exterminated almost to the soldier.

The Greys had taken form only a few weeks earlier in New Orleans under the spell of Halley's comet, whose remarkable tail stretched across one quarter of the western sky that long October.[2]

"Awesomely the clock in the Cathedral [of New Orleans] struck eight," recalled one witness attending the first of the save-Texas rallies, "and a Mississippi of people flowed toward the gigantic coffee-house, the Arcade."[3]

The keynote speaker at that rally was a War Dog from Texas, a lawyer and budding politician named Adolphus Sterne, who had come to Louisiana to raise money and volunteers. German by birth, Jewish by paternity, Sterne had smuggled weapons in bales of dry goods and barrels of coffee for the misguided rebels of the 1828 Fredonian Revolt. The Mexicans had caught him and ordered him shot for treason, but his Masonic lodge in New Orleans interceded and arranged a parole with his captors. With this sort of filibustering pedigree, Sterne was implicitly trusted by the War Dogs, and the provisional government had named him as one of their agents to beat the war drum in the United States.

Sterne was instantly successful. This first rally harvested thousands of dollars in pledges for the cause of liberty in Texas, and a list for volunteers provided the first of two companies of New Orleans Greys.[4]

Thousands attended public meetings throughout the South. Committees were appointed, money was subscribed, men stepped forward.

"A six-foot Kentuckian now ascended the speakers' platform," Ehrenberg reported, "and signed up at the top [of the list] under the thundering applause of the enthusiastic mass that surrounded him. 'Old Kentucky' was as always the first to seize the rifle when it was necessary to go into the field to struggle for the right.''[5]

A band calling themselves the Georgia Volunteers formed on November 12 at a spirited rally in Macon. An eighteen-year-old belle named Johanna Troutman presented the young lions with the first Lone Star flag, a white silk banner carrying a blue, five-point star and the time-honored inscription "Liberty or Death." The sight of 120 Georgia volunteers shouldering arms and basking in local glory in Montgomery, Alabama, prompted fifteen young men to join up on the spot. They were the beginning of several Alabama companies which eventually numbered 165 men wearing red jeans uniforms and bearing muskets borrowed from the Alabama state arsenal.[6]

The Texas Revolution could not have come at a better time for a generation of young militiamen steeped in Sir Walter Scott and the American Revolution. By 1835 the Indians of the South had been largely pacified, and the U.S. Army was becoming institutionalized as a professional fighting body. That left the local Southern militias with precious little to do except decorate themselves with uniforms, their town squares with fieldpieces, and their horses with military baubles. The closest they got to combat was firing off the town cannon on the Fourth of July.

Militias practically defined the South. The tradition of county militia musters was already old when seventeenth-century Englishmen brought it to Virginia with them.[7] Militias functioned as a glue between settlers scattered through a county. Muster days—held every few months— allowed elected captains and colonels to get head counts and gave militia troops a chance to practice rudimentary maneuvers.

Traveling from every point in the county, men showed up on muster day with their whole families. The militia was called to arms with the same cry used to bring Southern courts to order. "Oh yes! Oh yes! Oh yes!" a voice would call out, making the most of the corrupted French "Oyez" or "hear ye."

Many militias mustered in a riot of mismatched gear, dressed in calico, denim, linsey-woolsey, or buckskin and wearing moccasins, brogans, or nothing at all on their bare feet. They bore every form of gun from long rifle to shotgun and horse pistol, and for those too poor to risk damaging their hunting guns in practice combat, shaved branches or cornstalks sufficed (thus the term "cornstalk militias").[8]

While the men drilled to fife and drums playing "Yankee Doodle" or "The Jaybird Died with the Whooping Cough," their families would shop, gossip, and ready meats, cakes, and pies—and barrels of beer, cider, and corn liquor—for the afternoon picnic. As counties grew more stable and prosperous, the injection of money began to show up in militia appearances, and the drills themselves became something to watch. Plumes, scarlet sashes, insignias, flags, embossed buttons, matching uniforms, and other peacock flourishes did much to elevate the volunteers' self-esteem, but next to nothing to improve their groups' fighting skills.

In fact, by the 1820s and 1830s the actual combat value of these militias had become a matter of hot debate. As the national army grew in size and experience, regulars looked down upon militiamen as undisciplined, second-rate fighters who had cut and run just as often as they'd stayed and fought.[9]

Frontiersmen, especially Southerners, abhorred a regular standing army and attacked West Point as un-American and aristocratic. David Crockett went so far as to propose abolishing West Point on the grounds that its students were coddled, privileged, and "too nice to work; they are first educated there for nothing, and then they must have salaries to support them after they leave there."[10] He and thousands of others pointed to the much-cited Battle of New Orleans and countless skirmishes with forest Indians as proof that militias were and always would be the backbone of American defense. They went on believing that until the end of the Civil War. Now, as militia-trained volunteers flocked to Texas, their reliability seemed to confirm itself.

Volunteers rushed to Texas steeped in snowballing propaganda about defenseless Anglo-Americans and hordes of savage Mexicans. No matter how they arrived—dropped upon the coast of Texas by schooner or threading their ways up rivers on steamboats or through forests and prairies on foot or horseback—the volunteers showed up ignorant of the realities but happily spouting geysers of liberty talk.

The volunteers came for another reason beside that of defending the latest Anglo-Saxon beachhead. They came for land.

One of the first pieces of rebel propaganda was written by Sam Houston three days after the Gonzales cannon routed the Mexican cavalry along the Guadalupe River. In it he clearly tied gain to patriotism.

"If *volunteers* from the United States will join their brethren in this section [Texas], they will receive liberal bounties of land," Houston said. "We have millions of acres of our best *lands* unchosen and unappropriated.

"Let each man come with a good rifle and one hundred rounds of ammunition and come soon.

"Our war cry is 'Liberty or Death.'

"Our principles are to support the constitution, and *down with the usurper!!!.*"[11]

In return for their military service in the rebel army, volunteers throughout the United States were promised varying amounts of land. The amount was finally standardized.

The so-called auxiliary volunteers from the United States who remained in service until the end of the fighting were guaranteed 1,280 acres. A six-month stint with the rebel army earned a volunteer 640 acres; a three-month stint, 320 acres. These military bounties of land stood over and above any land claims an individual made under peacetime colonization laws.[12]

Land fever was at its absolute peak in 1835. Wherever one traveled in the United States men were talking about land.[13] Public lands in one state after another were snatched up by speculators. From the Wisconsin public lands to Mississippi, Louisiana, and Arkansas, vast sections of the nation were bought up in a matter of months. Land fever was hot and contagious. It drew Go Ahead men by the thousands, and when the land began running out, the Go Ahead men spilled over into Texas.

Texas beckoned as an open treasure chest. Naturally the Mexican government saw the swarm of patriot-volunteers as pirates. Then, one day, the British government did too.

On the evening of November 21, the brig *Matawamkeag* set sail for Texas. On board, she carried 180 volunteers under the command of a Col. E. H. Stanley. Nine days out, as the brig was passing Eleuthera in the Bahamas, the colonel took seventeen of his men ashore and plundered a plantation. The English brig *Serpent* captured the *Matawamkeag* and placed the volunteer company under the surveillance of a black West Indian regiment. The charge was piracy. (Ultimately the men were released.)[14]

One can argue that Colonel Stanley's batch was an aberration, that the volunteers entering Texas were sterling patriots. And for a while, the colonists and "gentlemen-squatters" of Texas would have agreed. But as more and more bunches of volunteers crisscrossed Texas rushing to and from various points, the settlers began to complain loudly about the theft of their property and violence. Inviting mercenaries into one's backyard proved to be a double-edged proposition.

But in the fall of 1835, war was still fun and the mercenaries were still welcomed with open arms. They brought with them more than weapons and itchy trigger fingers and a jaunty esprit de corps. They also brought innocence, and besides making for good cannon fodder, innocence reminded the settlers all over again that Texas was their Eden.

As the first company of Greys worked north by steamboat up the deep and narrow Red River, they peered down from the decks at alligators sunning among the river dross. Twenty-foot-high canebrakes fenced in the river, and mosquitoes hung in the dripping moss.

Finally the Greys freed themselves of the riverine forests and ventured out to the prairies, and they discovered a terrain so vastly similar that men had learned to use the wind as a directional.[15] The grass stood as high as a man in places, bent down here and there by buffalo or Comanche parties. Great black wolves called in the night, and during the day packs of curious coyotes trotted in rows beside the company.

Entering Spanish country, the boys encountered their first tastes of Hispanic culture.[16] Mexican food was distinctly unappealing to the newcomers. Corn made up the bulk of their diets in the form of johnnycakes, corn bread, roasted corn, and so forth. But they found corn tortillas odd, and the Mexican love of hot chiles unfathomable.

Spanish country held other wonders too. They heard it said that "Texas is bound together with rawhide" and found horses and cattle so abundant that when a wagon wheel broke they slaughtered a cow and mended it with fresh rawhide, and when they needed a rope they sharp-shot a wild mustang to harvest its hair.[17] They saw furniture, boats, and even whole oxcarts wired together with nothing but strips of leather. As did every Anglo-American coming to Texas, they recognized the Mexican *vaqueros* as horsemen without parallel.

As the Greys crossed toward San Antonio de Béxar, they found the countryside magnificent. Near Bastrop, gigantic pine trees broke the prairie. Pecans and hickories fell from the trees, and ripe persimmons lay on the ground. Trout, perch, and catfish drifted in the rivers, and honeybees swam through the sunlight.

Texas was a field of light. "The [sun's] gold hue . . . spread itself out over the majestic tree tops," Herman Ehrenberg marveled, "but it finally disappeared also." One night the Greys awoke to a huge purple cloud enveloping half the sky, a prairie fire. Another time, the Greys broke their boredom by lighting the grass on fire themselves.[18] They ate from the land. They slept on the ground. When townspeople offered them beds, the Greys declined, more comfortable on the grass and dirt.

And then one morning they reached the war.

"It was the last watch before the break of day, which I could barely await as I sat dreaming before the fire and gazing into the flames," said

Ehrenberg, "when—listen! The winged morning wind wafted the muffled thunder of the cannon of the Alamo over to us. . . . In a moment
everybody was on his feet, breakfast was prepared, coffee was cooked,
horses were saddled and everything was ready."[19]

Dawn unveiled a sight the Greys had never dreamed of, "in spite of
our active imagination and the descriptions and accounts of the War of
Independence in the States." Seven feet deep, twenty yards wide, the
warm waters of the San Antonio River slid quietly by on their left. The
magnolia and pecan trees crowding the riverbanks obscured their sight of
the town itself. But ahead, three quarters of a mile across prairie flats and
barren cornfields, looming among tall grass, mesquite, and fat clusters of
cactus, lay the Alamo, the mission that had become a fortress.

For almost as long as the Greys had been working their way across
Texas—and they had had five hundred miles to cover—the Alamo had
been under siege. The legends forget, but before the Anglo-Americans
spent thirteen days defending the Alamo from Mexican siege, the Mexicans spent forty-one days defending it from Anglo-American siege. Before the Mexicans struck down the Anglo-American flags in the Alamo,
the Anglo-Americans cut loose the Mexican flag.

The Greys arrived in San Antonio de Béxar on November 21, 1835.
By that time, Mexican forces under General Cós had been staving off the
tightening siege for three full weeks. After the Gonzales cannon fight, the
Anglo-Americans had patched together an army and selected Stephen
Austin their general. Some of the best advice Austin received was some
of the first. A planter-colonist named Eli Mercer stressed the importance
of fighting a guerrilla war. "Please to recollect," he said to Austin, "we
have not a man to lose, but must calculate on gaining our Victories with
out loss. . . . I think the only chance in our situation is to fight them from
the Brush, fight them from the Brush all the time; never take our Boys to
an open fight, our Situation will not admit of it. All must be deciplind
[sic] before we can fight in the open field."[20]

It was excellent advice. But General Austin ignored it. Later on, Sam
Houston would try to pull the Anglo-American forces back into eastern
Texas for a fight "from the Brush." Still later, as Santa Anna proceeded
against the rebels, it was exactly that kind of guerrilla war that the
Mexican general would fear the most.

But the rebel army kept acting like a conventional army capable of
fighting a conventional war. Besieging the Alamo was a conventional
tactic. Holding the Alamo—or attempting to—was a conventional tactic
too. With very few exceptions, every Anglo-American casualty in the

Texas Revolution resulted from militia-trained officers believing their rabble were a regular army. But that was later. In the beginning, all was confidence.

Realizing the crude and rowdy material with which they had to work, the drillmasters wasted no time on martial formations. Instead they hammered away at teaching the rebels not to fire their single-shot guns all at once.

On foot and horseback, the rebel army had closed in on San Antonio, cannon in tow. The cannon was next to worthless except as a large shotgun, and the carriage made for slow going. The oxen pulling the cannon had to be prodded along with customized file-head lances, and the cottonwood wheels and axles squealed and smoked. The rebels tried lubricating the axles with water until they ran out, then slathered on tallow, which didn't work. Finally they gave up on their solitary field-piece and buried it at Sandy Creek.

Approaching the chain of crumbling missions that stretched south below San Antonio, some of the rebels had developed second thoughts about taking on the Mexican army. Skirmishing with a hundred cavalry troops sent to observe them was one thing. Joining five hundred or more soldiers in real combat was something else again. "Boys," said one tentative warrior, "I don't like this. Ef thar's a big force of 'em they'll whop us." Immediately a big Pennsylvania Dutchman hissed back, "Shet up; don't say they'll weep us; you're weeped already!"[21]

Their first battle had come on October 28 at the old Concepción mission, where ninety Anglo-Americans found themselves face to face with four hundred Mexican troops equipped with a cannon.

Under James Bowie's command, the rebels scuttled down a six-foot-deep riverbank which became their ready-made breastwork. Rebel pickets came running in from the plain and the Mexicans opened fire. One picket felt a tug and, to his great annoyance, saw that his powder horn had been shot away. Another picket named Pen Jarvis dropped to earth, apparently killed. But upon examination, it was found that a Mexican musket ball had struck only Jarvis's knife, driving its blade into his leg: thereafter the lucky man was known as Bowie Knife Jarvis.

Three times the Mexicans charged. But hidden below ground level, the rebels were untouchable and calmly knocked away with their rifle fire. Mexican grapeshot slashed through the trees overhead, raining down ripe pecans, which the rebels casually gathered and ate for breakfast. "Keep under cover, boys, and reserve your fire," Bowie called out, "we haven't a man to spare." The sole Anglo-American casualty—the first of the

Texas Revolution—came when a knot of excited men climbed up out of the river cut and exposed themselves to Mexican fire. An immensely powerful young man named Big Dick Andrews promptly fell, gutted by a lead ball. Noah Smithwick, the blacksmith, found Big Dick "lying as he had fallen, great drops of sweat already gathering on his white, drawn face, and the life blood gushing from a hole in the left side, just below the ribs. I ran to him and attempted to raise him. 'Dick,' I cried, 'are you hurt?' 'Yes, Smith,' he replied, 'I'm killed; lay me down.' I laid him down and put something under his head. It was the last time I saw him alive. There was no time for sentiment. There was the enemy, outnumbering us four to one, charging our position, so I picked up my gun and joined my comrades."[21]

The firefight lasted only thirty minutes. Ravaged by rebel sharpshooting, the Mexicans had possibly sixty killed and as many wounded. The rebels raked the Mexican artillery crew one last time, then charged, panicking the soldiers. Without taking time to detach their mules from the caissons, the Mexicans fled, three to a mule. The rebels turned the Mexican cannon around and fired off a charge, "adding wings to their flight."

Then something happened which struck the Anglo-Americans as odd. The battlefield lay heaped with dead and wounded troops. The rebels had scarcely taken control of the field when the wounded Mexicans began pleading for mercy.

"I had approached a young Mexican of good appearance and above the average of intelligence," said Creed Taylor of the aftermath. "He lay where he had fallen with a broken arm and a bullet through his bowels. He held up his hand and begged me to spare him, saying that he was fatally wounded and wanted to see the padre before he died."[22]

It took the baffled rebels a few minutes to figure out what was going on.

"Having no knowledge of civilized warfare," Smithwick said, "the poor wounded wretches throught they were to be summarily dispatched, and it was pitiful to hear them begging for the miserable lives that no one thought of taking." Later, Anglo-Americans would bitterly accuse the Mexicans of betraying the mercy that was shown them at the Battle of Concepción.

After the Concepción fight, the rebel army slowly encircled San Antonio and the Alamo. On the night of November 3, from the cover of Mexican *jacales* (little huts made of wood and twigs), the rebels opened up on a picket guard stationed outside the south wall of the Alamo.

Feeling frisky and properly warmed up, the rebels urged their leaders to unleash them upon San Antonio to root out the Mexican army. However, a majority of officers counseled waiting for siege artillery before storming the Alamo and town. Sitting around and waiting rankled the volunteers, many of whom had already served out the thirty days militiamen traditionally owed a campaign. Desertions soon began eating away the army. Rumors that a cannon had been shipped to Velasco gave whimsical deserters their punch line. As they departed they facetiously declared, "I'm going after that cannon." No one stopped them. Colonel Fannin, the West Point dropout, had actively favored volunteers until this prolonged exposure to them. Quite suddenly, he changed his tune and was calling for a regular army.[23]

The officers were equally cantankerous and constantly jockeying for better rank and more power. The army was composed of numerous milita groups, and each group came with its own elected officers. These officers jealously maneuvered for power from the very start, and as events progressed their petty intrigues nearly wrecked the army altogether. As he watched his army melt away, Austin despaired.

Meanwhile, as "the Boys" were killing Mexicans in and around San Antonio, the delegates to the Consultation or revolutionary convention in San Felipe de Austin were also wrangling and equivocating. Though they formed their own provisional government—a revolutionary act—they were still not prepared to go whole hog and declare independence. Instead they went on pretending their rebellion was against Mexican rule, not against Mexico. They pledged to obey Mexico so long as Mexico obeyed its 1824 Constitution.[24]

For over a month Austin's army stagnated at San Antonio. Now and then some skirmishing broke out to declare the rebels' fighting spirit, or some minor gain occurred giving an appearance of progress. The irrepressible Travis dashed about on horseback. He burned vast stretches of grassland to cheat any approaching troops of forage, and he managed to capture 290 tamed horses and ten mules with the aid of an incredibly adept scout named Erastus "Deaf" Smith.

Toward the end of November, a rumor developed that General Cós had sent to Matamoros (on the Rio Grande) for his troops' payroll. When Deaf Smith spotted a pack train approaching San Antonio, Bowie and a hundred mounted volunteers intercepted the mule train and charged it repeatedly. When the running skirmish finally ended, the Mexicans had lost nearly fifty men and the Anglo-Americans had suffered two wounded. The surviving Mexican troops made it into San Antonio with their part of their pack train, and the rebels captured the remainder. Instead of gold or silver, the alleged payroll train turned out to be nothing but grass for the

Mexican army's horses and cattle. The bloody, ludicrous battle became known as the Grass Fight.

At dawn on November 21, the 1st Company of New Orleans Greys approached the Alamo, and "millions" of blackbirds leapt into the sky, circling in a swarm that darkened the sun. The rebels' horses and cattle grazed peacefully in the tall grass among the cactus. Puffs of dust drifted serenely toward the ramshackle camp, thrown up by ineffective Mexican grapeshot. In the nearby field used for butchering cattle, wolves and coyotes rooted among the heads, skins, and offal. Beaks open, wings cocked wide, vultures perched on pecan trees and basked in the morning sunshine. The youngest Grey, Ehrenberg, decided the sunning vultures were "a true picture of the Mexicans."

The Greys' arrival coincided with the morning muster. From a hodgepodge of tents and huts scattered "promiscuously here and there without any regard to order," half-dressed soldiers half assembled in front of their sergeants. Because the muster had caught them fixing breakfast, Ehrenberg said, "they were without firearms and most of them had in the one hand a friendly wooden frying spit ornamented with a smoking fry and in the other the famous Bowie knife. Several did not fall into line as their partially roasted meat did not permit them to leave it to its own fate or possibly the threatening condition of the coffee did not allow them to take their places." The sergeant proceeded with roll call, with men answering "here" from the line, from their cook fires, or from inside their tents. He did not need to dismiss the assembly, for the instant a man called out he took his own leave. The Greys looked on, dumbfounded.

Very quickly the Greys entered into the droll siege rhythms. Not a man among the rebels did any more or less than he wished, which probably explained why there seemed to be no orders being issued. The Greys put this laissez-faire to their rambunctious use. On their first morning several of them ran—literally—out to a small artillery entrenchment located close to the Alamo. There the 2nd Company of New Orleans Greys had set up two little four-pounder cannons. The 2nd Company had departed New Orleans well after the 1st Company, but with the advantage of sea travel it had reached San Antonio long before. Now men of the two companies mingled fraternally and enjoyed themselves with the cannons.

To great good humor and applause, the troops tried their hand at aiming the four-pounders. The Alamo's old masonry offered any number of targets. Boasts were made, bets placed. A spot midway between the third and fourth windows of the barracks was declared. One of the men stepped forward, offering a hundred ready-made bullets to twenty that he could hit the mark. He fired wide and lost.

Another aspirant took a turn, betting his brace of pistols against the two second-rate pistols tucked in Deaf Smith's pea jacket belt. "Well! Sir—reckon—can risk it," Deaf Smith stammered out. The ball missed and Deaf Smith collected. But he was a good sport. "Well, in order to give you revenge, comrade, I will take shot also. If this child doesn't hit either—well, comrade, you may have your pistols back again." As if aiming a rifle, he squinted down the cannon barrel, traced geometrical equations in the air, and finally reckoned he was ready. His shot obliterated the mark.

The rebel artillerymen gleefully punched holes in the Alamo, sometimes rolling down whole sections of the adobe walls with their iron balls. None of it fit into a strategy, for there was no strategy. They had no plans for storming the mission-fortress. "The whole thing was done for amusement," said Ehrenberg, "and every effective shot was accompanied with loud applause from the Greys."[25] Their recreation damaged the walls and prevented the Mexican soldiers from improving the fortifications. Later, when the rebels inherited the Alamo they had to shore up the walls they'd playfully shot apart. It was through one of these patched breaches that the Mexicans under Santa Anna would gain entrance on March 6.

The rebels' jolly nonchalance was contagious, and in no time the Greys decided to spring an impromptu invasion upon the occupied town. It was the afternoon of their first day in San Antonio. Like puppies drawn toward a noise, a band of thirty-five Greys started by firing at some snipers and soon found themselves charging headlong down the dirt streets of San Antonio with picket guards in retreat. The Mexicans had a reputation for abysmal marksmanship. Holding their faces away from the stock and squeezing their eyes shut—or simply firing from the hip or blindly from behind a wall—they would snap off shots twenty and thirty feet above their targets.[26] This instilled the Greys with further bravado and hilarity, and they raced around the town freely, looting whichever homes they wished.

"After we had penetrated a small part of the town in this manner and, drunk with victory, were loaded down with booty for the kitchen, we thought of retreating because we would soon have the whole Mexican army on our necks if we didn't," said Ehrenberg. But they had waited too long. Solid iron cannonballs began slugging at the houses around them and grapeshot rattled down the streets. The gang of Greys bowed low and ran back and forth, trying to escape. Beyond town, they saw the corn-

fields thick with blue-coated Mexican infantry, and this would have terminated their frolic if not for Deaf Smith.

For weeks, Deaf Smith had been urging an attack upon the Mexican
stronghold, but the rebel officers kept postponing a confrontation until
more reinforcements showed up. Now Smith saw his opening and took it.
Grabbing a Mexican tricolor flag, he mounted a horse and led the rebels
in the camp toward the cornfield. Like a wild man, he galloped from left
to right in front of the army while bullets whipped holes through his flag.
Playing "Yankee Doodle," the rebels appeared at one edge of the field,
and Deaf Smith prepared to lead them into the town and against the
Alamo and get the revolution over with. But the Mexican soldiers fled
back to their walls and breastworks, and that left the rebels with little
option except to retreat with their foolhardy Greys. Remarkably they had
not suffered a scratch.

"We were led back in triumph to our camp together with our welcome kitchen utensils," said Ehrenberg. "After that the Greys rose pow-
erfully in the esteem of the brave Deaf Smith, and he was accustomed to
call us by no other name than his boys."[26]

As more reinforcements showed up, more of the original rebel army
went back to their farms. This changed the army's chemistry, for the
mercenaries arriving from the United States were even more cocksure and
radical than the Anglo-Americans who had spent a few years in Texas.
The mercenaries had seen no real action and so could go on believing they
were somehow impervious to musket balls and grapeshot. Death was
something that happened to the craven Mexicans, not to them. They grew
hungrier for battle and all its rewards. Also they grew just plain hungrier.
It was not yet winter, and already San Antonio's food supply was dwindling. The locals were beginning to hoard their corn in secret caches, like
the fifteen wagonloads Ehrenberg and some Greys discovered in an ancient granary at San José Mission. The mercenaries' clothing was giving
out, and it was unfit for winter anyway. They had come for a lightning-
quick campaign, and instead faced an extended siege. They were not
pleased.

"Should [the Greys] lie in the colonies for three or four months?"
Ehrenberg questioned. "That was not the purpose for which they had
come to Texas. Why did they renounce the brilliant positions and prospects that were offered them in New Orleans? Why did many leave the
parental hearth? For honor, and not to become a soldier, because

the regular soldier is an object of contempt to the industrious citizens of the States; only seldom does one find the sons of Uncle Sam among them; they are mainly whiskey-loving foreigners."[26]

Travis left. Austin left, glad to leave the soldiering to other generals. Smithwick and scores like him left. Houston privately denounced the army for not breaking the siege and retiring east of the Colorado River into eastern Texas.[27] Colonel James Grant, an ex-Highlander from Scotland and an extraordinarily greedy land speculator, nearly succeeded in seducing the Greys to abandon San Antonio and ride with him to the coastal town of Matamoros, at the mouth of the Rio Grande. The Greys hesitated. In the space of their pause, the commanding officer lost control of the army.

After Austin's departure, the volunteers had voted Col. Edward Burleson to the top command position. Burleson was open to attacking San Antonio, especially after three Anglo-Americans living in San Antonio reported that the Mexican army's morale was sinking fast. The troops were readied for an attack on December 4, but then delayed for security reasons. The delay—one more in a long string of false starts—helped conservative officers persuade Burleson that the rebel army's best hope was to pack it up and retreat to Gonzales. At last it seemed the siege was going to break.

But then Ben Milam and Frank Johnson, two of the most persistent War Dogs, both of them land speculators, confronted Burleson in his tent. Unhappy with Burleson's decision, Milam and Johnson mutinied. With the mercenaries and what remained of the original rebels waiting outside, Milam threw back the tent flap and stepped out. He scratched a line in the dirt with his rifle stock, took off his slouch hat and waved it in the air. "Boys!" he called out. "Who'll go with old Ben Milam into Béxar?"

The boys answered with a deafening roar of "I will."

"Well," said Milam, "if you are going with me, get on this side." Three hundred men crossed his line.[28]

The deposed commander, General Burleson, made the most of the moment. He urged the troops who had not stepped forward to at least remain in camp as a reserve force.

That night a norther blew down off the high prairie, flattening tents and huts and demolishing campfires to the last spark. The men lay quietly under their blankets until two o'clock in the morning, when they were called to order. The roll call found only 210 of some 300 men still on hand. The rest had skipped south during the night. Wrapped in their blankets, the remaining rebels and mercenaries shouldered their guns and marched into the dark wind.

As they raced across the cornfields toward town, the Alamo reared upon their left, "a black colossus." A small, diversionary party of rebels snapped away at the Alamo walls and immediately elicited a thunderous response of Mexican cannon fire, drumrolls, and bugle signals. The main body dashed into town. Just before dawn, a load of grapeshot scoured the street and most of the rebels ducked into a nearby house.

This was the first time many had ever been in a Mexican house, and they found its thick stone and adobe walls curious. In the back patio a huge steer stood tied to a stake, lowing unhappily at the early morning trespassers. Soon he was cooking over a fire. With great excitement the division of Greys set up a six-pounder behind the lower wall. Every man kept his head down, for the Mexicans had directed more than a dozen six-pounders against their position with balls and grapeshot.

"The balls sang us a morning song of a singular kind," Ehrenberg recalled. "In countless tones from soprano down to bass like those of the harp and Aeolus they vibrated over our heads. Several of our men, who had taken position on the flat roof behind the wall, were compelled to keep themselves very quiet; they had never experienced a shooting of this kind before." Even tucked low, they were not safe because the enemy had mounted guns high in the tower of the San Fernando church on the edge of the town plaza.

Very suddenly something happened to sober the happy-go-lucky Greys.

A second division of rebel troops had taken cover in a distant house. Completely unaware of the first division's location, they opened fire when they spotted motion in Ehrenberg's refuge. Instantly the friendly fire dropped an enormous Mississippian to the earth. "The bullet tore the brain out of its cavity and spattered it on the walls and over us who stood near him," said a horrified Ehrenberg. "His colossal body twitched convulsively for hours in the thick clotted blood that flowed out of the wound. It showed us novices the battle of the body with the parting life."

Colonel Milam called for volunteers to run across and inform the second division of their error. Before they could identify themselves, another mercenary dropped his gun. "The wounded man, driven by a mighty force, made an involuntary movement, a puff of wind blew past him and a stream of blood issued from his sleeve. Pale as marble he looked about, clapped his hand on his left shoulder and remarked that he must be wounded, although he felt no pain."[29]

At last the second division quit firing upon the first division and the rebel army could get on with their attack. For two days the street battle seesawed between the rebels and Mexicans. All the while, the cold winter storm whipped the raging town with north winds. The rebels suffered more from thirst than from cold. The San Antonio River lay 150 yards distant and it wasn't long before Mexicans had the banks well covered. The price of water rose to three and four dollars a bucket, but finally no one would risk the Mexican bullets. At last, an anonymous, good-natured Mexican woman who had been in the house when the Greys first broke in offered to go for water. The chivalrous Southern officers forbade her to try, but she laughed and told the Anglo-Americans that as a woman she had nothing to fear from her countrymen, that they would never shoot a woman. She walked to the river in full view of the Mexican soldiers and filled her vessels. Then she stood to return. The Mexican soldiers shot her dead. The Greys were horrified. But not so horrified that they didn't rush down to the river and fill their buckets while the Mexicans reloaded.

Mexican gunfire kept the invaders pinned down. The Greys held their caps above the breastworks on ramrods and watched them twitch with each bullet hole. When the Mexican troops finally discovered the ruse, they quit firing. The Greys escalated the game by resting their caps on gourds and "peeking" over the walls. "This had the result that the enemy shot his powder away and occasionally exposed himself to the eyes of the backwoodsmen or the Greys," said Ehrenberg, "when, if he did not drop himself, he dropped his musket with a shattered arm."[29]

A more serious problem presented itself in the Mexican cannon fire, which was patiently gnawing away at the rebels' adobe walls and the flimsy *jacales*. Bit by bit, the balls eroded the Anglo-Americans' toehold in the town. Their vulnerability was dramatized when General Cós's troops unfurled a red flag from the San Fernando Church tower, signifying no quarter. The rebel army viewed it as colorful poppycock. The rebels found it ironic that now they alone were flying the Mexican tricolor. But their situation was serious. Outgunned by Mexican artillery, they had either to advance to houses with stronger stone walls or give up the urban street fighting and retreat.

At noon on December 7, the third day of battle, a Tennessee-born frontiersman, Henry Wax Karnes, hefted a heavy crowbar in his hands and considered. Opposite the second division's crumbling cover lay a large stone house with Mexican troops both inside and on the roof. Capture that stronghold and the rebels would not only eliminate a major source of suppressing fire but also position themselves directly upon the plaza, a strategic prize. Karnes was a scouting partner of Deaf Smith, and he shared Smith's go-ahead moxie. Finally he announced his decision. "Boys," he said, "load your guns and be ready. I am going to break open that door, and I want you to pour a steady hot fire into those fellows on the roof and hold their attention until I can reach the door, and when I break it in I want you boys to make a clean dash for that house."

When it was pointed out that Mexican *escopetas* (blunderbusses) stuck out every window and off the edge of the rooftop, Karnes snorted. "Damn the Mexicans and their *escopetas*. It's that house or retreat. You men do as I tell you."

With the crowbar in one hand, his rifle in the other, Karnes dashed through heavy gunfire and tore his way into the house. Right on his heels came his whole company. Mexican soldiers bolted through a partition door, though some were too slow and were captured.

The rebels could not spare any men to guard prisoners, which left them with no options but to shoot or release them. Without hesitation, they released them. But first the prisoners were required to promise not to raise arms against the rebels. "The paroling of a Mexican soldier required a slight knowledge of the Mexican character," said one captor. "To administer an oath after the American usage had no effect on a Mexican. He regarded it as a form of no value and, if a prisoner, he was liable to be found next day in line of battle, ready to shoot at you again. The Mexicans were Catholics, and no oath was binding upon them unless the Roman cross figured in the proceedings. So with a charcoal snatched from an abandoned 'brasero' it took Captain York but a few minutes to make a cross for each captive on the white lime-plastered wall. The men were marched up, the right hand of each on an outlined cross, their left hands on their breasts, and the oath was administered—and they observed it."[30]

Karnes's crowbar inspired a whole new approach to the battle. Its use freed them from moving down corridors of open and deadly space and allowed them to burrow *through* the houses. With crowbars to pry apart the stone and adobe walls, they could shape a long, protective tunnel anywhere in the city.

For the next two days, the rebels chewed their way through the mud and stone architecture. They would muscle a hole through the wall, discharge their guns into the connecting room, and finish knocking a crude doorway into the chamber. Oftentimes, the rooms held women and children, along with Mexican soldiers, all of whom begged for mercy. All were sent back through the chain of captured houses to safety and parole. Crashing through the wall of one room, Creed Taylor perceived what he called a beautiful little incident.

"A lovely little Mexican girl had concealed her pet kid from the Mexican soldiers. When we had driven them from her mother's room and while yet battering at the next partition, this little girl heard one of our men ask the mother if she could give him something to eat, as he was very hungry. The little girl hastened to bring her pet out of hiding and offered it to the hungry soldier, saying *'Acceptarlo, señor mio. Es todo lo que tenemos!'* ('Accept it, dear sir; it is all we have!')"[30] Given that the Anglo-Americans were in the process of wrecking and looting their homes and that bloodshed was staining their city, one may doubt whether the little girl acted out of some instinctive affection for the heretical invaders. But it was a familiar conceit. Anglo-American men habitually believed the Mexican female desired them above all others.

The rebels brought up a long twelve-pounder cannon and trained it on their ultimate source of grief, the high church tower that commanded the plaza. Dubbed "Langenheim" or Longarm, the twelve-pounder caved in part of the church dome, which the rebels considered fair warning to snipers in the tower. Then they quit firing at the church, Ehrenberg said, "in order to spare the venerable old ruin."[29]

Mesquite patches were set afire to reduce the enemies' cover. And when they ran low on six-pound cannonballs, the rebels would fetch expended balls lying on the outside of their walls and fire them back at the Mexicans "with our compliments."

House by house, the rebels pressed through San Antonio. They took the Garza house, the Navarro house, the priest's house, the Zambrano row, and, on the Calle de la Soledad bordering the river, the Veramendi "palace." This long, one-story stone residence had been owned by James Bowie's father-in-law, Governor Juan Martín de Veramendi, and Bowie had lived there off and on after marrying Ursula. Its prestige aside, the building commanded an important view of the city and it was a contested point. Deaf Smith was wounded on its rooftop. And on December 7, Ben Milam fell to a bullet that pierced his head.[31]

With one well-placed head shot, the rebel command had been decapitated. Milam had been the coup leader, and the men were devastated by the loss of him. A legend grew that when Milam's body was excavated, years later, it showed no signs of decay, one of the classic characteristics

of a saint. Even his boots could still be worn and the black silk handkerchief binding his head looked so fresh it could have been plucked from
the store shelf.[32]

An already confused offensive now verged on complete disarray.
General Burleson remained in camp with his "reserves," that is, the
troops who had not mutinied against him. And though Milam's friend
Frank Johnson was elected the new commander, the rebels felt themselves without a definite leader. The invaders remained a strictly volunteer outfit without orders. If a certain point needed to be stormed,
volunteers were called for.[33]

It was about this time that the rebels began gathering intelligence from
some of their prisoners too wounded to be turned loose. One badly
wounded Mexican captain told Creed Taylor in Spanish that General Cós
was near surrender. A body of six hundred conscripts and convicts had
shown up in bare feet and half-naked, many manacled to prevent desertion, next to none of them trained as soldiers. These men were nothing
but empty stomachs, a useless tax upon what few supplies remained in the
Alamo. Morale was low, ammunition had nearly run out. The Mexican
captain said matters were so bad that a large force of soldiers were
planning to abandon the Alamo at night.

If anything, the situation was worse than the wounded captain described. General Cós had over a thousand men packed within the Alamo
walls, along with many of their women and children who were refugees
from town. Not only had he acquired four hundred exhausted and untrained reinforcements, but his trained units in San Antonio kept pulling
back to the Rio Grande instead of into the Alamo. Near the end, the
refugees saw a group of Alamo soldiers stacking their arms at nightfall
and throwing their saddles and cinches over the walls to desert. Convinced the whole garrison was fleeing and they were to be left to the
Anglo-American wolves, the refugees panicked. They ran about in the
darkness, screaming, "Treason, they want to hand us over, we are lost."
General Cós was trampled and mauled by the mob before finally restoring
order. On December 9, the black flag of death was exchanged for a white
flag. At six o'clock in the morning, under cold, damp clouds, Cós authorized negotiations for surrender.[34]

Unarmed except for their swords, three Mexican officers approached
the enemy line with a lone bugler who sounded the call for a parley. The
rebels leapt from sleep and nearly shot the men out of ignorance of
military ceremony. Faced with dozens of cold rifle barrels, one of the

Mexican officers guessed the situation and waved a white handkerchief. Negotiations stretched on all through the day and into the night. Twenty hours after the bugler awoke the rebels, terms were signed and ratified. Upon their promise to evacuate Texas and never oppose the reestablishment of the 1824 Constitution, Mexican officers were allowed to retain their arms and private property. Any Mexican who wished to remain was free to do so, except for the six hundred convicts and conscripts, who Cós was to have escorted back across the Rio Grande. Private citizens were not to be molested. Searching for a shred of dignity, General Cós rejected the rebels' offer of provision for his retreat, declaring, "The Mexican army neither receives nor needs to receive anything given by their enemies."[34]

On December 13, the humiliated general started his long desert march to the presidio at Laredo. Of his total force of 1,500 to 1,600 men, he left San Antonio with 1,105. The rest had deserted, been killed in fighting, or been left to heal their wounds. They were the last Mexican troops remaining in Texas.[35] Now it was the rebels' turn to occupy the city and the Alamo. They did so with a vengeance, teaching the Béxarenos a lesson they had already learned, that nothing good came from revolution, nothing good for them.

The Greys moved into the ruins of the sprawling Alamo, each man seeking out the most comfortable nest he could find among the many empty rooms. Ehrenberg and eight others quartered themselves inside the old roofless chapel. General Cós had ordered the far end of the chapel filled with dirt and debris to create a mound for three cannons. In order to trundle these cannons into place, his engineers had built an ascending earthen ramp that began at the front doors. The doors were entered— quickly—under arches that looked precarious. Inside the chapel, several small covered rooms lined the walls, including the sacristy and baptistery. In these the Greys now made themselves at home, cooking up the day's venison, turkey, or beef, trading stories, hanging around.

On the front of the chapel, carved sandstone statues of St. Francis and St. Dominic occupied the niches. Every morning, pious women from town would cross the little wooden bridge over the San Antonio to kneel and pray before these statues. They ignored the volunteers who passed in and out of the chapel or who gawked at them. At least one of the volunteers was sure they weren't being ignored, however. "It was being said that the sandstone saints were being visited more now than ever before," said Ehrenberg, "and I have often wondered whether the black eyed

senoras became so pious because they were now in such close contact
with us heretics or whether it was the presence of the heretics themselves
that drew them into these desolate ruins."[36]

Nearly all of the original rebels returned to their homes. Nearly all of
the mercenaries stayed at the Alamo. They had won, and yet didn't seem
to know what their win really meant. Not gold, not silver, that was for
sure. People were saying that Santa Anna might visit next spring, so the
war was still not over. Having come this far with so little to show for it,
the Greys and other mercenary units stood little to lose by wintering in
Spanish country. And they stood little to gain by going home. That was
the way it was with Go Ahead men. So they hung on, waiting to see if
things might not break their way.

=6=

S ANTA ANNA WAS the worm that became a butterfly.
Mexico teemed with his species. They were mundane creatures, wriggling in Mexico's revolutionary mud until one or another would suddenly sprout iridescent wings and flutter recklessly along a sunbeam.

Santa Anna was not Mexico's first *caudillo* (military ruler) but he was among the most original and durable. Over his long lifetime, he served as Mexico's chief executive eleven times, living in palaces filled with mirrors. In a life of heady extremes, he also suffered tropical exiles for years at a time. From Indian fighting to revolutions to hunting bandits, he accumulated more combat time then George Washington and Andrew Jackson combined, and escaped death on a dozen occasions. He was a coward who more than once abandoned his army and ran from the enemy. But he could also be a splendid hero and patriot, giving his best to rally the nation against American invasion in 1846–47, especially at the Battle of Buena Vista where one horse was shot from under him. Mexico loved him. Mexico loathed him. In the end, Mexico barely survived him. Under his watch—during the Texas Revolution and the subsequent American invasion misnamed the Mexican War—the nation lost almost one half of her territory to the United States.

In the beginning an arrogant, quarrelsome schoolboy named Antonio López de Santa Anna rejected his father's attempt to place him as a clerk with one of the local merchants. He had spent all of his sixteen years in peace and ease, and it oppressed him. Jalapa, his hometown, was one of those exquisite whitewashed cities tucked into a steep green paradise. Santa Anna could not wait to leave heaven for earth. Declaring that he had not been born to become a ''counter jumper'' in a village store, Santa Anna fastened upon a military career. With his father's reluctant permission, he entered a prestigious Veracruz academy in 1810.

That same year the revolutionary priest Hidalgo descended upon Mexico City with his Indian and mestizo army. The bloodthirsty rabble was defeated, and a ruthless Spanish general named Joaquín de Arredondo set out to run Hidalgo's dwindling army to earth. With him, Arredondo took an energetic seventeen-year-old cadet from the Veracruz academy. Arredondo's battalion remained in northern Mexico for the next two years, exterminating pockets of rebels and suppressing Indian uprisings. The warfare was as severe as the desiccated land it traversed. Prisoners were shot or else horsewhipped and set to hard labor. Perched in town squares, the decapitated heads of rebel leaders blackened under the white sun. Lieutenant Santa Anna took to the brutal campaigning. He gained a reputation for recklessness and courage. Arredondo transferred his eager protégé from infantry to cavalry, a leap from foot to the cherished saddle.

In 1813, word came that an army of filibusters had entered Texas from the United States and captured San Antonio de Béxar. Arredondo—and nineteen-year-old Santa Anna—rode north to quash the invasion. Almost a quarter century later Santa Anna would try to duplicate his 1813 expedition into Texas.

Shortly after Father Hidalgo's capture and execution, a rebel named Bernardo Gutiérrez de Lara escaped to the United States and appealed to Secretary of State James Monroe for aid. From Washington, D.C., Gutiérrez sailed for Louisiana and began to raise an army to invade Texas. Even that early, New Orleans abounded with men eager to extend help, from Governor W.C.C. Claiborne to land speculators, businessmen, and others.[1]

As events progressed, Gutiérrez found himself a mere figurehead. As mercenaries and rebels gathered in Natchitoches, against the border of Texas, actual control over the army passed into the hands of the American military—covertly, of course. One of the brightest young officers in the U.S. Army, a tall, robust twenty-four-year-old West Pointer named Lt. Augustus William Magee, resigned his commission on June 22, 1813, and immediately took command of military operations for the rebel army.[2]

In early August the force crossed the Sabine into Texas "determined to besiege the Inferno itself."[3] It was led by American officers, funded by U.S. money, armed with U.S. firearms, and monitored by President Monroe's secret agent. Gutiérrez tagged along, "to give a Mexican character to the army."[4] It was, after all, supposed to be an army devoted to Mexican revolution. Three days after the army invaded Spanish territory, Governor Claiborne denounced the invaders' blatant breach of the U.S. Neutrality Law of 1794. In short, the United States invaded Mexico in 1813 . . . but avoided declaring war by using covert operatives and mercenaries.

Over the next nine months, the so-called Republican Army of the North flew a green flag and captured Goliad and then San Antonio. The ragtag army swelled from 150 in August to as many as 1,500 in April 1814, including 850 Americans. When Lieutenant Magee died of fever, he was replaced by a tavern keeper and professional adventurer named Samuel Kemper. Kemper was one of the famous Kemper brothers, a trio of Anglo-American border ruffians whom the Spanish had driven from West Florida back into the United States in 1804.[5] Seeking wider support from their countrymen this second time around, the Kemper filibusters spread propaganda warning that the Spanish were inciting American slaves to run amok.[6]

Under Samuel Kemper, the Republican Army of the North defeated Governor Manuel María de Salcedo's royalist troops and entered San Antonio. Governor Salcedo was a bright, humane *peninsulare* (that is, born in Spain), who believed in allowing certain handpicked aliens to immigrate to Texas.[7] Ironically, he excluded better-educated Anglo-Americans from immigrating. He argued that professionals such as lawyers, physicians, and traders tended to be the chief troublemakers in border disputes.[8] Twenty-five years later, the Texas Revolution would bear him out.

Governor Salcedo offered his sword in surrender directly to the American "general," but Kemper declined the honor. Instead he referred Salcedo to the nominal head of the army, Gutiérrez. In disgust, the royalist governor stabbed his sword into the ground at the Mexican rebel's feet.

Two days later, the Mexican rebels announced that Governor Salcedo and the other thirteen prisoners of war were going to be taken to the coast, and from there shipped to New Orleans for safekeeping. The prisoners were mounted on horses and escorted out of town by sixty rebels and locals.

Six miles out of town, the escort halted. Capt. Antonio Delgado had the royalists dragged from their horses, stripped, bound, and robbed.

While their executioners whetted their swords on their boot soles, the doomed royalists requested the holy sacraments. They were refused. Then the executioners closed on their prisoners like *vaqueros* working stock.

Salcedo's tongue was cut out. Each prisoner's throat was sliced open. The bodies were decapitated. The corpses were left to the animals.

Next morning Captain Delgado rode back to town and announced the executions. San Antonians cheered and applauded.

This barbaric slaughter stunned and outraged the American officers, some of whom, including Kemper, resigned. Their places were quickly filled with more American filibusters. The new crop of Americans was just as rough and ready as the original bunch. But without adequate leadership, the Republican Army of the North degenerated into an unwelcome mob. The Americans caroused at daily fandangos, drank, brawled, gambled, and feasted on the local señoritas. Their behavior drove three hundred resentful San Antonians south toward safety. It so happened these refugees ran into General Arredondo's army on its way to San Antonio. The unhappy refugees blamed the execution of prisoners on the Americans. This chilled the blood of their fellow Mexicans in the royalist army. According to one contemporary, it inspired "men to vow before the alter [sic] to devote their time and means, and the women to sell their trinkets to raise men and money to exterminate these inhuman barbarians."[9]

In mid-August the Republican Army of the North learned that Arredondo's army was approaching from the Rio Grande. Still quartered in San Antonio, the republicans were at their maximum strength with 850 Anglo-Americans, and as many Mexican rebels, local Tejanos, and friendly Indians. The filibusters were well supplied and thoroughly rested. They could have manipulated the coming battle with ease and safety from within the Alamo walls. Instead they marched out from Béxar to meet Arredondo in the field. It was a deadly decision.

The filibusters set up an ambush along the Laredo road near the Medina River. No sooner did a single royalist scout ride up than the trigger-happy American contingent opened up on him, exposing their ambuscade. Now the filibusters had little choice but to take the battle to Arredondo's army.

Unfortunately for them, Arredondo was encamped in a thick oak forest. Even more unfortunately, the filibusters had to cross a four-mile-wide plain of deep post oak sand. Their cannons bogged down in the sand. The August sun bullwhipped them. They had no water.[10]

The massed royalist troops didn't bother to aim, as usual, firing their escopetas from the hip to avoid the painful recoil. But with their cannons firing grapeshot, they didn't need to aim. The charging filibusters fell in batches. After two furious rallies and four bloody hours, the filibusters finally turned and fled. They had lost six hundred men. They soon lost more.

As the filibusters ran away, the royalist cavalry pursued them, cutting men down or taking them prisoner. Many of the Mexican soldiers who

had defected to the filibusters now defected back to the royalists and made
a gruesome display of their loyalty. "They butchered most of those
[Americans] who had broken down," wrote one American survivor.
Then the soldiers "cut them in quarters, and suspended them on poles and
limbs of trees like beef or pork for the packer; and when the enemy
[Arredondo] advanced, they displayed them as trophies of their
loyalty."[11]

Hundreds of fleeing filibusters—most of them American (*"la mayor
parte anglo americanos,"* wrote Arredondo)—were captured on or near
the battlefield. Arredondo wasted no time on them. They were shot, then
hung by the heels from tree branches. No quarter was given. As many
Americans died retreating as upon the battlefield. Of 850 who fought at
Medina, fewer than 100 were known to have made it back across the
Sabine.

Lieutenant Santa Anna earned an *escudo* (decoration) for "great bravery" during the battle. But by far the young lieutenant's greatest gain
from the Battle of the Medina was an education. He learned how to move
a large body of troops cross-country through northern Mexico into Texas.
He learned to suspect ambuscades and to value false retreats and aggressive attacks. He learned that bayonets were the final master of a battlefield.

And he learned that American filibusters were undisciplined, raggedy
amateurs. For decades after this battle in faraway Texas, Santa Anna
carried a scornful memory of American frontiersmen and their alleged
fighting prowess. He would remember that they died the way they
trespassed—in abundance.

Finally he learned how to squash a revolution. You began by destroy-
ing the rebel army on the field. Then you terrorized any remnants of the
enemy by shooting your prisoners and leaving them unburied as a sobering reminder.

Santa Anna rode into Béxar with Arredondo's army and did his part
in teaching the citizens to obey their king. The victorious army rounded
up two hundred of the local men, selected out one quarter of them, and
shot three every third day. The women of disloyal families were herded
into the Alamo prison building called the Quinta and were forced to grind
corn and cook tortillas for Arredondo's army for fifty-four days. During
seven hellish weeks, the women were whipped, raped, and abused by the
royalist soldiers, then turned loose. For many, little remained. Their men
were dead, their homes and property confiscated. Many families had fled
Béxar toward Louisiana, but Arredondo sent out cavalry troops to bring

them back for punishment. Among the refugees was the barbaric Captain Delgado, Governor Salcedo's butcher. He was shot, then stabbed repeatedly with lances before his mother's eyes. Finally he was stripped and left for the scavengers.

San Antonio de Béxar suffered grievously from this brush with revolution. The city lay in waste, depopulated, destitute, and terrorized. By 1820 the local troops assigned to defend Béxar from Indians were nearly naked and had few horses, worthless muskets, and neither food nor money. The city had twenty-four cannons, but the new governor doubted there were enough soldiers capable of spiking them, much less loading and firing them. Comanches rode imperiously through the streets, shooting Tejanos at whim as they sat by their doors. The Republican Army of the North had spelled Béxar's collapse.

After Arredondo's devastating campaign to Texas, Santa Anna was transferred to Veracruz. For the next seven years, he chased rebels, killed bandits, and pacified the countryside, winning hearts and minds by building eight villages for poor Mexicans dispossessed by the revolution. In short, he helped maintain the Spanish grip on Mexico. Then one day he helped break the Spanish grip.

In early 1821, Agustín de Iturbide, a charismatic thirty-eight-year-old *creole* (Mexican-born Spaniard) officer with muttonchops and an affinity for Napoleon, "pronounced." After many years of killing rebels, he became a rebel, calling for independence and an end to racial discrimination. The royalist command ordered Santa Anna to attack him. Instead, he joined Iturbide . . . and was promoted to full colonel. Soon after, Spain withdrew from Mexico. Independence was secure.

The triumphant Iturbide promoted the twenty-seven-year-old Santa Anna to brigadier general, a rather empty honor in light of a promotions glut that left fewer than two privates for every officer.

In 1822, when Iturbide borrowed a page from Napoleon and coronated himself emperor, Santa Anna accomplished one of history's greatest demonstrations of toadyism by writing the new emperor a letter of congratulations packed with seven hundred terms of specific flattery. But when he surpassed this exceptional feat by courting the emperor's sister—the Doña Nicolasa was then sixty years old—even a megalomaniac like Iturbide had his limits. Iturbide, sneering sarcasm, told Santa Anna he could never sanction such a morganatic union. The rejection cooled Santa Anna's ardor for Iturbide and his empire.[12]

Before the year was out, Santa Anna declared against Iturbide. His statement of revolt—published as the Plan of Casa Mata—forced the nation to decide between monarchy and republicanism. Choosing the latter, and borrowing heavily from the U.S. Constitution, leaders invented the famous 1824 Constitution. Simply put, Santa Anna was the unwitting father of the very constitution for which War Dogs and other Anglo-American rebels would fight and die in 1835–36. He would fight the children of his own creation.

All Mexico hung before Santa Anna.

Rose-colored flamingos sailed through the air. Lemons grew so thick upon the trees that orchard branches looped down to form tunnels. Coffee bushes yielded up red berries; oranges dropped from the trees by the thousands; bananas hung in fifty-pound clusters. Jungle fruits hung like small still animals; some animals passed as fruit.

Everywhere, it seemed, fields of green corn reached up beside unmoving whitewashed adobes.

Church floors lay freckled with thousands of flower petals strewn across dry brown drops of flagellants' blood: blood and flowers, the signature of Aztec and Mayan Mexico. The walls of village churches, constructed of building stones toppled by conquistadores, displayed carved hieroglyphics, some upside down or out of sequence. *Léperos*— the tens of thousands of Mexican street people—walked the Alameda in loincloths among elegant dons and military officers astride five-thousand-peso saddles. Vendors carried vegetables of every color and shape, live animals, sticks draped with pig guts, candies shaped like skulls. In the great cathedral of Mexico City starving folk knelt at altar rails of pure gold and silver and smiled shyly up at the Virgin Mary.

Mexico was the tree of life. And Santa Anna made himself its eagle.

From the rich layers of Mexico City and the palm and bamboo jungles of the *tierra caliente* (hot country) to the high chapparal of Texas, Santa Anna contained it all. He did not have a messiah complex. He skipped that level. He thought he was God.

As a very old and impoverished man with one wooden leg, Santa Anna remembered the fire of his youth. "How impatient I was to climb the stair of life! With the typical eagerness of youth, I wished to vault its steps two by two, four by four."[13]

It was an age when men believed they were God. It was the age of Napoleon.

Young Santa Anna pored through books by and about the Little Corsican. In between his rebel chasing, the vaulting young soldier educated himself. He attended lectures on the classics of Greece and Rome, studied the Gallic wars, but concentrated on Napoleon.[14] "He who wishes to make sure of everything in war, and never ventures, will always be at a disadvantage," Napoleon had declared. "Boldness is the acme of wisdom."[15] Here was the quintessential Go Ahead man. The man with a mission.[16]

Mexico had seen this kind of man before. Three centuries earlier his name was Cortés. Before him there had been El Cid. Spanish kings had learned to institutionalize these powerful figures and channel their super-human talents. It began in the early days of the Reconquest. The king would grant to *caudillos* (military strongmen) far-reaching powers and lands for retaking Spain from the Moors, bit by bit.[17] The most important *fuero* (privilege) was freedom from the laws that governed ordinary citizens.

In many important respects, the *caudillo* and his band were nothing but filibusters like Magee, James Long, Ben Milam, William Travis, and Sam Houston. The recruits were generally nonmilitary volunteers who fought for spoils even while they understood that their gains would somehow accrue to their mother country. Cortés's conquistadores, for example, were not soldiers, but civilians (mostly merchants, notaries, blacksmiths, tailors, and carpenters) who invaded Mexico for personal gain.[18] As her revolution evolved between 1810 and 1821, Mexico refined *caudillismo* to mean professional military leaders whose conquistadores were the professional or militia army.

Following Independence, the *caudillo* no longer owed allegiance to a higher authority.[19] That was when the *caudillo* became God.

Santa Anna's revolt against Iturbide spearheaded the coup that unseated Mexico's self-styled emperor. In 1823 Iturbide abdicated. He sailed into Napoleonic exile in Europe with his family. Precisely one year later he returned to "save" Mexico. He was picked up at the coast and summarily shot.

Over the next six years, Santa Anna carefully steered his course through the lethal rapids of Mexican public life. Between April 1829 and December 1844 fourteen different men occupied the presidency, which changed hands twenty times. The average duration of an administration was a breathtaking 7½ months. During the same period, the national treasury changed hands forty times.[20] Moving upon deep, speeding currents of their own, the turbulent factions engaged and released one another seemingly without logic. Santa Anna was politically illiterate—he didn't even know what a republic was when he declared for a republic.[21]

But he had the necessary survival instincts for knowing when to stand and when to hide.

In 1829 a Spanish fleet set sail from Cuba with three thousand troops. Its mission: to bring Mexico back into the imperial fold. One disaster after another tangled the Spanish army's progress. A storm wrecked one vessel along the Louisiana coast, leaving only twenty-six hundred troops. The army landed at the high point of yellow fever season in the middle of the yellow fever zone in Tampico. Coastal Mexicans knew from experience that disease could cost a hundred lives a day in the low-lying cities. The Spanish learned by experience. By the time Santa Anna showed up to do battle, the Spanish army was almost on its knees. After several weeks of fighting, truces, and more fighting, the Spanish counted up their losses—nine hundred men lost to disease and bullets. They capitulated and Spain never again attacked its ex-colony. Santa Anna had beaten the Father.

Instantly the "Victor of Tampico" was a national hero. He was showered with gold medals, honorary swords, cannon salutes, another promotion, and parades. The "Te Deum," an ancient hymn of praise to God, was sung at churches to celebrate Santa Anna, *Benemérito de la Patria* ("Well Deserving of the Native Land").[22]

The tall, athletic man with skin gone yellow from tropical diseases began calling himself the Napoleon of the West.[23] He combed his hair from back to front, the way Napoleon had when crossing the Alps. He kept aloof and confided in no one.[24] To Mexicans in the first decade of the republic, Santa Anna was a fascinating cipher.

"The soul of General Santana [*sic*] does not fit in his body," said Lorenzo de Zavala, a brilliant young statesman from Yucatán. "It lives in perpetual motion. It permits [him to be] dragged along by the insatiable desire to acquire glory. . . . One could say that his courage touches the summits of recklessness. On the battlefield he is a resemblance of Homer. He studies the enemy in his smallest movements. . . . He encourages his soldiers with the sensitive request of a friend. He is infuriated in moments of defeat. . . . He ignores strategy. Presented [with] the occasion, he unrolls in front of the enemy the immense resources of his genius."[25]

American diplomat Waddy Thompson once compared Santa Anna with his contemporary Andrew Jackson. "I have seen no countenance except that of General Jackson, whose range of expression was so great, where there was so great a difference between the quiet expression of the face when at rest and in a gentle mood, and its terrible ferocity when highly excited. The mildness of the lamb and the fierceness of the tiger would not much too strongly express this difference."[26] The lamb: the tiger. Santa Anna became a masterful shapeshifter, metamorphic and defiant of common men's rules.

During one siege, Santa Anna dressed in women's clothing and spied on his enemy. When his army ran short of cash, he dressed a unit of troops in death shrouds and had them rob a churchful of military opponents at mass, taking alms destined for the holy places of Jerusalem.[27]

After one of his revolutionary armies was overrun in 1832, Santa Anna escaped by following the enemy up a road, then stopping at the local *alcalde*'s house and claiming that he had won and was routing the soldiers who had just passed through town. He took the time to drink a cup of chocolate with the *alcalde,* then mounted his horse and took a detour to safety.[28]

Santa Anna escaped death in Texas, escaped death in Mexico after the Mexican War (the Texas Rangers tracked him and tried to assassinate him), escaped death during a French invasion of Veracruz (when he lost half of one leg). One moment, he was a determined presence, the next he was an escape artist . . . already gone. The man could be a disgraceful coward—as when he cut and ran from the French nearly nude one early morning, or, in Texas, dressed as a private and denied his identity. But he could also be contagiously indifferent to risk.

A German mercenary was with Santa Anna during one hot battle. The general had just distributed a basket of oranges among his officers when enemy troops suddenly opened fire on their bamboo hut. "For the next four hours it rained grenades, cannonballs, and grapeshot," the German said. "With cold-blooded composure, even as we joked and laughed, we saw the grenades land and explode among our troops. . . ."[29]

Santa Anna was not a particularly bright man. But he had a genius for finding the holes in reality. Somehow he escaped mediocrity, firing squads, assassins, lynch mobs, and anonymity.

In April 1833 Santa Anna first took executive office in Mexico. He was elected as a liberal—or federalist or states' rightist—but the wily, paranoid new president had his doubts about what the powers behind Mexican power really wanted. In order to test the waters, he installed his vice president Valentín Gómez Farías as president, and "retired" to his hacienda in Jalapa. It was customary in Mexican politics for individuals suddenly and strategically to retire from the public eye "due to illness." A master of this gambit, Santa Anna retreated to his estates in Jalapa over and over again. Besides lending him an aura of the martyr whose health

had been ruined in the service of his *patria,* these convalescences gave
Santa Anna the distance he needed from the capital's intrigues.

In Jalapa, Santa Anna led the life of a country gentleman. He was
married to a tall, thin woman named Ines Garcia who bore him five
children, one an "afflicted" child whom Santa Anna rejected. Her husband was not a faithful man. In the tradition of warrior kings, Santa Anna
inseminated a fair share of Jalapa's Indian girls and sired any number of
other children. Deciding she'd been underpaid for her favors, one tart
stole the medals from Santa Anna's uniform jacket and pranced through
Mexico City's slums bestowing the Order of Guadalupe upon one peon,
the Order of Charles III upon another, the Cross of Tampico on yet
another; Santa Anna had to pay several thousand pesos to retrieve his
medals.[30] When he was not womanizing, Santa Anna spent his country
time raising and training fighting cocks. He took enormous pride in their
combat skills and once left a Cabinet minister waiting while he attended
a favorite bird.[31] Between his dalliances and his cockfighting, Santa
Anna let Mexico clarify its crises and orchestrated his encores upon the
public stage.

As expected, once his vice president Gómez Farias floated a number
of progressive reforms in 1833–34, the capital began rumbling. Among
other things, Gómez Farias had dared to attack the sacred *fueros.* The
conservatives cried out for his head.

Power in Mexico was made up of two ossified interests: the Church
and the military. Only a madman would deprive one or the other. Gómez
Farias had deprived them both. He got Congress to pass laws abolishing
the military *fuero* that excluded soldiers from civil or criminal prosecution in ordinary courts, as well as laws overhauling the Church and its
privileges.

With cries of *"Religión y Fueros"* thundering in the air, Santa Anna
returned from his convalescence in April 1834. Calling his vice president
a *sansculotte,* a derogatory term used for the popular or liberal party and
meaning a bum too poor to buy breeches, Santa Anna expelled Gómez
Farias.[32] He dissolved the liberal Congress and began all over again with
conservatives. Liberal governors were replaced. The federal system gave
way to Santa Anna's centralism. Powers that the states had enjoyed for
years were now stripped away. The popular reforms legislated by Congress were revoked.[33]

Santa Anna's measures did not go down well in certain parts of
Mexico. Distant Yucatán with its tradition of autonomy and wealthier

mining states like Querétaro and Zacatecas were particularly strident in their objections. These states formed a loose confederation, with their power in their state militias. Originally envisioned as a citizen bulwark to the regular army, some state militias had evolved into standing armies in their own right, making certain governors into minipresidents and the states into small countries.[34]

These Mexican militiamen were little different from their American counterparts. Comparing them to "troops of boys," one Mexican commentator said, "You've seen them. They elect their leaders and they obey them while they feel like it, and when they don't they boot them out and change." Most of them were undisciplined. But to the centralists, they were pools of tomorrow's dangerous rebels. In 1830–31 most of the militias had been eliminated. But in 1832 Zacatecas revived its dormant militia with drastic consequences.[34]

When Santa Anna returned to the capital in 1834 to scuttle liberal reforms and consolidate centralism, the militia of Zacatecas was the best organized, most lavishly outfitted in all of Mexico. It was trained by top-notch foreign officers. Its arsenals were full with arms and munitions. The state boasted twenty-five heavy artillery pieces, a fort, and a recently constructed citadel.[35] Zacatecas could afford the expenditure, for much of Mexico's silver came from Zacatecan mines. With a population of three hundred thousand, the Zacatecan militia could field twenty thousand men, a ratio of one militiaman for every fifteen civilians. The centralists proposed that the militia forces not exceed one for every five hundred civilians. The Zacatecans defied them. Obviously, Santa Anna had to answer back.

In May 1835, Santa Anna descended upon Zacatecas. He set his thirty-five hundred troops brilliantly, matching them against a fortified, heavily armed army of thirteen thousand militiamen. His strategy, a high-speed maneuver against the rear, came straight from the Napoleonic primer. Within a mind-boggling two hours, the battle of Zacatecas was over. Santa Anna had won at a cost of less than a hundred dead and wounded centralist troops.

In the city of Zacatecas alone he captured twenty-four hundred prisoners and over a hundred officers. Santa Anna decreed that all foreigners with the Zacatecan army be shot on the spot, but his own officers protested so loudly that he rescinded the order and allowed them to be marched in shackles to Mexico City.[36] No one has finally determined the number of rebels killed in battle or executed as prisoners, but Mexican historians continue to treat the brutal suppression of Zacatecans as a dark, shameful episode. Estimates of rebels and civilians killed in the ensuing rape and massacre range from the hundreds to twenty-five hundred. Plunder was the order of the day, and a special hatred was shown toward the few English and U.S. citizens in town. Their property was destroyed, some of the men were killed, and the women were treated shamefully.[37]

Everywhere Mexico went still, horrified. The reduction of Zacatecas collapsed all opposition to centralism for a period of years, and firmly established Santa Anna as a formidable *caudillo*. It also provided his so-called Army of Operations with invaluable combat experience. Fully a dozen of the highest-ranking officers who fought at Zacatecas would soon, very soon, accompany their commander in chief to Texas.[38]

Santa Anna had barely returned from crushing Zacatecas when the cafés and drawing rooms began buzzing with rumors that El Presidente would soon be teaching the Anglo-Americans in Texas a lesson. On the verge of his release from Mexican imprisonment, Austin met with the general. "Gen. Santa Anna told me he should visit Texas next March [1836]—as a friend," Austin related back to the United States. "His visit is uncertain, his friendship still more so. We must rely on ourselves and prepare for the worst."[39]

Until that "friendly" visit the following spring, Santa Anna meant to retire to his hacienda at Jalapa, this time leaving his presidency in the hands of a conservative, Gen. Miguel Barragán. But near the end of February, Santa Anna left his lush green retreat and rode north through the barren winter to raise an army against the Anglo-Saxon rebels whom he called the *tumultuario* of the Mississippi Valley.[40] He had been led to expect a glorious army of thirty thousand men: He found a total force of two thousand, not counting Gen. Ramírez y Sesma's fifteen hundred already on their way to Texas.[41] He also found an empty war chest.

The Mexican government was barely afloat upon a sea of loans, some foreign, others internally generated.[42] The chief lenders were the Church, pawnshops, and private moneylenders.[43]

The whole nation was in hock. Revenues from individual customhouses were pledged for years into the future.[44] The Fresnillo mine in the state of Zacatecas had just paid one million pesos to the government, but, with what Santa Anna called "incredible speed," every peso vanished into the maw of debt payments.

Santa Anna realized that he would have to fight just to put together an army to fight. His generals were already conscripting troops who required food, supplies, and arms . . . but he had no money to pay for any of it.

"A dark horizon, indeed," Santa Anna concluded, "that foretold the storm!"[45]

In late November, Congress authorized the government to raise 500,000 pesos "by the least onerous means."[46] Santa Anna attempted to wring forced loans from various states, but none displayed much charity. The most generous contribution came from San Luis Potosí: 576 pesos, 4 reales, and 3 cuartillas.[47] At an average cost of 1 peso per man per day, 576 pesos would not even cover drawing a battalion up into military formation on the parade ground, much less pay for Santa Anna's 7,000-peso sword or the special Legion of Honor crosses ordered struck for the Texas campaign—silver for the cavalrymen, gold for the officers. Less than 600 pesos would not even begin to cover the graft one needed to factor in for a campaign of this size.

In desperation Santa Anna negotiated a loan from the firm of Rubio and Erraz. Not only did the firm demand—and receive—a lucrative contract for providing the army with supplies (at double their street value) but also interest payments on the 400,000-peso loan (half in silver, half in vouchers) at a staggering 4 percent *per month,* or 48 percent annually.[48] Congress took one look at the arrangement and rejected it, but by then Santa Anna had departed north with his army.[49]

Santa Anna had an extraordinary touch for mounting armies at a moment's notice. It took a very special talent to pull together men and material and lift them from one square on the chessboard to another. He guarded his tasks, as if only he could accomplish them. He worried that his officers might not treat the tiniest details with his same compulsion. He delegated powers but never gave them away. Part of his secret was in arranging his whole army on paper, right down to the shako straps upon each private's chin and the extra pair of sandals for their feet.

In early December, Santa Anna rode to San Luis Potosí where major elements of the Army of Operations were gathering. Along the way he put finishing touches on a ten-point set of instructions. Several of the points came directly from his mental textbook of the 1813 Battle of Medina.

He remembered that the filibusters had nearly ambushed Arredondo's army, and instructed, "On the march from Laredo to Béxar exercise all caution against a surprise attack."

He remembered the doomed rebel charge across a sandy plain, and instructed, "If action is met with the enemy, consider position; if unfavorable, try to move to another place, but pass them on to Béxar or make a false retreat."

He remembered the breakpoint of Medina, and instructed, "At the first sign of weakness by the enemy there should be a charge with fixed bayonets. . . . Once action is begun, any hesitation is dangerous."

Finally, he remembered General Arredondo's terrorist policy, and instructed, "Since the foreigners are making war, they are due no consideration and will be given no quarter."[50]

One of the energized *caudillo*'s most respected advisers, an older general named Manuel Fernandez Castrillón, took the upcoming Texas campaign lightly. He joked that it had all the makings of a military parade and wondered whether the enemy would fire even a single shot.[51]

Santa Anna was just as cavalier. For a change Mexicans would not be killing Mexicans. The enemy this time was Mexico's traditional enemy, a rabble of Anglo-American scofflaws, mercenaries, and peasants inviting the gleaming sword stroke.

Before leaving gay, glittering Mexico City, Santa Anna predicted an early, easy win. He went so far as to boast to British and French ministers that if he found the U.S. government had aided the rebels in Texas, he would continue his march all the way to Washington and plant the Mexican flag upon the American capitol.[52]

The campaign was designed for a blitzkrieg sweep across Texas . . . nothing protracted, nothing ambiguous. Napoleon had preached the rapid formation and deployment of an army that would travel light and live off the countryside. "The strength of an army, like the power in mechanics, is the product of the mass by the velocity," Napoleon said. "A rapid march augments the morale of an army and increases its means of victory."[53]

What Santa Anna was about to learn was that blitzkriegs worked best in short, high-voltage pulses, and they required a fertile environment for the army to feed upon. The Army of Operations was aimed at a bleak geography in a bleak season. When Santa Anna had last visited Texas, in the summer of 1813, the grass was tall, the cattle fat, the sun warm, and the ground dry. Winter in northern Mexico differed radically from the Mexico of his memory.

Noting Santa Anna's Napoleonic obsession, several Mexican journalists ruffled the *caudillo*'s composure by wondering if Texas might not prove to be his Russia.[54]

=7=

"**Y**OU MAY ALL go to hell," David Crockett bitterly told his Tennessee constituents when they turned him out of office in August 1835, "and I will go to Texas." He had just turned forty-nine. His waist was thickening. He was sick and tired of being broke. Texas seemed like a good solution.

On the first of November, Crockett left with his nephew, a brother-in-law, and a neighbor. The *Niles Register* marked his exit like an obituary. "Col *Crockett* has proceeded to *Texas*—to end his days there."[1]

Crockett didn't go to Texas to fight a revolution. He didn't go to sharp-shoot tyrants and defend liberty. He went for himself.

He wanted land.

He wanted money.

And he wanted to catch that monster.

It was his monster and it was out there. Everywhere Crockett rode—all along his leisurely arc from the United States through the eye-popping Red River Country—the ungrateful beast had preceded him.

In the beginning the poor creature had been as tentative and spindly as a newborn foal. In the beginning it had been utterly dependent on its creator.

But over the years, it had packed meat on its bones and swing in its stride. It took a name all its own—Davy, not David. While Crockett grew older and no more lucky, Davy grew bigger and faster and wilder. He became a folk hero. But instead of slaving for his creator like a grateful (or even ungrateful) son, the monster broke loose of his maker and loped west with the popular imagination. The annoying part was that by then, Crockett had become dependent on his creation.

The little party of hunters shipped down the Mississippi and up the Arkansas by steamboat, then rode off overland, taking their time, savoring the autumn country. They ate well off the fat game. At night they listened to the resin pop and hiss in their campfires. Coming upon settlers in frontier Arkansas, they jawboned about how it was in the deeper regions.

The West deepened and opened to them, willing and seductive. Rocking gently in his saddle, rifle nested across the horn, Crockett cogitated on the new life opening before him and tried to put away his past.

Half-horse, half-alligator, in the spirit of amphibious pioneers, his creation was out there, roaming through the wild frontier, haunting its maker. The creature had first stirred in 1821 when a well-dressed legislator in the Tennessee state congress baited the freshman congressman David Crockett as "the gentleman from the cane." Crockett got even. He found a fancy cambric ruffle in the dirt just like one his tormentor was wearing, and pinned it to his coarse shirt. On the next opportunity Crockett quietly stood in the chamber and let the satire speak for itself. The congressmen laughed heartily. And Davy was born.

Tentatively at first, but with growing savvy, Crockett made bumpkinhood a badge of honor. Just the way America was learning to do, he quit denying his roots in log-cabin poverty and took pride in what he was. Bragging was already a recreation among the corn-and-cabin set; Crockett made it an art. Davy used words to skewer pompous dandies the way he used lead to knock down varmints. Regardless of how the Anglophiles and European tourists sniffed at him, Crockett brought America's backwoods hick into the open air and sunshine.

"I don't want it understood that I have come electioneering," he once announced to an election crowd. "I have just crept out of the cane, to see what discoveries I could make among the white folks."[2] With tremendous good nature, he found the ordinary world every inch as curious as it found him. To Crockett's great surprise, his bastard creation gave him legitimacy. Remarkably, it also allowed a poor man who could barely read to transcend his insecurity.

Crockett's life to date had been one long string of hard knocks and miscalculation. His first love had married another man, his first wife had died, his mills had gotten flooded out, his barrel stave enterprise literally sank on the Mississippi River, and he was perpetually in debt. The mild-looking son of a Revolutionary War veteran, Crockett fought as a volunteer scout during the gut-wrenching Creek War of 1813–14. He hired a substitute to finish out his term of enlistment, thereby missing the climactic Battle of Horseshoe Bend, at which Sam Houston took an arrow and musket balls and first came to Andrew Jackson's attention.

Crockett had worked at farming for two years, lost one wife, gained another, then had "removed" with his family to the headwaters of Shoal

Creek, only to remove again to western Tennessee. There among the "harricane"—where fierce winds had piled the trees so thick a man could scarcely walk through, where a set of earthquakes had temporarily reversed the Mississippi's flow—Crockett made a stand. He knocked together a cabin, stabbed in some corn among the stumps and windfall, and laid in some gunpowder, cornmeal, salt, and whiskey. He called it home for the next thirteen years. From this tangled forest country, he mounted expeditions into both the wilds and political life.

He proved to have a talent for the hard, dangerous labor of bear hunting. Like some great prehistoric hunter, his confrontations sometimes originated in a dream. "I told them," Crockett said, "I had dreamed the night before of having a hard fight with a big black nigger, and I knowed it was a sign that I was to have a battle with a bear; for in a bear country, I never know'd such a dream to fail. So I started to go up above the harricane determined to have a bear."

On the occasion of his dream hunt, he came close to getting mauled. "At the crack of my gun here he came tumbling down; and the moment he touched the ground, I heard one of my best dogs cry out. I took my tomahawk in one hand, and my big butcher-knife in the other, and run up within four or five paces of him, at which he let my dog go, and fixed his eyes on me. I got back in all sorts of a hurry, for I know'd if he got hold of me, he would hug me altogether too close for comfort. I went to my gun and hastily loaded her again, and shot him the third time, which killed him good."[2] His reputation spread. Incredibly, he killed 105 bears in a single season.

Around the same time, Crockett entered politics, using bounty money he collected from wolf scalps to help foot the expenses of American-style campaigning. "I [had] me a large buckskin hunting-shirt made, with a couple of pockets holding about a peck each; and . . . in one I would carry a great big twist of tobacco, and in the other my bottle of liquor; for I knowed when I met a man and offered him a dram, he would throw out his quid of tobacco to take one, and after he had taken his horn, I would out with my twist and give him another chaw. And in this way he would not be worse off than when I found him; and I would be sure to leave him in a first-rate good humour."[2]

His trademark became a few horns of home-distilled "creature," a mouthful of chew, and an earful of story for every voter. They were folk stories about the people and land, stories about dangerous migration and intense poverty. Crockett was instinctively connected to the land. He knew how to make it work for him in more ways than one. When an opponent on the stump once paused in midspeech to chase away a noisy flock of quail, Crockett leapt to his feet and appreciated how the quail were gabbling his name, "crockett crockett crockett."

Crockett gave his creation a leg up on life. He furnished Davy— through lower-class folk tales—with the luck of a cat and the vision of a sharpshooter. He made Davy smart enough to humble any two Yankee peddlers. He gave him muscle and fists and heart. Best of all, he gave Davy a silver throat for bragging. Out of that throat-high organ pipe, he sang out a plain dream in plain words . . . he wanted more. Existence was hard. But Crockett's creature didn't complain. He celebrated. He didn't ask to have it easy. He just wanted it abundant and full.

Standing upon stump after stump, the aspiring politician unloaded a storehouse of frontier tales upon the electorate with his bewildering, comical drawl. He was elected to the state House in 1821 and 1823, and to the U.S. House in 1827, 1829, and 1833. Along the way Davy became an American Odysseus who could stare wild animals to death, outfight Indians, river pirates, and bears, and undo every brand of superior fool. There was not a Western expansionist worth his powder who could resist Davy's catchall motto Be Sure You Are Right, Then Go Ahead. For if you went ahead you were right, and there was far, far to go out there.

Crockett's recipe for turning his hickory roots into political hay was inspired, but not completely original. In the 1820s and 1830s, the eighteenth-century pioneer Daniel Boone stood gigantically in the public mind as a forest-busting entrepreneur at one with nature and yet unconverted by it, eager to colonize "Old Kentucke" and bring fire to her long, cold night. Americans were hungry for a homegrown hero, someone distinctly American.[3]

His popularity gained.

The Whigs took notice. They were looking for a man of the people with whom they could unhorse the omnipotent Man of the People, Andrew Jackson. They encouraged Crockett's attacks on King Andrew. They planted in Crockett's ear the thought of himself as president. Nicholas Biddle, president of the endangered Second Bank of the United States, loaned him money, then graciously struck the loan from his books.[4]

The Whigs courted and flattered the naïve backwoodsman. They put coin in his pocket. They fed his monster. Whigs began ghostwriting his speeches and books. A "biography" called the *Sketches and Eccentric-*

ities of Colonel David Crockett of West Tennessee appeared in 1833 (written anonymously by Matthew St. Claire, clerk of the House of Representatives, a Whig and friend of Biddle. Interestingly, this biography plagiarized an immensely popular play called *The Lion of the West* (1831) by James Kirke Paulding, which in turn had plundered Crockett's own tall tales. Crockett's creature was spinning off so many imitators that they had begun to collide.

St. Claire "quoted" his subject as bragging, "I'm that same David Crockett, fresh from the backwoods, half-horse, half-alligator, a little touched with snapping-turtle; can wade the Mississippi, leap the Ohio, ride upon a streak of lightning, and slip without a scratch down a honey locust; can whip my weight in wild cats—and if any gentleman pleases, for a ten dollar bill, he may throw in a panther—hug a bear too close for comfort, and eat any man opposed to Jackson."[5]

The biography offended Crockett, even though he probably helped write it and it propelled his popularity. For one thing, he received none of the royalties from the lucrative biography. For another thing, being offended gave him a chance to correct the record with his autobiography . . . issued to coincide with his 1835 campaign for reelection. ("I Consider that Justice demands of me to make a Statement of facts to the amirican [*sic*] people I have no doubt but you have Saw a Book purporting to be the life and adventers [*sic*] of my Self that Book was written without my knowledge and widely Circulated and in fact the persons that took the first liberty to write the Book have published a Second addition and I thought one inposition [*sic*] was enough to put on the Country and I have put down the imposition and have promised to give the people a Correct Statement of history of my life.")

Crockett didn't mind self-caricature; that was the essence of his tall tales. But finding himself caricatured by others in propaganda and on-stage felt like theft. He was David Crockett, a real man with a real life, not some plagiarism of a plagiarism of a tall tale for drunken voters.

A story surfaced that Crockett had made a fool of himself at a White House dinner by sipping water from his finger bowl. It was the kind of gaffe Crockett might have boasted about, but published as an attack on his manners, the story stung. Crockett got two Whigs to publicly vouch that he'd done no such thing.[6]

On the streets of Washington and in the legislature, Crockett dressed like a politician, not a yokel. He was verbally outrageous, but left the wilder fashion statements to peacocks like Sam Houston. Crockett was not an extravagant man. His favorite piece of clothing was neither the sainted linsey-woolsey hunting shirt nor a buckskin jacket with fringe, but a long, fashionable wool overcoat presented to him by an admiring Boston manufacturer.

In the space of one year (1833–34), Crockett sat for five different portraits of himself. The first four showed a somewhat homely, decent-looking man with sideburns, a long thin nose bracketed by rosy cheeks, blue eyes, and ruffled brown hair that was parted in the middle, tucked behind his ears, and fell below his collar. In each of these portraits he wore a vest, a high stiff white collar, and a dark, high-necked frock coat. This was his congressional look, respectable and mainstream.

Yet the four portraits bothered him. He complained that they made him look like ''a sort of cross between a clean-shirted Member of Congress and a Methodist Preacher.'' A fifth portrait was commissioned, a life-size oil painting. For this ultimate portrait, Crockett bowed to his rustic creation. With the help of artist John Gadsby Chapman, Crockett hunted all through Washington for a genuine hunting shirt, a knife, a hatchet, and a scarred, worn-looking muzzle-loader, none of which the bear hunter had. Insisting on authenticity, he even rounded up three alley mongrels to pose as hunting dogs.[7] The hat he waved over his head was a battered brimmed hat, not the coonskin cap of legend.

In real life, Crockett probably never wore a coonskin cap. Like much of the bizarre language attributed to him, the coonskin cap grew from between the layers of fiction and plagiarism that Davy inspired. In Paulding's *The Lion of the West,* a character named Col. Nimrod Wildfire was played by a popular actor named James Hackett. Night after night, Wildfire boomed out rip-roaring boasts dressed in animal skins and a bobcat-skin cap.[8]

Crockett never quite understood that he was nothing but a mule to pull along the Whig party and undermine the patriarchal Jackson. There in his looking glass, he saw blue-eyed Presidential timber with the bark still on it. He envisioned himself as a grand usurper, the man who toppled King Andy . . . but his Whig handlers saw him as nothing more than a spoiler. They puffed him up only to use him.[9] It wasn't that a bankrupt bear hunter from the harricane couldn't dream of becoming President. Rather Crockett was a mediocrity.

Crockett witnessed the extraordinary flowering of his alter ego, he saw the crowds and heard the applause, and he forgot what he really was . . . an aging, semiliterate squatter of average talent. The worst part of this celebrity who believed in his own fame was that his hubris was attached to a cartoon figure of his own making. He was a Go Ahead man, but not *the* Go Ahead man.

Crockett's record in Congress was downright sorry. For six years he sat in office, and he accomplished nothing. In three terms of national office, he failed to get a single bill passed. His pet concern—fair land laws and preemption rights for poor settlers and squatters—went belly up in Congress. And not only was he stubborn and ineffective, he was truant. In 1834 he took an ill-advised three-week tour of the Eastern seaboard to promote his autobiography. Unfortunately those were three weeks at the height of the congressional session, and the Jacksonians made sure his constituents heard about it.

In 1835 the first of a long, wildly popular series of fifty Davy almanacs appeared, lofting Davy from politics into a commercial fantasy world of violent, racist configurations. Crockett's west Tennessee became a riotous Eden in which the giant wilderness clown "pinked" Indians, hugged bears, and outtalked, outdrank, and outfought every man he ever knew.

It was Davy, not David, who brayed a path through the thicket of vulgar paperbacks known as the Nashville Crockett Almanacs. By then Crockett's uncopyrighted persona was in the hands of a stable of New England hacks published out of Boston, albeit with the "pedigreed" imprint of Nashville, Tennessee. "I was born in a cane brake," Davy declared in one of these almanacs, "cradled in a sap trough, and clouted with coon skins; without being choked by the weeds of education which do not grow *spontinaciously*—for all the time that I was troubled with *youngness,* my cornstealers were *na'*trally used for other purposes than holding a pen; and *rayly* when I try to write my elbow keeps coming round like a swingle-tree, and it is easier for me to tree a varmint, or swallow a nigger, than to write."[10]

The almanacs reached absurd, vicious lows in the 1840s and 1850s. Davy thrashed and gouged "Paddies" and Yankees alike, beat and killed blacks (claiming he could "swallow a nigger whole without choking if you butter his head and pin his ears back"), and visited pornographic savagery upon Indians, or "red niggers." In one story he mowed down a band of Indians stealing some hay, and observed "the red nigger's sap both watered an manured my field, till it war as red an striped as Uncle Sam's flag. . . ."[11]

Crockett's downfall was swift.

Keen-eyed among his native windfalls, he proved to be blind in the political wilderness of Washington. Jackson's political machine made sure the voters back home heard about Crockett's self-service, his Whiggish antics, and his book-promotion truancy. In August 1835 Adam Huntsman, a Jackson man who had lost a leg in the Creek War, turned him out of office.

In early January, Crockett crossed the Red River and entered Mexico. He was not the first illegal alien to enter Texas, but he was certainly one of the most distinguished.[12] Crockett wasn't even the first "wetback" congressman in southwestern history. Sam Houston had crossed before him.

Moving south through Red River country, Crockett and his three friends entered vast plains that typically staggered the Anglo-American mind. Giant herds of buffalo and horses moved across the land in cloud banks, and at night, sometimes, enormous wildfires turned the sky orange. Crockett luxuriated in what he called "the richest country in the world."

He wrote a letter to his oldest daughter. "The best land and the best prospects for health I ever saw, and I do believe it is a fortune to any man to come here. . . . Good land and plenty of timber and the best springs and will [wild] mill streams, good range, clear water and every appearance of good health and game aplenty."

Riding from settlement to settlement, Crockett discovered that Davy had preceded him everywhere. "I am hailed with hearty welcome to this country. A dinner and a party of ladys [sic] have honored me with an invitation to partisapate [sic] both at Nacing docher [Nacogdoches] and at this place. The cannon was fired here on my arrival."[13]

The sudden appearance of a national celebrity augured well for the rebellion. Crockett's presence gave definition and stature to the dogfight with the Mexican government. And they welcomed him. The irony was that Crockett himself was in search of legitimacy and definition. He knew that the cannon smoke of San Augustine saluted Davy as much as it did David.

On January 9, Crockett took an oath of allegiance to the rebel government and joined its army—thereby gaining a grant of land. Better still, newly arrived mercenaries were allowed to vote. That meant a second crack at public office.

"I have taken the oath of the government and have enrolled my name as a volunteer for six months," he wrote from "Saint Agusteen," "and will set out for the Rio Grande in a few days with the volunteers of the U.S., but all volunteers are entitled to a vote for a member of the convention and these members are to be voted for; and I have but little doubt of being elected a member to form the Constitution of the Province."[13]

So Crockett felt inspired to become a founding father of the sovereign nation of Texas . . . once it became sovereign, of course. In other words, he volunteered to fight . . . but not to fight.

The Creek War, he once said, "closed my career as a warrior, and I am glad of it, for I like life now a heap better than I did then; and I am glad all over that I [survived], which I would not have done if I had kept fooling along in war, and got used up at it."[14]

He had no intention of becoming cannon fodder for someone else's army and government, especially not for some Jacksonian politico like the rebel general Sam Houston. For that reason, he inserted the word *republican* into his oath of allegiance to the "provisional government of Texas, or any future *republican* government that may be hereafter declared. . . ."[15]

Crockett joined a foreign army to qualify for election to the upcoming constitutional convention to be held in March. If he could not become President of the United States, at least he could act like one and shape this new country.

But he lost his gamble. Davy's celebrity did not translate into a slot at the convention for David. Instead they sent the forty-nine-year-old storyteller off to the western front.

=8=

THERE WERE ESSENTIALLY two waves of mercenaries, the first large group arriving just before and after the capture of San Antonio, the second arriving after the Texas Revolution was over. Throughout the revolution, Americans came in, some on foot, some armed to the teeth. There were those, like Crockett, who trickled across the prairie in little batches almost as an afterthought. Others marched to the front in uniformed militias, full of mission. All through the southern states, and in a few eastern cities, a call to arms reaped mercenaries and money, though never enough of either.

From tip to tip of the Christmas holidays in 1835, New Orleans was lit with Texas war fever. Rebel propaganda shouted from every corner: Broadsides on lampposts and in store windows, news articles, torch-lit public meetings with agents and speakers begged money and recruited. Barely had the city learned, in mid-December, of San Antonio's fall to the Anglo-American rebels before a play opened in one local theater. Entitled *The Fall of San Antonio,* it warned that Santa Anna was coming. No one knew when, for sure, but Texas was sure to be visited by "the colored hireling of a cruel and faithless despot."[1] Night after night, Old Ben Milam suffered martyrdom all over again on the curve of a Mexican musket ball. It is impossible to know how many young volunteers arrived in Texas that winter led by a skull-shot ghost.

In the midst of the young gallants milling about in New Orleans was a twenty-eight-year-old schoolteacher named Mary S. Helm. The wife of an Anglo-American settler, she had been living in Texas for six years and was on her way back home from a Stateside visit. Like the majority of mercenaries gathering in New Orleans, she was going to travel by schooner to a Gulf port in Texas—a trip of only a week or so.[2]

After a few days at sea, tensions began to run high. A Mexican man-o'-war named *Montezuma* was said to be plying the coastal waters off Texas in search of precisely this kind of revolutionary cargo—mercenaries, suppliers, and weaponry. On board, the ladies were put to work making up cartridges for the little cannon they were carrying and the volunteers kept their firearms close, bracing for a battle upon the high seas. "As we approached the Texas coast," Helm recalled, "every old cutlass was put in fighting order, our cannon mounted, and our spy glasses constantly looking for the enemy."[3]

Just off the Texas coast, three vessels suddenly appeared on the horizon. The rebels were sure they were the *Montezuma* and other Mexican warships, against which the American schooner was nearly helpless. Some of the passengers pressed for retreat, but the overwhelming odds seemed to incite most of the American mercenaries. What Mexican could possibly stand up against American sharpshooting and the mission of democracy?

As Helm would later evaluate, "The instinct of races never dies out any more than individuals. The Anglo-Americans are hardy and enduring beyond all other races. Endowed with an incredible and inexhaustible energy, they never turn back or yield to reverses however severe or crushing. On the other hand, the modern Mexicans are, as it were, the debris of several inferior and degraded races; African and Indian crossed and mixed, and even the old Spanish blood was mixed with the Moorish and demoralized by a long course of indolence and political corruption; both physically and mentally they are the very antithesis of the Anglo-Americans. They are as weak as he is strong; they run where he fights. . . ."

Ramrods slammed home charges of gunpowder. Orders were given, advice received. The moment stretched on, marked by the endless slapping of waves against the wooden hull.

Alone among his agitated passengers, the schooner's captain was unfazed by the impending clash. He steered directly for the three ships.

Because the three "ships" were his landmark: three summer residences upon the Texas beach. With this introduction to the illusions of Texas, the volunteers disembarked and hurried inland to join Colonel Fannin at Goliad. Some would go to the Alamo. Nearly all of them would join Old Ben Milam in the afterworld.

Ultimately it would cost the Anglo-Americans about $1.25 million to put on their Texas Revolution.[4] That was a good $4 to $9 million less than what the United States had offered Mexico for clear title to the region. But it was still $1.25 million more than was available in the rebels' war chest. As the rebellion heated up, tens of thousands of dollars were subscribed by patriotic Americans. Some of the largest subscriptions came from New York, which raised $100,000 on the first day of its drive, and another $100,000 on the second day.[5] But as one rebel propagandist swiftly pointed out, $100 in real cash was worth more than $1,000 in subscription.[6] In fact, actual cash donations to the rebel cause never amounted to more than $25,000.

A more lucrative source of cash for the fight came from American land speculators. Speculators in Cincinnati, Kentucky, Virginia, New Orleans, and, of course, New York, stepped forward to lend the strapped rebels real money at 8 percent interest. The terms of the loan specified that repayment could be taken in either cash or land. The lenders meant to take land. The land would be surveyed and plotted and be apportioned at $.50 an acre. Among themselves the speculators determined not to sell their lands for less than $1.25, meaning they would make 150 percent on their investment. Hundreds of thousands of dollars were subscribed upon these terms, but only $100,000 was actually collected.

The troubles in Texas were by no means a national rallying point. Texas generated enormous excitement, but also tremendous cynicism. The rebellion was perceived by many as a criminal land grab, and also a Southern attempt to spread slavocracy into a region that might yield as many as four to five more states when annexed. The *Baltimore Gazette* excoriated the rebellion, calling it a land speculators' scheme that had jumped its own gun.

"They cannot as yet count enough American riflemen to drive the rightful lords of the soil out of their own country; and therefore they make up a pitiful face and cry oppression, and call upon individuals to shoulder their rifles and come to their aid, and inform them as an inducement to do so that they have millions of acres—of Mexican land, let it be observed— which they will bestow on those who aid them to conquer them. So long as this matter rested solely with individuals we took no part in the controversy. If American citizens thought fit as individuals to go forth on this crusade, running the risk of being hanged, and acting on their own responsibility, the government could not well interfere. If these chivalrous individuals had been caught warring against the Mexican authorities, proceeded against as robbers, murderers and land pirates, and such had been ordered for execution, our government would of course have left them to their fate. . . .

"This affair is now however changed in toto; Mr. Caldwell, Bogart and Co., whose principals we doubt not may be found in Wallstreet, propose organizing, arming and importing at their own or their employers expense an American force into the territories of Mexico for the avowed purpose of supporting armed rebels against a friendly nation.''[7]

Naturally, Mexico protested against American citizens' underwriting, manning, and arming military expeditions into her territory. It was not the first time American neutrality was at issue, but the Texas Revolution most nakedly exposed neutrality as a hollow word. This was particularly unfortunate, for the United States had been the first nation to specify that certain acts violated neutrality and to put those acts into a criminal code. Among others, George Washington had feared that strong American sympathy for the French Revolution might produce drastic entanglements. The Neutrality Act of April 24, 1800, made enlistment or recruitment in the service of a foreign power a high misdemeanor punishable by a fine of up to a thousand dollars and imprisonment for up to three years. For mounting or outfitting a military expedition, the fine was up to three thousand dollars. In 1817 the Neutrality Act was broadened to include service under "a foreign prince, state, colony, district or people"—which the provisional government of rebels in Texas certainly qualified as. But American filibusters and mercenaries continued to mount expeditions against Latin America, unconcerned by the Neutrality Act.[8]

On November 4, 1835, Secretary of State John Forsyth circulated a formal warning to U.S. district attorneys in Louisiana, New York, Massachusetts, Pennsylvania, Maryland, and Alabama stating that it was the "fixed determination of the Executive" to prevent citizens from embroiling themselves in Mexico's domestic affairs. That meant Texas. The district attorneys were instructed to be "attentive to all movements of a hostile character which may be contemplated or attempted."[9]

Nevertheless, throughout the Texas Revolution, district attorneys watched armed volunteers parade—literally—into Texas. "With drums beating and fifes playing," one company of recruits descended the Mississippi past two district attorneys who insisted that nothing exhibited them as an armed force, and they were therefore qualified as legitimate emigrants bound for Texas. The Nashville district attorney was himself secretly responsible for raising a company of mercenaries.

Furthermore, while the secretary of state's attempt at neutrality seemed in good faith, President Jackson's own conduct spoke more clearly. On its way to Louisville, Kentucky, a band of patriotic volunteers crossed paths with a steamer bearing Old Hickory. The mercenaries lowered their company flag in salute and roared out three cheers for Andy. One of the mercenaries wrote that a prominent abolitionist was on board the steamer and "demanded of the President why it was that armed bodies of men were allowed to recruit in the United States to make war on Mexico. To which General Jackson replied, 'That Americans had a lawful right to emigrate and to bear arms.' "[10]

American neutrality laws were a joke to the mercenaries streaming westward, who got around them by calling themselves "emigrants" and their firearms "hollow-ware." Recruiting agents for the rebels were instructed to go through the motions of concealing their activities. "You will also advertise for passengers for Texas" read one set of instructions from the rebel government, "and charge them such reasonable price for passage as in your judgement [sic] should be proper, and if any should take passage in said Boat, with intention of entering the service of Texas, they shall have their passage money refunded to them, on being received into service."[9]

The volunteers were sensitive about charges that they were hired guns, and could become strident in their own defense. "'Tis no filthy lucre that promotes us to the battle field of Texas; no desire to enrich ourselves in land, which has been deluged in patriots blood," one mercenary crowed as the Ladies' Legion of Lexington presented his bunch with a flag. "Ours is, I trust, a far purer and nobler aspiration. . . . Kentucky has gained a reputation for deeds of chivalry, which the proudest might envy. Scarcely a battle field of the late [Revolutionary] war does not bear testimony of the honorable bearing, the lofty and unbending patriotism, and the magnanimous bravery of her Sons."[11]

But the fact remained that Texas needed fighters and was luring them with the same currency offered to wealthy lenders—land. Until almost the last day of the Texas Revolution, the rebel army had no more than a hundred "regular" troops. The ranks were composed of volunteers, and only a fraction of the volunteers had lived in Texas for more than a few months or years. Almost all of the men gathering in western Texas at the Alamo and at Goliad were freshly arrived mercenaries from the United States. The use of mercenaries eventually created problems for Anglo-American Texas.

Only a few months after the revolution ended, the first president of Texas, David Burnet, called the volunteers still pouring in from the United States "mere Leeches. They never have and never will do Texas any good; but much evil, independent of the cost, results from them." The bulk of these American soldiers of fortune signed on for only a three-month hitch, and Burnet said that demonstrated greed, not sacrifice. Besides that the three-month mercenary tended to desert, get drunk, and raise hell. "We have no use for such," he said, "and do not want any men for a less period [sic] than one year or during the war. Such we will be happy to receive."[12]

Indeed, once the fighting was over, the rebel government quickly withdrew its lavish recruiting incentives. Just as quickly, embittered and landless volunteers began returning to their homes in the United States with their silk flags limp, blustering about Texan deception.

However necessary the mercenaries' presence was, it wore thin very quickly. The rebel officers, though glad for the extra manpower, were distinctly unhappy with the constant threat of mercenary mutiny. From the outset, the mercenaries balked at committing themselves to any sort of time period or discipline. Most joined auxilary corps, and a three-month commitment turned them cold.

Their officers were just as whimsical. On Christmas Day, six mercenary captains rebelled against the rebels, declaring that their companies had not volunteered for regular army service and would not take regular army commands.[13] In late January a large body of the mercenaries decided to invade deeper into Mexico, with or without permission from the provisional government. In the face of that kind of carte blanche it was almost impossible to build a cohesive fighting force, and the wonder was that the rebel army did not self-destruct before Santa Anna ever arrived.

Factionalism raged among the Anglo-American patriots. Travis called the army a mob.[14] Houston called the rebellious volunteers exactly what Santa Anna called them—pirates. One of the mercenary officers, J. W. Fannin, declared that volunteers should be paid through despoiling the enemy, to which Houston angrily responded, "This, in my opinion . . . divests the campaign of any character save that of a piratical or predatory war." He went on to say that plundering Mexican civilians would only cause greater enemy resistance. "In war, when spoil is the object, friends and enemies share one common destiny. This rule will govern the citizens of the Matamoras in their conclusions, and render their resistance desperate. . . . They will look upon [the Anglo-American army] as they would look upon Mexican mercenaries, and resist them as such."[15]

Houston, Austin, and other rebel leaders were not alone in their disenchantment with the volunteers. Even before the U.S. mercenaries showed up to plunder Mexicans, Anglo-Americans living in eastern Texas arrived in western Texas to plunder Anglo-Americans.[16]

Anglo-Americans had preyed on their countrymen even during the worst, most binding moments of the revolution. But with the fall of San Antonio in December, the plundering became a practice.

"For two weeks after the fall of Béxar the soldiers who garrisoned the town enjoyed a season of almost utter abandon," said Creed Taylor, who had fought to evict General Cós. "They were mostly volunteers from the 'states' [*sic*]—nearly all of the Texans having gone to their homes—and being disappointed in not having their promised rewards, they soon learned to regard the property belonging to Mexican citizens as lawful prey and so acted accordingly. Each day a detail was sent out to round up beeves and fat cows for food for the garrison, and when a Mexican appeared in town with a good horse, ownership of the animal was promptly transferred to a needy *American*. Reliable Mexican citizens have told me of many of the practices of the volunteers while in San Antonio, all of which were a shame and a disgrace to the American name."[17]

In Goliad (La Bahía), the town next to the fortified presidio, drunken Anglo-Americans went on a rampage, breaking into Tejanos' homes, raping the women, and looting. The town's population plummeted from one thousand to ten as citizens fled to surrounding ranches. The mercenaries took up "ample and comfortable" quarters, sharing the rest of the deserted town with cats and dogs.[18]

The bad blood between civilians and warriors was a classic portrait of an army lacking clear command. Houston was designated commander in chief, but he could only complain about, not control, men like Fannin who were bent on a war for spoils. The result was a dearth of discipline, leading to chaos. Civilians—Anglo-American, but to a much greater degree, Tejano—were helpless. They were resentful. And the volunteers resented their resentment.

The young lions from Stateside prowling along the advance line in anticipation of blood mocked the Anglo-American settlers. They resented the settlers' absence from the front, stung that their heroism was no longer being celebrated.[19]

One rebel officer wrote that despite an abundance of livestock, the local civilians volunteered no meat to the rebel army. Not only did the officer have to go out and purchase cattle, he had to butcher them too.

Fannin, the West Point dropout, guessed that only twenty-five citizens would muster upon call—"Nay, I am informed that there is not half that number." Fannin despised the colonists he'd delegated himself to champion. He was bewildered by their apathy. As the revolution crashed around him, he wrote, "I have but three citizens in the ranks and tho' I have called on them for six weeks, not one arrived, and no assistance in bringing me provisions, even Texas refused me. I feel too indignant to say more about them." Just the same, he added, "If I am lost, be the censure on the right head, and may my wife and my children and children's children curse the sluggards forever."[20]

"Our affairs are gloomy indeed," Travis complained. "The people are cold and indifferent—They are worn down & exhausted with the war, & in consequence of dissensions between contending & rival chieftains they have lost all confidence in their own gov't and officers."[21]

When Travis called senior officers "chieftains," he was not far wrong. The various factions, units, and geographical bodies of fighting men in Texas acted largely as separate clans, each carving out its own territory. There had been discord from the outset. But once the enemy was banished from San Antonio, the rebels' disharmony turned ugly and threatened to eat the revolution out of sheer spite.

Sensing this, the rebel command dreamed up an attack upon the Mexican port city of Matamoros three hundred miles due south of San Antonio. Virtually the entire rebel army was made up of mercenaries now, and the command reasoned that they needed action in order to stay out of trouble. From a strategic point of view, Matamoros was a juicy target. Beside that, a land speculator named Dr. James Grant had convinced large numbers of volunteers that Matamoros was the key to unlock all of Mexico.

Grant's real motive in channeling the fighters into deeper Mexico was to regain his land holdings. Under the corrupt Coahuila-Texas legislature, he had compiled huge tracts of real estate with a voracity that brought down the wrath of the Mexican government. At Santa Anna's orders, General Cós had arrested whatever speculators he could get his hands on, including Ben Milam and Dr. Grant.

Grant escaped, and then audaciously set about reassembling the old, favorable status quo. He knew that under the independent Republic of Texas the War Dogs were pressing for, his shifty land titles would be as null and void as they were under Santa Anna's centralist regime. His only hope was to revolutionize Mexican federalists and resurrect the old state legislature. By maintaining states' rights, he might still advance his real estate schemes.[22]

Grant had been talking up an invasion since late November and had almost seduced a number of besiegers into leaving San Antonio for Matamoros. Only Milam's rousing, "Who'll go into Béxar with Old Ben Milam," had prevented the rebels from heading south at that time. Once

San Antonio fell, however, Grant's description of silver and glory danced in the soldiers' heads.

A week before Christmas a Matamoros invasion suddenly seemed like a grand idea to the rebel command. Houston ordered one of the few men he trusted, James Bowie, to lead an expedition south.[23] But Bowie didn't receive the orders, and Houston soon changed his mind. But Dr. Grant put together an invasion anyway.

Designating himself the commander in chief of the volunteer army, Grant stripped the Alamo of supplies, arms, hospital supplies, and all but a hundred men. He had been loosely commissioned by the revolutionary council, which was at noisy odds with the revolutionary governor Henry Smith. The council compounded the problem by authorizing someone else as commander in chief of volunteers, a land speculator named Francis Johnson. Altogether, Grant and Johnson rallied some five hundred mercenaries. Yet another commander in chief, James Fannin, added his Georgia Battalion, which was bearing arms furnished by the state of Georgia.

Not a man to hedge his words, Governor Smith called the rabble "a mob nicknamed an army." He predicted doom for the mutinous expedition. "I will ere long throw them a fall which will break their own damned necks and they shall welter in their own blood."[24]

The invaders were acting in defiance of Governor Smith and his own commander in chief, Sam Houston. With a coup d'état hanging overhead, the governor dissolved the council ("a damned corrupt Council") and the council retaliated by impeaching the governor for libel, embezzlement, and treason. Now Houston went public with his doubts and thundered that the Matamoros expedition was unauthorized. Grant and Johnson declared that Houston had no authority over the volunteers. And Fannin allowed that Houston did have authority, but only if he attacked Matamoros.

By the end of January there was so much strife among council members that a quorum could not be raised and the government disintegrated altogether. Through the next crucial month—as Santa Anna crossed northern Mexico into Texas—every man acted at whim.

By this time, rumors were flying that Santa Anna was in northern Mexico and the regular army command, that is, Houston, was firmly opposed to raiding Matamoros. Even if Matamoros fell to the rebels, it was hundreds of miles beyond reinforcement and supply. Even if the rebels won Matamoros and sparked a federalist revolution in Mexico, Texas would merely resume its place as a Mexican state, not an independent republic. On the other hand, if the rebels were defeated at Matamoros, the Anglo-Americans would be left without an army and Texas would rapidly sink back into the Mexican orbit. No matter how Houston and his party looked at it, Matamoros promised to be a strategic disaster.

Wearing one of the only pair of boots in Texas, Houston rode across to southwestern Texas where the mercenaries were massing in mid-January. He was in an odd position. Of the four supreme commanders now claiming authority, Houston had the least support among the mercenaries. Realizing how senseless it would be to demand the army back from Grant, Johnson, or Fannin, he simply rode along with the troops, talking with them individually, warning them of the dangers lying at Matamoros, and arguing against Grant's bid to reestablish Mexican federalism.

"Comrades, Citizens of Texas!" he sermonized to the wayward troops on January 15. "Let us . . . sever that link that binds us to that rusty chain of the Mexican Confederation; let us break off the live slab from the dying cactus that it may not dry up with the remainder; let us plant it anew that it may spring luxuriantly out of the fruitful savannah. Nor will the vigor of the descendants of the sturdy north ever mix with the phlegm of the indolent Mexicans, no matter how long we may live among them. Two different tribes on the same hunting ground will never get along together. The tomahawk will ever fly and the scalping knife will never rest until the last of either one tribe or the other is either destroyed or is a slave. And I ask, comrades, will we ever bend our necks as slaves, ever quietly watch the destruction of our property and the annihilation of our guaranteed rights? NO!! Never! Too well I know my people. The last drop of our blood would flow before we would bow under the yoke of these half-Indians."[25]

The handsome giant was a charismatic figure, but the mercenaries were inflamed by dreams of wealth, black-eyed señoritas, and more violence. They had not traveled thousands of miles to serve as garrison troops under the command of a cautious regular army. Houston was learning what Mexico already knew, that no matter what color their flag or uniform, filibusters came for profit, not patriotism. Houston was disgusted. He turned his horse back toward eastern Texas, leaving the men to their fate.

"The evil is now done," he wrote to Governor Smith. "I trust sincerely, that the first of March [the date set for a constitutional convention] may establish a government on some permanent foundation, where honest functionaries will regard and execute the known and established laws of the country, agreeably to their oaths. If this state of things can not be achieved, the country must be lost."[26]

On January 16, Houston got word from the Alamo. Lt. Col. James Clinton Neill had loyally remained in the mission-fortress with roughly one hundred men who had either rejected Grant's rainbow chasing or else been too wounded or sick from the San Antonio siege. The situation was grim and getting grimmer.

"The men all under my command have been in the field for the last four months," Neill wrote. "They are almost naked, and this day they were to have received pay for the first month of their last enlistment, and almost every one of them speaks of going home, and not less than twenty will leave to-morrow, and leave here only about eighty efficient men under my command. . . . We are in a torpid, defenseless condition, and have not and cannot get from all the citizens here horses enough to send out a patrol or spy company. . . . I hope we will be re-inforced in eight days, or we will be over-run by the enemy, but, if I have only 100 men, I will fight 1,000 as long as I can and then not surrender. . . ."[27]

The entire western front was crumbling. The presidio at Goliad, too, had been stripped of men, munitions, and horses. The Anglo-American army of over six hundred was about to march off to Matamoros, leaving the interior of Texas completely exposed. Houston decided to consolidate what forces he had left at Gonzales. On January 17 Houston dispatched James Bowie with about thirty men to San Antonio. Bowie's mission was to prepare the destruction of the Alamo.

"I have ordered the fortifications in the town of Béxar to be demolished," Houston reported to the governor. "And, if you should think well of it, I will remove all the cannon and other munitions of war to Gonzales and Copano, blow up the Alamo and abandon the place, as it will be impossible to keep up the Station with volunteers, the sooner I can be authorized by letter the better it will be for the country."[28]

Not much later, Houston furloughed himself and left the western front to fend for itself. When he departed, most of the mercenaries did too, many of them taking refuge at the Goliad presidio. Grant and Johnson retained only about 150 men, and in the end they never got close to Matamoras.

As Bowie approached San Antonio, Houston received news of the Alamo from a Kentucky-born lawyer named Green B. Jameson who was serving as the chief engineer. His communiqué reiterated the dearth of men and payroll: There were 114 troops at the Alamo, of whom only 80 were healthy enough to serve. Of those, the officers had carried the lion's share of patrolling and standing guard.

"We have had loose discipline untill [sic] lately," Jameson wrote. "Since we heard of 1000 to 1500 men of the enemy being on their march to this place duty is being shown well and punctually in case of an attack we will move all into the Alamo and whip 10 to 1 with our artillery.

"If the men here can get a reasonable supply of clothing, provisions and money they will remain the balance of the 4 months, and do duty and fight better than fresh men, they have all been tried and have confidence in themselves."[29]

They had received a hundred bushels of corn and forty-two head of cattle: sufficient for two months, but hardly a complete diet. The one hundred bushels of corn were probably those discovered by young Ehrenberg in the ruins of San José Mission, hidden underground by locals to avoid confiscation by the Anglo-American or Mexican soldiers. If so, it was corn forcibly "purchased" from the long-suffering Tejanos, who had no choice in the matter. There were almost no Tejanos who volunteered services to the Anglo-Americans. In his letter to Houston, Jameson specifically mentioned one who did, local rancher Juan Seguín.

A good-looking, self-possessed *criollo,* with family money and land, Seguín got along remarkably well with the racist Southerners who were pressing the revolution. His own goal was an independent republic of Texas, free of Mexico and also equally free of the United States. The Mexicans considered him a traitor of Benedict Arnold's dimensions, but the Anglo-Americans found him useful. He formed up a company of two dozen Tejanos, which performed invaluable intelligence work for Houston, Travis, and Bowie, effectively screening thousands of square miles between the Rio Grande and San Antonio. Though he fought in almost every campaign of the Texas Revolution and buried the remains of the Alamo defenders with high honors, Seguín was repeatedly and brutally betrayed by the Anglo-Americans. A decade hence, he would be fighting against the Americans in the Mexican War.[30] Besides Seguín and his twenty-five men, next to no Tejanos joined the Anglo-Americans in fighting Santa Anna.

Bowie arrived in the town of his dead wife in late January, ready to evacuate and demolish the Alamo. In his company of volunteers rode a strikingly handsome, high-minded young South Carolinian named James Butler Bonham. Bonham and Travis had grown up only a few miles apart, but the plantation hierarchy had kept them separate. Travis came from a poor, if proud family, while Bonham descended from wealth.

Bonham was nevertheless a born rebel—extravagant, contrary, and chivalrous. He was expelled from South Carolina College for rebelling against school authorities in defense of nullification, or states' rights. He showed up at Charleston in 1832 as a captain of the artillery, all ready to fight the North and secede.[31] The fiery paladin had arrived in Texas a few days after San Antonio fell. As a member of the Mobile Greys, he was just one more mercenary knocking about in search of an opportunity.

Colonel Neill cordially welcomed Colonel Bowie and his twenty or thirty volunteers. The two colonels discussed the notion that the Alamo should be razed and came up with their own reasons why it should not be. While calculating that it would take a force of one thousand men to adequately hold the walls against a siege, Bowie declared that the Alamo was a vital defense against the Mexican army.

"Our force is very small," he freely admitted, "the returns this day to the Comdt. is only one hundred and twenty officers & men. It would be a waste of men to put our brave little band against thousands." Just the same, the two colonels determined to make their stand at the Alamo. It was not their decision to make. But, in keeping with the anarchy characteristic of the rebel army, they made it anyway.

"Col. Neill & Myself have come to the solemn resolution that we will rather die in these ditches than give it up to the enemy." Bowie's reasons were earnest and for the most part candid.

"The salvation of Texas depends in great measure in keeping Bejar out of the hands of the enemy," Bowie wrote. "It serves as the frontier picquet [sic] guard and if it were in the possession of Santa Anna there is no strong hold from which to repel him in his march towards the Sabine." He also argued that the Béxarenos deserved protection.[32]

And so, rather than ready the Alamo for demolition, Bowie added his voice to Neill's in calling for reinforcements, money, and food. One thing Bowie was not candid about was how a remote command, like the Alamo, meant both prestige and autonomy. Above all, the Alamo command meant limelight, for it was positioned upon the bowhead of the Anglo-American warship. It stood clean and separate from the hurly-burly.

On February 13, Colonel Neill abruptly left the Alamo on furlough to tend his sick family. That should have left Colonel Bowie with his very own plum of a command. But by then another colonel, one of the only regulars in the country, had shown up at the Alamo: William Travis.

Three and a half months earlier, when Bowie was a full colonel, Travis, fourteen years Bowie's junior, had been a mere lieutenant. Travis was a War Dog of great energy and panache, but he had almost no following or charisma. All the same, he thought the Alamo was meant to be his own command.

Travis and Bowie knew each other. They'd served together during the fall campaign, though Travis had done little actual fighting, while Bowie had been neck-deep in battles. Austin had bestowed the rank of lieutenant upon Travis in October, and by the end of the month the lieutenant had catapulted to a captaincy.

For the most part Travis galloped around the countryside, setting the prairie grass on fire to deprive any Mexican reinforcements of forage. He was allowed a dozen or so men to command and assigned to range about in the direction of the Rio Grande. His prairie duty kept Travis out of trouble and also kept him out of camp where he was apparently not liked.

After failing to find a *caballada* of three hundred Mexican horses, Captain Travis resigned in the first week of November. "Believing that I can not be longer useful to the army without complaints being made, I herewith tender to your Excellency [Austin] my resignation. . . ."[33]

The same day he resigned, Travis dove back into the prairie grasses in search of the grazing *caballada*. He took exaggerated pride in never turning back or failing. There were a lot of young men running around in Texas with overblown codes of honor, but it was Travis's in particular that ultimately affected the course of the revolution.

On the fourth day out, Travis and a detachment of twelve men cut the trail of the *caballada*. They followed the hoofprints to the Mexican camp, spent an uncomfortable cold, rainy night without water, and next morning surprised the soldiers. Not a shot was fired. Five Mexicans surrendered, two escaped, and Travis returned in minor glory with three hundred saddle-broken horses.

In wrapping up his report to Austin, Travis added, "I have nothing further to add, than that during ten days of arduous service, my men have had to mount guard every night, & to be on fatiguing duty during the day, without any other food than meat without salt; & that most of them have conducted themselves with a heroism & firmness worthy of the great cause of liberty in which they are engaged, & the satisfaction they enjoy of having rendered some service to their country, more than compensates them for the fatigues & privations they have undergone in a bleak wilderness, amidst cold & rain."[34]

By late November Travis had grown disenchanted with the siege. His small cavalry company had too. His morning report for November 26 recorded the bare bones of a command—seven cornets, one private, and three desertions.[35] Sometime between November 26 and December 3, Travis departed the army and returned to San Felipe and his law practice.

But in early December the effusive lawyer contacted Governor Smith and the council with his ideas about forming a regular army. In the midst of much prose about "usurpations & Tyranny of a dictatorial army & bigoted clergy" and "a storm is impending over us—The time that is 'to try men's souls' is yet to come," Travis proposed an army of three infantry battalions and one unit of cavalry. He specified that the cavalry should be commanded by a lieutenant colonel "who should be subject alone to the orders of the commander in chief for the time being."[36] For a Walter Scott addict like Travis the command of mounted soldiers was a dream of exquisite completion. In addition, a senior military rank would practically guarantee political office in the future.

In mid-December the rebel government was pleased to appoint Travis a position in the embryonic regular army. But to his enormous disappointment, he was offered neither the lieutenant colonelcy nor a place in the cavalry. Instead, he was assigned the rank of major in the artillery.

Travis fired back a letter. "I feel highly sensible of this mark of distinction," he wrote, "and I return my sincere thanks . . . for the honor [the council has] intended me; yet believing that I could not be so useful in the artillery as elsewhere, I beg leave to decline the office, or if I have been commissioned to resign the same."[37]

On Christmas Eve, 1835, Travis got his wish. Governor Smith appointed him lieutenant colonel of the cavalry.[38]

Travis threw himself into creating a cavalry over which he could command. He ordered himself a complete colonel's uniform from New Orleans, along with uniforms for his Legion of Cavalry: The basic troop was meant to sport a gray coat with yellow bullet buttons, cowhide boots, brass spurs, and a broadsword. His horses would carry Spanish saddles, his troops would carry a brace of horseman's pistols and a shotgun. The volunteer cavalry militias of the South poured money into trappings for themselves and their horses. Uniforms ran between twenty to seventy-two dollars apiece, an expense borne by the wearer. A standard rifle cost fourteen dollars. And then there was the expense of gleaming rig for their steeds.[39] The aristocratic cavalry was no place for poor men, one more reason Travis coveted his assignment. But Travis's uniform did not arrive before Santa Anna did.

As sketched out by the rebel government, the Legion of Cavalry was to have a full complement of officers, 14 musicians, 5 saddlers, 5 boot-makers, and 286 privates. Travis had been ordered to raise 100 men, but quickly found few people shared his enthusiasm for the war or his cavalry. Night and day he "strained every nerve" to transform the cavalry from paper to flesh, using his personal credit for expenses, laboring to interest settlers in joining his corps.

"The people are cold and indifferent," he reported to Governor Smith. "They are worn down and exhausted with the war, & in consequence of dissentions between contending & rival chieftains, they have lost all confidence in their own Govt. & officers. A regular army is necessary—but money, & *money* only can raise & equip a regular army—Money must be raised or Texas is gone to *ruin*—without it—war cannot be again carried on in Texas."[40]

Travis was badly discouraged. His fanaticism had failed to attract more than a third of his cavalry, and even the few he'd mustered were deserting.

In the frosty, waning days of January, Travis rounded up his cavalry and headed off to reinforce the Alamo. On the first or second day, nine of his followers deserted. Their chief complaint seems to have been Travis himself, for several of the men later showed up at the Alamo under their own steam, and five had no qualms about fighting under Houston at San Jacinto. All of this gored Travis's pride and contributed to his spiraling depression.

On the day after he reported the desertions, the fickle, high-strung Travis decided that commanding a cavalry legion was not all it was cracked up to be and demanded to be relieved of leading these particular troops. "I am willing, nay anxious to go to the defence of Bexar, and I have done every thing in my power to equip the Enlisted men & get them off," he wrote to Governor Smith. "But Sir, I am unwilling to risk my reputation (which is ever dear to a soldier) by going off into the enemy's country with such little means, so few men, & them so badly equipped—In fact there is no necessity for my services to command these few men—The company officers will be amply sufficient." In closing, Travis said he would be better employed in superintending the recruiting of soldiers.

Travis set aside his pride and continued on to San Antonio. On February 3 he rode into the bullet-marked town at the head of his cavalry. The addition of his thirty or so cavalrymen brought the rebel forces up to about 140 men.

Probably the most pressing issue among the troops was the election of delegates who would go to the convention slated to begin on March 1, their mission to make sense of the revolution, to clarify just what the rebels were fighting *for,* as distinct from what they were fighting *against.*

All across Texas, Anglo-Americans came together on February 1 and voted. Houston was among the fifty-nine delegates elected, one of several who brought with them congressional experience at the state or national level. Only three delegates were Mexican-born. In other words, though Mexicans formed 16 percent of Texas's population, their representative voice formed only 5 percent of the conventional body. In future years, the imbalance would grow even grimmer.

The provisional government had ruled that any volunteer who took an oath of allegiance to it could vote, but the election judges in San Antonio, including the pro-revolutionary Juan Seguín, rejected the idea that the 120-odd mercenaries and regulars camping out in the Alamo had any right to dominate local politics. Except for the few who had settled in town before the autumn siege, the Anglo-Americans were not citizens of the municipality. Less than a quarter of them were even citizens of Texas or Mexico. In short, the rebels were ineligible to vote in their own revolution. The thought of getting disenfranchised—and by a pack of swarthy Mexicans—struck the rebels as offensive and absurd.[41]

A physician attached to the Alamo garrison, Dr. Amos Pollard, wrote a furious letter to Governor Smith about the Tejano shenanigans. "Four Mexicans are to represent this Jurisdiction in the convention although we might with great ease have sent the same number of Americans, had it not have been that a few of our people through Mexican policy perfectly hoodwinked headquarters, making them believe that it was unjust to attempt to send any other than Mexicans. . . . Perhaps I have said enough," Pollard started to close. Then he added, "However, I intend that those representatives shall distinctly understand, previous to their leaving, that if they vote against independence, they will have to be very careful on returning here."[42]

Not to be denied their natural Anglo-Saxon rights, the Alamo garrison went ahead and held its own election on February 5. Bearing a petition for their acceptance, Samuel Maverick (who later lent his name to stray cattle and saddle tramps) and Jesse Badgett rode off to represent the Alamo company at the convention.[43] The convention accepted these two last-minute delegates without debate.

When Colonel Neill took a twenty-day furlough from the Alamo to attend to his sick family in eastern Texas, he left the command in Colonel Travis's hands—or thought he did—and departed on horseback with Deaf

Smith. Travis's authority lasted at most a matter of hours, perhaps only minutes.

"I feel myself delicately and awkwardly situated," Travis confessed to Governor Smith on the day after Neill left. "I therefore hope that your Exclly [*sic*] will give me some definite orders, and that immediately—"[44]

His problem stemmed from the factional strife between the regulars and the volunteers. Thinking he could breast his way through the conflict, Travis told the mercenaries that if they were dissatisfied with his command they could elect one of their own. The mercenaries promptly named Colonel Bowie to lead them. Travis had miscalculated but could not back out. He called for a company election. Only the volunteers voted, and not even all of them. They formally elected Bowie to command.[45]

Once again Travis found himself slapped with evidence that leadership was more than romantic wishes and fantasies. Rough-and-ready fighting men plainly were not drawn to him. Still the proud young lawyer refused to submit to Bowie's control.

For his part, Bowie threw a wild party, turning San Antonio into an animal house for the next several days. It was a disgraceful, stumble-drunk orgy of power and corn liquor.

"Since his election [Bowie] has been roaring drunk all the time," Travis complained from the sidelines. "If I did not feel my honor & that of my country compromitted I would leave here instantly for some other point with the troops under my immediate command—as I am unwilling to be responsible for the drunken irregularities of any man."[46]

As if celebrating the collapse of all order in Texas, Bowie applied himself to anarchy. Like Sam Houston, he was a notorious alcoholic and now proved his reputation. To loud "huzzahs," he released a cavalry trooper who had been convicted of mutiny. He emptied the jails of Mexican prisoners and released prisoners from their labor gangs. When Juan Seguín ordered one prisoner remanded to jail, Bowie furiously confronted the Tejano captain and demanded the prisoner's rerelease. Seguín refused; Bowie summoned a body of mercenaries who drunkenly paraded under arms in the main square.

Bowie ordered his followers to halt all the huge, ox-drawn Mexican carts that were trundling out of town laden with Tejanos and their valuables. Reports had been flying that Santa Anna and his army were massing along the Rio Grande for a counter-invasion. The citizens of San Antonio knew too well what that would mean and were quietly fleeing town to let the revolutionaries trade gunsmoke with the government forces. Bowie understood what their departure signified. Like a king ordering the ocean to halt its waves, Bowie arrested a few oxcarts.[47]

Travis finally had a bellyful of the mob and removed his dozen or so faithful regulars to the Medina River. On February 14 the two colonels reached an understanding. Travis would have command of his regulars and the volunteer cavalry. Bowie would command the volunteers of the garrison. All correspondence and general orders would be signed by both commanders, at least until Colonel Neill returned from furlough.[48]

The first thing the joint command of the Alamo signed was a letter to Governor Smith. They needed money. They needed men, supplies, and munitions—but first they needed money. Without that the few troops they had under arms would desert. They were desperately close to losing San Antonio, even though the enemy was still hundreds of miles away on the far side of the Rio Grande. And no one had even fired a shot.

=9=

WHILE THE ALAMO garrison defiantly tallied the votes of its unauthorized election, the once-and-wishful congressman David Crockett was rocking in his saddle a hundred miles east of San Antonio. Clouds threatened rain, but the weather was unseasonably warm. Frogs sang along the waterways and butterflies tagged small flowers poking up through the prairie soil.[1]

By now Crockett understood that his last-minute bid for office had crumbled. He was stuck. There was no way a man of his prominence could back out of military service, not with the eyes of future voters upon him. He had one consolation anyway. He was traveling with a bunch of Tennesseeans, the best possible audience for a Tennessee tale spinner.

They were a strange set of mercenaries. Not one of them was a professional soldier; several were gentle, cultured men probably still wearing their city clothes. Three were lawyers, two were physicians, and there were two teenagers in the group. Though the dozen or so men came to be dubbed the Tennessee Mounted Volunteers, only half of them even came from Tennessee, the rest being from Kentucky, Pennsylvania, and Ohio. And finally, these volunteers were only just mounted, many of them having walked 115 miles through winter rain, mud, and water from Natchitoches to Nacogdoches. Crockett had joined them almost by accident, having arrived in Nacogdoches and taken his oath of allegiance at the same time they did. He was not their leader though. They called him Colonel Crockett: That was just the old Southern honorific. The company's designated commander was a twenty-five-year-old captain named William B. Harrison.

Like many of the volunteers streaming toward the western front, Crockett and his companions saw themselves as pious, radiant champions, not soldiers of fortune. Daniel Cloud, a twenty-four-year-old lawyer from Kentucky wrote a letter home that was almost hysterical with tightly wound patriotism. "The tide of emigration will be onward and irresistible," he wrote, "and he whose life is spared fifty years will see the apostles of liberty and republicanism, the sons of our blessed country descending the western declivities of the Rocky Mountains, bearing in one hand the olive branch of peace and the implements of husbandry—in the other, the weapons of defense and security to shed on that benighted region the light of Christianity and the blessings of civilization and free government, then the mighty waves of the monarch of oceans which wash the East Indies, the hoary empire of China and the islands of Polynesia on the east, shall waft all their stores of plenty into the republican ports of our mammoth confederacy of the west."[2]

Most of the Tennessee Mounted Volunteers descended from Revolutionary War soldiers.[3] Their genealogies were resplendent, and they practiced high-mindedness with a passion. The accusation that land hunger motivated them kept mercenaries like these on constant defense.

One of the first things Crockett declared in one speech was his selfless intent. "I have come to your country," he orated, "though not, I hope, through any selfish motive whatever. I have come to aid you all that I can in your noble cause. I shall identify myself with your interests, and all the honor that I desire is that of defending as a high private, in common with my fellow citizens, the liberties of our common country."[4]

But the reality of the volunteers' motives clashed markedly with their red-white-and blue gasconades. In their private correspondence the desire for Texas land was abundant and unabashed.

Daniel Cloud and his classmate James Bailey, for instance, were less drawn to Texas than pushed along to it. Having recently graduated from law school, they left Lexington, Kentucky, to make their fortunes. Neither of them was looking for dragons to slay. All they wanted was a juicy law docket. They traveled to Illinois, Missouri, Arkansas, and Louisiana in search of a community that could support them. In one state after another, the prospects were discouraging and they moved along. "The reasons which induced us to travel on, were briefly these," Cloud reported about Illinois. "First our curiosity was unsatisfied, second, Law Dockets were not large, fees low, and yankee lawyers numerous, Third the coldness of the Climate."[5]

Cloud's zealotry—from his sanctimony to his romantic verbiage—was a mirror image of the man he was going to serve under, Lieutenant Colonel Travis. Born in the same generation in the same sector of the United States, both were literate and ambitious, both were lawyers, both smelled opportunity in Texas, and both wrapped themselves in flamboyant language. Crockett's generation tended to be blunt and to the point. As the excited crew neared San Antonio, Crockett would have recognized himself more clearly in the only other man over the age of forty, Micajah Autry. To them Texas represented a chance for two bone-weary Go Ahead men to try their luck one more time.

Like Crockett, Autry was sick of poverty and debt. Like Crockett, he was one more Tennesseean pilgrim with a reputation for marksmanship living in the shadow of Andrew Jackson, the state banks, and an idea that life ought not be so hard. He had a rich tenor voice, played the violin well, wrote poems, and sketched pictures. He tended toward teaching the arts, but practicality nudged him into studying law. In 1830 Autry removed his family and slaves to Jackson, Tennessee. There he entered a partnership with another lawyer, and he flourished. Like Crockett with his river mills and his barrel-stave enterprise, Autry made a stab at business. Autry plunged all of his and his partner's money into merchandising dry goods purchased in Philadelphia and New York. Like Crockett, he ended up bankrupt. On one of his trips to the North for dry goods, he heard Stephen Austin speak about Texas. Determined to make good for his wife, daughters, and son, Autry headed west on the steamboat *Pacific*.[6]

Like Crockett, Autry was aiming for Texas land, not Texas revolution. The thought of fighting Mexicans was a smoky abstraction. It was far from certain there was even any more fighting to be done. "The fighting will be over before we get there," he wrote in one letter.[7] In another he reported, "Some say that Santa Ana [*sic*] is in the field with an immense army and near the confines of Texas, others say since the conquest of St. Antonio by the Texians and the imprisonment of Genl. Cos and 1100 men of which you have no doubt heard, that Santa Ana has become intimidated for fear that the Texians will drive the war into his dominions and is now holding himself in readiness to fly to Europe. . . ."

The rigors of frontier travel wore hard on the middle-aged Autry. The young bucks storming toward the front could ignore their blisters, the weather, and a variety of illnesses, but Autry found the adventure exhausting. On top of that he was homesick and desperately missed his family. "We stand guard of nights and night before last was mine to stand two hours during which the moon rose in all her mildness but splendor and majesty. With what pleasure did I contemplate that lovely orb chiefly because I recollected how often you and I had taken pleasure in standing in the door and contemplating her together. Indeed I imagined that you might be looking at her at the same time. Farewell Dear Martha.

"P.S. Col. Crockett has just joined our company."[8]

Autry kept his focus tight and tangible. He had not come to Texas to harvest a warrior's credentials. He'd come for land. "I have become one of the most thorough going men you ever heard of. I go the whole Hog in the cause of Texas. I expect to help them gain their independence and also [shades of Crockett] to form their civil government, for it is worth risking many lives for. From what I have seen and learned from others there is not so fair a portion of the earth's surface warmed by the sun.

"Be of good cheer Martha I will provide you a sweet home. I shall be entitled to 640 acres of land for my services in the army and 4444 acres upon condition of settling my family here. . . ."

In between northers and frost snaps, the weather was downright summery. As Crockett and his party worked along toward the front, lime dust powdered their horses' legs, taking the hair off. At crossings, when the rivers were swollen by overnight thunderstorms, the men swam their mounts. The pines grew scarce and they entered cactus and mesquite country. Altogether their journey from Nacogdoches to San Antonio took about three weeks.

The men reached their destination on Monday, February 8, 1836. According to Antonio Menchaca, a Béxareno, Crockett and the volunteers entered town at the old Mexican graveyard on the west side of San Pedro Creek. There they halted and sent word to Bowie to receive them. Bowie and Menchaca escorted the reinforcements into town to great fanfare.[9]

The excited rebels took Crockett off his saddle, set him on the stump. They set him upon a packing box in San Antonio's Civil Plaza and demanded one of his famous speeches. To great applause and "profound" silences, the cheery traveler with the sunburned cheeks delivered.

"The full-toned voice of the distinguished speaker rose gradually above the audience and fell with smooth and lively accent upon the ears of all," said Dr. John Sutherland, a physician with the Alamo garrison. "Its sound was familiar to many who had heard it in days past, while the hearts of all beat a lively response to the patriotic sentiments which fell from his lips."[10]

Crockett gave them well-worn anecdotes about his life and career. Then he humbly declined any military title, declaring himself a "high private, in common with my fellow-citizens." It was just as well Colonel Crockett demoted himself: The Alamo command was already overdosed on colonels.

Two nights later, a dance was thrown in Crockett's honor. Several Tejanos were invited, among them Antonio Menchaca, a relative of José Menchaca who died fighting Arredondo's royalist army in 1813. Antonio was asked to bring along "all the principal ladies in the City." The dance was probably a hybrid affair, part Mexican fandango, part Southern frontier ball.

One and all, the American boys were pleasantly scandalized by the women of San Antonio who wore loose blouses with jaw-dropping décolletage under their rebozos and danced with a gypsy eroticism unknown to the belles back home. "The vulgar speech and suggestive positions of each filled us with amazement," related Herman Ehrenberg the first time he witnessed a pair of Mexicans dancing the fandango. "The senor was smoking a real Havana and the senora a lovely little cigarito, which was very becoming to her neat mouth, pretty enough to kiss, and to her whole person. The [musician] . . . stood enveloped in terrible fumes, and over the heads of the very respectable dons and donnas hovered a grey mass of smoke clouds."[11]

At around one o'clock in the morning, a courier came galloping into town with the latest word from the Rio Grande. He had been sent by a sympathizer and sought to convey the intelligence to Juan Seguín. Seguín was gone, but Menchaca received the message.

"At this moment I have received a very certain notice, that the commander in chief Antonio López de Santa Anna marches for the city of San Antonio to take possession thereof," the message read. Ten thousand of the men were allegedly infantry, the remainder cavalry.

Bowie, seeing Menchaca with the courier, approached to hear the news. As Travis passed by, Bowie called him closer. According to Menchaca, Travis said that he was dancing with the most beautiful woman in San Antonio and could not stay to read letters. Bowie insisted. Then Crockett came close too. The men studied the message, and then Travis dismissed the urgency. It would take thirteen thousand men a fortnight to reach San Antonio, he said. "Let us dance to-night and to-morrow we will make provisions for our defense," Menchaca quoted him saying.

They were still dancing when the sun rose the next morning.[12]

= 10 =

Santa Anna's military "family" of officers was an odd assortment. Some were talented and keenly patriotic professionals, others were corrupt, incompetent, or stupid. They included some of the best-educated men in the Americas, and also some of the most ruthless and greedy. A number of them weren't even Mexican, at least not by birth. Through a quarter century of fighting with—and sometimes against—these men, Santa Anna knew them well. Through the coming months of the Texas campaign, he would demonstrate that he trusted none of them. This distrust was most clearly evident in the extraordinary barrier Santa Anna kept between himself and his senior staff. But it was also evident in his Machiavellian selections for command.

The general whom Santa Anna elevated to his second-in-command—the officer he trusted most—was a man none of his other officers trusted: Vicente Filisola, an Italian by birth. Filisola had enlisted in the Spanish army in 1804 at the age of fifteen. By his twenty-first year, he had fought in over twenty battles and made second lieutenant. Like Agustín Iturbide, his commanding officer during the revolution, and like another young officer named Santa Anna, Filisola had declared for Mexican independence at the exact right moment.[1] By 1835 Filisola was a veteran not only of combat but also of Mexico's political intrigues, both equally dangerous. He would be imprisoned for his political sympathies in 1840, then released. He would run for the Senate in 1843, but lose. And during the Mexican War he would command a division against the United States. Despite this service to Mexico, Filisola always remained a foreigner in his adopted land. For this reason, Filisola was invaluable to Santa Anna, for he could use the man's talents without having to fear his influence.

Another officer of exceptional quality was Santa Anna's old colleague, Manuel Fernandez Castrillón, a tall leonine Cuban.[2] As the Texas campaign progressed, Castrillón would repeatedly argue for the humane treatment of prisoners of war. There was a simple reason for this. Following one of Santa Anna's failed coup attempts (1832), he had once been a prisoner of war himself.[3]

Another officer destined to go to Texas with Santa Anna shared the same dungeon cell with Castrillón. But Anglo-Americans soon came to know Nicolás de la Portilla as a butcher, for he would personally oversee the worst atrocity of the entire Texas campaign: the mass execution of over four hundred Anglo-American prisoners of war. At the time of his imprisonment in 1832 he was only a twenty-four-year-old lieutenant, mercurial, with a fierce expression; before his death in 1873, he would have climbed to the post of Minister of War.[4]

By the time he entered Texas, Portilla had been promoted to colonel, and he was under the command of a no-nonsense general named José Urrea. With a bristling widow's peak and jaw-length sideburns, General Urrea had the aspect of a wolf and the instincts of a tiger. Throughout the Texas campaign, he would demonstrate a fluid, deadly efficiency that put to shame Santa Anna's curious strategies. In keeping with his origins (bordering on Zacatecas, Durango was also a federalist hotbed), Urrea firmly believed in states' rights.[5]

Less flexible and mobile than Urrea, in fact downright flat-footed, was Santa Anna's star-crossed brother-in-law, Gen. Mártin Perfecto de Cós. Just as Santa Anna had courted Emperor Iturbide's sister, so Cós curried favor by courting Santa Anna's sister (he eventually married her). Standing five feet nine, Cós cut a dashing figure with brilliant black eyes, a well-groomed mustache, long black sideburns ''sun-burnt at the ends,'' and a high broad forehead. His most distinctive features were *''remarkably short''* fingernails, and a tiny gold earring in each ear. Certainly he had a dashing past. Cós had fought under the revolutionary hero José Morelos as early as 1811. But the man was a born loser. Even before Santa Anna learned Cós had lost San Antonio to the Anglo-American rabble in December, the Mexican army had marched north in large part to bail Cós and his bedraggled troops out.

Among the other foreign-born officers was Antonio Gaona, a haughty Cuban general, and a wandering French mercenary, Gen. Adrian Woll, who had joined the Mexican army after failing to gain a spot through Winfield Scott in the U.S. Army.

Though some of Santa Anna's officers were inept, like Cós, and others, like Joaquín Ramírez y Sesma, timid and corrupt, some were practically holy in their courage. Among these nerveless warriors was José Vicente Miñon. In 1822 he and 30 men had withstood the onslaught of an enemy column in Jalapa; in 1832 he and 60 men had charged 400 enemy cavalry troops; soon after, he and 120 men had captured an enemy battalion of 350. He and his men would be the first on the Texas campaign to enter San Antonio, and also the first to gain the interior of the Alamo.[6]

But one of Santa Anna's best and brightest officers in the Texas campaign did not even exist officially. This soldier's name was José Enrique de la Peña. Born in Jalisco and trained as a mining engineer, de la Peña had chosen to make a career of the military.[7] He was articulate and provocative and enormously idealistic. He believed—fervently believed—in his new nation. De la Peña, who had been assigned as a military attaché to a European legation, threw his safety to the wind at the first word of war in the autumn of 1835 and secured permission to head north for Texas.[8]

Wherever he found Mexico's enemies, de la Peña fought them. He took on Spanish invaders at Tampico in 1829 and Anglo-American invaders in Texas in 1836. And when he perceived corruption and incompetence closer to home, he took that on too. At the age of nineteen, he had dared to publish a series (in *El Sol*) exposing the anti-Mexican antics of Adm. David Porter, a former U.S. commodore who became a mercenary and took a position with the Mexican navy.[9] Ten years later, following his dusty, bloody participation in the war in Texas, de la Peña would find cause to speak out once again against his superiors. But this time he would dare to criticize the president of the nation (". . . those in command deceived themselves [about Texas] and have endeavored to mislead the nation. Let us undeceive her!") and his punishment would be erasure from every record of the campaign.

A navy man by training, de la Peña envisioned the Texas campaign in terms most familiar to himself. "The Texas expedition should have been considered as a fleet taking to the high seas. . . ." The image of a naval fleet implied structure and self-containment, and a clear dependence upon one's comrades for survival. They were heading off to war, but also they were heading into the heart of a Texas winter. They could win, but first they had to survive.

"War was the one thing that could least frighten Mexicans, who seemed to have sworn not to live without it," de la Peña wrote just months after the campaign, "but the distance of the country in which it would be waged, its climate, and the local conditions, not only in the general but in the particular topography as well, were factors of considerable weight in the eyes of the thinking person. It was the first time that our soldiers would be dealing with men of a different language and a different religion, men whose character and habits were likewise different from theirs. All was new in this war, and although it was happening on our soil, it seemed as if it were being waged in a foreign land."[10]

The expedition that de la Peña wished to resemble a fleet of men-o'-war looked like nothing less than a colorful exodus from Mexico. If the officers were an exotic collection, their recruits were fabulous, an anthropologist's dream of tribals and hybrid peoples. On paper the Mexican army had thirty thousand soldiers. In reality it had barely one tenth that number. What army units actually existed tended to be scattered all across Mexico, watchdogging neighboring units that had an aggravating penchant for mutiny.[11]

The thirty thousand ghosts in Mexico's paper army did exist, though, as potentiality. The Mexican army was built around an outsized officer corps. In times of peace, the Santanista-era military was glutted with strutting generals and their aides, who had scarcely any troops to command. But when war threatened, the officers quickly activated the draft and patched together an army.[12]

The ghost soldiers were drawn from what the Mayans, in their pre-Columbian Nahuatl tongue, called *mazehualob* or the common people. Traditionally *mazehual* designated any commoner between a noble and a slave, but by the 1830s it referred to anyone of the masses. During this period, the Mexican masses were almost exactly the reverse of the American masses. In the United States roughly 18 percent of the population was wholly or partly of African blood, with the remaining 72 percent of unmixed European blood. In Mexico, only 18 percent were pure European, the remainder Indian or of mixed blood.[13] Though the rigid *limpieza de sangre* (purity of blood) had begun to corrode by the 1800s, *casta* continued to be a derogatory term for people of mixed blood.[14] Oddly enough, the formation of Santa Anna's army for the Texas campaign was a step toward fusing Mexico's multiracial identity by serving as a sort of melting pot.

At least half of Santa Anna's sixty-five-hundred-man expedition had to be conjured up virtually overnight, many from the northern states of San Luis and Querétaro.[15] Next to no one volunteered for service, and so conscription was employed. In Mexico the draft was known as the *sorteo*, which, technically speaking, was a drawing of lots. In fact the *sorteo* was a mass kidnapping, and there was no quicker way to empty a town of people than to announce a military lottery. As a result press-gangs descended upon towns unannounced, raiding dances, *pulquerías*, and homes and rooting through the jails. Top-priority candidates were often vagrants and "pernicious" men, followed by bachelors, unhappily married men *(mal casados)*, and childless widowers. Entrapment and decoy were considered legitimate tools for filling regional quotas. After one such roundup, an observer counted fourteen young blades tied together, freshly borrowed from a local fandango. *Léperos* were plucked from the alleys. Convicts and silent Indios found themselves chained together and dropped into geographies almost unbearably alien.[16]

At least three thousand of the army's empty slots were filled "by recruits [versus *permanentes*] snatched away from the crafts and from agriculture, by heads of families, who usually do not make good soldiers, by men in cells awaiting the punishment of their crimes, at times by men condemned by one corps yet finding themselves as part of another. . . ." de la Peña said of the draftees. "There were many too young, some too old, some of these succumbing under the weight of their weapons and knapsacks. . . ."[17] He later estimated that nearly one tenth of the expeditionary force either deserted or fell sick before a shot was ever fired in Texas.[18] So many deserted that de la Peña regretted turning captured deserters back to their units, and it was considered "barbarous" when Santa Anna ordered deserters to be executed.[19] (In later years, deserters were simply sent to Veracruz for duty: Because of tropical diseases like yellow fever, it was considered a death sentence.[20])

The average soldier stood a little over five feet tall (each was measured to a sixteenth of an inch), considerably smaller than the average Anglo-American. The difference led one American minister to Mexico to sneer, "I do not think that the Mexican men have much more physical strength than our women."[21]

Almost to a man, the recruits were illiterate, impoverished, and superstitious. Many were Indian, and as such were considered little better than animals, much the same way Anglo-American Southerners viewed black slaves. It was the opinion of Mexican Creoles and even mestizos that the Indio was a dumb brute genetically suited to work in climates that would kill a white man. There was a saying that Indios heard only through their backs, meaning the overseer's whip had a tongue. Indios were considered honest (because they were so religious), lazy, docile, and humble . . . and they were famous for despising military service.[22]

Among the shanghaied troops bound for Texas was a unit of three hundred Mayan Indians plucked from the jungles of Yucatán. They were a proud people who were scrupulous about cleaning themselves, bathing whenever the weather and rivers permitted. The Texas campaign was extremely unpopular with the Mayan conscripts, for they had a profound dread of leaving their home territory.[23] On top of that, they didn't know Spanish, couldn't handle a rifle,[24] and were being sent far away with no provision for their return upon discharge.[25] With the help of their H-men, or pagan priests, they looked into the future through their dreams (to dream of a falling sky suggested disaster, to dream of marriage predicted one's own death) and color-coded mankind, with whites ranking highest and blacks and Chinese lowest. Around their necks they wore amulets of oyster and snail shells and bone and deer's toenails against ever-threatening evil winds and the evil eye.[26] But they were also fervent Christians, believing that Jesus Christ impelled their rain *chaacs* (spirits) to action and that the Virgin Mary rode a black horse and caused torrents of rain.[27] They had a deeply-rooted horror of the desecration of religious objects.[28] As fate would have it, Anglo-American troops in Texas would burn Christian santos and torch a church at Goliad in March 1836, and these very same Mayans would be assigned to execute them.

Much the same religious fervor and superstition dominated other soldiers in the Mexican army, many of whom practiced the hybrid Christianity that early priests had constructed on top of the Aztec religion. In churches across Mexico a public penance called the *Desagravios* was held annually for a period of thirty-five days. It was just one step removed from Aztec blood rituals. Upon a signal whole churchfuls of *penitentes* would whip themselves with iron- and thorn-tipped scourges. The self-flagellation would continue for half an hour until the church floor was covered with blood.[29] On New Year's Eve, the Zapotecs of Oaxaca still visited the ruins at Mitla, ''the Town of Souls,'' bearing flowers, candles, and incense to the souls inhabiting the old stone city.[30] In mid-January, on St. Anthony the Abbot day, domestic animals throughout Mexico were blessed at village churches. From miles around, people would bring to the plazas their cattle, chickens, burros, pigs, and dogs brightly colored with vegetable dyes and with flowers and streamers tied to their horns and tails.[31] Once traveling priests left their villages, the Indios reverted to their pre-Columbian ways. ''For the rest of the year, then, the Indian is on his own,'' Eduard Harkort, the German mercenary, summarized. ''He christens his children himself and buries his dead. All alone he goes to the caves and mountain peaks, where he still has a hidden altar to his former gods and where he still offers sacrifices among the broken idols of his ancestors. He sprinkles his fields with the blood of parrots or turkeys and with their blood he marks, too, the door of his house, as the children of Israel did with the blood of the lamb. Before his death he buries his money in places that to him are still sacred."[32] Such was Mexico. Beneath its uniform, such was the Mexican army.

Each soldier was supposed to be issued a knapsack, a pair of shoes, a pair of extra sandals, two changes of clothing, a cape, a canteen, a plate, one round of cartridges, one flint, and one gun.[33] They had towering leather shakos for their heads, and many wore white cotton or linen clothing completely unsuited for Texas winters. They were supposed to be paid 20 pesos 8⅔ granos per a twenty-five-day month, meaning it cost about 1 peso per man-day to keep the troops heading north. The farther north they reached, the more Santa Anna's blitzkriegers looked like refugees. Their shoes and sandals gave out. Their shirts rotted, leaving them to wear their uniform jackets against their skin. And they hungered.

Food was provided to soldiers below the rank of first sergeant, but only half rations: one pound of meat and some beans or corn per day. For the final thirty days before reaching San Antonio, soldiers ate only eight ounces of toasted corn cake daily.[34] Soldiers begged for tortillas from the civilian mule drivers transporting supplies.[35]

Officers all had to purchase supplies out of their wages which, as it turned out, did not include a promised combat bonus. The order created a real hardship for many of the career soldiers, for food had to be bought from the scalpers accompanying the huge, long train of soldiers and camp followers. The notion that officers had to pay to play in this war outraged and demoralized them from the outset. Just at the time Santa Anna should have been cultivating the greatest respect of his officers, he insulted their whole strata.

The officers had to pay sky-high prices to feed not only themselves, but their families who trailed along. When supplies ran low, officers bribed the quartermasters for food. When their money ran out, officers dipped into their troops' rations.[36] The deeper the expedition ventured into the North, the higher prices spiraled.[37] The most outrageous fact was that Santa Anna and several of his officers were apparently skimming profits from the sale of goods to their own soldiers.

As the army—spread over two hundred and more miles—marched northward, it became evident that Santa Anna had economized in one other vital way. On paper he had provided for a mobile hospital system staffed by physicians.[38] In reality, there was no medical care available for the sixty-five-hundred-man expedition. Two physicians and three interns were assigned to various posts along the route, but only one physician actually accompanied any of the marchers, and he quickly revealed himself to be a fraud. "No one in the army is unaware that the surgeons assigned to its corps are generally indifferent men of meager education, wretched, many of them ignorant, who have taken no notice of the advances in their profession," said de la Peña. "No able professional is going to exchange the comfort he enjoys in society or the fees he derives there for the fatigues of the camp or the miserly salary."[39]

Surging ahead to relieve General Cós, the vanguard under Gen. Ramírez y Sesma suffered an accident. A horse kicked Capt. Blas Esnarrega in the leg, breaking the bone four inches below the right knee. Casting about, Ramírez y Sesma discovered a physician nearby, a nameless Anglo-American, "a sort of North American quack who called himself 'doctor,' as all of those from that republic are in the habit of doing, although generally they do not even know how to use a lancet." The supposed doctor didn't even bother to untwist the poor captain's leg in order to set it, and inflammation set in. The captain nearly died before a Mexican physician showed up to save him. Nevertheless, the Anglo-American had said he was a doctor and the Mexican troops needed a doctor, so he was employed, the sole medic traveling with them. Fortunately for the troops, the Anglo-American caught a fever near the Rio Frio and died soon afterward.[40]

Besides having no physicians, the expedition was provided with no beds, no medicine, no utensils or surgical equipment, no stitching thread, no stretchers. The adjutant inspector stated that the entire expenditure upon medical supplies for the army was three hundred pesos.[41] Near Monclova a dysentery epidemic—or food poisoning—struck down the marchers, costing several lives. Hypothermia cut down more soldiers. Contaminated drinking water took more. Soldiers brawled, cutting and stabbing one another with knives. Often they fought over women or because they were drunk on *pulque,* but another probable cause was a strange tropical skin disorder. According to a medical report issued in October 1836, troops from southern low-lying regions brought with them a repulsive spotted itch. "When their skin is perspiring, [they] exhale an insufferable stench very much like the foul and disagreeable fetidity of vultures . . . noxious to the health of those who breathe it, and because of the revulsion this ill odor causes to the healthy, frequent brawls arise between the latter and the afflicted."[42] Once hostilities actually began with the Anglo-Americans in Texas, the absence of physicians became especially desperate. Scores of wounded men died for simple lack of care. And as they approached death and cried for spiritual consolation, one more failing appeared. In the whole Catholic army, there was not a single priest.[43]

Many more women and children probably died along the way of disease and the elements than did the soldiers, but not being a formal part of the army they were never counted among the casualties. The presence of camp followers disturbed some of the officers, but overall they were accepted as a natural and necessary limb of the army.[44]

De la Peña estimated that there were three thousand camp followers, "a family much like the locusts that destroy everything in their path."[45] Officers complained that, besides consuming precious supplies, these civilians distracted the soldiers, carried venereal diseases, caused fights and even killings, clogged retreats, and slowed advances.[46] But no one was more devoted than a soldier's woman, and the camp follower was a permanent fixture of the nineteenth-century Mexican army.

De la Peña mixed his criticism of them with praise. "The women who followed the army merited all consideration, as they did all they could to help the soldier. Some carried knapsacks, and they would leave the road for a mile or two in the hot sun seeking water; they prepared their food and even attempted to build huts that would protect them from the elements."[47] Called *soldaderas,* they sometimes died in battle beside their husbands, and not uncommonly gave birth and raised families upon the trail.[48]

One thing Santa Anna's expedition did not lack was firepower. He was transporting twenty-one pieces of heavy artillery, including two 12-caliber cannons and four 8-caliber cannons, and though his soldiers might go barefoot or coatless, they each carried a firearm. Most of these guns were British army surplus. Though the Spanish had operated a Mexican weapons factory which produced superior muskets and pistols, it had fallen into disuse after Independence. The British had stockpiled—and condemned—440,000 of their Tower factory India Pattern smooth-bore flintlock, better known as the Brown Bess musket. Mexico purchased the weapon by the thousands, and stamped their eagle-and-snake motif on the lock plate above the trigger. The Brown Bess was functional, if old, throwing a .753-caliber ball about a hundred yards with any accuracy. But in order to load the gun, the Mexican army prescribed eighteen motions—counted out by the number—performed in eleven commands. Firing the weapon required four more counts and commands, though this complicated lockstep ritual could be streamlined for rapid fire in combat to four sets of commands.[49]

American minister Waddy Thompson observed, "There is not one in ten of these soldiers who has ever seen a gun, nor one in a hundred who has ever fired one before he was brought into the barracks. . . . Their arms, too, are worthless English muskets which have been condemned and thrown aside. . . . Their powder, too, is equally bad; in [one recent battle] which lasted the whole day, not one cannon ball in a thousand reached the enemy—they generally fell about half-way between the opposing armies."[50] He did not exaggerate.

A young Mexican soldier of the period described his own first fearful encounter with a gun. He was stuck in the rear rank with a druggist clerk in front of him. When the order was given to load and fire, "I closed my eyes . . . and said under my breath to the druggist 'God help you!' . . . When I opened my eyes, the druggist was getting up off the ground badly frightened and bruised. I had singed his bushy hair and he wished to devour me. . . . On returning to the barracks expecting arrest or some such thing I found I had been made a sergeant—so as to prevent me from firing any more guns. . . ."[51]

It was unnecessary, even undesirable, for these soldiers to be accurate, for they were just cannon fodder. Their purpose was simply to provide mass to the shock tactics borrowed from European tactics of the day. The Mexican infantry lined up, lowered their muskets, walked forward, and fired on command. Called "volley firing," this tactic made a body of foot soldiers into a giant, moving shotgun. In the classic two-deep, shoulder-to-shoulder formation, a unit could present one musket every twelve inches, and could throw a mutilating barrage of lead balls into enemy ranks. It was a highly inaccurate delivery of gunfire, but military leaders swore by it.[52]

Now and then, while one section of the Texas-bound army waited for other sections to catch up, the recruits were drilled. But they received no firearms training. This was by order of Santa Anna. "All the efforts of the brigade chiefs to instruct the recruits and train them in firing were useless," de la Peña reported, "because the commander in chief maintained that they would become accustomed to gunfire during combat."[53]

This and other decisions very soon frustrated and worried Santa Anna's officers. They were beginning to see that their leader's quirks were having an insidious influence upon the expedition. The problem lay in deciding which minor decisions an officer dared to oppose and when. It was one thing to suspect—even to dread—a commanding general's ability to make decisions, quite another to openly challenge it. An undercurrent of suspicion about Santa Anna's leadership ran throughout various Mexican officers' accounts, but these were professional soldiers. And on the several occasions when his officers did dispute Santa Anna's decisions, he simply retired into seclusion and went ahead with his plans.

Furthermore, none of his officers dared forecast defeat. Certainly his expedition had the energy and momentum of a victorious juggernaut.

"There is much activity by way of preparation. . . . There are many troops and [there is] much noise," reported José Juan Sánchez Navarro, the adjutant inspector, "but I see no indications of good political, military, and administrative systems." All through the Texas campaign Santa Anna pretended to hold the reins, when in fact he had nothing but two handfuls of air. His greatest secret was his illusion of control. Even as his wild horse plummeted into the abyss, Santa Anna looked serene. But lest anyone learn how vaporous his grasp really was, Santa Anna developed a habit of doing everything himself, delegating as little as possible to more competent men.

Sánchez Navarro noticed this. "His Excellency himself attends to all matters whether important or most trivial. . . . What will become of the army and of the nation if the Most Excellent President should die? Confusion and more confusion because only His Excellency knows the springs by means of which these masses of men called the army are moved. The members of the army in general have no idea of the significance of the Texas war, and all of them believe that they are merely on a military excursion. If, when questioned, one tells the truth about what one has seen there [in Texas], one is considered a poor soul. As if the enemy could be conquered merely by despising him. . . .

"It is said that His Excellency is very economical, even miserly. Those close to him assert that whoever wants to, can make him uncomfortable by asking him for a peso; and they add that he would rather give a colonel's commission than ten pesos. Can all this be true? Even if it is, would it not be better not to mention it? I believe so."[54]

One result of the meek silence practiced by Sánchez Navarro and many of the officers was a deformed army. Soldiers did not have "sufficient shoes or other articles of clothing and coats with which to replace those which were being worn out daily—only what they were wearing," complained General Filisola. "However, on the other hand out of all proportion to the number of men and the purpose was the number of chiefs and officers, artillery, ammunition of all kinds, empty sandbags and an endless number of useless items carried by the troops. . . . the brigades appearing to be immense convoys of equipment rather than troops that were on their way to fight a campaign. . . ."[55]

It was the studied opinion of most officers that Santa Anna should bypass San Antonio and Goliad—the two places where the enemy would be expecting an attack—and strike into the heart of the colonies. Filisola urged Santa Anna to transport the expedition soldiers by boat, and to keep them close enough to the coast to be supplied by sea. As de la Peña observed, "The map of Texas itself indicated the path to be followed." It would have saved time and money, and would have eliminated the burdensome camp following.[56] The suggestion found favor with a majority of the generals on Santa Anna's fifty-man staff, and was recommended by the governors of Nuevo León and Coahila y Tejas—two men who knew the territory very well.

But Santa Anna was insistent. He wished to tackle San Antonio first. There was logic to his insistence: For one thing, Mexico had no navy, and the Texas coast was "held" by the Anglo-American navy of four ships, including one originally built for the African slave trade. To attempt a sea-based strike at Texas without naval superiority—or even equality—would have been risky. In addition, the best maps to be found of this unsettling nightmare land to the north had been drawn by enemy hands (Stephen Austin's maps were the most accurate and recent), in itself an unsettling thought. Better by far, Santa Anna reasoned, to follow the geography of personal experience. Overland to San Antonio, Santa Anna had helped suppress adventurers in Texas in 1813. Overland through San Antonio, he would suppress them again.

As the campaign progressed, Santa Anna's decisions became increasingly monolithic: fixed, one-man edicts that brooked no dissent. Moreover, the senior officers detected in their commander a mystifying peevishness that had no explanation. "Ill humor," de la Peña called it. The president was "quite obsessed . . . he refused to listen to reason. . . ." Thrust into daily contact with Santa Anna (or at least with his commands), the officers saw conduct that alternated among paranoia, depression, and rage.

In the words of General Filisola, "His forehead had clouded over. . . . Some interpreted it as discouragement, others as despair, and not a few as rudeness, scorn or indifference towards all the persons that he had to deal with or met with for some reason or other." The mood swings deepened the farther they penetrated the wilderness.[57] Santa Anna made outrageous snap judgments, then reversed himself. He ranted and raved at nearly everyone. He was self-indulgent and imperious. His attention span was a joke; though he cast himself into every detail, he seemed "unable by temperament to concentrate on any one thing. . . ."[58]

Entering a region of prairie which Travis and Deaf Smith had burned off the previous autumn, the starving cavalry mounts became too weak to carry their saddles, much less their riders. When Santa Anna saw his proud cavalry troops on foot and hauling along their saddles, he flew into a rage. It had been his own decision not to provision fodder or grain for the cavalry—as per the Napoleonic blitz, he had decided they could eat off the land. All along the way, cavalrymen had been forced to sacrifice to their hungry horses the grass they would have used to pad their beds. Now Santa Anna saw the consequences, and he was not pleased. Apoplectic, he ordered the cavalry commander sent back to Mexico City for court-martial. Then, just as suddenly, he changed his mind and revoked the order.[59]

Incidents like that were common. Even before crossing the Rio Grande his temper cost the Mexican army its professional mule and oxen drivers. A representative party of these civilian outfitters made the mistake of approaching Santa Anna and requesting more supplies for the drivers and more corn for the animals. Santa Anna insulted and abused them "in a truly harsh and cruel manner highly unworthy of the purpose of the men and the circumstances." Though the muleteers were finally issued a bit of corn and money, at the first opportunity they deserted. Some took their livestock and harness, some left the harness behind, some abandoned their oxen, mules, herds, and carts. "Wherefore it was necessary to replace them with soldiers who knew little or nothing about that sort of thing."[60]

Another of Santa Anna's eccentric decisions cost him the finest desert fighters in Mexico. These were the *presidio* troops stationed in forts along the way, the closest thing to special forces upon the northern Mexican landscape. "They know how to read all sorts of tracks, how long they have been there as well as signs and clouds of smoke. . . ," Filisola recommended them. "Likewise they are familiar with the weather signs, changes in temperature and the time of night by the course of the stars. They are excellent riflemen, horsemen and swimmers, untiring in hardships, extraordinarily sober, admirable caretakers of all sorts of animals, cautious against the tricks of the savages, good oarsmen and canoe handlers, most apt in the handling of carts and pack mules, in the killing of beef, and unequaled as guides and couriers in that wilderness and those paths which no one understands or knows the way they do." But Santa Anna decided he didn't want them. "Not only did the commander in chief not accept [them]," an astonished Filisola said, "but he treated those [presidial] companies with the greatest scorn." In the end, Santa Anna selected a small fraction of the presidio troops to serve under him, which only caused more trouble because every division commander fought to have the specialists in his unit.[60]

Santa Anna was fixed on crushing the Anglo-Americans in Texas, in good part to confirm to all of Mexico his far-reaching personal power. The campaign had a military face but a political brain. To him the Anglo-Americans were an opportunity rather than a serious enemy. He actually feared that one of his generals might steal his thunder by defeating the rebels before he could arrive on the scene. He went so far as to instruct his vanguard generals to wait for him before achieving the inevitable victory.[61]

More and more isolated in his monomaniacal cocoon, Santa Anna slipped away from reality. He seemed bent against tapping the wisdom of any adviser, from experienced generals and governors down to savvy Indian fighters and muleteers. But even his most critical officers did not guess how wild Santa Anna's horse really was. For the truth was, Santa Anna was an opium addict. The Mexican army was in the hands of a junkie.

In those days, opium laced some of the most respectable drugs available. One of the most popular elixirs was laudanum, a mixture of opium dissolved in liquor. It was used for everything from soothing drunks suffering delirium tremens to relieving pain for broken bones and chronic infections. Medical wisdom stated that opium acted as a stimulant when taken in small doses, and as a soporific and anesthetic in larger doses. The most authoritative "how-to" medical book for Jacksonian Americans, *Gunn's Domestic Medicine*, said, "Taken in proper quantities, [it] introduces order, harmony and pleasurable serenity."[62]

There is no record of when or why Santa Anna started taking opium. None of the Mexican accounts mentions his narcotics dependency, but several of the American accounts of Santa Anna in captivity make it clear that the general swallowed opium, especially in periods of stress.[63] As the campaign ended, the first thing Santa Anna requested was some opium. As it turned out, he asked the right man, for it so happened that Sam Houston was also an addict ("he had long been accustomed [to it]," said one of Houston's physicians[64]). In certain respects, both of these substance abusers manifested remarkably similar behavior during their war with each other. They were idiosyncratic to the point of eccentricity, they kept their own counsel, and they insisted upon their own visionary strategies so obstinately that serious concerns circulated among their subordinates. Conditioned to obey hierarchies, the Mexican officers talked only among themselves. But, in the coming days, Houston's odd behavior and his reputation for serious alcoholism would almost fracture the Anglo-American army. Houston barely averted mutiny. Despite his excesses and corruption—and his many enemies—Santa Anna was almost never accused of drunkenness.[65] But as Texas loomed about them, the *caudillo* came closer and closer to losing control of his army.

"We have mentioned earlier that the commander in chief had already brought upon himself the ill will of the army," de la Peña remarked as the expedition extended deeper north. "The hatred for him was found even among his friends and intimates, for his aides frequently would try to avoid serving as his guards or being near him. General Castrillón, one of Santa Anna's most loyal officers, finally declared his unwillingness to follow the commander in chief. Others did the same. On another occasion when Santa Anna castigated his staff, Castrillón openly challenged him. Realizing he'd gone too far, Santa Anna tried to make amends, "admitting that it was not within his power to control his irascible character, which circumstances had only made worse. He lamented the indifference with which his military family looked upon him and begged indulgence, and thus succeeded in quieting animosities and in winning over to his side his aides-de-camp."[66]

The skeleton acquired flesh. The few became many. Edging northward, the army touched the major towns that lay between the arms of the Sierra Madre ranges like a rosary strand.[67] When they reached the staging ground of San Luis Potosí, they waited, gathering strength and numbers. Haciendas thrived there, stocked with large herds of horses and other livestock, and spiky maguey plants gave juice for *pulque* and nopal cactus yielded a spiny fruit called *tuna*.[68]

After that, across the long, thin San Luis valley, lay desolation and pools of brackish fetid water. Wolves and coyotes abounded, and the high altitude desert hung bare and miserable, cut by ravines. Gradually the plain dipped lower into corridors of mountains that funneled down to the once and future capital of Coahuila, Saltillo (or Leona Vicario).[69]

The army consolidated itself. Battalions from surrounding states joined with the main expeditionary force, swelling the number of troops and aggravating the logistics. Santa Anna staggered his march, spacing each brigade two days apart.[70]

From Saltillo onward, the journey took on new gravity. As they entered the northern winter, the troops received a cold reception from locals who had seen armies come and go. Civilians fled from the draft. They hid food and supplies from the requisition officers who scoured the countryside, and towns and haciendas refused to admit General Ramírez y Sesma who tried to buy provisions with worthless chits.[71] Undaunted, the army stripped small towns and ranches along the way, confiscating food, livestock and carts, horses, pack mules, and rigging. Hapless civilians were impressed to transport goods to forward points with barren promises of future payment. Of the eighteen hundred mules in the army, a thousand were seized along the way. For many northern Mexicans this midwinter trespass represented centralism at its worst. Robbed and shanghaied, they received no recompense and no thanks. Already this region was a hotbed of federalism, and Santa Anna only fueled local resentments.

Under foot and hoof, limestone paved the way. Steep mountains channeled the army to Monterrey. Above Monterrey, the land flattened out.

In reaching for Laredo and beyond, the army's suffering magnified. The marchers were plagued by diarrhea and blistered feet. The watering holes along the route barely sufficed. Where there was water at all, thirsty troops and livestock stirred it into mud. Pools and wells were often polluted with animal carcasses, but the army drank from them anyway.[72] This was a desiccated region in which *vaqueros* had learned to singe off the thorns of old cactus, producing fodder for their longhorns.[73] The army's livestock simply expired on the hoof. Since there was little or no graze, they atrophied almost before the soldiers' eyes. The horses' and mules' tongues swelled and split from an inflammation the Mexicans called *telele,* and their masters bled them and split their ears with knives to release the heat from their blood. At night, Comanches and Lipan Apaches drove them off to ride or eat. And, mirroring their human masters, the equine urge to desert was constant, especially when the army passed through a wide band of country that Stephen Austin had identified on a map with "immense Droves of Wild Horses." Stampedes could suddenly ignite at the mere smell of high-velocity mustangs in the far distances.

The cattle had their own special pain. By day, their hides ran red with blood drawn by frustrated soldiers, who used the points of their bayonets to drive the stumbling beasts forward. An ox required eight hours for cud and eight hours for rest, leaving a well-paced eight hours for work.[74] After the professional teamsters deserted and the soldiers took over their care, the oxen were driven to death. When they collapsed and died, there was not even enough meat left on their bones to bother butchering them. Wildlife was abundant, especially once they crossed into Texas, but the laboring army put all animals to flight except for the coyotes and turkey buzzards that fed upon the soldiers' leftovers and excrement.[75] The sol exception came the day the army crossed the Rio Grande. That was a day of almost blessed abundance, for upon fording the river the soldiers and camp followers found themselves surrounded by thousands of hopping jackrabbits, so abundant that "soldiers could catch them by hand as easily as chickens from a hen [coop]."[76] After that, they returned to their hunger.

The far northern towns like Laredo were already so impoverished that the army had to move right on through or they would perish in place. Heat and thirst hammered the marchers. Dust clotted their nostrils and throats. "It broke one's heart to see all this," said Filisola, "especially many women with children in their arms, almost dying of thirst, crying for water. The tears that they were shedding were all that they could give them to drink."[77]

On the day after Christmas, General Cós's retreating soldiers met up with Santa Anna's sunbaked vanguard brigade at Laredo. There were only 815 of Cós's bunch, roughly half the men he had left San Antonio with, "most without clothes and poorly armed."[78] By far the worst off of these were the pitiful conscripts who had been marched to reinforce General Cós in San Antonio. They had reached San Antonio just in time to turn around and retreat with him, with only one day to rest. Technically speaking, these men weren't soldiers-in-arms, for none had the slightest bit of training. All they knew about army life was walking, already having covered a thousand miles, some in chains all the way. Filisola took one look at them and wanted to send them south for two weeks of recuperation and training. But all momentum was toward Texas.

Santa Anna angrily ordered Cós to violate the terms of his parole, that is, that he would not bear arms against the Anglo-American rebels. The bony remnants of Cós's command were promptly herded in with the Army of Operations. No sooner did these limping skeletons reach Laredo than they were turned around and driven back toward San Antonio. While others in the army thirsted and hungered, these cannon fodder merely died. "They were so weak and so little accustomed to the fatigue of the marches that they had fallen far behind," Filisola recorded. "Although water was sent to them with all haste, several of them never managed to drink because they were already dying; others died as they drank; and others finally got through with a thousand difficulties after having drunk."[78]

The thousand difficulties included lightning, hail, northers, and finally a killing blizzard. "The snowfall increased and kept falling in great abundance, so continuous that at dawn it was knee-deep," said de la

Peña. "It seemed as though it wished to subdue us beneath its weight. Indeed, one could not remain standing or sitting, much less lying down." Few of these soldiers, women, and children had ever seen snow, and with first daylight they were astounded. "What a bewitching scene!" de la Peña recounted. "As far as one could see, all was snow. The trees, totally covered, formed an amazing variety of cones and pyramids, which seemed to be made of alabaster."[79] It was beautiful, but also terrible. Looking closer, the soldiers saw that the white snow was covered with brilliant blood. The blood was from their mules and horses which had been overloaded by the snow and had fallen down, cracking their skulls. Many of the animals had slipped beneath the surface and essentially drowned, their muzzles packed with snow. The cavalry lost horses, the mule team was thinned out, and fifty oxen died of the intense cold.[80] The virtually trackless North now turned completely blank, every trail buried. De la Peña was reminded of Napoleon's bloody, frozen retreat from Moscow.[81]

= 11 =

THE EARLY WEEKS of February passed in a state of constant false alarm. Some skittish accounts had Mexican soldiers massed in impossible numbers just west of the Rio Grande. Conversely, people bragged that, broken to the dirt by General Cós's brush with Anglo-Saxon marksmanship, the Mexican army was never going to come. During the month of February, as nerves stretched tight and still no Mexican hordes appeared, the propagandists beat their drums louder and louder.

"Texas Forever!!" shouted one New Orleans broadside. "The usurper of the South has failed in his efforts to enslave the freemen of Texas."[1]

"Captain Jack" Hall made a public address. Hall was an old War Dog, a fifty-year-old land speculator who had filibustered in the 1812–13 invasion of Texas and was about to rent to the constitutional delegates a drafty building in which they would declare Texan independence. He had a special gift for casting buzzwords guaranteed to hook the average Southern Anglo-American.

"Fellow Freemen," he said. "The despot dictator, and his vassal myrmidons, are fast displaying their hostile columns on the frontier of our heretofore happy and blessed Texas. Their war cry is, 'death and destruction to every Anglo-American, west of the Sabine;' their watchword, actually, 'beauty and booty' . . . . And will you *now*, as Texian freemen, as fathers, as husbands, as sons, and as brothers, suffer the *colored* hirelings of a cruel and faithless despot, to feast and revel, in your dearly purchased and cherished homes? . . . . Your beloved wives, your mothers, your daughters, sisters, and helpless innocent children given up to the dire pollution and massacre of a band of barbarians!!"[2]

In early February the slave trader Colonel Fannin cried out from Goliad, "What can be expected for the *Fair Daughters* of chaste *white women* when their [the Mexicans'] own countrywomen are prostituted, by a licensed soldiery, as an inducement to push foward into the Colonies, that they may find *fairer game?*"[3]

151

If any rapes were committed upon white women—and there is a strong suggestion that some were—they were by white men. Capt. Almeron Dickinson's wife, Susannah, moved to San Antonio from Gonzales after a band of Ayish Bayou "soldiers" rampaged through the town. In La Bahía, the town next to Goliad (aka Fort Defiance), white mercenaries raped Tejano women. The same thing may have happened to the Tejano women in San Antonio. But the fact stands that not a single rape by Mexican soldiers was reported throughout the entire period.

Their propaganda aside, the Anglo-Americans in Texas dangled in ignorance for a second reason: their own racism. At great risk to themselves, Tejanos carried generally accurate intelligence from points along the Rio Grande to San Antonio. But to the very end the Anglo-Americans would not believe their information because they had a deep distrust of darker races.

At one point Travis counted up three Tejanos who had allied with his group, and condemned all others living in San Antonio. "All the citizens of this place that have not joined us are with the enemy fighting against us," he said. "Let the government declare them public enemies, otherwise she is acting a suicidal part. I shall treat them as such, unless I have superior orders to the contrary."[4] He proposed confiscating their property to help pay for war debts.

Down in the Goliad presidio, Fannin held the same grudge. He arrested the local priest and thirteen Tejano soldiers attached to the presidio, declaring "*This man of God* is the blackest of old villains—a murderer, adulterer, &c., and his influence is almost unbounded. . . . There is more danger from these spies, who are so intimately acquainted with the country, than from twenty times the number of armed soldiers. I again tell you, we must not rely on Mexicans. It would be a fatal delusion."[5]

On February 20 Juan Seguín's cousin, Blas Herrera, returned from the Rio Grande. Seguín had posted his cousin there as an early warning device, and on February 18 Herrera observed Mexican troops crossing the river. Risking death as a spy, he inquired about the coming army, then spurred his horse on to San Antonio. At nine o'clock Travis convened a candle-lit council of war in his quarters upon the Civil Plaza. Seguín introduced Herrera, who told the assembly that Santa Anna's army was five thousand strong. Of these, thirty-five hundred were slow-moving infantry, but fifteen hundred cavalry were making a forced march to take the rebels by surprise.

"This created some considerable discussion," said Dr. John Sutherland. "Some held that it was more authentic than anything that had reached them before, whilst a majority declared it was only the report of a Mexican, and entitled to no more consideration than many others of a like character that were daily harangued throughout the country. The council adjourned without coming to any conclusion as to whether it was necessary to give any heed to the warning or not."

Seguín and his company of vaquero-scouts made the Anglo-Americans' revolution their revolution. Lorenzo de Zavala, the Mexican politician, sat at the constitutional convention with two other Mexicans, all of them betraying their nation of birth for the ideal of liberty. But none of them was trusted because they were not Anglo-Saxon.

"Such was the universal distrust of Mexican authority," Dr. Sutherland explained, "that no report coming from it ever received due consideration. So many false alarms had been given by a degraded class of 'Greasers' continually passing to and fro through the west, that no credence was given any rumor, however plausible, and no danger was apprehended. Many had persuaded themselves that Santa Anna would never attempt to conquer Texas and the most general reply to any argument to the contrary was that he was afraid to meet us. 'He knew better.' "[6]

The Anglo-Americans were functioning blindly and fearfully. They were becalmed and adrift. Fannin sat in Goliad with 420 men. Travis and Bowie sat in San Antonio with a third that number. Grant and Johnson had vanished into the region between La Bahía and Matamoros with less than 100 men, and no one was quite sure what they were doing. The longer they floated upon the calm chaparral, the more nervous the fortress commanders got. Fannin called for Houston to send 1,200 to 1,500 men to San Antonio and 500 to 800 to Goliad, and to post a reserve army along the Colorado River, "and then all will be well."[7]

Fannin didn't indicate where Houston was supposed to get these thousands of troops. All he knew was that his soldiers were in rags, many of them were barefoot, and none had been paid since the start of the campaign. Fannin had a rock-solid fort with thick walls, bastions on each of the four corners, and adequate artillery. When the rebels had first captured Goliad back in October, they had taken ten thousand dollars' worth of military stores including six hundred stands of arms. Even after arming men without guns, the Goliad garrison found itself in possession of over four hundred surplus firearms. One of Fannin's officers started tinkering and invented a makeshift machine gun by mounting sixty-eight of the old muskets side by side. With a single match the contraption could fire all barrels simultaneously. (It was never put to use.)[8] All Fannin lacked was a full-size army of clothed, well-fed men with which to invest the weapons and structure. Again and again, he cursed the Anglo-Americans in Texas for not joining his mercenaries.

Fannin's military experience consisted of two years at West Point Academy and a single battle, beside Bowie, at Mission Concepción in October. Travis, on the other hand, had essentially no experience at all. He had served briefly in a militia, fired upon a few Mexican soldiers during his War Dog shenanigans, and had missed the Gonzales cannon fight that opened the revolution because he had had the flu. He wasn't there at the Concepción Battle, and he went home before the San Antonio invasion in December. He was eager, brave, and patriotic. But he was also young, fickle, and saturated with romantic fantasies. The Alamo garrison rewarded his leadership with only lukewarm support. The alcoholic Bowie seemed far more to their liking than Travis's semiaristocratic mannerisms.

Besides teetering under an amateur and uncertain leadership, the Alamo fortress was not really a fort. After the Alamo was secularized by the Spanish back in 1793, a company of hot-pursuit cavalry called the Second Flying Company of San Carlos de Parras was transferred to San Antonio for Indian fighting. These were the original Texas Rangers—mobile, fast, counterguerrilla—and they brought with them a new name for the Mission San Antonio de Valero. They came from a town called Alamo, and the name stuck to their new home. Over the years the mission metamorphosed into a fortified headquarters for military troops, but lacked the basic design to ever become a full-fledged presidio like Goliad.

It was not only Houston who considered the Alamo worthy of demolition. The chief engineer, Green Jameson, who labored to strengthen the walls and produce more artillery positions, also viewed the Alamo as a strategic write-off. On February 16 Jameson sent a letter to Governor Smith in which he condemned the Alamo; "The mexicans [sic] have shown imbecility and want of skill in this Fortress as they have done in all things else." He went so far as to suggest abandoning the Alamo and building a whole new fort.

"If I were ordered to construct a new & effective Fortress on an economical plan," he proposed, "I would suggest a diamond with two acute & two obtuse angles—with few men & Guns with a sufficient entrenchment all around such a Fortress with projecting redoubts & Bastions would command all points—if you are not too much perplexed with other business I wish you to write me officially on this subject."[9]

The garrison, some of which lived in town, numbered 142 or so.

Almost a fifth of this number was sick. Dr. Amos Pollard had exhausted his supply of medicine, and Dr. Sutherland had to dip into his private supply just to stabilize the group.[10] Some of the men never did recover. The garrison was subsisting on nothing but beef and corn, and like Fannin's mercenaries they had not been paid, their morale was wilting, and many wore clothing that was falling to pieces on their backs.

Meanwhile, supplies were starting to arrive upon the coast from New Orleans. One warehouse was *"full, very full,"* and on February 17 the schooner *William A. Turner* was sent back with most of its cargo for lack of storage space. The quartermaster listed goods including hundreds of barrels of flour, sugar, beans, and salted pork, tobacco, bags of coffee, casks of liquor, boxes of sperm-oil candles and soap, and blacksmithing equipment. There was medicine, bacon sides, hardware, woolen socks, 161 coats, 120 live pigs and more, all waiting for a destination.[11] It looked like the western front was going to get supplied, even if not paid, after all. The logistical pipeline from the United States to the rebels had finally opened. Help was on the way.

Pragmatists in the rebel ranks held that Santa Anna could not realistically invade Texas until spring grass began greening the prairies. He would need forage for his livestock and *caballadas* of cavalry horses. Since spring came no earlier than March, local Anglo-Americans forecast that the Mexican army wouldn't appear until almost April or later. By then the rebels would have enjoyed their constitutional convention, law and order would be restored, leaders (not just delegates) would be elected, and Independence would be declared. The revolution would take on a formal shape. Rather than having four supreme commanders scattering manpower and resources all over the map, a single commander in chief would determine whether Texas should mount an offensive or prepare a defensive. Garrisons would be stocked and manned. They would quit flying random flags—the San Antonio garrison was currently sporting a red, white, and green Mexican tricolor with two stars, which represented Texas and Coahuila, that is, federalism[12]—and unfurl a flag of sovereign design. And maybe Travis's uniform would arrive from New Orleans. So while a fog of desperation and cold ignorance hung upon the mercenaries and regulars in San Antonio and Goliad, there was also the promise of restored sunlight. Everything depended on a few more weeks of peace.

On Tuesday, February 23, Travis awoke to the sound of oxcarts squeaking out of town. It was not yet dawn on a day Béxarenos ordinarily came to San Fernando Church dressed in their white cotton blouses and finest accessories.

But on this day, even before dawn, the townspeople were leaving in droves. "The citizens of every class were hurrying to and fro through the streets with obvious signs of excitement," said Dr. Sutherland. "Houses were being emptied and their contents put into carts and hauled off. Such of the poorer class who had no better mode of conveyance, were shouldering their effects and leaving on foot."

In his heart, Travis knew precisely why San Antonio was emptying out. Santa Anna was coming. But Travis resisted the truth. He wanted information presented to him through channels that were familiar and controllable. He wanted authorized scouts—Anglo-Americans—to issue him dispatches. Watching the populace turn itself into refugees before his eyes was simply not an acceptable communication.

Like Bowie had during his binge ten days earlier, Travis ordered the populace to remain in town. He demanded an explanation for this fearful scene. But the Tejanos' evasive answers only magnified Travis's apprehensions.

"Orders were issued that no others be allowed to leave the city, which had the effect of increasing their commotion," said Dr. Sutherland. "Several were arrested and interrogated as to the cause of the movement, but no satisfactory answer could be obtained. The most general reply was that they were going out to the country to prepare for the coming crop. This excuse, however, availed nothing for it was not to be supposed that every person in the city was a farmer."

Twice now Travis had been warned by Tejano scouts that the army was approaching: once at the welcoming ball for Crockett on February 10, once by Antonio Menchaca on February 20. Both times he had rejected the reports. Now, he tried to assimilate the horrifying truth. But the local Tejanos were of no help to him this time around.

"Colonel Travis persisted in carrying out his order and continued the investigation. Nine o'clock came and no discoveries were made," Dr. Sutherland related. "Ten o'clock in like manner passed and finally the eleventh hour was drawing near and the matter was yet a mystery. It was hoped by Colonel Travis that his diligent investigation and the strict enforcement of the order prohibiting the inhabitants from leaving the city would have the effect of frightening them into a belief that their course was not the wisest for them to pursue."

Just what measures Travis meant to coerce the Tejanos with remains uncertain. He and his mercenaries and regulars had already forcibly occupied the town, stolen cattle and other goods, and committed unspecified "shameful" acts against the residents. Any delusions of Béxareno

solidarity with the revolution evaporated as Travis angrily—and vainly—
pried for information.

Remarkably the secret—which was shared by hundreds or thousands
of townspeople—remained confidential despite hours of investigation. At
last a Tejano friendly to the rebels revealed the cause for alarm. On the
night before a body of Mexican cavalry had reached the León Creek just
eight miles outside of town. A messenger had brought word to the Tejano
civilians to evacuate town at dawn next morning, for San Antonio would
be attacked that day.

Not only that, but the Mexican troops had almost sprung a surprise
attack upon the rebels a day or two earlier, while the Anglo-Americans
were engaged in yet another fandango. But chance had intervened in the
form of a heavy cloudburst which swelled the river and prevented fording. In short, the partying rebels were so far from being alert that San
Antonio nearly returned to Mexican control without a battle. Among
locals a legend grew that Santa Anna himself had entered town in disguise
and spied on the rebels at a fandango on Soledad Street.[13] It was not true,
but it epitomized the degree to which Travis and his command were in
both local disfavor and disarray.

Unbelievably, even as the sky was crashing down around his toes,
Travis continued to doubt. "This statement [by the Tejano source] seemed
altogether plausible, and substantiated the statement in the report given
by Herrera three days before," said Dr. Sutherland, "yet it wore the
countenance of so many of their false rumors that it was a matter of doubt
that there was any truth in it."[14]

Despite repeated warnings that the enemy was advancing on San
Antonio, Travis didn't even have a regular system of patrols. Before he
could dispatch scouts to investigate the report, Travis had to borrow a
horse to send a rider out to the pasture where his cavalry mounts were
grazing.

In the meantime, Travis, Dr. Sutherland, and a "reliable" soldier
climbed up the San Fernando Church's wooden staircase into the squat,
octagonal belfry tower. The three men squinted out across the sweeping
flats and up a long gentle slope west of town known as the Alazan
heights. Travis's cynicism about Mexican reports was confirmed by the
blank landscape. Nothing moved out in the distances. Just the same, the
soldier was posted as a sentinel with orders to ring the bell if he spotted
anything.

Travis went back to his room. Then the church bell began ringing.

"The enemy are in view," yelled the tower sentinel.

A crowd of soldiers, including Travis, quickly gathered in the plaza fronting the church. Several of them scrambled up into the tower to confirm the sighting and count the enemy.[15] As extra pairs of eyes scanned the distances, there was nothing to see.

"False alarm," one of the men shouted down. The whole tale was a lie, he called out. Their fears were baseless. The embarrassed sentinel cursed and swore that he had seen troops, that the figures had hidden behind a row of brushwood. But the crowd dissolved. It seemed that the whole nerve-racking morning had been another Mexican trick.

Dr. Sutherland volunteered to ride out and check around if someone familiar with the countryside would accompany him. John William "El Colorado" Smith, aka Redhead, a local merchant and a future mayor of San Antonio, offered his services.[16] The two men mounted up and readied to swing through the barrens. "If you see us returning in any other gait than a slow one," Sutherland told Travis, "you may be sure that we have seen the enemy."

They cantered west out of town along the old Laredo branch of the Camino Real and worked to the top of the Alazan hills a mile and a half outside of town. Riding at a moderate clip, they suddenly reined short, face to face with a nest of several hundred Mexican cavalry. The troops were "well mounted and equipped; their polished armor glistening in the rays of the sun as they were formed in a line between the chaparral and mesquite bushes mentioned by the sentinel; the commander riding along the line, waving his sword, as though he might be giving directions as to the mode of attack." The advance unit of fast-moving cavalry numbered 369 or less.[17] Less than 150 yards from these crack horsemen, Sutherland took one quick look and calculated that 1,500 troops were poised to charge.

Immediately, Sutherland and Smith wheeled their horses around and spurred for town. The rainstorm that had helped prevent the Mexican army from springing a surprise attack upon the rebels on the dawn before had also turned the dirt road into a greasy mud slick. Whipped to full speed, Sutherland's smooth-shod horse went into a fifty-yard scramble of slipping and sliding, concluding with a horrifying somersault. Sutherland pitched loose from his saddle, landing ahead of his horse which landed on him. The horse lay stunned and still across Sutherland's legs, pinning him to the earth. Smith frantically tried to pull the animal off Sutherland without luck. Finally, after a few minutes, the horse revived and clambered to its feet. Smith helped his shaken comrade to stand. Limping badly, Sutherland picked up the broken parts of his gun, remounted, and descended into town.

The two scouts' pell-mell gallop from the hillside road alerted the rebels well before they arrived back in town. As they galloped into the Civil Plaza, Crockett met the two men and told them Travis had already pulled his headquarters out from the town and across the river into the Alamo. The entire rebel garrison was taking position in the patchwork fortress.

Crockett accompanied the excited doctor across a ford. On their way into the Alamo, they met up with Philip Dimmitt, a Kentuckian who had married a Mexican woman and naturalized in Texas.[18] Dimmitt was not at the Alamo to fight. It was his opinion that "there were not enough men at Béxar to defend the place, that it was bound to fall."[19] Dimmitt tried to persuade Sutherland to depart with him immediately. The two of them could spread the alarm throughout the countryside, raise a force, and victoriously return with reinforcements.

"I should go and report to Colonel Travis," Sutherland replied. He would not commit himself to leaving San Antonio. Dimmitt said he would wait for Sutherland down the street at his house.

Sutherland dismounted in front of Travis's headquarters at the Alamo, only to collapse in a heap to the ground. Until this moment adrenaline had masked the full extent of his injuries. Now he realized that his fall had damaged his knee quite badly. It took Crockett's helping shoulder for the doctor to limp into Travis's room.

Sitting at a wooden table, the young colonel was intensely scratching his quill across a sheet of paper, unleashing the first of his famous series calling for help. It was addressed to Colonel Fannin down in Goliad and would serve as the stereotype for all of Travis's future communiqués. "We have removed all our men into the Alamo. . . . We have one hundred and forty-six men, who are determined *never to retreat*. We have but little provisions, but enough to serve us till you and your men arrive. We deem it unnecessary to repeat to a brave officer, who knows his duty, that we call on him for assistance. . . ."[20]

Grant and Johnson's Matamoros expedition had stripped the Alamo garrison nearly empty of food, leaving behind only a pittance of coffee, sugar, and salt. Over the past month these meager supplies had been consumed, leaving the garrison with whatever cattle they drove in from the prairie. They butchered only enough cattle to feed them for a twenty-four-hour stretch, they kept no extra livestock on hand. Over the coming days, this would have spelled starvation for the rebels. Besides beef, the garrison had been reduced to just three bushels of corn.

But as the garrison was hurriedly retreating from town to the Alamo, a drove of twenty or thirty lowing beeves, probably the property of some vacating Tejano, suddenly appeared on Alamo Street. The rebels were quick to appropriate them and herd them into the Alamo. Their cupboard was buttressed by the discovery of eighty or ninety bushels of corn in some of the *jacales* near the Alamo. These hastily abandoned stick-and-mud huts would also provide firewood for the defenders over the next two weeks.

The last minute "gift" of cattle and corn struck the messianic Travis as a divine afterthought. The miraculous coincidence was proof, as Travis was quick to point out, that "the Lord is on our side." Over the coming days, Travis would need to dig ever deeper to find any more such proof.

At two o'clock the Mexican cavalry began their long, glittering descent from the Alazan hills in full view of the town. Rebels and civilians alike raced around. Many fled to outlying ranches or other settlements, some stayed in town to show their loyalty to Santa Anna or profit from the military payroll. Some of the rebels and Anglo-American civilians dove easterly toward safety. Most poured into the Alamo. No one knew quite what might happen.

Among the Tejano refugees from town, a few threw their lot in with the Anglo-Americans. Most of them had attached themselves to the rebels in one way or another and had reason to fear Mexican treatment for their disloyalty. Probably a dozen or more took sanctuary with the rebels. Several were wives of Anglo-Americans. Only a month before, Juana Navarro had married a Kentuckian colonist named Dr. Horatio Alsbury. She and her younger sister Gertrudis had been orphaned as little girls, then been adopted by their uncle, the wealthy Juan Veramendi. Juana had been married to a Tejano gentleman who gave her one son before dying of cholera. Now, as her new husband departed to round up more fighters for the Alamo, Juana found herself alone with a toddler and Gertrudis. She was not all alone, however. Through a complicated weave of relationships, James Bowie was her brother-in-law. As the town desperately reassembled itself in the face of Mexican occupation, Bowie took responsibility for the frightened woman and her family in the Alamo.

At the same time, Capt. Almeron Dickinson was trying to bring his own wife and child into the Alamo. Dickinson was the blacksmith who had been placed in charge of the tiny Gonzales cannon during its brief, glorious combat back in September. Since then, the Tennesseean had graduated from baby-sitting a six-pounder to command of the eighteen-gun artillery of the Alamo, which included the largest piece in all of Texas, a massive eighteen-pounder. Only fifteen years old, his wife, Susannah, was a black-haired Tennessee girl with blue eyes, and had joined her husband sometime after the Ayish Bayou rabble ransacked Gonzales back in October. Together with their infant daughter, Angelina, the Dickinsons had set up house in San Antonio. Now mother and child were in danger there.

The church bells were ringing as if it were Christmas Day, and Mexican troops had magically materialized in certain street corridors. With growing fear, the young Susannah cradled her baby and waited for rescue. Suddenly Captain Dickinson came galloping up to their house. "The Mexicans are upon us," he said. "Give me the babe, and jump up behind me."

Portero Street, which led to the footbridge, was already occupied, and Dickinson was afraid the Mexican soldiers would open fire on him. He galloped south of the bridge to a common fording point and urged his horse forward through the shallow water. As Captain Dickinson rode through the southern entrance of the Alamo, he brought with him the only Anglo-American females in the whole compound.[21]

It was just after three o'clock in the afternoon. San Antonio now belonged to the Mexicans by default. No one had fired a shot.

Travis found the transition aggravating, but beyond his control. Had Houston simply forwarded the troops he'd requested, Travis could have held the town and used the Alamo as a fallback position. But Houston—and Texas—had failed him.

Travis determined not to fail them. He would lead by example. After years of being eclipsed by larger, more dramatic figures, the lawyer finally saw his chance and grabbed it.

First he sent a young messenger named Johnson off to Goliad with the message for Fannin to send troops. Then, while Dr. Sutherland rested in the corner, he penned a second letter to the people of Gonzales: "The enemy in large force is in sight. We want men and provisions. Send them to us. We have 150 men and are determined to defend the Alamo to the last. Give us assistance."[22]

Shortly after three o'clock, Dr. Sutherland climbed back onto his horse with Travis's dispatch.[23]

Dr. Sutherland rode down the river to find Dimmitt, but Dimmitt had already left. "El Colorado" Smith linked up with Sutherland, but just as the two men readied to leave for Gonzales, they were paralyzed by the sight of enemy soldiers marching into the Military Plaza in regular order. While they sat on horseback gaping at the exotic scene, merchant Nat Lewis came trudging up on foot. Over his shoulder he'd slung big leather saddlebags filled with stock of his store delicacies; he was quitting town for safer territory. What remained in his store, he philosophically dismissed as a contribution to the enemy.

Freighted with his precious saddlebags, the hardy merchant trekked off into the mesquite and chaparral brush on foot. Sutherland and Smith turned south along the old Goliad road in order to throw any Mexican soldiers off their scent. Sutherland's injured knee began to stiffen and his pain grew more and more acute. His saddle became a hard, undulating torture device and all he could think of was returning to the Alamo. The temptation to go back dogged him with each hoofbeat. Just then he and Smith heard a single cannon shot resound across the still prairie. The battle had begun and retreat was now out of the question. They did not know it, but Travis had just had his way.

He had an entire fortress from which to posture, but his dramatic license was exposed almost immediately.

The short winter afternoon was drawing shadows sometime after four o'clock, when the rebels saw a chilling patch of color in midtown. Up in the belfry of San Fernando Church, soldiers tied a large red banner on the Alamo side of the tower. It was plainly visible and it signified no mercy.

Despite his former arrangement with Colonel Bowie, Colonel Travis didn't bother to consult his co-commander in the Alamo with whom all decisions were to be jointly shared. On this first significant issue facing the Alamo command, Travis alone decided. Trading one dramatic gesture for another, Travis ordered the eighteen-pounder to be fired.

The big cannon boomed. It was aimed directly at town, a half mile distant, but the cannonball had no particular target. Rather it was a loud exclamation mark.

Bowie and others in the Alamo were horrified by the opening shot. It accomplished absolutely nothing and only committed them further to this ridiculous fortress.

The Mexicans opened up with a five-inch howitzer, lobbing four grenades into the Alamo compound. They ceased firing when a lone rider emerged from the Alamo under a white flag of truce. This was Green Jameson, the garrison engineer, and he was bearing a dispatch from James Bowie.

"Because a shot was fired from a cannon of this fort at the time that a red flag was raised over the tower, and a little afterward they told me that a part of your army had sounded a parley, which however, was not heard before the firing of the said shot. I wish, Sir, to ascertain if it be true that a parley was called. . . . God and Texas!''[24]

Bowie clearly wanted to talk. He all but renounced Travis's noisy cannon shot, and politely invited the Mexican army to negotiate. While waiting for a reply, Jameson chatted with Col. Juan Almonte, Santa Anna's talented, bilingual aide-de-camp. Jameson explained that the Alamo was not in good condition and reiterated Bowie's desire that some sort of honorable surrender be worked out.[25] The Mexican siege of the Alamo was barely an hour old, and already the rebels were having second thoughts about a confrontation. Soon Jameson and Bowie had their answer. Santa Anna had delegated his response to an officer of Bowie's rank, Col. Don José Batres.

"As the Aide-de-Camp of his Excellency, the President of the Republic," Batres wrote, "I reply to you, according to the order of his Excellency, that the Mexican army cannot come to terms under any conditions with rebellious foreigners to whom there is no other recourse left, if they wish to save their lives, than to place themselves immediately at the disposal of the Supreme Government from whom alone they may expect clemency after some considerations are taken up. God and Liberty!"[26] In short, the only surrender Santa Anna would accept was "at discretion," meaning unconditional.

Travis was offended that Santa Anna would dare to call the Anglo-American rebels holed up in this Mexican outpost "rebellious foreigners."[27] But he was even more offended by James Bowie. Even though Travis had fired the cannon without Bowie's consent, he was infuriated that Bowie had contacted the Mexican army without *his* consent. Bowie's action had effectively erased the sensitive young colonel's very presence. Furthermore, Bowie's dispatch had been written in Spanish and signed by Bowie alone. The Mexicans didn't even know that Colonel Travis of the Legion of Cavalry was on the premises. That was unbearable.

Travis trotted out his own emissary to treat with Santa Anna; twenty-eight-year-old Albert Martin, formerly a clerk from a New Orleans business house. Martin spoke directly to Almonte, inviting the Mexican colonel to negotiate with Travis.

Travis had several reasons for talking with Almonte: Almonte spoke fluent English . . . Travis only halting, pidgin Spanish; Almonte was closely connected with Santa Anna; Almonte had been schooled in the

United States and had toured Texas only the year before. On the other hand, Almonte had no reason to speak with Travis. "I answered," Almonte recalled, "that it did not become the Mexican Government to make any propositions through me, and that I had only permission to hear such as might be made on the part of the rebels."[28]

Travis couldn't bluster and bully Mexican officials this time around, because for a change he was in the minority. To the professional soldiers in Santa Anna's army, he was a silly, pompous man.

Martin returned to the fortress. The sun washed yellow, then pink upon the west-facing adobe and stone walls. Night came on.

According to a confused summation of this opening day of the siege, Travis told Houston that he opened fire with his cannon after, not before, Colonel Batres's response to Bowie (". . . [they] demanded a surrender at discretion, calling us *foreign rebels*. I answered them with a cannon shot"[29]). That was not so. He mentioned sending his messengers Johnson and Sutherland after, not before, the cannon shot. That was not so. He stated that the Mexicans opened up a relentless bombardment of the Alamo. That was not so.

According to Almonte, the Mexican army fired only four grenades in the afternoon. Following Bowie's and Travis's attempts to parley, there was no more firing.

San Antonio bustled through the night. There were artillery batteries to be readied and positioned, units to be fed, horses to be watered and grazed, enemy effects to be inventoried. The occupation army settled upon the town. From the Alamo, the Mexicans' torches, cook fires, and candle flames lit the city like a constellation fallen to earth.

Sixteen miles out upon the dark prairie, Dr. Sutherland eased from his saddle, gritting his teeth. He and his companion spread their blankets on the ground and lay down. "Being somewhat relieved of my suffering," he said, "I was soon asleep."

"I was born for a storm. Calm does not suit me." Andrew Jackson in a lithograph based on a Mathew Brady daguerreotype. (*Courtesy Library of Congress*)

Stephen Austin, called the Father of Texas, controlled vast land holdings under Mexican law and opposed the War Party for years. (*Courtesy Texas State Capitol, Austin; and UT Institute of Texan Cultures, San Antonio*)

One of the most fanatical of the War Dogs, lawyer William Travis demanded—and got—a command in December 1835, the same month this sketch was made. (*Courtesy Daughters of the Republic of Texas History Research Library, San Antonio*)

R. M. "Three-Legged Willie" Williamson, like many of the War Dogs, was a lawyer and a land speculator. After the revolution, Williamson prospered as a judge and politician. (*Courtesy Texas State Capitol, Austin; and UT Institute of Texan Cultures, San Antonio*)

Vol.I." *Go Ahead!*"No.3.

Davy Crockett's
18 ALMANACK, 37
OF WILD SPORTS IN THE WEST,
Life in the Backwoods, & Sketches of Texas.

O KENTUCKY! THE HUNTERS OF KENTUCKY!!!
Nashville, Tennessee. Published by the heirs of Col. Crockett.

David Crockett probably never wore an animal skin cap, but "Davy" did. This woodcut was copied from a poster of a stage character who in turn was based on a highly embellished biography of Crockett. (*Courtesy National Portrait Gallery, Smithsonian Institution, Washington, D.C. Published in* Davy Crockett's Almanack for 1837)

David Crockett complained that portraits like this 1834 painting made him look like "a sort of cross between a clean-shirted Member of Congress and a Methodist Preacher." (*Courtesy National Portrait Gallery, Smithsonian Institution, Washington, D.C. On loan from Katherine Bradford in honor of her mother, Dorothy W. Bradford*)

Above: When Houston sat for this photo two years after the revolution, he was the proud president of a republic. (*Courtesy Daughters of the Republic of Texas History Research Library, San Antonio*)

Left: In 1831, while struggling to rise from alcoholism, Sam Houston had himself painted as a Roman senator. (*Courtesy State Preservation Board, State Capitol, Austin*)

Sly and ruthless, Antonio López de Santa Anna was the ultimate *caudillo* or strongman. Under his command, Mexico lost one third of its territory. (*Courtesy Nettie Lee Benson Latin American Collection, UT/Austin*)

Months before Travis drew his fight-to-the-end line in the Alamo's dirt, old-time filibuster Ben Milam scratched a line of his own for volunteers ready to attack San Antonio. (*Courtesy Texas State Library, Austin; and UT Institute of Texan Cultures, San Antonio*)

James Bowie, shown clenching the handle of his famous knife, is said to have died of his illness hours before the Alamo fell. (*Courtesy Daughters of the Republic of Texas History Research Library, San Antonio*)

This silk flag of the New Orleans Greys was one of two or more flags at the Alamo. When Santa Anna captured it, he sent it to Mexico City as clear proof of Anglo-American mercenary activity. (*Courtesy Daughters of the Republic of Texas Alamo Museum*)

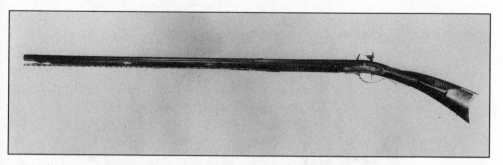

Legend has it that long rifles like this .58 caliber Pennsylvania model found in the Alamo's rubble helped keep the Mexican army at bay for thirteen days. In actuality, there were but a few long rifles at the Alamo, and they did nothing at all to hold back Santa Anna. (*Courtesy Daughters of the Republic of Texas Alamo Museum*)

Manuel de Mier y Terán, scientist and general, warned in 1828 that Anglo-Americans were overrunning Texas. (*Courtesy Nettie Lee Benson Latin American Collection, UT/Austin*)

El Alamo by Jean Louis Theodore Gentilz. Dated 1844, this painting shows the famous chapel much the way it looked during the battle. The distinctive "hump" that today caps the front was added in 1848 by the U.S. Army. (*Courtesy Daughters of the Republic of Texas History Research Library, San Antonio*)

A general without a country, Italian-born Vicente Filisola was able, but distrusted by all but Santa Anna. (*Courtesy Nettie Lee Benson Latin American Collection, UT/Austin*)

The son of a Mexican revolutionary, Juan Almonte was educated in the United States. He served as Santa Anna's aide, and later as the Mexican minister in Washington, D.C. (*Courtesy Nettie Lee Benson Latin American Collection, UT/Austin*)

José Urrea destroyed the Anglo-Americans' southern defenses, capturing hundreds of mercenaries from the United States. (*Courtesy Nettie Lee Benson Latin American Collection, UT/Austin*)

Under orders from Santa Anna, Nicolás de la Portilla (here shown many years after the campaign) executed most of Urrea's prisoners. (*Courtesy Nettie Lee Benson Latin American Collection, UT/Austin*)

"It is not in the nature of things for the superior race to long remain under the domination of the inferior." Noah Smithwick, blacksmith and smuggler, shown forty years after the revolution. (*Courtesy Eugene C. Barker Texas History Center, UT/Austin*)

A native Tejano, Juan Seguín sided with the Anglo-Americans, but they turned on him, forcing him to flee to Mexico. (*Courtesy Fannie Ratchford Collection, Archives Division, Texas State Library*)

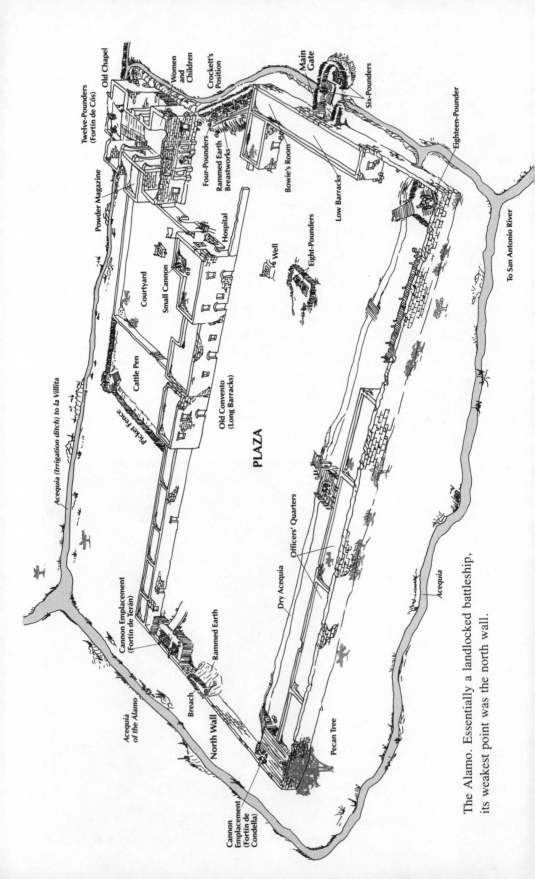

The Alamo. Essentially a landlocked battleship, its weakest point was the north wall.

Acequia (Irrigation ditch) to la Villita

Twelve-Pounders (Fortín de Cós)

Old Chapel

Women and Children

Crockett's Position

Main Gate

Six-Pounders

Eighteen-Pounder

Four-Pounders

Rammed Earth Breastworks

Powder Magazine

Bowie's Room

Low Barracks

Hospital

Small Cannon

Courtyard

Well

Eight-Pounders

To San Antonio River

Cattle Pen

Picket Fence

Old Convento (Long Barracks)

PLAZA

Officers' Quarters

Dry Acequia

Acequia

Cannon Emplacement (Fortín de Terán)

Rammed Earth

Acequia of the Alamo

Breach

North Wall

Pecan Tree

Cannon Emplacement (Fortín de Condella)

Fall of the Alamo by Jean Louis Theodore Gentilz. Except for the bright daylight, this representation of the battle is one of the more accurate. (*Courtesy Daughters of the Republic of Texas History Research Library, San Antonio*)

Fall of the Alamo---Death of Crockett.

With time, Crockett's death in battle was depicted with an epic ferocity. In actuality, he was captured, then executed. (*Courtesy National Portrait Gallery, Smithsonian Institution, Washington, D.C. Published in* Davy Crockett's Almanack *for* 1837)

Susannah Dickinson spent bitter decades trying to forget the Alamo, but finally became its grande dame. (*Courtesy Daughters of the Republic of Texas History Research Library, San Antonio*)

Angelina Dickinson, the "Babe of the Alamo," was unable to receive a penny of state aid and ended as a prostitute. (*Courtesy Daughters of the Republic of Texas History Research Library, San Antonio*)

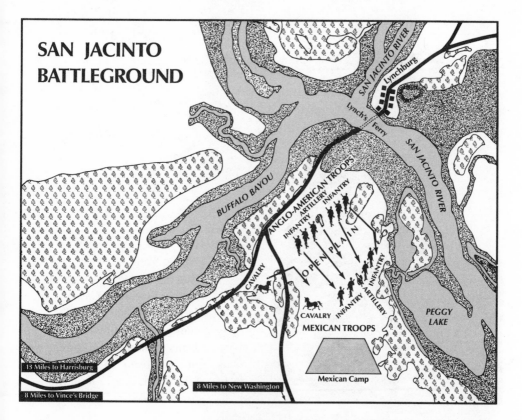

SAN JACINTO
BATTLEGROUND

SAN JACINTO RIVER

Lynchburg

Lynch's Ferry

SAN JACINTO RIVER

BUFFALO BAYOU

ANGLO-AMERICAN TROOPS

INFANTRY ARTILLERY INFANTRY

O P E N   P L A I N

CAVALRY

INFANTRY ARTILLERY INFANTRY

CAVALRY

MEXICAN TROOPS

PEGGY LAKE

Mexican Camp

13 Miles to Harrisburg

8 Miles to Vince's Bridge

8 Miles to New Washington

Santa Anna's inept brother-in-law, Martín Perfecto de Cós, surrendered the Alamo, but later helped regain it. (*Courtesy Texas State Archives, Austin; and UT Institute of Texan Cultures, San Antonio*)

For a half century after the Alamo battle, Andrea Ramírez Villanueva, known locally as Madam Candaleria, insisted she nursed James Bowie in his final hours. (*Courtesy Daughters of the Republic of Texas History Research Library, San Antonio*)

The Surrender of Santa Anna by William Huddle shows a wounded Sam Houston offering a seat to his enemy. A lynch mob forms in the background, while Deaf Smith tries to hear in the front. (*Courtesy Texas State Capitol, Austin; and UT Institute of Texan Cultures, San Antonio*)

= 12 =

THE SHADOW OF the church bell tower dropped upon Enrique Esparza like a dark angel as he entered San Antonio's Main Plaza. Eight years old, Esparza was a frail and delicate boy for whom San Antonio was the entire universe. He had been born in an adobe hut on the east side of El Calle de Acequia, the Street of the Irrigation Ditch. From the moment Santa Anna entered his town, the boy's world changed shape. At the age of ninety, he told of this incredible day and the war it spawned.

"You ask me do I remember it," he said. "I tell you yes. It is burned into my brain and indelibly scarred there. Neither age nor infirmity could make me forget, for the scene was one of such horror that it could never be forgotten by any one who witnessed its incidents."

For the Esparza family these "incidents" had their beginning with the friendship between Enrique's father, Gregorio, and El Colorado Smith, the red-headed norteamericano carpenter and merchant who had emigrated to Texas and planted roots in San Antonio. When the revolution flowered, Gregorio decided that he had more in common with El Colorado than with his El Presidente. He joined the company of Tejanos under the ranchero Captain Juan Seguín.

From the start of the troubles, Smith had intended to send his young Tejano wife, María de Jesus Curbelo, and their children[1] east to Nacogdoches. Smith invited Gregorio to send his family along in the same wagon. But the wagon was delayed in returning to town. It was during this delay that Santa Anna arrived.

At the time, Enrique was playing with some friends in the Main Plaza. "I saw Santa Anna when he arrived. I saw him dismount. He did not hitch the horse. He gave his bridle reins to a lackey. He and his staff proceeded immediately to the house [the Yturri house] on the Northwest corner of Main Plaza."[2] El Presidente entered town with his general staff, well guarded by three companies of light infantry under Colonel Morales, three companies of grenadiers, two mortars, and a unit of cavalry.[3]

The children fled. Enrique ran to his home and told his father and

181

mother of the astounding event. His parents received the news with alarm. El Colorado's wagon had failed them. There was no time to evacuate the family. That left just one option. "My father was told by Smith that all who were friends to the Americans had better join the Americans who had taken refuge in the Alamo. Smith and his family were there and my father and his family went with them."

Some Béxarenos bravely stayed put. Some wished to protect their property or try to profit from the army. A few, like the *alcalde* Francisco Antonio Ruiz, whose father had fought Santa Anna at the Battle of Medina in 1813 and who was attending the revolutionary convention in Washington-on-the-Brazos, remained to protect the rights of the citizens at large. Other Tejano civilians heeded the Mexican army's warning and removed from town until the hostilities ended. One of these was six-year-old José María Rodríguez: "My father being away with General Houston's army, my mother undertook to act for us, and decided it was best for us to go into the country to avoid being here when General Santa Ana's [*sic*] army should come in. We went to the ranch of Dona Santos Ximenes. We left in ox carts, the wheels of which were made of solid wood. We buried our money in the house, about $800.00; it took us nearly two days to get to the ranch."[4]

Only a few of the locals—perhaps twenty or thirty of a population of more than two thousand—joined the Anglo-American rabble in the Alamo. Several of these were the wives or women of the rebels. Some were sympathizers. A few were probably *vaqueros* under Capt. Juan Seguín's immediate command. All of these Tejanos were considered traitors by the Mexican army.

"It was twilight when we got into the Alamo," said Enrique Esparza, "and it grew pitch-dark soon afterward. All of the doors were closed and barred. The sentinels that had been on duty without were first called inside and then the openings closed. Some sentinels were posted upon the roof, but these were protected by the walls of the Alamo church and the old Convent building. We went into the church portion. It was shut up when we arrived. We were admitted through a small window.

"I distinctly remember that I climbed through the window and over a cannon that was placed inside of the church immediately behind the window. There were several other cannon there. Some were back of the doors. Some had been mounted on the roof and some had been placed in the Convent. The window was opened to permit us to enter and it was closed immediately after we got inside."

For the next thirteen days he was sheltered in the chapel with his mother. His father manned one of the cannon. Sometimes the little boy heard cannonballs strike the wall of the chapel. Sometimes he heard the Mexican soldiers jeering from far away.

The Alamo floated upon an ocean of grass and mesquite, a virtual gunboat in contested waters. To the Mexicans it represented a sort of ark at the far edge of their defensible realm. To the Anglo-Americans it bobbed upon the prairie, a gothic wreck that should have sunk under the weight of its stone long before. When Mexican soldiers were besieged in the Alamo, their distant countrymen viewed the situation as remote and desperate—one that required rescue. Now that Travis and his little army sat besieged in the Alamo, Anglo-Americans saw it the same way. All too clearly, the Alamo was a liability.

It had been built to shelter Christianized Indians from unconverted tribals, not to withstand a European-style siege against several thousand troops. Nevertheless, the Spanish, then the Mexicans, then the Anglo-Americans had all tried to adapt the mission to resemble a presidio, a fire base designed to survive and suppress the heathen, whoever the heathen might be—Moors, Comanches, or filibusters.[5] But except for its long windowless walls facing the outer world, the Alamo had few real features of a presidio.

It lacked some of the most basic requirements of a fort: No bastions reached out to protect the exterior of the walls; banquettes or terraces were scarce or nonexistent along some walls; and there were few gunports or embrasures through which riflemen or artillery could pick off the enemy in safety. Little distinguished the Alamo as a defensive point beyond its crumbling adobe and limestone walls—and those the rebels themselves had gleefully blasted full of holes during the autumn siege of San Antonio.

Just the same, Travis and Bowie visualized the Alamo as a landlocked battleship. Boasting an eighteen-pounder setpiece plus other cannons, it came as close as any Mexican structure east of the Rio Grande to "bristling" with artillery. It held between thirty and forty pieces of artillery of various calibers, but only half that number were mounted.[6] Even so, the Alamo displayed more firepower than even the Goliad presidio. Numerically, it outgunned Santa Anna's expedition, which had a total of twenty-one cannons and howitzers. The Alamo's eighteen-pounder, the biggest gun in Texas, had been emplaced to overlook San Antonio and could throw a solid iron ball more than half a mile beyond the town's western outskirts. Heavy artillery like eighteen- and twenty-four-pounders were used like long-distance battering rams to demolish buildings and walls. In Santa Anna's hands, such a weapon would have knocked the Alamo's walls to pieces in a day. But a cast-iron eighteen-pounder weighed thirty-five hundred pounds and had limited mobility. The largest artillery Santa Anna lugged along were two twelve-pounders. Though not as imposing as the eighteen-pounder, they promised significant punch. But these two guns straggled weeks behind the vanguard, and in the end they played no role in the battle.

Instead Santa Anna relied on his nine-pounders as the workhorse artillery. With its two-wheeled limber, each weighed two tons and could fire two aimed rounds of solid shot per minute to a distance of 1,400 yards.[7] On the morning of February 24 the Mexicans dug an entrenchment 350 yards from the Alamo on the opposite bank of the San Antonio River. Early that afternoon, they nestled two nine-pounders into the earthworks.[8] The battery was an instant success. In the artillery duel that broke out before dusk, the Mexicans scored direct hits on the massive eighteen-pounder, which commanded the town, and on a second cannon. Both pieces were dismounted.[9]

The Alamo's highest point was its thirty-foot-high chapel. Lying open to the sky, the chapel's nave was filled with dirt and rubble that sloped up from the doorway to form a cannon ramp to the battery at the front of the church. While the chapel walls were made of cut stone and well-preserved mortar, the majority of the fortification was constructed of adobe and unquarried limestone, hardly an imposing barrier. And the average height of the nearly half mile of walls was a moderate eight to ten feet.

The north wall was particularly weak. It was in ruins even before the rebels besieged the Alamo the previous fall. Under General Cós, the Mexicans had shored the wall up with wooden logs five and six inches thick.[10] But after Anglo-American snipers had put a halt to all work outside the walls, the exterior of the braces had never received its thick facing of earth. The standard of the day prescribed a 1.5-foot thickness of rammed earth to stop a musket ball, and 8.5 to 10 feet to protect against a twelve-pounder cannon.[11] Obviously, there was a lot of earth moving to accomplish at the north wall, but the mercenary garrison refused to work until they were at least clothed and fed. It was a reasonable enough demand,[12] but their labor strike resulted in neither clothing nor food, and it left the bare wooden "patch" on the north wall as a massive, inviting ladder.[13] The Mexicans knew from their earlier possession of the fortress just where the structure was flawed.[14]

Ordinarily one dug entrenchments on the outside of the wall, not the inside. But the rebels had no choice. They would have been exposed to enemy fire on the outside, and so they labored to pack dirt against the weak wall. "However this operation was more harmful than useful to them," Gen. Vicente Filisola later observed. "Since they had no walkway [along the interior of the wall] it was necessary for them on the day of the assault to stand up on it in order to fire with their guns, and thus they presented an immense target for our fire."[15]

Travis made his headquarters in an adobe house along the west wall, a position tucked at the deepest interior of the plaza. Playing through the various configurations of the upcoming assault, Travis saw his location in the fort as ideal. He was next to the two northern batteries and could pitch in there if the enemy threw itself at the north wall. And if the enemy gained entrance through the south gate, Travis would be guaranteed a heroic body count. Trapped in the rear of the fortress, he could fight until the bitter end and go down like a tiger, one of the last to die. In addition, his quarters were out of the way and gave him a measure of privacy. Over the coming days, he exploited that privacy, growing more and more reclusive. Travis had much to think about.

For one thing Bowie had fallen ill. No sooner had the rebels withdrawn to the Alamo than Bowie collapsed, too weak to walk, almost too weak to sign his own name. Bowie's drunken binge two weeks earlier had seriously weakened his immune system and on February 23 the big knife fighter was poleaxed by "a disease of a peculiar nature," tuberculosis, pneumonia, typhoid fever, typhoid-pneumonia, or some other debilitating ailment. He immediately recognized how serious his illness was and wasted no time in quarantining himself. He had undertaken the protection of his Tejano sisters-in-law, Juana and Gertrudis, and suddenly the best protection he could offer them was his absence.

"Sister," Bowie told Juana, "do not be afraid. I leave you with Colonel Travis, Colonel Crockett, and other friends. They are gentlemen, and will treat you kindly." Then he had two soldiers carry him off to a room near the makeshift infirmary. There he was attended by a Mexican woman named Andrea Castañon Ramírez Villanueva. Susannah Dickinson later declared Señora Candaleria, as she was called, a fraud; Candaleria "snappily" countered that Dickinson was a racist who hated Mexicans. In her testimonials, the Tejana swore that she had tended Bowie on his sickbed. There is no reason to disbelieve her: The tradition of *curanderismo* lends credence to her claims. A *curandero* was a Mexican folk healer, part shaman, part herbalist, part psychiatrist, who specialized in medieval Spanish medicine and Native American remedies.[16]

Since Bowie had been baptized and married into Hispanic culture, it would have been perfectly natural for his Mexican relatives to bring a local healer in to nurse him. Besides that, even though the Alamo held six physicians, they had little or no medicines to treat a patient with Bowie's symptoms.

Every *curandero* practiced differently, but certain treatments seem to have been standard: the use of herbs, prayers, massage, sucking, sweating, and gifts or distractions aimed at Christian and pagan deities. Brightly colored clay and wooden toys or food were sometimes used to bribe spirits.[17] A fairly common diagnostic tool was an egg. Rubbed over the patient's entire body and then cracked open, the egg could be "read" and the cause of illness analyzed. Some *curanderos* took the patient's pulse to ferret out foul play by a witch. Blood spoke to *curanderos,* and they used the pulse as a sort of lie detector while asking the patient questions.[18]

If Candaleria was practicing her arts on Bowie, as she claimed,[19] then Bowie's last days would have seemed to him, at times, hallucinatory as he felt chicken eggs "cleaning" his body, smelled and tasted strange herbs and teas, and watched the flame of a candle guarding his bed.[20] But whatever the *curandera'*s ministrations, Bowie certainly was spared from the "heroic" cures of Anglo-American medicine popular at the time. Called "puke, purge and bleed," this regimen consisted of harsh emetics, purgatives, and bloodletting. American doctors equipped themselves with quinine, calomel and blue pills (made with mercury), and laudanum (the alcohol-opium mixture), and generally bled their patients with leeches, lances, or spring-triggered scarificators. The treatment was so unpleasant that slaves often hid their maladies for fear of the treatment. Since the physicians fighting at the Alamo had run out of medicine, Bowie's last days were relatively free of pain.

Two or three times Bowie had himself carried on his cot from the hospital to the room in which Juana and Gertrudis were staying.[21] Chatting in Spanish, they probably discussed the latest news about the Mexican army's occupation of the town. A number of townspeople traveled back and forth between town and the Alamo, visiting friends and relatives.[22] It was advantageous to both contending armies to have this kind of traffic, for the visitors' gossip provided valuable intelligence about the opposing side's condition.

Through such visitations, and from their own observances upon the Alamo walls, the two Tejana sisters knew that their dead stepfather's beautiful house, the Veramendi Palace, had been converted into one of the first strategic installations. Mexican troops walked along its flagstoned *zaguán* (hallway) and its lovely *sala* (parlor) echoed with war talk. Near the patio cannons slammed rounds into the Alamo.

Bowie's condition worsened and in terms of command, he was already dead. Without any comment to his own superiors, Travis absorbed Bowie's contingent of volunteers and from February 24 onward signed all dispatches as the commanding colonel. Except for his attempt to parley with the Mexican army on the first day of the siege, Bowie contributed nothing to the garrison's leadership. Travis mentioned numerous other figures in his dispatches, but never Bowie. If Travis ever bothered to consult with Bowie after his collapse, it was not recorded. Bowie was hauled out into the sunlight on warm days to encourage the men, but this was on a small scale at best. Bowie spiraled deeper into illness.

The loss of Bowie as a co-commander was a blow to the rebels' dynamism. He had been an aggressive, charismatic fighter, and he knew the western Texas terrain intimately. He had even been on the receiving end of a siege once. In November 1831 Bowie, his brother Rezin, and nine other treasure hunters had been pinned down near the ruins of San Luis de las Amarillas by 164 hostile Caddo Indians. After a fourteen-hour stand in which they killed 50 Caddos and lost one of their own men, Bowie's party had driven their attackers away. Bowie had known how to command men unused to following orders, when to organize them, and when to let them alone. He had something else Travis lacked, too: judgment.

Equally important to his combat experience, Bowie had appreciated the Mexican mind-set better than did most Anglo-Americans. He could speak and write Spanish and was related through marriage to two of the most powerful families in Texas. Though he'd tried to defraud various Mexicans, Bowie had understood their motivations and formalities, something few ethnocentric Anglo-Americans ever attempted. Following Travis's hasty shot with the Alamo's eighteen-pounder on the first day of their siege, Bowie had instantly tried to open negotiations with the Mexicans in hope that the rebels could surrender.

Travis was just the opposite. For him unremitting defiance was the coin of power. He had never learned the difference between bravado and courage, nor the meaning of diplomacy. He had long aspired to military leadership, but he lacked any real connection with his men. More crippling still, he had no respect for the enemy. His fantasy about Anglo-Saxon supremacy replaced plain good sense. In the face of a grim and overwhelming situation, his reaction had been to exacerbate events by firing off the biggest cannon he had. He had always dreamed of riding the wild horse of power, but once mounted on its bare back he could only clutch at its mane.

Now that Travis had complete authority within the walls of the Alamo, he seemed bewildered by the demonic speed of being stationary. His letters flowered with excited prose and confused facts. But where he had seen an empire of grass and adobe, he now watched a thousand, then several thousand Mexican soldiers in red and blue and white uniforms wheeling about in parade formation. And when he turned and looked down from the walls, he saw his own pathetic army: mercenaries and ragtag troops with the shoes rotting off their feet.

Travis spent the remainder of the siege trying to square his hopes with the diminishing odds. Every day more troops poured into the town across the river. He estimated the numbers at between fifteen hundred and six thousand. Though he had enough food to last another twenty days, his garrison was fast running out of gunpowder and cannonballs. He begged Houston to send "at least five hundred pounds of cannon powder, and two hundred rounds of six, nine, twelve, and eighteen pound balls, ten kegs of rifle powder and a supply of lead."

When the rebels had defeated General Cós's troops in December, they had seized more than 12,000 cartridges, powder, hundreds of old muskets, 166 bayonets, 10 bags of grapeshot, and 112 Mexican duck jackets.[23] At first glance, they seemed to have acquired all the fixings to press their war. But the munitions proved to be a sorry illusion. "We looked upon their [Mexican] cartridges as the greatest prize, and eagerly seized their cartridge boxes," one rebel said. "But on examining the powder, we found it little better than pounded charcoal, and, after a trial, rejected it as altogether useless. It was by far the poorest powder I ever saw, and burnt so badly that we could clearly account for the inefficacy of the enemy's fire. Compared with the double Dupont, with which we had been furnished, it was evident that we had vastly the advantage over our enemy in this particular. We therefore emptied all the cartridges, and saved only the bullets."[24]

But the rebels did not throw the Mexican gunpowder away. Instead they stored several hundred pounds of it in a fireproof room on the north side of the Alamo chapel, protected by masonry two feet thick. If things reached bottom and the garrison were overrun, the last man would torch the powder room and blow everyone up.

The irony was that the Alamo contained more than enough powder to commit suicide, but not enough to prevent it. Their good powder steadily dwindled. After a week or so, the rebels were limited to touching off an artillery round only three or four times a day.

For two solid months now the various commanders at the Alamo had been dunning the provisional Texas government for supplies and reinforcements. For just as long they had received nothing at all.

From the beginning Travis had used the Alamo and San Antonio as bait. He was baiting the Mexicans with his presence, but he was also baiting the rebel government, challenging the provisionals to come west to him. It was a dangerous maneuver, for he was pitting himself against not only Santa Anna, but against Sam Houston, who wanted to consolidate his forces on Anglo-American turf.

Houston was not fooled by Travis's machinations, but until he had the authority of an established government he could not bring into line the Fannins, Bowies, and Travises showboating on the western front. So until he obtained absolute authority over the army, Houston issued no significant orders. And until Houston did issue orders, Travis went right on making up his own strategy.

"If [supplies] are promptly sent and large reinforcements are hastened to this frontier," Travis said, "this neighborhood will be the great and decisive ground. The power of Santa Anna is to be met here or in the colonies; we had better meet them here than to suffer a war of devastation to rage in our settlements."[25]

The concept of a western front extending from San Antonio through Goliad to the Gulf coast was logical. But it was impossible. There were no large reinforcements to hasten to the frontier. Supplies were stockpiling on the coast, but without any logistical order. The rebels had no standing army prepared to reinforce the western line. Every man under arms was already on the western line, and dispatch after dispatch described them as nearly naked and destitute. One of the primary tasks of any military is to bring the enemy to battle on your own terms and make the enemy fight by your rules, not theirs. As Travis quickly learned, holding the Alamo with a skeletal grip was not fighting by his own rules. To Travis's unpleasant shock, the Mexican army held complete control of the battle. He had absolutely no choices in determining how, when, and where the Alamo would be taken away from him. In short, Travis had lost the Alamo even before the first gleaming Mexican cavalryman had descended from the Alazan hills.

Travis faced defeat like a mystic facing a mountain. It stood before him, an undeniable barrier. But by closing his eyes, it was no longer in front of him. Travis turned his back on reality. He took to his white-washed room in this former mission and retreated to the only religion he knew: propaganda. He propagandized the colonies, the States, the world. He even propagandized his own men.

"To the People of Texas & all Americans in the world," he wrote on the second day of the siege. "Fellow Citizens & Compatriots—I am besieged by a thousand or more of the Mexicans under Santa Anna. . . . The enemy has demanded a surrender at discretion, otherwise, the garrison are to be put to the sword, if the fort is taken. I have answered the demand with a cannon shot, & our flag still waves proudly from the walls. *I shall never surrender or retreat.* Then, I call on you in the name of liberty, of patriotism & every thing dear to the American character, to come to our aid with all dispatch. . . . If this call is neglected, I am determined to sustain myself as long as possible & die like a soldier who never forgets what is due his own honor & that of his country. VICTORY OR DEATH."[26]

This message has been called one of the masterpieces of American patriotism. Certainly it was Travis's masterpiece, romantic, pointed, and abundant with ego. Travis repeated its suicidal melody in the next (and last) four dispatches he sent from the Alamo, but never quite captured the high tragedy of this February 24 message.[27]

The day before Travis had used the injured Dr. Sutherland as his courier. This time he selected another limping man, twenty-eight-year-old Albert Martin, to carry his dispatch. Obviously Travis was saving all able-bodied men for combat. Martin had gashed his foot badly in a wood-cutting accident, but had sufficiently recovered by late December to pack an assortment of smuggled Spanish goods to Béxar on horseback.[28] There he had been drawn into the revolutionary doings. With Travis's rousing dispatch in his saddlebags, Martin galloped off in search of a nonexistent army.

At ten o'clock on Thursday morning, February 25, the Mexicans probed the Alamo defenses with a small frontal assault. Two to three hundred unfortunate soldiers advanced under the cover of a ramshackle slum of jacales, then broke into the open ninety yards from the southern wall. The rebels waited until the soldiers were at point blank, then opened up with a heavy discharge of canister and grapeshot along with small arms fire. The Mexicans fell back to the dubious shelter of the jacales, dragging their dead and wounded with them. Under the encouragement of their three artillery captains, Dickinson, Carey, and Blair, the rebel cannons held their own. The "high private" David Crockett "was seen at all points," Travis said, "animating the men to do their duty."

Two men sallied out through the south gate on horseback with torches in hand. With enemy lead streaking by on every side, they fired the jacales behind which Mexican soldiers were trying to stay alive through the long afternoon. Deprived of their cover, the enemy gradually pulled back.[29]

Whenever positions were advanced within musket shot of the Alamo, the Mexicans took a few more casualties. Soldiers manning some of the Mexican artillery nearest the Alamo had to expose themselves to reload their guns, and there was no telling when some Anglo-American sharpshooter might be waiting for a target. One night a party of five or six Mexican soldiers under Col. Juan Bringas raced across a small footbridge in an attempt to press the encirclement, but the rebels opened up, killing one man and spilling Bringas into the cold river.[30]

On several other occasions, the rebels sallied out through the south gate to open fields of fire and burn nearby jacales that would provide the enemy with cover. They also pulled the miserable wood and straw shacks to pieces and carried sections in to use for their fires. The rebels tried to fetch water from the *acequia*. They had dug a second well in the Alamo plaza, but apparently wanted greater quantities. But Mexican marksmen, probably armed with the new and accurate Baker rifles, opened up on the men, and so the forays outside the Alamo walls remained more adventurous than profitable.

The February 25 "battle" was only a halfhearted skirmish to test the Alamo's defenses. Travis realized that a full-scale assault would not go so well for him. But the skirmish lifted his spirits for it seemed to confirm that Mexicans were inferior in everything they did, including making war. A number of Mexicans had been killed and wounded, and the rebels had suffered nothing but a few scratches from flying bits of rock. To a crusader like Travis that came very close to divine protection. It certainly allowed him a certain amount of optimism despite the louder realities.

More and more cannons and howitzers sprouted upon the riverbanks and in the prairie surrounding the Alamo. Unknown to the rebels, Santa Anna was personally reconnoitering the area on horseback to determine where to dig entrenchments and deploy resources.

"The enemy have been busily employed in encircling us in with entrenched encampments on all sides," Travis reported. Besides the battery of nine-pounders along the San Antonio, there were artillery and troops in La Villita, a suburb three hundred yards to the south that commanded the road to Goliad. Troops of cavalry were posted on the hills east of the Alamo and at the Casa Mata Antigua one thousand yards away on the road to Gonzales. These troops were to guard against any mass retreat by the defenders and to prevent any mass reinforcement from the eastern Texas colonies. As it turned out, they were not up to either task. Because of the immense terrain they had to guard, the Mexican lines remained porous and messengers passed freely back and forth from the Alamo.

A siege is always nerve-racking for those trapped within, but for the Anglo-Americans in the Alamo it was also a bewildering experience. They were psychologically unprepared to be garrison troops, much less the object of a siege. Their form of warfare tended to be aggressive and mobile, loosely regimented, and highly individualistic. They were masters at semiguerrilla warfare, which allowed them to engage and disengage the enemy rapidly and at will. Getting herded into an adobe pen where they were deprived of all offensive motion confounded them.

Crockett was plainly unhappy with the situation. Captain Dickinson's wife, Susannah, recounted that his discontent bordered on claustrophobia. "I heard him say several times during the eleven days of the siege: 'I think we had better march out and die in the open air. I don't like to be hemmed up.' "[31]

Without question, they were hemmed up. Each morning the rebels looked out from their walls and found the Mexicans a little closer than the day before. Piece by piece, the Mexican army wrapped gun and troop positions around the Alamo in a giant horseshoe. Only the north remained clear. Any reinforcements from Houston or Fannin were conceptually blocked on the east and south, while the logistics pipeline feeding more soldiers and supplies up from the Mexican interior was wide open.

The weather deteriorated on the third night. A cold norther rushed down through the mouth of this horseshoe and poured over the weak north wall. The temperature dropped to 39 degrees by morning and failed to climb above 60 for the next week. The rebels did the only thing they could. They built small cook fires and stayed warm. They whittled and gossiped, sang and cursed. Like ghosts, they hung upon the edge of reality. They waited.

=13=

WARMED BY THE sun, Susannah Dickinson sat against a stone wall, her infant, Angelina, sucking at one breast. The fifteen-year-old girl stared off across the muddy plaza, joyless and perplexed. She was a beautiful young woman with shining black hair and the kind of blue eyes that could stop a man in his tracks and had gotten many looks over the past weeks from these garrison bravos. Some of them, like Colonel Travis, had even begun to treat her with a chivalry and reverence that confused her. Part of it, of course, was the fact she was the sole white woman in the compound.

She was a woman of duty, and yet duty had given her few rewards. Dutifully she had followed her husband, Almeron, from the green womb of Tennessee to this all-consuming Texas. Dutifully she had trailed after him to San Antonio and handed up her baby and climbed onto the horse for their dash into the Alamo. She had been terrorized by the Ayish Bayou volunteers before Almeron brought her over from Gonzales last autumn. Now, according to Travis, she was on the verge of being raped by the Mexican army.

The norther had finally blown out and it was warmer today, though rain was threatening from the south. People were emerging from their dark, pungent rooms. Their flesh was blue from the mesquite and oak-wood smoke of their cook fires, and their eyes glowed with a preternatural whiteness. Every pair of pants, every skirt was crusted with mud. The men who normally bothered to shave had mostly quit. At the mouths of various hovels and doorways, men were searing pieces of fresh beef and Mexican women squatted by their coals, patting out tortillas or sampling greasy red chili sauce heating in earthenware pots. Back by the corral, a group of men had gathered to see about butchering the latest cow. Cattle bones, hides, and offal lay in a heap to one side.

During these lulls in the shelling, people avoided the open spaces of the plaza, hugging the walls in case more rounds came whistling down. They had lived through the last seven days of often intense bombardment amazingly well. Grenades and solid balls had dug the plaza to pieces, leaving it ravaged like a smallpox face. Some two hundred shots had rained down into the Alamo. But except for a horse, no one had been killed or even injured. Now a few men wandered across the plaza hunting out expended cannonballs that could be wiped off and fired back at the enemy.

Though a week of siege had produced no casualties whatsoever, the garrison's spirits were sinking. Travis and Bowie had put out the word that help was on the way . . . but where was it? And how could reinforcements hope to cut their way through the swelling encirclement? There were at least two thousand soldiers out there now.

Besides fear and wonderment, there were other insults to the garrison's psychology. The rebels had been treated to nightly music by Mexican military bands, interrupted every now and then by false assaults. Mexican troops would shout and light off their artillery as if attacking. After a week of invaded sleep, the rebels were running on bare nerves.

The Anglo-Americans were reduced to irrelevance. Sometimes they managed to sting the Mexicans but no matter what they did, the garrison troops never diminished the flood of soldiers all around them. To break the monotony and imbue themselves with some small suggestion of menace, the rebels threw curses and an occasional Comanche bullet toward the campfires flickering in the distance. "These men," one Mexican soldier remembered, "were defiant to the last. From the windows and parapets of the low buildings, when taunted by the Mexican troops, they shouted back their defiance in the liveliest terms."[1]

On a fairly recreational basis the men also sniped at Mexican soldiers who trespassed within their rifle range. One frustrated man in particular caught the Mexicans' attention. "A tall man with flowing hair was seen firing from the same place on the parapet during the entire siege," remembered Capt. Rafael Soldano. "He wore a buckskin suit and a cap all of a pattern entirely different from those worn by his comrades. This man would kneel or lie down behind the low parapet, rest his long gun and fire, and we all learned to keep at a good distance when he was seen to make ready to shoot. He rarely missed his mark and when he fired he always rose to his feet and calmly reloaded his gun seemingly indifferent to the shots fired at him by our men. He had a strong, resonant voice and often railed at us, but as we did not understand English we could not comprehend the import of his words further than that they were defiant."

Captain Soldano even went so far as to embellish this recollection (ten years after the fact) by adding, "This man I later learned was known as

'Kwockey.' "[1] Ever since, Alamo fans have leapt to the conclusion that this deadeye sniper in buckskins was David Crockett. The Mexican captain did indeed mean to suggest this character was Crockett, for he was being interviewed by an Anglo-American at the close of the Mexican War in 1848 and knew by then precisely what an American audience wanted to hear. But unfortunately for the Davy-addicts, the sniper whom Soldano described could not possibly have been Crockett. Crockett did not have flowing hair, he was not wearing buckskins, and his position was at the log palisade by the chapel, not a low parapet behind which he could kneel or lie down.

The long-range sniper in buckskin could have come from anywhere in the South, where marksmanship enjoyed ritual status.[2]

But, then, marksmanship was a national obsession distinguishing the New World Anglo-Saxon from almost every other class of human being in the world. It was considered a fundamental skill not only to the individual hunter but to national security. Honing a sharp eye became a patriotic duty. One advertisement for a shooting match made it clear: "Let us practice sharp-shooting and encourage excellence by offering competent rewards to those who are eminent, until we not only astonish the natives on the other side of the waters, but show them that it may be dangerous to stand in battle array before western militia, who, in the heat of action cannot only hit a man aimed at, but place the ball on the very spot chosen, even the eye."[3] One can be certain that whoever the Alamo sniper was, he probably had an appreciative bunch lounging near him laying bets on his prowess.

Legends would grow about Anglo-American marksmanship and the long rifle at the Alamo. In fact there were few high-quality long rifles at the Alamo. Austin had earlier complained that "we have more men than guns,"[4] and the quality of the firearms available tended toward the laughable. Noah Smithwick, the journeyman blacksmith, threw some light on the sorry state of weaponry in the Anglo-American colonies when he said, "I fixed up many an old gun that I wouldn't have picked up in the road. . . ."[5] The rebels besieging San Antonio in the autumn had actually envied the Mexicans' British-surplus weaponry dating back to 1809.[6] Depending on the gunpowder used and how it was used, a musket could reliably throw a lead ball about fifty to seventy yards. A rifle of the type called Pennsylvania or Kentucky long rifle could reach twice that far, an advantage for the Alamo sniper, but of little use to shorter-range siege fighting. Austin recognized this—and Travis followed his lead—in ordering shotguns and yagers for the rebel cavalry.[7]

Much of the long rifle's quasi-religious glamour was born on January 8, 1815, the final day of the myth-laden Battle of New Orleans. There sharpshooting frontier riflemen (known to the British as "Dirty Shirts") tucked themselves behind cotton bales and mud parapets and supposedly obeyed Andrew Jackson's orders to aim just above the white leather crossbelts on the chest of the British uniform. "That leaden torrent no man on earth could face," one English lieutenant recalled.[8] Most likely it was the American artillery and grapeshot that shredded the British lines.[9] Even what credit American rifles could take for the victory was due less to marksmanship than simple volume of gunfire. Jackson had arranged his frontier troops in three constantly rotating lines that could pour gunfire into the advancing British. At the Alamo there were not enough men to compose even one full line, much less three rotating lines. A hundred or two hundred or three hundred more long rifles would not have made any difference to destiny as it quietly shaped for the defenders.

Travis knew this. He sent more messengers out, pleading for reinforcements. The garrison didn't see much of Travis. Now and then he materialized upon the walls or spoke to someone. Otherwise he kept an unremarkable profile.

The men occupied themselves as best they could. Crockett cursed their predicament, but he did not mutiny. There was no reason not to believe Travis's assurances that help was coming. Moreover, Crockett dearly loved the company of men, and these men took enormous solace in his company. According to one story passed down from the teenage girl Susannah, Crockett possessed some small talent with a fiddle. When the Mexican bombardment slackened, Crockett would pull out his fiddle and hold a musical competition with John McGregor, a thirty-four-year-old Scot who inflated his bagpipes to awful effect.[10] Between the two of them, enough music issued forth to distract, if not relax, the garrison for short patches of time.

Once in a while the rebels loaded up one or another of their cannons with a precious cannonball and shelled the occupied town. On March 1 a twelve-pound ball demolished part of the Yturri house on the Main Plaza where Santa Anna had established his headquarters. He was gone that afternoon, surveying the old mill site eight hundred yards north of the Alamo for the next artillery emplacement. But the attack confirmed in the Mexicans' minds that the rebels knew exactly where Santa Anna was staying. Only a few days earlier he had been fired upon by rebel riflemen.[11]

In fact, Travis and his men had no idea Santa Anna had even entered

San Antonio. Their sniper fire was happenstance and the shelling seems to have been random. It was not unlikely the rebels had simply undershot the San Fernando Church tower, which still showed the red flag and was in the same line of fire as the Yturri house. Their lucky hit upon the Mexican headquarters was just not lucky enough.

The Alamo's response to Mexican artillery diminished to infrequent, mostly symbolic cannon fire. There were plenty of targets, but the garrison was running low on ammunition. Travis requested large amounts of gun powder, cannon balls, and lead for musket balls.[12]

In all, sixteen couriers departed from the Alamo carrying Travis's alternately excited or angry—always desperate—requests for help. The man upon whom Travis pinned the most hope was Lt. James Bonham, the lofty, foursquare lawyer and radical from South Carolina who had helped form the Mobile Greys back in October. Arriving in Texas well ahead of the Greys, Bonham had offered his services to General Houston "without conditions. I shall receive nothing, either in the form of service pay, or lands, or rations."[13] He was strikingly handsome, strikingly principled, and strikingly melodramatic. Naturally he became a favorite of young men like Fannin and Travis, both of whom trusted and admired him. And so Travis had chosen the dashing rebel as his bridge to Fort Defiance in Goliad. He knew that if any man could impress upon Fannin the skeletal condition of the Alamo, it would be a mutually appreciated Southern gentleman and officer.

Bonham had barely returned from a futile delivery of requests to Fannin on February 23 when Santa Anna had invaded the town. On February 27 Travis dispatched Bonham to Goliad once again, this time stressing the urgent need for reinforcements. Fannin's garrison of 420 men was the closest, most sizable source of men in all of Texas, and Travis felt certain that if aid was going to arrive, it would come from Goliad. Everyday he looked out from the walls, scanning the horizon for Fannin's troops. From three sides all that met his eye was the spreading stain of more Mexican emplacements and battalions.

But to the north was open land—no town, no army of tiny soldiers. Nothing but cottonwoods and live oaks lining the serpentine river. North lay a landscape of hope, or at least a landscape empty of reasons not to hope. But then as the month of February closed out, Travis's heart sank lower still. There, inevitably, eight hundred yards to the north, he spied activity at the old mill upon a loop of the San Antonio River. Mexican engineers were directing soldiers in an attempt to cut off the water supply to the Alamo.[14] The attempt failed, but a battery was planted there, and then a sister battery was established equidistant from the Alamo on the east side of the *acequia*.[15] Now there was no direction free of the enemy. No room for fantasy. No hope of reinforcement.

Only then did the reinforcements arrive.

= 14 =

THE MOST RELUCTANT soldier in all of Texas was the thirty-two-year-old slave trader from Georgia named James F. Fannin, Jr. His partial education at West Point had elevated him high above the amateurs posing as officers throughout the Texas Revolution. The revolution exposed Fannin as an amateur too. But by then it was too late.

As captain of a Texas colonial militia called the Brazos Guard, Fannin had fought alongside Bowie at the thrilling Concepción battle in October. Then, like Travis, he had withdrawn from the muck and tedium of revolution and waited with civilian patience to be commissioned a colonel in the soldierless regular army. This he brokered into the title ''commander in chief,'' one of the four such chasing around in Texas. Virtually addicted to uncertainty, Fannin had joined then quit the Matamoros Expedition, and on February 12 had pulled back to the only bona fide presidio east of the Rio Grande, the fortress called Goliad.[1] Fannin had enough military training to see that if Goliad had been San Antonio's lifeline for the Mexican army, it would be for the Anglo-American army also. Once installed on the presidio, Fannin received orders from the spurious provisional council and *its* choice of governor *not* to retreat any further. He was urged to accomplish his original mission, which was the invasion of Matamoros. Just the same Fannin made himself comfortable at Goliad.

The presidio of Goliad contained three and a half acres surrounded by eight- to ten-foot walls. In this spacious and well-constructed outpost, Fannin presided over some 420 men, most of them volunteers from the States who had lunged toward Matamoros and then gotten cold feet after Sam Houston's cautionary lectures. Grant and Johnson, two other ''commanders in chief'' in the fractious rebel army, had chosen to meander westward with their Matamoros Expedition now composed of 60 hopelessly quixotic men. As for Houston, the fourth rebel commander in chief, he lacked any staff or men at all. In fact Houston was nowhere to be found. He was off with his Indians, arranging a treaty to guarantee they wouldn't ally with the invading Mexicans.

Soon after Mexican forces swarmed into San Antonio, a young rider named Johnson rode through the gates of the Goliad fortress with Travis and Bowie's urgent dispatch. "We have removed all our men into the Alamo, where we will make such resistance as is due to our honour, and that of the country, until we can get assistance from you, which we expect you to forward immediately. In this extremity, we hope you will send us all the men you can spare promptly."

Fannin did not hesitate. He instantly slapped together a relief expedition of 320 men, four cannons, and several wagonfuls of the few supplies and ammunition he had available. Only a few of his men still had shoes, and many were hard pressed to cover their nakedness. They had run out of coffee, corn, and salt—those barest of Southern essentials— and for several days had eaten nothing but fresh bull beef. Ammunition was embarrassingly low: only twelve cartridge rounds per man. And there were no saddle-broken horses to haul the cannons or wagons, much less to carry the men. Resorting to oxen for drayage, they discovered there were just enough to provide a yoke per vehicle. As if these deficits needed punctuation, a strong norther slammed the fort at nine o'clock that night. By dawn the temperature had dropped close to freezing.[2]

Fannin realized that his beggarly gang was in no shape to march cross-country and cut its way through an unknown number of enemy forces. "I am well aware that my present movement toward Bexar is any thing but a military one," he candidly admitted. "The appeal of Cols. Travis & Bowie cannot however pass unnoticed—particularly by troops now on the field—Sanguine, chivalrous Volunteers—Much must be risked to relieve the besieged—"[3]

Accordingly, Fannin and his ragged, barefoot little army set off into the teeth of bitterly cold weather to rescue Travis, Bowie, Crockett, and the Alamo a hundred miles away. Fannin left behind a company of one hundred soldiers to hold Goliad against any supplemental Mexican action.

The pathetic column managed to travel only two hundred yards before the first wagon broke down. Within a mile or so two more wagons broke down. The men wrestled their four cannons across the San Antonio River but were unable to bring over the ammunition wagon. To make matters worse, several of their oxen meandered off overnight.[4] It became clear the men would have to proceed on foot without supplies, without food, without artillery, and without winter clothing in order to join their comrades in the Alamo. Their closest hope of food lay seventy miles northwest at Juan Seguín's ranch, meaning they would be starved and emaciated by the time they got within striking distance of San Antonio.

While the half-naked men swung their arms back and forth to keep warm, Fannin held a war council with his officers in the bushes along the San Antonio's bank.

Just then a messenger came galloping up with fresh information. A shipment of long-awaited supplies had been landed at Matagorda Bay, but it lay unguarded. Without those supplies the whole rebel front line would vaporize like so much Texas mist. Fannin was already convinced that the Mexicans intended to attack Texas by sea as well as land. He now anticipated that the enemy might put ashore right upon the rebels' precious stockpile of food, clothing, and ammunition. The impromptu war council unanimously voted to suspend their rescue of the Alamo garrison and return to Goliad.[5]

No sooner had the bedraggled troops hauled their cannons and wagons back to the presidio than a courier arrived with chilling news. Fifty miles to the southwest at San Patricio, Col. Frank Johnson and about fifty men, out to catch wild horses to mount their wishful Matamoros expedition, had been surprised by the Mexican general José Urrea and one hundred cavalry.[6] At three o'clock in the morning, February 27, Urrea and his men materialized from a driving rain and surprised Johnson's tiny army of horse catchers. The Mexican cavalry killed sixteen rebels outright and captured twenty-four, including five Tejanos. Johnson and four others escaped into the darkness and reached the safety of a nearby *rancho* with tales of brutality and the execution of all the prisoners. Actually Urrea remanded eighteen of the prisoners to Matamoros, where they were sentenced to death but spared and eventually released. Nevertheless, when the Goliad garrison heard the bloodcurdling description of murdered prisoners, a blast of terror sliced through them.

"[Urrea] put the whole garrison under the command of Col Johnson to the sword," John Sowers Brooks wrote to his family. One of Fannin's most energetic aides, it was Brooks who invented the sixty-eight-barrel "volley gun" at Goliad. "Five of them have reached this place [the presidio], and they are probably all that have escaped. Capt. Pearson of the Volunteers, was killed with several others, after they had surrendered. The war is to be one of extermination. Each party seems to understand that no quarters are to be given or asked."[7]

Fannin and his men got busy. Only a few weeks earlier, Fannin had complained that his men were lazy ("I have been greatly troubled to get my militia to work or do any kind of garrison duty"[8]), but now the horrified garrison was stung into industry. Day and night they picketed, ditched, buttressed, and fine-tuned the fortress. To stymie any assault against the stone walls, they dug a trench four feet deep and six feet wide all around the presidio. Then, for good measure, they dug a second trench on the outside of the first trench. They enlarged the block house. And they installed Brooks's volley gun.

They arrested a number of local Tejanos, including an old priest, suspected of espionage. One was scheduled to be shot. Patrols were sent out for early warning, but the garrison continued to operate blindly, unsure of where or how numerous the enemy really was: One estimate held that fifteen hundred to three thousand were on the way, and that if the Alamo fell more thousands would descend upon Goliad. Nighttime guard duty turned deadly serious. When a guard was caught sleeping, Fannin decided to make an example of him. "He will be tried by a Court Martial," Brooks said. "The penalty is death." Andrew Jackson had done that once, setting a hungry, cantankerous young militiaman before a firing squad for an exceedingly minor infraction. The execution had worked wonders for discipline. Where one could not rule through persuasion, one ruled through might.

Certainly Fannin was not ruling through persuasion. By the time the Mexican army arrived, Fannin's command over his men was in trouble. "Our commander is Col. Fannin, and I am sorry to say the majority of the soldiers don't like him," a private named J. G. Ferguson wrote to his brother. "For what cause I don't know whether it is because they think he has not the interest of the country at heart or that he wishes to become great without taking the proper steps to attain greatness."[9]

Like Travis, Fannin's desire to lead outstripped his abilities. He was baldly ambitious and, at least to all appearances, had come to Texas to make huge profits. In civilian life he had traded in slaves, but even the slave-owning farmers in Texas seemed to find his practice of bringing over Africans unsavory. His position as commander at Goliad struck men as profiteering also. He mastered human beings for money. Now there were ugly rumors among the troops that he mastered human beings for his private ascension as well. Southerners understood slavery. Not one would knowingly brook being any man's slave, not even for the glory of Texas.

The disenchantment ran both ways. Fannin distrusted militias and he detested the militia habit of holding elections for officers. He saw the world in terms of obedience. He scorned the idea of a military organization entertaining any sort of democratic process. Democracy ruined hierarchies, and men like Fannin thrived on the insulation a hierarchy provided. Fannin's greatest failing was that he perceived too late that he was in command of a bunch of mercenaries, not a neatly organized regular army. He needed structure, and all that surrounded him was chaos. The situation called for a man who could, like a horsebreaker, bully and ride the chaos into a semblance of order. Fannin was a tame man in a wild storm surrounded by barbarians. As the north wind shrieked against his fortress walls and the Mexicans approached, he painfully realized that he was destined to fail. In all but body, he had already quit and left Goliad.

"Will you allow me to say to you . . . that I am not desirous of retaining the present, or receiving any other appointment in the army," he wrote to the council. "I did not seek, in any manner, the one I hold, and you well know, had resolved not to accept—and but for [several friends' advice] would have declined. I am a better judge of my military abilities than others, and if I am *qualified* to command an *Army, I have not found it out.* I well know I am a better *company* officer than most men *now* in Texas, and *might do with Regulars* &c, for a *Regiment.* But this does not constitute me a commander. I also *conscientiously* believe that we have *none fit* for it *now* in the country;—at least their talents have not been developed."[10]

In letter after letter, Fannin asked to be relieved of command. All he wanted now was to go home to his wife and children. To his credit, however, the star-crossed colonel was resolved to make his stand at Goliad . . . at least until the council furloughed him.

"I will never give up the ship, while there is a pea in the ditch," he declared on the day after his rescue expedition to the Alamo collapsed. "If I am whipped, it will be *well done*—and you may never expect to see me."

He was outraged that Texas was treating him and the Goliad garrison as ghost warriors who required no food, no shoes, and no gunpowder. Fannin lost his faith in the people he was fighting to save.

"They [the Anglo-Americans in Texas] have been called on and entreated to fly to arms and prevent what has now been done," he said on February 28. "I have but three citizens in the ranks, and tho' I have called on them for six weeks, not one yet arrived, and no assistance in bringing me provisions, even Texans refused me. I feel to indignant to say more about them. If I was honorably out of their service, I would never re-enter it. But I must now play a bold game—I will go the whole hog. If I am lost, be the censure on the right head, and may my wife & children and children's children curse the sluggards for ever. I am too mad, and too much to do—any thing but fight."[11]

Bonham had slipped loose of the Mexican siege and brought the latest word from Travis. He arrived at Goliad on the same day the garrison straggled back into its stony womb. His news was bad but also heartening.

"The Mexicans have made two successive attacks on the Alamo in both of which the gallant little garrison repulsed them with some loss," stated Fannin's aide, John Brooks. "Probably Davy Crokett [*sic*] 'grinned' them off."[12]

The Alamo still held. Travis and Bowie and Crockett had repulsed the Mexicans twice, meaning they could repulse them again and again. The legends of Anglo-Saxon superiority were actually bearing out. A band of 150 white men really could stop an army of 2,000 Mexicans. And if that few could deter so many from such an inferior defense as the Alamo, then how much safer and more secure were 420 men in the muscular presidio of Goliad. If the Alamo could hold, then Goliad was solid beyond question. Bonham's news went far toward diluting the terror of Colonel Johnson's rout at San Patricio.

Fannin recalculated his strength. Now that Urrea's troops were nearing, he dared not send three quarters of his garrison to rescue Travis. But sending half seemed feasible, especially if the Mexicans encountered other Texas roadblocks.

"If the division of the Mexican army advancing against this place has met any obstructions," Brooks said, "and it is probable they have been attacked by the Comanche Indians, and their advance much retarded by the loss of their horses and baggage, 200 men will be detached for the relief of Bexar. I will go with them. Our object will be to cut our way through the Mexican army into the Alamo, and carry with us such provisions as it will be possible to take on a forced march. Our united force will probably be sufficient to hold out until we are relieved by a large force from the Colonies."[12] Brooks estimated the two hundred crusaders would depart for the Alamo on March 2 or 3.

The men had every reason to be grim. Reduced to eating nothing but unsalted meat and to drinking cold water, they were becoming scarecrows. The Mexican army was reaching for their throats. They had no horses for long-range patrols. The weather was terrible. And there was the usual fracturing of egos among the rank-greedy officers. Yet the volunteers' mood was almost circuslike. "I have never seen such men as this army is composed of," said one soldier (B. H. Duval). "No man ever thinks of retreat, or surrender, they must be exterminated to be whipped—Nothing can depress their ardour—we are frequently for days without anything but Bull beef to eat, and after working hard all day could you at night hear the boys crowing, gobling, barking, bellowing, laughing and singing you would think them the happiest and best fed men in the world.''[13]

They were about to get their fight. Two hundred of them were going to dog it north to the Alamo and whip Mexicans in San Antonio. An equal number were going to stay here at the presidio and whip Mexicans in the trenches. At last the volunteers were going to have their adventure.

But while Fannin's men hooted and caterwauled themselves into a happy battle frenzy, Fannin refused to smile. Like Travis, a hundred miles to the north, he fell into a depression that isolated him from his men. Like Travis, he kept waiting for hundreds of heavily armed colonists to appear from the mesquite and oak forests surrounding his fortress.

"Hoping for the best, being prepared for the worst," he growled. "I am in a devil of a bad humor."[14]

"This is not imaginary," Governor Smith cried out to the colonists on a nearly freezing Thursday in San Felipe de Austin. That same morning Launcelot Smithers, a young rider who had left the Alamo on Sunday afternoon for Gonzales and then volunteered to relay this second dispatch further still, had thundered into town with Travis's appeal "To the People of Texas & all Americans in the world."

Governor Smith responded. He had no army to dispatch to the Alamo. He had no money with which to buy or send arms and ammunition. He had no real authority. But he did what he could do. He wrote some propaganda of his own.

"I call upon you as an officer, I implore you as a man," he called out to the colonists, "to fly to the aid of your besieged countrymen and not permit them to be massacred by a mercenary foe. I slight none! The call is upon ALL who are able to bear arms, to rally without one moment's delay, or in fifteen days the heart of Texas will be the seat of war."[15]

William F. Gray, the hustling Virginian land hunter, was on his way to Washington-on-the-Brazos for the upcoming constitutional convention, and witnessed in San Felipe the reaction to this first word about the Alamo. "The people now begin to think the wolf has actually come at last," he said.[16]

The colonists were shocked, for most predictions had placed Santa Anna's earliest arrival in March or April. And some prepared to march for the Alamo, among them Col. Sidney Sherman and his band of fifty-two mercenaries from Kentucky. At the age of thirty-one years, Sherman had sold his cotton-bagging plant and sunk the money into outfitting a

company of volunteers bound for the Texas Revolution. He was trouble
from the day he arrived. Though they arrived scarcely twenty-four hours
before the election of convention delegates, his company bullied the
election officials into allowing them to vote. He and his mercenaries were
destined to commit some of the worst Anglo-American atrocities of the
entire war at San Jacinto.[17] But now, when he heard that the Alamo was
under siege, Sherman instantly aimed his bunch toward Gonzales to try
and relieve Travis.

For the most part, however, the colonists in San Felipe and elsewhere
reacted to Travis's plea with much the same energy they had exhibited all
winter. They stayed put. To the naked eye there was little to indicate that
a war was even close. The farmers were out on their farms. The lawyers
were still jockeying for political office. There were still two governors
claiming (provisional) supremacy, and Smith and the council were still
brawling about treason and power. Semitropical diseases, especially malaria, continued to knock men down with regularity, but no epidemics of
the cholera proportion were loose that season. The land speculators were
abundant and industriously sniffing out juicy titles, stockpiling their
claims. Down along the coast and up the slender river channels, slavers
were landing more African labor than ever before. "About fifty of those
poor wretches are now here," Gray reported, "living out of doors, like
cattle. They are all young, the oldest not 25, the youngest, perhaps, not
more than 10; boys and girls huddled together. They are diminutive,
feeble, spare, squalid, nasty, and beastly in their habits. Very few exhibit
traits of intellect. . . . An old American negro stood over [a killed beef]
with a whip, and lashed them off like so many dogs to prevent their
pulling the raw meat to pieces. This is the nearest approach to cannibal-
ism that I have ever seen."[18] In short, despite Santa Anna's approach, it
was business as usual in Texas.

Until Travis's dispatch arrived, the most exciting event by far was the
constitutional convention about to take place in Washington-on-the-
Brazos. This Texan Philadelphia was, Gray said, a disgusting place. "It
is laid out in the woods; about a dozen wretched cabins or shanties
constitute the city; not one decent house in it, and only one well defined
street, which consists of an opening cut out of the woods. The stumps still
standing. A rare place to hold a national convention in. They will have to
leave it promptly to avoid starvation."[19]

The elected delegates were riding in from all points, and all held an
opinion about the Mexican siege of the Alamo. A few wanted to postpone

the convention and go fight, but cooler heads argued that Texas could not survive any more provisional government. In fact, Travis's message elicited more hot air than actual aid. "Some are going," Gray noted, then added with disgust, "but the *vile rabble* here cannot be moved."[20]

Word about the Alamo siege seemed to have stalled altogether in Washington-on-the-Brazos. Launcelot Smithers was becalmed, too penniless to carry the alarm any further. For two days he waited, then several locals thought to take up a contribution, to which Gray donated a dollar. While Smithers plunged eastward through the cold drizzle, the delegates jammed into an unfinished house without doors or windows. Some thoughtful soul stretched cotton cloth across the glassless windows to cut the cold wind. On March 1 the convention was called to order.

There were fifty-nine delegates. Three quarters of them were natives of U.S. slave states, a guarantee that there would be no talk of manumission. Only one delegate had been a member of Austin's original settlers in 1821 and only ten had lived in Texas more than six years. Almost one third of the delegates had resided in Texas less than six months. In Velasco's election for delegates, eighty-eight men had voted, of whom forty-seven had been in Texas less than a week.

There were only two native Texans, both from San Antonio: Francisco Ruiz and Antonio Navarro. The one other native Mexican—who was not a native Tejano—was the cosmopolitan revolutionary and land speculator, Lorenzo de Zavala. It was surprising that any Mexicans had been permitted to participate at all. A few months earlier, Governor Smith had vetoed a public ordinance providing for the election of delegates because it had allowed all Mexicans opposed to a central government to vote, "as well as all free white men." It was Smith's belief that all Tejanos near San Antonio were suspect. "I consider it bad policy to fit out or trust Mexicans in any matter connected with our government," he said. "I am well satisfied that we will in the end find them inimical and treacherous."[21]

By far the most popular delegate was a bedraggled giant in buckskin pants and a Mexican poncho who looked like he'd barely survived his latest hangover. "Gen'l Houston's arrival has created more sensation than that of any other man," Gray recorded. "He is evidently the people's man, and seems to take pains to ingratiate himself with everybody. He is much broken in appearance, but has still a fine person and courtly manners; will be forty-three years old on the 3rd of March—looks older."[20]

On the first day of nation building, the convention elected a president and secretary, appointed a committee to write up a declaration of independence for the Republic of Texas, and then fell into their old brawling over the powers of Governor Smith versus Governor Robinson and the council.

Next morning, the Texas declaration of independence was read to the assembly at large. It was lifted wholesale from the U.S. Declaration of Independence and endowed with as many complaints as could be invented overnight. Among the rebels' peeves were the absence of trial by jury and of a public system of education, the "invasion" of Texas by a mercenary army, the attempted arrest of War Dogs like Travis and the imprisonment of "one of our citizens" Stephen Austin, the stationing of military troops in Texas, the dissolving of the Coahuila y Tejas legislature, and government "by a hostile majority, in an unknown tongue."

The complaints, as already noted, were absurd. Mexico was already introducing trial by jury into Texas; under Mexican law, public education was not the federal government's responsibility; to say that Mexico was "invading" Mexico was ludicrous. And it was grotesque that a host of squatters, land speculators, and short-term colonists should expect the Mexican government to grant them government conducted in the English language. Mexico had not forced the Anglo-Americans to come to Texas. Mexico had most certainly *not* promised those who did come "that they should continue to enjoy that constitutional liberty and republican government to which they had been habituated in the land of their birth, the United States of America." To the contrary, those settlers in Texas who were legitimate had pledged themselves to a set of regulations extended by a whole new authority.

In short, the delegates built a house of cards. Then, before a breeze of fact might nudge it into collapse, they instantly voted on their delicate fabrication. With a haste that astonished Gray, the document "was received by the house, committed to a committee of the whole, reported without amendment and unanimously adopted, all within less than one hour. It underwent no discipline, and no attempt was made to amend it." Independence would have taken even less time to declare, but Houston couldn't resist making a speech about it.

Because there were no printing presses in Washington-on-the-Brazos, assistant clerks were assigned to handwrite copies of the document to be circulated in various points in Texas. A copy was sent across the Sabine to the United States so that a thousand copies could be printed for public consumption.

Now that the pro forma declaration of independence had been accepted, the convention turned itself to the matter of creating a government with laws. But first a motion was made that the members should strap on their weapons for the remaining sessions of the convention. The motion failed. Santa Anna still seemed far away.

That night a third express arrived from the Alamo, dated a week earlier. Travis and his men had survived bombardment and an assault. So far they had sustained no killed in action. The convention learned that Colonel Fannin had started on foot toward San Antonio with most of his men. "It is believed the Alamo is safe," Gray wrote of the general opinion.[22]

On March 3, the declaration of independence was read again and signed by all present. The Republic of Texas was now official. Next day Houston was appointed commander in chief of its army, and on March 6 he saddled up and left for the seat of war. He expected to find seven hundred men in Gonzales, among them Fannin's troops, armed and howling to be unleashed.[23] He meant to rescue the Alamo garrison and then retreat. Houston did not believe in forts and stationary garrisons. By pulling his forces back into eastern Texas, he planned to pull the Mexican army farther and farther from its source so that the Mexican logistics would fail. Meanwhile Houston could deploy his untrained fighters for a mobile guerrilla war in the swamps and forests close to their suppliers in the United States. And, Houston fervently hoped, the United States would send American troops across the Sabine. It was a dangerous strategy, for it required battling the Mexicans while baiting the Americans. But it was no more dangerous than the piecemeal chaos that was passing for a strategy at the moment.

On Saturday evening the enemy arrived in Washington-on-the-Brazos—in the form of two prisoners under the guard of a New Orleans Grey named Capt. William Cooke. Fannin was charging the two Mexicans with spying and had sent them to Goliad for safekeeping. The conventioneers took a close look at what they were up against and saw only the same men they'd already fought. Gray regarded them as harmless specimens. "One of them is an old priest named José Antonio Valdez," he said, "a miserable, meagre, squalid looking creature, who is said to be a very immoral character, and yet a man of considerable property. The other is a young man named Eugenio Hernandez, a lieutenant in the late army of Cós, and on parole."[22]

However desolate the prisoners looked, their keeper looked even worse. Captain Cooke's ragged wardrobe prompted Gray and another gentleman to donate their spare clothes to the destitute soldier.

As Houston galloped west toward Gonzales and a seven-hundred-man army that didn't exist, the convention moved along, item by item. The delegates had slammed through their declaration of independence in record time, but now progress was mired in arguments and politicking. "What with the advance of the Mexicans on one side and the Indians on the other, and the organization of a new government, this Convention would seem to have enough on their hands to do," Gray observed. "Yet they get on slowly. The evil spirit of electioneering is among them for the *high offices* in prospect. And the land quest also requires much *log rolling,* to make it suit the existing interests or selfish views of members."[24]

The land quest was Gray's sole reason for being at the convention. An astute and handsome gentleman-lawyer from Virginia, Gray had come to Texas in late 1835 as a personal agent for two Washington, D.C. land speculators, Thomas Green and Albert T. Burnley. In the contemporary parlance Gray was a land hunter, and he hunted tirelessly. His journal notes throughout the convention were interlarded with all the latest prices, quantities, bargains, and opportunities for real estate as speculators readied to scoop up the best of Texas. The trick was to withhold actual purchase until the self-declared Republic of Texas truly won its independence.

After failing to get himself appointed secretary of the convention, Gray simply hung around observing. His probing interrogations finally made delegates nervous and it was suspected he was a spy and that Texas real estate was going into speculators' pockets. He was and it was. Land deals among the delegates—including the Mexican delegates—were fast and furious as the true scope of profits became clearer.[25]

Gray's central mission was to press the rebel government to accept a $200,000 loan at extraordinarily bad terms for Texas. The lenders were required to extend only 10 percent of the loan, that is, $20,000, until the terms were solidified. Their loan was to be redeemed in land at $.50 per acre, that is, 400,000 acres. At the time public lands in the United States were selling for $1.25 per acre, making the Texas redemption worth roughly $500,000. Furthermore, the lenders were to receive a premium of 32 leagues, or 141,696 acres, worth another $70,000 (at $.50 per acre).[26] Midway through the convention a body of delegates began to object to the terms of the loan. Gray groaned, "I learn there will be serious opposition to [the loan], arising from the wretched selfishness of members, who regard the terms of the loan as too favorable to the lenders, the land being *too low,* in their opinion. To national faith and credit they are insensible. I begin to find myself uncomfortably situated here."[24]

Nevertheless, Gray stuck it out. He had no choice. The days blurred as delegates debated and motioned and wrangled, trying to hammer together a constitution. Every now and then various land questions arose, including the loan approval. "The President went out of his way this afternoon to give the loan a blow," Gray said. "He distinctly pronounced it a bad bargain, said it should be confirmed in order to preserve the public faith, but hoped no more such would be made." Still, opposition to the terms persisted.

Some 1,100 leagues, or 4.9 million acres of land, had been granted by the corrupt Coahuila y Tejas legislature in 1834–35 to John Mason and others. James Bowie had helped distribute packets of this land grant to yet other speculators. To the distress and loathing of Gray and the other land speculators attending the convention, the delegates now declared the Mason grant null and void.[27] That seemed to bode ill for the Texas loan.

As the days passed, some members went home, some saddled up and left for the war theater. Men got drunk and the convention began showing signs of erosion. "Great confusion and irregularity prevailed in the Convention to-day," Gray reported. "The President has lost all dignity and all authority."

Disgusted delegates liquored up and slandered one another. Like victims of cabin fever, they were getting crazy and rambunctious. Gray recorded that delegates had turned adolescent. "The proceedings of the house to-night were disorderly in the extreme, and boyish. Nearly all the members were sometimes on the floor at once, some calling *'question,'* some laughing and clapping, etc. The President, by his manifest partiality, egotism and alarm, has lost the respect of the house. He frequently argues questions from the chair."[28]

On the morning of March 6, another dispatch arrived from Travis. It had been carried out of the Alamo by El Colorado Smith, who had crawled out through Mexican lines on his hands and knees. The letter was dated just three days earlier and was addressed directly to the convention. Travis described the tightening siege and again begged for aid. He had despaired of Fannin ever coming with reinforcements. "I will, however, do the best I can under the circumstances; and I feel confident that the determined valor and desperate courage, heretofore exhibited by my men, will not fail them in the last struggle; and although they may be sacrificed to the vengeance of a Gothic enemy, the victory will cost the enemy so dear, that it will be worse for him than defeat. I hope your honorable body will hasten on reinforcements, ammunitions and provisions to our aid so soon as possible.''

Travis requested rifle and cannon powder, lead, and cannonballs, and repeated his belief that the Alamo would decide the revolution once and for all. ''The power of Santa Anna is to be met here or in the colonies; we had better meet them here than to suffer a war of devastation to rage in our settlements. A blood red banner waves from the church of Bejar, and in the camp above us, in token that the war is one of vengeance against rebels; they have declared us as such; demanded that we should surrender at discretion, or that this garrison should be put to the sword. Their threats have no influence on me or my men, but to make all fight with desperation and that high-souled courage that characterizes the patriot, who is willing to die in defence [sic] of his country's liberty and his own honor.''[29]

After that, the convention members heard nothing more from the Alamo. Daily they remarked on the silence. ''No news yet from the Alamo, and much anxiety is felt for the fate of the brave men there,'' Gray said.

The weather turned warm but gloomy, and the delegates braced for rain. A friendly wind blew from the Gulf. Gray looked at the sky and saw signs that winter was breaking apart. ''The wild geese are mustering for the North,'' he said. ''Large flocks are seen flying over, but in very militia-like style. They have not yet got drilled into a regular echelon form of march.''[28]

Another week passed. Still there was no word from the Alamo.

= 15 =

OLD HICKORY FUMED. He wanted Texas. But Texas was slippery, like a root that kept changing into a snake. One moment he seemed to have it tight in his hands, the next it was sliding right out of his arthritic fingers. His unprincipled minister, Anthony Butler, was still in Mexico City crudely trying to bribe and bully the Mexicans into selling Texas. And then many weeks before Stateside Americans learned that Santa Anna had thrown an army across the Rio Grande, a rumor coursed through Washington, D.C. that the Mexican minister finally wished to sell Texas.[1] True or not—and it was not—Jackson felt certain Mexico would sell at some point. With time it wouldn't even matter if Mexico took payment, for the Anglo-American population in Texas was steadily reaching strategic proportions. Soon the fruit would ripen and drop from its branch directly into the American basket. All Jackson needed was time. Then, quite suddenly, Texas revolutionized. Jackson saw nothing but doom.

When Stephen Austin wrote to Jackson requesting an open show of support for the revolution, Old Hickory snorted derisively. Despite his warrior instincts, the President took his office seriously. He was not some common filibuster and he knew he could not simply reach out and grab a territory, not from a nation-state recognized by European powers. There were, at the very least, certain appearances that needed to be kept up. "The writer does not reflect that we have a treaty with Mexico, and our national faith is pledged to support it," he said. "The Texians before they took the step to declare themselves Independent, which has aroused and united all Mexico against them, ought to have pondered well—it was a rash and premature act, our neutrality must be faithfully maintained."[2]

The one thing Jackson could not afford was a war with Mexico. Any such war risked antagonizing the British and French and Spanish, all of whom were waiting for a brash U.S. action to justify their own intrusion into the region. As a sometimes berserk and always headstrong general, Jackson had trampled international relations. But now that he was Pres-

ident, Jackson needed to act responsibly. He rejected Austin's appeal for
U.S. government money and soldiers. He instructed federal district attorneys in the South to be alert for mercenary recruitment. He spoke of
neutrality and pretended diplomacy. He appeared aloof. But Jackson was
not about to let Texas escape his grip.

On January 23, just as Santa Anna's army was massing along the Rio
Grande for its push eastward, Jackson turned loose yet another of his
peculiar agents. This was an apparently senile general named Edmund
Pendleton Gaines, an old war chum whose lust for Texas rivaled Jackson's hard desire. Ten years younger than his sixty-nine-year-old President, Gaines looked remarkably like Jackson, and their past held more in
common than it did not. Both were Southerners, both had practiced law
on the frontier, both were ferocious Indian fighters, and both had distinguished themselves in the War of 1812. Most important, as military
commanders both had a habit of extrapolating from their orders. Given
the proper circumstances, neither was afraid to overstep his authority and
take matters into his own hands.[3]

In modern terms, Jackson needed an agent willing to commit an
illegal, off-the-shelf operation without explicitly being ordered to do so.
In General Gaines, he had his man.

Gaines comprehended the use and abuse of political language. He had
watched Jackson commit outrageous acts in Florida and then get sainted
with double-speak like "defensive acts of hostility." He had seen how an
extraordinary breach of conduct could be rewarded with extraordinary
fame and rank. He could read between the lines of an order and decipher
the will behind the words. Also, having arrested and testified against
Aaron Burr for his dreams of empire in 1807, Gaines understood both the
machinery of frontier conquest and the necessity for discretion.

And Gaines knew Texas. His cousin James Gaines, born a year earlier
in the same Culpeper County, Virginia, had filibustered on the ill-fated
Magee Expedition of 1812–13, had emigrated to Texas in the early 1820s,
and was serving as a delegate to the constitutional convention at
Washington-on-the-Brazos. He not only signed the declaration of independence, he helped draft it.

In short, General Gaines had the proper portfolio for the job Jackson
wished to see done. He had a sense of international politics, appreciated
the delicacies of empire and opportunity, and had elite insights into the
Texas situation.

"Sir," read his orders, issued January 23, "I am instructed, by the
President, to request that you would repair to some proper position near

the western frontier of the State of Louisiana, and there assume the personal command of all the troops of the United States who are or may be employed in any part of the region adjoining the Mexican boundary. . . . Public considerations demand the exercise of great discretion and experience."[4]

The instructions stressed that the United States was an entirely neutral neighbor, and that the troubles in Texas were to be confined to Texas. If either of the feuding parties tried to cross the border under arms, they were to be resisted with military force. Gaines was also instructed to help enforce any neutrality laws *if* called upon by local civil authorities. Since local authorities, including at least one U.S. district attorney, were energetically aiding mercenaries in reaching Texas, it was unlikely any would be calling upon Gaines.

Toward making perfectly clear, if not credible, the stationing of Gaines and the 6th Regiment of the U.S. Army along the Sabine River, the orders further explained the thirty-third article of a U.S.-Mexican treaty. According to this article, the United States was required to prevent all Indian activities that originated in the United States and were harmful to Mexico. This was a blatant smoke screen. The only people in Texas worried about Indian trouble were the Anglo-Americans. The Mexican army was fully capable of taking care of itself. By citing this article, however, the Jackson administration was able to justify massing troops along the eastern frontier of Mexico. At best, Jackson was playing at brinkmanship. At worst, by loading the 6th Regiment with a man like General Gaines, Jackson was preparing to launch an invasion of Mexico.

The menacing buildup of U.S. troops across the Sabine River was no secret. Well before Gaines and the 6th Regiment approached Louisiana, the *New Orleans Bee* published the story of their coming, and the Mexican government read about it. In Mexico City, the Mexican secretary of state sent a letter from the Palace of National Government across to the U.S. legation, requesting an explanation for the troop buildup.[5] The U.S. minister, Anthony Butler, responded by spitting in the Mexican eye.

He found it mysterious that the Mexican government might be concerned about a troop buildup. "It seems strange," he said, "that the present movement—a military movement completely within the ordinary regulations of exchange of commands, so usual in our army . . . should have created suspicions and alarm."[6]

When General Gaines received his orders to proceed to the Mexican border, he was in Florida, wrapping up the second Seminole war. He took his time crossing the southern states to Fort Jessup at Natchitoches. By the time he got there, he had interpreted his mission with the sort of breadth and creativity Jackson had hoped for.

"Should I find any disposition on the part of the Mexicans or their red allies to menace our frontier," he wrote to Secretary of War Lewis Cass, "I cannot but deem it to be my duty not only to hold the troops of my command in readiness for action in defence [*sic*] of our slender frontier, but to anticipate their lawless movements, by crossing our supposed or imaginary national boundary, and meeting the savage marauders wherever to be found in their approach towards our frontier."

Supposed or imaginary national boundary: Jackson could not have dreamed up a more pugnacious approach to geopolitics. Gaines also took it upon himself to call out various militias along the way. His goal was to amass an army of eight thousand to twelve thousand soldiers, both regulars and volunteers. He was preparing an outright invasion of Mexico.

The beauty of all this was that Gaines was at least a week or more distant from the fastest communication between Washington, D.C. and the frontier. In the gap, Gaines could accomplish enormous destruction before the President could catch the leash and pull his war dog back. Gaines was aware of this.

"Should I err in this view of this subject [the impending invasion]," Gaines wrote, "I shall be gratified to receive the views of the President, to which I shall scrupulously adhere."[7]

Jackson had chosen the right man.

=16=

I F NOT FOR a rainstorm, the Alamo probably would have fallen on George Washington's birthday while Travis's garrison lay drunk. Only the day before, at 1:45 P.M. on his own birthday, February 21, Santa Anna had reached the Medina River. At around five o'clock the rest of General Ramírez y Sesma's fifteen-hundred-man Vanguard Brigade had caught up with him, but before they could cross the river and set up camp, a heavy downpour soaked the column to the bone. And the storm swelled the river, which put an early crossing next morning out of the question. That, in turn, brought Santa Anna's breakneck forward momentum to a halt, and he gave his troops the day off.

The brigade spent much of February 22 clearing the wet powder from their guns and drying their clothes in the clear sunshine. While they rested and ate freshly killed beef, Santa Anna accepted that the Anglo-Americans knew of his army's presence by then. How could they not? Certainly the local Tejanos knew, for a number of them visited the troops camping among the oak and cottonwoods.[1] Among these visitors was an officer in the local presidio company, Lt. Manuel Menchaca, who updated Santa Anna on rebel activities in town.[2] As a result, Santa Anna ordered General Ramírez y Sesma to mount a high-speed cavalry unit of sixty chasseurs upon the best horses in camp and race toward San Antonio.

Had Ramírez y Sesma acted boldly that night, the Mexican army would have cut the Alamo off from its defenders. Almost to a man the Anglo-Americans were in town across the San Antonio River, partying to celebrate Washington's birthday. The fortress held only ten men.[3] There would have been no siege, no battle, and possibly no bloodshed.

Unfortunately Santa Anna chose the wrong man to act as his lightning bolt. A fellow officer castigated Ramírez y Sesma as "a timid and irresolute commander, dilatory in his judgment and apathetic in his movements. . . ."[4] Instead of swooping down upon the partying rebels, Ramírez y Sesma meekly halted on the back side of the Alazan hills. It was the commander in chief himself who led the army down into town and began the siege. As they descended the long slope, Santa Anna had much time to watch the Anglo-Americans scamper for cover like jack-rabbits. Passing the Campo Santo cemetery, which he would soon fill with bodies, Santa Anna entered town unopposed.

History reads that the siege impeded Santa Anna's pell-mell progress, that if not for the Alamo the Mexican army would have surged across Texas and crushed the Anglo-Americans as they slept in their colonies. The purpose of this view is to give value to the waste of Anglo-American life at the Alamo and to make sense of Travis's weird fanaticism. But the Alamo siege did not arrest the Mexican advance, nor did it spell Santa Anna's defeat. The Alamo did not command some narrow mountain pass through which the Mexican army had to pass. The Alamo garrison was just a nuisance. Too few in numbers and too poorly equipped, the Alamo rebels were incapable of cutting the enemy supply train or attacking the Mexican army. With very little manpower, the Mexicans could monitor the sprawling old mission and starve the garrison into submission.

The reason Santa Anna paused in San Antonio was elementary. He had to wait for his army to catch up. On the day he entered San Antonio, General Gaona and the sixteen-hundred-man 1st Infantry brigade were just arriving at Presidio de Rio Grande, two hundred miles behind.[5] Gaona was hauling along the expedition's largest pieces of artillery, two twelve-pounder cannons. While on the march, Santa Anna had predicted his army would occupy San Antonio by March 2.[6] He had reached it on February 23. For all intents and purposes, Santa Anna was a full week ahead of schedule. Down south, his exquisitely capable General Urrea was consolidating the Gulf crescent, sweeping away all resistance. Santa Anna's forceful and timely approach had largely exposed the Anglo-American "revolution" for what it was, a land grab, just one more Anglo-Saxon invasion of Hispanic territory. Not only Tejanos, but also Irish (that is, Catholic) colonists from San Patricio would contribute both information and fighters to Santa Anna's army.[7] In short, even while he was stationary, Santa Anna was in motion. Every day he waited in San Antonio, his army got larger and more war materiel arrived. Within the month, his army (plus camp followers) would quintuple the Hispanic presence in Texas to over eleven thousand, a temporary increase that Santa Anna wished to make permanent.

Santa Anna spoke at times about turning Texas into a dead zone. According to de la Peña, the general said, "It should be razed to the ground, so that this immense desert . . . might serve as a wall between Mexico and the United States."[8] But as they passed through Texas on their demolition mission, Mexican officers and soldiers saw that this was a place of beauty and prosperity. They became enthusiastic about the idea of establishing military colonies in Texas, and several officers criticized Santa Anna for treating Texas only as a geopolitical Alamo, a fortress possessed by unfriendly spirits.

Santa Anna himself was one of the most vigorous proponents of recolonizing Texas with military men once the Anglo-Americans were expelled. In a freewheeling letter to his secretary of war, Tornel, he proposed that colony leaders be drawn from Mexico's military and civil service, and that they be required to draw colonists from among Mexicans. "In any case," he said, "I am firmly convinced that we ought not to risk allowing either Anglo-American or European colonists to remain on the frontier, much less along our coastline."[9]

Santa Anna proposed granting land bounties to Mexican officers and soldiers who wished to stay in Texas after the campaign ended, giving out a square league for staff officers, half a league for subordinates, and a *solar* (173 acres) for common soldiers . . . units that were considerably smaller than the generous grants colonists had been enjoying up to then.[10] One of his officers, Col. Francisco Gonzalez Pavón, proposed forming a new colony with his Tampico regiment. The energetic man went so far as to corral three hundred Anglo-American dairy cows as part of his colony herd, and through the remainder of fighting and marching he would "fuss and curse" if told to release another cow to the army's butchers.[11]

One thing was certain, Anglo-Americans were to be driven out of Mexican territory. Even Anglo-Americans who had remained loyal to Mexico would be removed to the interior of Mexico, away from the magnetic force of the United States. As for the actual combatants, Santa Anna was adamant.

"I neither ask for nor give quarter," he repeatedly told his staff in San Antonio. He stated it verbally and wrote it in official documents. He enunciated it publicly for he wanted the public—Mexican, as well as Anglo-American—to hear him. The rebels must die. Not one should survive.[12] In case there remained any question, he reiterated his stance while his cannons spoke against the Alamo walls in late February. *"En esta guerra sabe vd. que no hay prisioneros"* (As you know, in this war there are no prisoners).[13] He even authorized one aide to pistol-whip him if he deviated from this resolution.[14]

Many years of revolutionary violence had inured Mexicans to the habit of shooting prisoners of war. The practice had become so embedded that one revolutionary leader, Nicolás Bravo, became practically a saint for his refusal to shoot a single prisoner of war, even after the royalists executed his own father.[15] Quite apart from the horrific Mexican custom, there was an American precedent for executing war captives: Andrew Jackson. Acting as a *caudillo* during his invasion of Spanish Florida in 1818, Jackson had summarily ordered one British subject shot, and another hanged. Secretary of State John Quincy Adams had defended the executions, quoting international law that declared that a commander contending with an inhuman enemy "may take the lives of some of his prisoners and treat them as his own people have been treated." Adams had gone a step further, stating that "the justification of these principles is found in their salutary efficacy for terror and example."[16]

Despite the legal and historical precedents, several of Santa Anna's officers strenuously objected to a policy of killing prisoners of war in Texas.[17] There were practical reasons not to execute prisoners of war, chief among them that the enemy tended to execute their captives if you executed yours. General Filisola also pointed out that prisoners of war could be used on public works to help defray the expenses of war.[18]

Though Filisola argued against execution, he could not help but argue for it, too. Old habits were hard to put down, particularly in a conflict like the one in Texas. "The war in Texas was exceptional," Filisola would later reflect, "it was not a civil war; nor was it a war of one nation against another. In it the thief was fighting against the owner, the murderer against his benefactor, and nothing was more natural than that these hordes of assassins and thieves should be done away with." In addition, the Mexican army was unequipped to treat its own wounded and sick, to say nothing of feeding, housing, and guarding prisoners of war.[19]

At various staff meetings, General Castrillón and Colonel Almonte argued to spare prisoners, voicing "principles regarding the rights of men, philosophical and human principles which did them honor."[20] But Santa Anna always overruled them, citing the example of General Arredondo. Under Arredondo, Santa Anna had first come to Texas and crushed Anglo-American rebels. Arredondo had executed hundreds of men at the Medina River and in San Antonio, after which the 1812–13 filibuster had disintegrated like smoke. From that experience Santa Anna had learned that terror ruled.

But it was another matter altogether—a matter of love, not death—that scandalized Santa Anna's staff almost to the man. Common wisdom had it that the women of north Mexico possessed greater beauty and more desirable shape than those of the south. One day, according to the tale, while timbers were being taken from San Antonio homes to build a bridge across the river, General Castrillón entered a house and found inside it the widow of an ex-presidio officer and her beautiful daughter, ''well-bred, intelligent, though poorly clad.'' Castrillón mentioned this young northern beauty to Santa Anna, who developed ''a great fever to see the pretty girl.'' He ordered Castrillón to obtain the girl for him, but Castrillón refused on the grounds it was not a military matter. A second officer quickly made himself available for the task.[21]

Back home in Jalapa, Santa Anna's tall, thin, angelic wife watched over family and farm. Quiet, nurturing, steady, the señora was like corn, however, and sometimes a warrior chieftain wanted fruit plucked ripe from the vine. *Barragania* (concubinage) was another of those medieval Spanish institutions that had found roots in Mexico,[22] so the idea of a local girl opening her body to the greatest *caudillo* of the day was not objectionable. But the girl's mother proved to be an obstacle, ''not only inflexible, but defiant.'' Hers was a respectable family, she said, and Santa Anna could gain her daughter through nothing less than marriage.

In relaying this bad news to His Excellency, the staff officer proposed a ruse. He had in his company a well-educated rascal adept at ''all sorts of tricks, even the personality of a priest.'' Dressed in vestments obtained from a local priest, the rascal solemnized an artificial wedding and Santa Anna honeymooned while the Alamo was under siege. But to the Catholic generals, concubinage was one thing, and the sacraments something else entirely. The incident was treated as a dark and sinful disgrace. Later the girl was sent by Santa Anna's carriage to San Luis Potosí with two thousand pesos out of the war chest. Legend has it that she was installed in a good house just a few doors from the public square in Jalapa, where she did—or did not—bear Santa Anna's illegitimate child. As Santa Anna's private secretary, Ramón Caro, summarized it in a whisper, ''Decency and respect for public morals do not permit further details to be given.''[23]

For Santa Anna, Texas was an exercise in will and imagination. He regarded Mexico as his destiny and vice versa. This was clear in the final days of the Alamo siege when he called a staff meeting on March 4. Part of his army was still on the march, but several thousand troops were then in town. Down south, General Urrea was scoring victories and gaining glory, while Santa Anna was paused before the Alamo. It was time to smash the enemy. Santa Anna could wait no longer. A victory would raise troop morale to a fiery pitch.[24]

His officers agreed . . . and yet disagreed. They agreed that honor required the reduction of the Alamo garrison. Their dispute lay in how such a reduction should be accomplished. "There was no need to fear that the enemy would be reinforced," said de la Peña, "for even though reinforcements had entered because of our lack of vigilance, we were situated so as to do battle with any other possible arrivals one by one. We were in a position to advance, leaving a small force on watch at the Alamo, the holding of which was unimportant either politically or militarily, whereas its acquisition was both costly and very bitter in the end."[25]

Castrillón, Almonte, and Romero argued that if an assault was to be made they should wait for the heavy artillery to come up the line. General Gaona was only one to three days away, and with his two twelve-pounders and the other artillery, they could tear the Alamo walls to scrap in a matter of eight to ten hours. An artillery barrage would at least open a breach and possibly force a surrender. Either way it would save Mexican blood. The issue of what to do with prisoners of war was also raised once again. In short, the war council concluded without unanimity and without a resolution to attack.

Santa Anna was not pleased. Urrea was stealing his thunder with his streaking advance toward Goliad. His officers were less than lockstep in their military advice, quibbling about prisoners' lives and his wish to assault the Alamo. And, finally, Santa Anna feared that the enemy garrison was about to surrender. According to de la Peña, "It was for this reason that he precipitated the assault, because he wanted to cause a sensation and would have regretted taking the Alamo without clamor and without bloodshed, for some believed that without these there is no glory."[25] If Travis surrendered, it would cheat Santa Anna of the terrorism with which he hoped to empty all the Anglo-Americans out of Texas.

At noon on March 5, disregarding the advice of his cautious general staff, Santa Anna ordered the long-awaited attack upon the Alamo. It was set for the early morning of Sunday, March 6.

According to Capt. Fernando Urizza, one of his aides, Santa Anna had a final discussion with Castrillón over a midnight meal of chicken. Castrillón pressed him to wait and spare Mexican lives. But Santa Anna held up a leg of chicken. "What are the lives of soldiers more than so many chickens?" he said. "I tell you, the Alamo must fall, and my orders must be obeyed at all hazards."[26]

Napoleon could not have put it better.

=17=

THE WEST WIND swung Gulfward, plunging the temperature far below the freezing mark. Not far distant, Mexican soldiers were too cold to sleep, and next morning their officers would be unable to write their reports before thawing the ink in their bottles.[1] But the reinforcements spurred on through the blackness. Scoured by wind, the night turned nude: no clouds, a million stars. The men urged their horses through midnight. They clutched their cold gun barrels with bare hands. Wolves moved in the darkness.

At last they neared San Antonio. The twinkling mesquite campfires of Mexican units stationed at the Powder House and along the road served as distinct landmarks. At the head of the reinforcements rode three men who had each left the Alamo within the last week: redhaired John Smith; Charles Despallier, Travis's favorite aide; and Capt. Albert Martin, the messenger who brought Travis's message to the world. Skirting the Powder House campfires, El Colorado led the troops in single file through the wind.

The night was pinned in place by points of light. The trick was to find a way between the points, beneath the stars, and arrive at the south gate of the Alamo. At one o'clock on Tuesday, they reached the edge of the city. Without warning, like a fairy-tale archangel, a lone man on horseback appeared from the darkness and spoke to them in English.

"Do you wish to go into the fort, gentlemen?" he asked. Assured that they did indeed wish safe passage, the mysterious horseman said, "Then follow me."

He turned his horse to take lead of the company. But for some reason, Smith suspected evil. "Boys," Smith called out, "it's time to be after shooting that fellow."

Before anyone could train his gun upon him, though, the guide touched spur to horse. Like some underworld apparition, he vanished into the brush, one more Texas illusion. "Some supposed this was General Woll, who was an Englishman in the Mexican service," Dr. Sutherland later recorded. However Woll was French, not English, and no matter how fluent his English, the idea of a general patrolling the Alamo perimeter alone in the middle of the night defies belief. At any rate, the company escaped false guidance and continued on toward the fortress.

The Alamo walls took shape above the bosky labyrinth. Smith sent a messenger ahead with word of their arrival, and the reinforcements strung along in single file, winding quietly through the wind. Smith's messenger apparently failed to communicate his news, or else the Alamo guardians were made more anxious by it. Without bothering to hail the men, a sentinel spontaneously banged off a shot from the walls. One of the weary, frozen reinforcements yelled and reached down his leg, a lead ball lodged in his foot. The reinforcements were in danger of being exterminated by the garrison they'd come to aid. Then the riflemen were called off.[2]

At three o'clock in the morning the relief company entered through the fortified south gate. The Gonzales Ranging Company of Mounted Volunteers had successfully infiltrated Mexican lines.[3] They had not needed to cut their way through the Mexican ring. They simply married with the illusory night.

But what Travis greeted in the fire-lit plaza was not Houston's 700 soldiers. It was not Fannin's 320 men or his second projected column of 200. All Travis found huddled against the wind were 32 tired souls. And three of this number were men he'd sent forth from the Alamo as couriers. Furthermore, the Gonzales volunteers had failed to bring gunpowder or supplies. Travis looked around and saw more hungry stomachs when what he needed were wagonloads of munitions, clothing, and food. Worse, the men brought dismal news. They were the only reinforcements they knew about.

The Gonzales reinforcements shared a common origin, the ten-year-old settlement of Gonzales. When there was fighting to be done over the Gonzales cannon back in October, they had fought. Some of them had been among the original eighteen who had stood off the Mexicans until more colonists could rally. Some had helped besiege San Antonio through the autumn.

They were neighbors and they were bound. Some were joined by business or debt. Some by a woman. Some had money, most didn't. All had faith in the Go Ahead credo of property as an expression of self. Two generations of menfolk, the majority of Gonzales's adult male population, dismounted while Travis watched. A number of them weren't even adults, just fierce teenagers. Others were men past forty with families of up to eight children. One, Isaac Millsaps, had kissed good-bye six children and his wife, who was blind. George Kimbell, the hatter-turned-militia-captain, had left behind his Prudence pregnant with twin daughters. Now that they were inside the Alamo walls, the reinforcements were joyously greeted by friends they had lived beside, people like Almeron Dickinson, the artillery captain, and his teenage wife, Susannah.

For weeks and months, the Alamo garrison had been defined by the dissimilarity of its parts, by lonely men and boys missing their families.

There were, for instance, the two Scurlocks, William and his older brother Mial, who had brought their slaves to Texas for a stab at fresh land near San Augustine. Both had fought at the Siege of Béxar, but after December only Mial had remained at the Alamo. William had joined Dr. Grant's Matamoros Expedition and was even now facing death a hundred miles south.

There was Joseph Kerr, a twenty-two-year-old volunteer from Louisiana who had come from Lake Providence with his brother Nathaniel. Within a fortnight of their arrival at the Alamo in early February, Nathaniel had dropped with some disease. He died on February 19, leaving Joseph just four days to bury and mourn him before Santa Anna appeared on the Alazan hills above San Antonio.

Charles Despallier was also missing a brother, Blaz Despallier, who had been wounded at the Siege of Béxar and had returned to Louisiana. And John Goodrich's brother, Briggs, was gone too, off to the convention at Washington-on-the-Brazos.

Here and there family ties bound tight some of the besieged and gave them comfort. Three Tennessee brothers, Edward, George, and James Taylor, had migrated to Liberty, Texas, and come in a pack to San Antonio.

Bowie's in-laws, Juana Alsbury and her sister, Gertrudis, quietly watched after Juana's infant and prayed to Maria and the saints, terrified by the fury around them. By her own admission, Juana never knew all of the Tejanos forted up in the Alamo.

Across the plaza, the Esparza family was staying close to the chapel, where Enrique's father, Gregorio, manned a cannon. Enrique was too young to wield a gun, but he was not the only child in that frustrating situation.

There were two more boys, possibly the sons of Avram or Abraham (Anglicized version: Anthony) Wolfe. Wolfe was an English Jew who had migrated from London (bound for "Teksis," according to synagogue records) and settled in Nacogdoches in 1835. His departure for the New

World, with his young sons, Benjamin and Michael, had followed the
death of his wife, Sarah.

But each of these connections spelled out the underlying separateness
of the garrison population.

Now, with the arrival of the Gonzales volunteers, the dynamics of a
whole town was transplanted to the Alamo. The garrison took on the
dimensions of a community, and its tales dovetailed into a whole frame-
work of local history.

There was Thomas Miller, for example, a forty-one-year-old merchant and road surveyor: Originally from Virginia, he had been living in
Texas for six years. He owned a number of slaves, sat upon the local
ayuntamiento, and ran a large general store, which had been looted of a
hundred dollars and "a newe hat" by a pack of volunteers during the
November campaign and from which he had helped furnish supplies to
the Alamo. What really stitched Miller to the town was not his business
or civic contributions but a girl named Sidney Gaston.

Sidney Gaston was a Kentucky-bred emigrant whose seventeen-year-
old brother, John E. Gaston, aka John Davis, was already inside the
Alamo. John and Sidney's father, John L. Gaston, had died, and their
mother had remarried a George Davis, and the boy was apparently listed
under both his father's and stepfather's surname.

Like Susannah Dickinson, Sidney had married a man old enough to
be her father—Thomas Miller—when she was only fifteen or sixteen and
had quickly borne him a child. In July 1833 their marriage had crumbled
and their infant died shortly afterward. Sidney was careful to select a boy
her own age the second time around. In 1835 she married John Kellogg,
who was nineteen years old. So it was that Sidney's husband, Johnny,
rode in company with her ex-husband to relieve her brother, Johnny, in
the Alamo.

Along with the two teenage Johnnys from Gonzales came Galba
Fuqua, a sixteen-year-old descended from a French Huguenot refugee.
His grandfather had fought at Brandywine and Cowpens in the Revolu-
tionary War. In the same year the Fuqua family removed to Texas, 1828,
Galba's mother had died. When Galba was fourteen, his father died too.
But his uncle Benjamin Fuqua linked Galba to the Alamo. Benjamin had
been one of the Come and Take It fighters defying the Mexicans over the
Gonzales cannon, and Benjamin's brother-in-law, sixteen-year-old
William Phillip King, rode for the Alamo with the reinforcements. One
may be certain the two young boys rode together and fought together.

The connections were overt, here mundane, there poignant. There was James George, to whom at least three of the Gonzales men now in the Alamo owed money: Jesse McCoy owed eighty dollars for two cows and calves, John Tumlinson owed fifteen on a note of land, and Almeron Dickinson owed eight. James George had married a tiny, hundred-pound Dutch woman named Elizabeth Dearduff, whose brother William had come to Texas also. Elizabeth had hugged both her husband and brother good-bye the afternoon the Gonzales Ranging Company of Mounted Volunteers rode for the Alamo. Just as they started off, George had called down to a crippled man named Rowe who was renting a room from him and asked him to keep his wife and children safe. Rowe bartered. He would watch over the family in return for free room and board. As it was, George never returned from the Alamo and Rowe married Elizabeth.

Some of the reinforcements had nothing to do with Gonzales except in their desire for a place in the world. One of these was Jonathon Lindley, who had come to Gonzales through the Alamo, and now returned to the Alamo through Gonzales. One of eleven children, he had come to Texas a few years earlier and learned one of the most secure jobs available on the frontier: land surveying. By the time of the revolution he had accumulated eighteen head of cattle, eleven hogs, and 640 acres of Mexican grant. Besides that he owned very little: an ax, a branding iron, a hoe, and his drawing chains for surveying. Clearly he aimed at the future. During the fall campaign, he had joined the rebel army, and along the way saw the countryside around Gonzales. When word arrived that help was needed, Lindley joined with the reinforcements and returned to the Alamo.

A party of eleven other soldiers had left San Antonio in mid-February bent on snapping up the best lands available. Of that party, a mercenary from the States named David Cummings had returned with Lindley to the Alamo. Less than seventy days earlier, Cummings had arrived from Pennsylvania to fight and make his fortune. He had presented to Sam Houston a box of rifles and a letter from his father, who had fought and suffered imprisonment in the War of 1812. Houston had advised Cummings to get a horse and head west for the front. No sooner did Cummings reach San Antonio than he returned to Gonzales to select the land he meant to take as his military bounty once the fighting was over. "Great speculation is going on in Lands," he enthused to his father and brother Jonathan.[3]

But Santa Anna cut short David Cummings's fortune seeking. When he heard of the Mexican siege, Cummings joined the Gonzales group to take up a gun. There he rejoined a boyhood friend, John Purdy Reynolds, who was the same age and had grown up in the same town, Lewiston, Pennsylvania, but had emigrated to Texas separately.

All around the plaza, in the two-story Long Barracks housing the men and in the officers' quarters where Travis debriefed Captain Martin and John Smith and others, a tremendous sense of fraternity warmed the garrison. It muscled their morale higher than it had been in days. But Travis knew that a couple dozen reinforcements were more symbolic than effectual, and he knew by then that he had miscalculated by making this Alamo stand. Not only had Fannin and Houston and Texas failed him, so had the fictions powering his vision.

"The love of battle is the food upon which we live," Scott's *Ivanhoe* had once informed Travis. Ivanhoe and Waverly and Napoleon . . . Byron, Paulding, and Scott . . . all had whispered to the reclusive Travis, never more clearly than when he visited Susannah Dickinson and little Angelina. He sensed doom and wished desperately to be remembered, if only by a memento. Hopelessly attached to the chivalric gesture, Travis tied a string through a gold ring with a cat's-eye stone. This was probably the same ring his fiancée, Rebecca Cummings, had given him in exchange for a broach, and now Travis looped it around Angelina's neck.[4]

While the garrison's spirits seemed to be holding,[5] Travis found himself staring at the bony face of extermination. It wasn't supposed to have been this way. Texas should have rallied to him by this point.

The Alamo was alive with rumors, of course, and there were any number of explanations as to why the Mexicans had not yet pressed a full assault and when they might. Every man who sighted along the notches cut in the breech and muzzle rings of the cannons or drew a practice bead upon the distances debated these issues. They imagined situations and rehearsed their reactions. With their neighbors and with themselves, they asked questions of the land, the architecture, time and will. No one could say how many enemy troops now crowded the adobe and stone city across the river. Some kept their estimates low, only fifteen hundred. Others explored the ceiling of their own dread, guessing that six thousand men had arrived for the attack. But everything reduced to conjecture, and that stranded each and every one of them on islands of prophecy.

Real information eluded the garrison, or at least the Anglo-Americans, to a profound extent. They never did learn that the Texas independence for which they were fighting had been declared.

Many of the Mexicans who had taken refuge with the rebels in the Alamo had begun to disappear. Travis reported that only three remained, though the number was more likely a dozen. The "desertion" of friendly Tejanos diminished the Alamo's manpower. And it injured morale. Obviously the Tejanos knew something the Anglo-Americans did not, and their disappearance was ominous. As much to deny his own fears as to protest the Tejanos' change of heart, Travis made a wholesale condemnation of Tejanos. "Those who have not joined us in this extremity, should be declared public enemies," he recommended, "and their property should aid in paying the expenses of the war."

Travis didn't even know that the most powerful man in Mexico, the most significant figure to visit Texas in over a century, had been in town since the first afternoon.[6] Fully ten days passed before Travis believed Santa Anna arrived. On March 3, he wrote that "a report was circulated that Santa Anna himself was with the enemy [in San Antonio], but I think it was false. A reinforcement of about one thousand men is now entering Béxar from the west and I think it more than probable that Santa Anna is now in town, from the rejoicing we hear."

This was a good deduction, since the Mexican soldiers were shouting "Santa Anna, Santa Anna."[7] But what they were really rejoicing about was the latest news from General Urrea. A few days earlier, Urrea had crushed Colonel Johnson and his horse catchers. Then on March 3, word arrived in San Antonio that Urrea had search-and-destroyed Colonel Grant's roving band. Santa Anna and the Mexican troops in San Antonio were jubilant. Fannin was horrified. Already tentative, he grew paralyzed. There was no longer any question about his sending aid to the Alamo.

By March 3, Travis had quit looking for Fannin's reinforcements. At eleven o'clock that same morning, Travis's "special messenger," James Bonham, had ridden between the Powder House and a Mexican artillery position and entered the Alamo after trying in vain to stimulate Fannin into relieving Travis.

Bonham was the last man to enter the Alamo. He unfolded the bad news before Travis. Fannin was not coming. There were no more reinforcements in sight. They were alone. They were even uncertain about what they were fighting for, since news of the declaration of independence never would reach them.

Travis dipped his pen in ink and addressed another letter to the convention expressing his determination and needs. In it he mentioned the thirty-two reinforcements from Gonzales, but only in passing. He asked for a small wagon train of munitions and "large reinforcements." Try as he might, Travis was unable to hide his disgust for Fannin. . . . "I have *repeatedly* sent to him for aid without receiving any.'' Jutting his chin bravely, he assured the convention that with aid he could run the enemy out of Texas.

Then he wrote a more fatalistic letter to his friend David Ayres, a merchant and fellow War Dog, who had been removed from active service with the rebels because of his deafness.

"Take care of my little boy," Travis asked. "If the country should be saved, I may make him a splendid fortune; but if the country should be lost and I should perish, he will have nothing but the proud recollection that he is the son of a man who died for his country."[8]

Travis sent instructions for all future reinforcements to bring with them ten days' rations; the Alamo could afford no more men arriving without supplies. Finally Travis said that he would fire the eighteen-pounder three times a day, once each at morning, noon, and night, so long as the Alamo still stood. The cannon's deep boom could be heard as far away as Gonzales.[9]

Once again Travis secluded himself in his adobe quarters along the west wall. Next night, on March 4, Mexican engineers crossed the *acequia* to the northeast and planted a battery within 250 yards of the walls. The Alamo was now at the mercy of Mexican artillery. The two twelve-pounders Santa Anna had hauled along were only two or three days back on the road. By Monday, March 7, according to Mexican predictions, the twelve-pounders could be positioned and their cannons could easily knock the Alamo into a pile of rubble.[10]

Travis did not have access to these details, but it was plain that the fort was encircled. Every indication forecast an assault, and soon.

Contemporary strategy argued against Travis trying to hold the Alamo any longer. A West Point professor named D. H. Mahan had written a book on field fortifications filled with advice especially for militia officers like Travis. "Finally, in an isolated post, if the enemy, after having been repulsed, makes a show of blockading it, or of renewing his attack, and there is no prospect of succor arriving, the garrison should attempt an escape by night."[11]

Travis could not have read Mahan's book, which was just being published. But he was well aware of the military wisdom at large. Crockett, among others, had repeatedly raised objections to staying in the Alamo.

There remained alternatives to a bloody last stand. To date every individual approaching or leaving had safely passed through Mexican lines, and that included the long file of thirty-two men from Gonzales.

Escape was at least conceivable, if not palatable. But Travis took pride in never turning back. Scotch-Irish to the core, he treated obstinance as a virtue, compromise as defeat. Just the same, the idea of escape intertwined his meditations like an evil thought.

Another alternative, equally repellent, was surrender. The Mexicans were now flying two red banners, one from the church tower, the other at the northern entrenchments. Like Travis's defiant cannon blast from the eighteen-pounder on the first day, the Mexicans' no-quarter flags were for show. From Travis's perspective, they had to be. One simply did not kill prisoners, not in 1836. The Anglo-Americans had demonstrated the kind of fair play with which they expected their Mexico clashes to be conducted. Over the past several years, especially over the past several months, they had let Mexican blood, but they had never killed a Mexican prisoner of war. To the contrary, as many of the soldiers now besieging the Alamo could have testified, the Anglo-Americans treated their POWs well. They tended the sick and wounded. And they scrupulously paroled their POWs. The example was radiant: mercy to prisoners. The enemy's red flags provided Travis with nice color in his pleas for aid, but he did not take the threat of no quarter seriously. No Anglo-American did.

As cannonballs continued to pound away and rip through the Alamo walls, the thought of surrender tantalized Travis. He had only to show the white flag and his garrison would be stripped of its weapons and marched off to the Gulf for a boat back to New Orleans. Travis might face imprisonment, or possibly execution, but other rebel leaders like Stephen Austin and Ben Milam had been spared to fight another day. The empty north prairie was filled with Mexican artillery emplacements and troops. It was time to choose between the options: stand, escape, or surrender.

Travis chose. He attempted to surrender.

Two separate Mexican accounts spoke of the attempt, both credible sources. One was Colonel de la Peña, who said, "Travis's resistance was on the verge of being overcome; for several days his followers had been urging him to surrender, giving the lack of food and the scarcity of munitions as reasons, but he had quieted their restlessness with the hope of quick relief, something not difficult for them to believe since they had seen reinforcements arrive from Gonzales. Nevertheless, they had pressed him so hard that on the 5th he promised them that if no help arrived on that day they would surrender the next day or would try to escape under cover of darkness. . . . The enemy was in communication with some of the Béjar townspeople who were their sympathizers, and it was said as a fact during those days that the president-general had known of Travis's decision. . . ."[11]

According to General Filisola, "On that same evening [March 5] about nightfall it was reported that Travis Barnet [William Barret Travis], commander of the enemy garrison, through the intermediary of a woman, proposed to the general in chief that they would surrender arms and fort with everybody in it with the only condition of saving his life and that of all his comrades in arms. However, the answer had come back that they should surrender unconditionally, without guarantees, not even of life itself, since there should be no guarantees for traitors."[12]

It was at this point that Travis let his men know how precarious their grip really was. He pretended to give the garrison its choice of fates. It wasn't much of a choice.

The only witness to what happened was a historically elusive Frenchman named Louis Moses Rose. Rose may or may not have fought under Napoleon, may or may not have been Jewish, and may or may not have been the man Susannah Dickinson later identified as "Ross."[13] But he did exist and apparently did escape from the Alamo before its fall. Unfortunately, he was illiterate and his tale was embellished by the people who wrote it down for him.

According to Rose, Travis arranged the garrison in a single file.[14] He stood front and center of the line, and took a moment to compose himself before speaking. The written word, not oratory, was Travis's strong point and he had to nerve himself to address the gathered men. Apparently he had not been idle in his quarters. His speech, as memorized and told by Rose, and then rememorized and retold by a woman whose son finally transcribed it, was lengthy and florid. Even after so much handling, the spirit of Travis's language peeks through.

"My brave companions. . . ." Travis supposedly began. "I must come to the point. Our fate is sealed. Within a very few days—perhaps a very few hours—we must all be in eternity. This is our destiny, and we cannot avoid it. This is our *certain* doom.

"I have deceived you long by the promise of help. But I crave your pardon . . . in deceiving you, I also deceived myself, having been first deceived by others."

According to the transcription of the speech, Travis then explained how Fannin and Texas had failed them. Emphasizing the number of Mexicans surrounding the Alamo, he then asked the garrison if they wished to surrender or try to escape ("We should all be slain in less than ten minutes''), and answered that they should stay and not just fight, but kill and kill and kill. That, at any rate, was his own preference. But Travis wished to leave every man to his own choice. Anyone who wished to attempt escape was free to go. Even if everyone left, Travis said that he would remain alone and fight.

And then he drew his sword and walked from one end of the garrison to the other, scratching a line in the dirt. All who would stay, he declared, should cross the line.

As theatrical as the gesture was, Travis was not the first commander to give his men a choice of leaving or fighting. As a younger man, Crockett had been told by his militia leader that any man who wanted to go home was free to vote with his feet and leave.[15] In those days, militia officers (like Capt. Abraham Lincoln in 1832) were frequently elected by soldiers who physically voted with their bodies, crossing a line or standing in a group to show their support for a man or an issue.[16] Some of the men crossing Travis's line had already crossed a similar line drawn by Ben Milam in December. The sight of a military unit mustering to one side or another of a line in the dirt would have struck no one as extraordinary. Rather it appealed to their democratic tastes. They viewed it for what it was, an election.

According to Rose, a twenty-six-year-old man named Tapley Holland, the proud son of a War of 1812 veteran, was the first to bound across the line, and he was followed by every man in the garrison but one. Even sick men rose from their cots and staggered across. Bowie was too sick to stand, but he allegedly said, "Boys, I am not able to come to you, but I wish some of you would be so kind as to remove my cot over there." Four men lifted the cot and carried it across.

Travis had tested his men and they confirmed him and renewed his faith. They had elected to stand and fight. They had acted as if they really had a choice.

Only Rose did not cross the line. Over fifty years old, he sank down upon the ground and covered his face. For the next century and a half, those who accepted his existence would be ashamed of this quiet figure. He would be labeled the only coward in the Alamo. Bowie supposedly looked at Rose, who was a friend, and said, "You seem not to be willing to die with us, Rose." Rose affirmed the remark. Crockett said something to the effect that, "You may as well conclude to die with us, old man, for escape is impossible."

Rose didn't bother to debate. Gathering his unwashed clothes into a

pouch, he mounted one of the walls and jumped down. He claimed to
have landed in a puddle of Mexican blood. Then he headed circuitously
through the land, making for the colonies. To his great agony, as he
trekked on through the night he ran into large patches of prickly pear
which tore his legs with their thorns.[17] The thorns worked deep into his
flesh as he struggled to survive in the wilderness.

=18=

THERE WERE PREMONITIONS.

The month of March had just opened and the sky was dark when a ten-year-old girl named Dilue Rose heard a sound like hurricanes and thunder all wired together. Her family lived at Stafford's Point near Harrisburg, over two hundred miles from the Alamo. But as the minutes gathered and the roar swelled, it could have been the Mexican army descending upon them as well. It was a mysterious noise which grew no less frightening once they determined that it was a stampede of several thousand buffalo.

"They passed in front of our house," Dilue remembered, "but we could see only a dark cloud of dust, which looked like a sand storm. Father tried to get a shot at one, but his horse was so fractious that it was impossible. As the night was very dark we could not tell when the last buffalo had passed. We were terribly frightened, for it was supposed that the Indians were following the herd. The buffalo passed and went on to the coast, and the prairie looked afterwards as if it had been plowed."[1]

People would never see vast herds of buffalo in those regions again.[2]

Far away in Philadelphia, a mother named Mary Irvine Lewis came to breakfast that same morning, or one very close to it. She was in tears, mourning though she had no reason to mourn except for a dream. These had been melancholy times for her. During a trip to one of the Carolinas, her cherished twenty-three-year-old son William had dropped from sight. By now she may have learned that he had answered the call for volunteers and gone to Texas. She may even have learned that William had joined the Tennessee Mounted Volunteers, Crockett's bunch, in San Antonio. But it would be weeks or months before she learned that he was at a place called the Alamo and what it was. All the same there was last night's dream to explain, and at the breakfast table she related it with the tears still wet upon her face. She had seen William surrounded by smoke and flame.[3]

And then there was Don José María Heredia, a young officer in the Zapadores (Sappers) battalion drawn up before the Alamo. From the opening of the Texas campaign, the boy had frequently predicted his death in the North, and had firmly resigned himself that he would never see his family again. When word came down that they were finally going to storm the Alamo, his fellow officer José Enrique de la Peña sought him out with his own morbid fears. The officers would be wearing white hats into combat, and de la Peña was certain that Anglo-American marksmen would pick him off, along with Heredia.[4]

Other Mexican officers reacted to the promise of combat with outright joy and congratulated one another on their good fortune. "There is no doubt that some would have regretted not being among the first to meet the enemy, for it was considered an honor to be counted among the first," said de la Peña. "Once the order was issued, even those opposing it were ready to carry it out; no one doubted that we would triumph, but it was anticipated that the struggle would be bloody, as indeed it was."[5]

Santa Anna had several thousand men to choose from for the assault, and he chose the best. Some of the soldiers had served in the Zacatecas campaign the summer before, others were veterans of various Mexican revolutions or the fight with Spain at Tampico or had fought bandits and Indians. He specifically commanded that "recruits deficient in instruction will remain in their quarters."[6]

Saturday, March 5, was a warm day, with the mercury reading 68 degrees, and so the soldiers had superb weather in which to prepare their equipment and their minds. Each unit's officers groomed and guided the troops for the moment. They had walked well over a thousand miles to test their destiny. Gung ho officers applied themselves to keying their men tight with patriotic speeches, borrowing from speeches Santa Anna had delivered along their way through the wilderness. Other officers, like de la Peña, were more philosophical, realizing that the enemy had heard exactly the same speeches in their own language.

"For their part," he said, "the enemy leaders had addressed their own men in terms not unlike those of our commander. They said that we were a bunch of mercenaries, blind instruments of tyranny; that without any right we were about to invade their territory; that we would bring desolation and death to their peaceful homes and would seize their possessions; that we were savage men who would rape their women, decapitate their children, destroy everything, and render into ashes the fruits of their industry and their efforts. Unfortunately they did partially foresee what would happen, but they also committed atrocities that we did not commit, and in this rivalry of evil and extermination, I do not dare to venture who had the ignominious advantage, they or we!"[5]

Santa Anna had lavished his usual fanatical attention to the general orders for attack. Besides stating which sections of which companies would be positioned at this or that point, he meticulously defined the minutiae normally left for noncommissioned officers to attend. Not only did he specify how many ladders would be applied to which walls, he also described how he wanted the ladder carriers to carry their guns ("[they] will sling their guns on their shoulders, to be enabled to place the ladders wherever they may be required"). He addressed himself to the issue of ammunition, even the way he wished headgear worn.

"The companies of Grenadiers will be supplied with six packages of cartridges to every man, and the centre companies with two packages and two spare flints. The men will wear neither overcoats nor blankets, or anything that may impede the rapidity of their motions. The Commanding Officers will see that the men have the chin-straps of their caps down, and that they wear either shoes or sandals. . . . The arms, principally the bayonets, should be in perfect order."[6]

Throughout the balmy afternoon the six-cannon battery, now only 250 yards off the northeast wall, slammed away at the Alamo. The targets of choice were several artillery emplacements arrayed along the northern and eastern walls, particularly two multiple-gun batteries commanding the upper prairie. The Mexicans had christened one of these fortlets Fortín de Terán, after Manuel de Mier y Terán, whose scientific/border expedition had first called attention to the Anglo-American threat. Composed of two cannons aiming northward, it perched eleven feet above the ground and was protected by two-foot walls girdled by a wooden palisade rammed tight with a five-foot thick arc of dirt. Fortín de Terán's sister battery on the northwest corner held three cannons and was dubbed Fortín de Condelle, after Col. Nicolás Condelle, commander of a unit under General Cós.[7]

The third battery in the Alamo to be distinguished by a Mexican nickname was the three-gun battery poking over the chancel at the far end of the chapel. Mexican troops under General Cós had built this battery the previous autumn, and it was aptly named Fortín de Cós. The fifteen-foot-high battery had been built to accommodate the eighteen-pounder. But the rebels had lowered the eighteen-pounder down the ramp inside the chapel and replaced it with three smaller pieces, which now shared the somewhat awkward north-sloping battery terrace.[8]

Undermining any one of these three *fortines* meant, in effect, sinking two or three guns at the same time. Each of the Alamo's various cannon emplacements was built atop old adobe or stone houses filled with earth and rubble. But a lucky hit, or simply enough pounding away at the walls underneath these batteries could collapse or at least structurally weaken the positions. That may be how the Mexicans had dismounted the eighteen-pounder in the southwestern battery on the second day of the siege.

By now, it was obvious the Mexicans were going to assault the fort and had targeted the north wall for their entrance. The rebels desperately threw more dirt up along the inside of the north wall to cushion it against the cannonballs, creating a ten-foot-high hill that sloped down into the plaza. One could reach the top of the wall simply by walking up the hill. The north wall was finally made cannon-proof, but after strengthening it, the defenders had no way to stand and safely fire.

The north wall was the Alamo's weak point, and the positioning of Mexican artillery informed the rebels that Santa Anna knew it. The brisk cannon fire also informed the rebels that Santa Anna was about to close in. In response, the garrison waited. The eighteen-pounder was fired off three times a day according to signal, announcing as far away as Gonzales that the Alamo still stood. But the rebels' powder supply was too low to engage in an artillery duel. Besides, the Mexican engineers had done their work well and it would have been futile trying to uproot the menacing north battery.

While their artillery softened the Alamo walls, some Mexican officers muttered among themselves that two or three more days would give them the twelve-pounders to knock the walls to bits. Instead, they would now have to climb over the walls or excavate holes through them with axes and crowbars, and that would cost extra lives. Nevertheless, the decision had been made. "Once the order was issued, even those opposing it were ready to carry it out," one of those unhappy officers said. "No one doubted that we would triumph, but it was anticipated that the struggle would be bloody, as indeed it was. All afternoon of the 5th was spent on preparations."[5] Twenty-eight ladders had to be constructed. The wood was bound together with rawhide. But time was short and the bindings were clumsy. No one would know how clumsy until next morning.

At sunset Mexican activity paused. The north battery ceased fire. The assault forces were sequestered to sleep, or at least rest. "Night came," said de la Peña, "and with it the most sober reflections. Our soldiers, it was said, lacked the cool courage that is demanded by an assault, but they were steadfast and the survivors will have nothing to be ashamed of. Each one individually confronted and prepared his soul for the terrible moment, expressed his last wishes, and silently and coolly took those steps which precede an encounter. It was a general duel from which it was important to us to emerge with honor. No harangue preceded this combat, but the example given was the most eloquent language and the most absolute order. Our brave officers left nothing to be desired in the hour of trial, and if anyone failed in his duty, if anyone tarnished his honor, it was so insignificant that his shortcomings remained in the confusion of obscurity and disdain.''

The moon—almost full[9]—rose up behind a skyful of clouds, at which time the Active Battalion of San Luis silently retired from their position along the siege line. Unimpeded, the teenager James Allen rode through the line toward Goliad with yet another plea to Fannin. Travis drew his line, and Moses Rose slipped over the wall to make his escape. After nearly two weeks of nerve-racking bombardment and false alarms, the garrison was seduced by the quiet night. Nearly everyone fell asleep.

Travis had posted three sentries outside the walls to give early warning of any attack.[10] But they apparently fell asleep or simply didn't detect any unusual movement in the night. At any rate, they gave no alarm though half the Mexican army was on the move.[11]

At midnight Mexican officers began circulating among their troops, rousing those who had managed to fall asleep. Squad by squad, the companies and battalions assembled with their equipment, forming into columns. Working the cold, nervous men into their proper groups, largely unaided by torchlight, took an hour or two. Finally, at about one or two o'clock, the combatants moved out and crossed the San Antonio in single and double file over wooden bridges. At the same time, cavalry troops under General Ramírez y Sesma began saddling up at the Alameda, their mission to scout the countryside during the battle and cut off any attempts at escape. Bullfrogs lay motionless along the steaming river. Cavalry horses exhaled silver frost and the cold Texas moon hung in a cage of clouds. At that hour the doves still slept.

Once across the river, the four columns fanned out, giving wide berth to the sleeping Alamo. According to Santa Anna's plan, each column stationed itself at a musket shot's distance from a different wall. The first column, composed of under five hundred men drawn from two separate battalions, was commanded by General Cós and had the west wall as its objective. If Cós fell none other than the Supreme Commander himself would take over the column.

Arrayed against the north wall, Col. Francisco Duque commanded the second column, with another five hundred men. Facing the looming east wall with its high black silhouette of the chapel and convent, the third column had three hundred riflemen drawn from three battalions, and was commanded by Colonels Salas and Romero. The fourth and smallest column, under the command of Colonels Morales and Miñon, with only a hundred or so men, was charged with taking the south gate and the wooden-stake palisade that ran diagonally from the chapel. This was the point Crockett had been assigned to defend on the very first day of the siege.

Up at the Mexicans' north battery, Santa Anna gathered with all the members of his general staff who were not participating in the first thrust. He had with him a fifth column. Pulled together as a reserve force, this final column was made up of the elite Zapadores (corps of engineers) plus five companies of grenadiers, in all about four hundred men. Slowly, some eighteen hundred soldiers took their places upon the chessboard arranged in Santa Anna's mind.

Risk all, gain all. Maybe lose all. It was madness as an art. He was the nation. The nation was him. As the units positioned themselves for battle, Santa Anna believed that they were about to sacrifice themselves for him. But, like his Napoleon, he could not afford to care. "The first object of a general who gives battle . . . is the glory and honor of his arms," Santa Anna had learned, "the safety and consideration of his men is but secondary."[12] Eyes dry, heart steeled in the Napoleonic tradition, he tended to his name.

Silence was repeatedly ordered. Smoking was forbidden. The attack had been ordered to begin at four o'clock. However no one was to move until a bugle signaled from Santa Anna's position at the north battery. For thirteen days, the rebels had waited for this attack. Now it was the Mexicans' turn to wait.

"The moon was up," said de la Peña, "but the density of the clouds that covered it allowed only an opaque light in our direction, seeming thus to contribute to our designs. This half-light, the silence we kept, hardly interrupted by soft murmurs, the coolness of the morning air, the great quietude that seemed to prolong the hours, and the dangers we would soon have to face, all of this rendered our situation grave; we were still breathing and able to communicate; within a few moments many of us would be unable to answer questions addressed to us, having already returned to the nothingness whence we had come; others, badly wounded, would remain stretched out for hours without anyone thinking of them, each still fearing perhaps one of the enemy cannonballs whistling overhead would drop at his feet and put an end to his sufferings. Nevertheless, hope stirred us and within a few moments this anxious uncertainty would disappear; an insult to our arms had to be avenged, as well as the blood of our friends spilled three months before within these same walls we were about to attack."[13]

Lying and sitting about on the ground, the soldiers fiddled with their guns and huddled close for warmth and security. They had no ponchos or blankets because of Santa Anna's concerns about speed during the charge, and so they shivered. An hour passed, then another. After a while, some loosened their chin straps and took off their black, bucket-shaped leather shakos. Others tightened their sandal thongs. Men began to doze.

"Light began to appear on the horizon, the beautiful dawn would soon let herself be seen behind her golden curtain," de la Peña remembered.

Then it came, the notes of a bugle. There were seventy bugle calls used by the Mexican army, fifty-seven of them common to both the cavalry and infantry branches.[14] The field command "at attention" was one of them. Sometime between five and five-thirty, one of the Zapadores' buglers, José María Gonzalez, stabbed his notes into the silence. Fourteen hundred Mexican soldiers rose in one mass from the quiet soil.

Through the preceding hours, Mexican artillery could have been pummeling the walls with cannonballs and arching grenades into the plaza to further soften the Alamo for attack. The iron balls might have caved in a palisade or opened breaches, and the grenades might have caused a few enemy casualties. By the Mexican adjutant inspector's estimate, it would have taken only two hours to knock a breach through the north wall with sustained cannonade.[15] But any such advantages had to be weighed against the element of surprise. Santa Anna opted to drop upon the enemy like an eagle. The cold iron barrels lining the battery entrenchments stood silent. To avoid hitting their own troops, Mexican artillery would not fire throughout the assault.

The three picket guards outside the Alamo walls never did sound an alarm. They may have been killed in their sleep, or have woken in time to scramble inside. The first man to notice the Mexican charge was Capt. John J. Baugh. A stickler for military formalities, Baugh was the officer of the day. He had just begun his rounds at five o'clock when he heard the Mexican bugle, followed by a distant smattering of vivas. He turned to face the Alamo plaza, drew a deep lungful, and bellowed out, "The Mexicans are coming."[11]

The massed Mexican columns rushed pell-mell toward their assigned walls. Almost immediately, their neat, uniformed regularity—so carefully sculpted by Santa Anna—fell into pieces. Their darkened lines bent and waved as running men were slowed by the terrain or detoured around foliage or tripped. Despite Santa Anna's picture-perfect battlefield array, the order began to break down. Officers had been instructed to open fire while still over a hundred yards away from the fortress. But now that the columns were launched and streaming inward, some officers took matters in their own hands and disregarded the command. They held their fire at least until the troops got within musket range.

As the soldiers raced forward, Santa Anna's military bands were ordered to start playing the "Degüello," a cavalry tune that was as unfamiliar to the infantry troops as it was to the Anglo-American rebels. The name of the brassy medieval song dating back to Spain's long war with the Moors, *degüello* meant "cut throat" or "behead." But scarcely any of his army had ever heard the "Degüello,"[14] and so the song accompanied, rather than signaled, the atrocities that were about to occur.

Inside the Alamo, in a room along the west wall, the slave Joe was asleep with Travis. When Captain Baugh shouted the alarm, both men jumped to their feet. The room was pitch-black, but Travis knew exactly where he'd placed his shotgun and sword. Grabbing these weapons, he told Joe to follow him. Joe took a gun and sprinted after his master. Travis made a beeline across the plaza for the fragile north wall, taking a position at the battery the Mexicans called the Fortín de Terán. "Come on, boys," Travis called out, "the Mexicans are upon us, and we'll give them *Hell.*"[11]

The columns of rushing Mexicans were nearly indistinguishable from the dark landscape. Here and there the rebel garrison estimated the position of the columns from the flash of their musket fire. Above all the rebels could hear them.

Whipped to a patriotic frenzy by some of their officers, the Mexican troops kept breaking out with loud cheers. The enthusiasm gave point to their adrenaline, but it also betrayed the soldiers' positions. The Toluca Battalion in the second column northwest of the Alamo uncorked a reckless burst of vivas hailing their republic and their president-general. Standing with the Zapadores reserve column, de la Peña witnessed the consequences. "The officers were unable to repress this act of folly," he said, "which was paid for dearly."[13]

A minute later, the Fortín de Terán answered back. Tracking the second column by its cheers, the gunners at Travis's station touched off a blast of grapeshot. That single blast of shrapnel devoured half the chasseurs of the Toluca Battalion, dozens of men and boys in one mangling bite. Capt. José María Herrera was killed, and his lieutenant, Vences, was wounded. Capt. José María Macotela was wounded and died soon afterward.[13] Shrapnel from another blast caught the column's commander Col. Francisco Duque in the thigh, dumping him to earth. Lying in the dirt, he was trampled by his own men, yet continued cheering them on until his backup, General Castrillón, managed to take over.[16] Two more blasts from the northwestern battery gouged forty men from the ranks of the Aldama Battalion under General Cós.

Later, in describing the loss of so many of their officers and men, Mexican officers like de la Peña would suggest that the Anglo-American sharpshooting had caused many of the early casualties. "Travis, to compensate for the reduced number of the defenders, had placed three or four rifles by the side of each man, so that the initial fire was very rapid and deadly. Our columns left along their path a wide trail of blood, of wounded, and of dead."[13] Always eager to promote American marksmanship, American commentators would pick up on this theme and declare that backwoodsmen always shot for braid. But, it was simply too dark and—after the initial volleys—too smoky to pick off individual soldiers wearing officers' uniforms. So the vaunted long rifle gave the Alamo no advantage whatsoever on this particular Sunday morning. If anything, the long rifle would prove to be a liability during the battle, for its stock extended all the way out to the muzzle and a bayonet could not be mounted on it.

It may have been, as de la Peña claimed, that each of the defenders kept three to four guns stockpiled at his position. But muzzle-loaders were difficult to keep loaded for any length of time. Dew, night rains, even ordinary humidity quickly dampened and ruined the charge in the pan. It was not uncommon for men to discharge their guns periodically in order to reload them with fresh powder. With gunpowder supplies running low at the Alamo, it seems unlikely that the garrison kept its firearms loaded and primed for long periods. If the attack had occurred during daylight hours, giving them enough advance warning, the garrison might have had time to load multiple guns. But this predawn attack came so quickly that men barely had time to run to the walls, much less load three or four muzzle-loaders in the dark.

The bulk of the initial Mexican casualties were caused by grapeshot. And the Alamo artillery was less deadly than it might have been. There simply weren't enough men, especially trained artillery crews, to man all eighteen cannons mounted in the Alamo. To load and fire a muzzle-loaded cannon took five men: a rammer, a loader, a thumbstall, a gunner, and a powder monkey. The maintenance and firing of eighteen cannons would have tied up ninety men, more than half of the healthy male population in the Alamo.[17] Besides having inadequate manpower, the Alamo artillery suffered for being amateur.[18] Just the same, the Alamo had teeth, at least for a few minutes.

From where Gen. Antonio López de Santa Anna stood at his north battery, the Alamo looked like a cup of summer lightning. The old mission walls blossomed with gunfire. The eastern horizon splintered with dawn.

Outlined by incandescent gunfire, fourteen hundred inky silhouettes surged hard toward this grail of light. Around their necks they wore homemade rosaries of string and seeds, simple crucifixes, and Indian charms made of vegetation, feathers, and animal bone. Some of the magic worked. Much didn't.

From the dirt to higher than a man could jump, the air sang with metal. The soldiers sang back. Their skyful of vivas and *muertas* and cries to María and her Son met a curtain of one-ounce musket balls, of grapeshot, chopped horseshoes, scrap iron, and shotgun pellets. Singly and in ragged batches the soldiers fell to earth. The troops wavered and tried to retreat.

Herded by their shouting officers, the soldiers turned back to attack again. Waving his sword, de la Peña's friend in the white hat, Don José María Heredia, urged his platoon forward. Two inches above his right nipple a bit of metal nipped in through his uniform. It would take the young Mexican thirteen agonizing days to die. All around him men lay in one or another attitude of suffering or death.

The second column raced on for the north wall where a sanctuary, of sorts, awaited them. The Alamo cannons' barrels could not be depressed below a certain angle, meaning the soldiers finally reached an umbrella of sorts beneath which the rain of grapeshot could not touch them. It was a mixed blessing, for the ladders needed to gain the wall were nowhere to be seen. Either the ladder carriers had been shot or they had dropped their burdens in search of speed or to run away. Only one ladder made it to the north wall, and that one was poorly built. Having run the gauntlet of cannon fire, the soldiers were now trapped against the wall, with the enemy overhead and a swelling flood of comrades on every side. Now the slaughter began in earnest. The cruelest irony was that Mexican bullets took the greatest toll of Mexican lives.

With very few exceptions, marksmanship did not exist in Santa Anna's army. Not only were soldiers not trained to aim their *escopetas* (muskets), they were discouraged from aiming. To add to their poor aim, their Brown Bess muskets were heavy pieces that kicked hard. The Brown Bess threw a .75 caliber ball, and had to be packed with a very heavy charge of powder to compete with an American musket's range.[19] The average Mexican conscript was considerably smaller than a British troop, and the recoil bruised his shoulder. Wishing to subtract from their miseries, Mexican soldiers would undercharge their shot, which reduced the ball's range. They further spared their shoulders by firing from the hip. Mexican soldiers were notorious for shooting five and ten feet above their targets, much to American scorn. But on this Sunday morning the beehive of Mexican musket balls found at least one distinguished subject among the rebels holding the north wall.

After galloping up the embankment to the dirt terrace of the northeast battery, Travis yelled encouragement to his men and triggered his shotgun at the rushing Mexican line. He had spent thirteen days and a lifetime of novels readying for his final stand. He had no idea it would last only a few seconds for him. There was just time for his slave Joe to fire his own gun down into the enemy. And then, almost instantly, Travis was toppling backward down the earthen hill with a single bullet lodged in his forehead. He was possibly the first Anglo-American to be killed during the entire siege, though his death would take a few more minutes. Stunned by the wound, Travis managed to sit up in the dirt, sword in hand. Joe saw his master fall down the hillside. Still clutching his gun, Joe ran off to find refuge in one of the rooms.

Off the eastern wall, Colonel Romero's three hundred riflemen ran straight into a hail of grapeshot from the artillery mounted at the end of the towering chapel. The left flank of their column was torn apart, and Romero's column swung to its right, away from the source of pain.[20] Meanwhile, over on the west wall, General Cós's column was being raked not only by enemy grapeshot, but by bullets fired haphazardly at the north wall by what remained of the Toluca Battalion and the San Luis companies.[21] Cós's men stampeded to their left to join with the bloodied second column. In a few minutes they were joined by Romero's panicked column. Three columns were now fused beneath the murderous north wall in a nightmarish scene worthy of Goya. "All united at one point, mixing and forming a confused mass," said de la Peña, who was one of the hapless soldiers.

From his distance, Santa Anna viewed the dark jammed chaos with alarm. The battle was less than ten minutes old and as the light of day came up on his setpiece, all he could discern was snarled disaster. Believing the three columns were being routed, Santa Anna panicked. Highly agitated, he ordered his reserve unit under Colonel Amat to rush the walls. Then, for good measure, he threw in his whole general staff and everyone at his side. "This gallant reserve merely added to the noise and the victims," de la Peña later described with disgust. "[It was] the more regrettable since there was no necessity for them to engage in combat. Before the Sapper Battalion, advancing through a shower of bullets and volley of shrapnel, had a chance to reach the foot of the walls, half their officers had been wounded."

As they ran toward the Alamo, the four hundred reserves blindly fired off their weapons. Their high bullets slapped and pattered against the wall like hailstones. Low bullets raked the shoulders and heads of troops in front of them, mowing down more Mexican soldiers.

General Filisola and others were horrified by the friendly fire. "Since they attacked in a closed column," Filisola said, "all the shots, the direction of which was turned somewhat downward, aimed the bullets towards the backs of those ahead of them. Thus it was that most of our dead and wounded that we suffered were caused by this misfortune. It may be said that not a fourth of them were the result of enemy fire." In other words, by Filisola's count, fully three quarters of the Mexican casualties—a number well in the hundreds—were caused by Mexican bullets.

In the kill zone all was frenzy. Those lucky enough to reach the walls huddled against the adobe and limestone. "A quarter of an hour had elapsed, de la Peña observed, "during which our soldiers remained in a terrible situation, wearing themselves out as they climbed in quest of a less obscure death than that visited on them, crowded in a single mass." With the addition of the reserves, the press of humanity at the north wall numbered probably thirteen hundred to fifteen hundred. Several hundred dead and wounded—perhaps as many as four or five hundred—lay heaped in a huge crescent fanning out from the north wall.[22] No one was counting as the assault continued, but it was horribly clear that the Mexicans were getting mauled. And yet they went on fighting.

At the opposite end of the Alamo, the fourth column under Colonel Morales had made a sweeping stab at the palisade and south wall, without luck. David Crockett's "boys" apparently bit a chunk out of the small unit, firmly repelling their assault. Under Morales's direction, the chasseurs bucked away from the gunfire at the south wall and regrouped in the jacales off the southwest corner of the Alamo. But here they came face to face with the Alamo's Goliath, the huge eighteen-pounder. The big cannon had been remounted and now dominated the townscape. But for all its power, it proved impotent against Morales and his fourth column. Hidden behind the jacales, they stayed under the cannon's declination angle long enough to revise their attack plan.

The crisis at the north wall had begun to draw defenders away from their posts, but Morales had no way to know that. Still when he and his small column made a daring second lunge at the walls, they encountered little resistance. Either by storming the platform directly, or by first capturing the front gate, they managed to seize the eighteen-pounder. The Mexican soldiers killed or dispersed its crew, and then raced down the ramp to press their rupture of the Alamo's defense. They were advancing across the plaza toward the north wall when suddenly the troops of four combined columns swelled up and over, cresting the wall.

"Our *jefes,* officers, and troops, at the same time as if by magic, reached the top of the wall," said Lt. Col. Sánchez Navarro.[23] If luck is magic, then magic deposited them at the top of Travis's north wall, where the bare timbers and wooden braces that had never been covered with earth presented the Mexican soldiers with a crude but effective ladder.

"There was therefore a starting point," said de la Peña, "and it could be climbed, though with some difficulty. But disorder had already begun; officers of all ranks shouted but were hardly heard. The most daring of our veterans tried to be the first to climb, which they accomplished, yelling wildly so that room could be made for them, at times climbing over their own comrades. Others, jammed together, made useless efforts, obstructing each other, getting in the way of the more agile ones. . . . A lively rifle fire coming from the roof of the barracks and other points caused painful havoc, increasing the confusion of our disorderly mass. The first to climb were thrown down by bayonets already waiting for them behind the parapet, or by pistol fire, but the courage of our soldiers was not diminished as they saw their comrades falling dead or wounded, and they hurried to occupy their places and to avenge them, climbing over their bleeding bodies. The sharp retorts of the rifles, the whistling of bullets, the groans of the wounded, the cursing of the men, the sighs and anguished cries of the dying, the arrogant harangues of the officers, the noise of the instruments of war, and the inordinate shouts of the attackers, who climbed vigorously, bewildered all and made of this moment a tremendous and critical one. The shouting of those being attacked was no less loud and from the beginning had pierced our ears with desperate, terrible cries of alarm in a language we did not understand.''

Maddened, the army jammed through the breaches into the Alamo's interior. From his hiding place, the swarm of Mexicans seemed to Joe to come pouring over the wall ''like sheep.'' He later claimed to have fired his gun several times at the enemy, taking aim from his hiding place. Those defenders at the north batteries and wall now fled for the protection of the rooms lining the east and west sides of the plaza. They had taken the precaution of digging loopholes through the walls of some of the rooms, and so the Mexicans descended into more gunfire.

As he peeked out through a loophole or a crack in the wall, Joe saw—or imagined he saw—a Mexican (whom he identified as Gen. Ventura Mora of the Dolores Regiment) approach his stunned master. The Mexican general supposedly threw a cutting sword blow which Travis parried with his own sword. Although wounded in the head and sitting on the ground, Travis summoned up a superhuman effort and skewered this final opponent, then expired.

There were other accounts of the Great Heart's death. De la Peña mistook some other Anglo-American for Travis (''a handsome blond, with a physique as robust as his spirit was strong'') and described his machismo with admiration. ''Travis was seen to hesitate, but not about the death that he would choose,'' de la Peña said. ''He would take a few steps and stop, turning his proud face towards us to discharge his shots; he fought like a true soldier. Finally he died, but he died after having traded his life very dearly. . . . Travis behaved as a hero; one must do him justice, for with a handful of men without discipline, he resolved to face men used to war and much superior in numbers, without supplies, with scarce munitions, and against the will of his subordinates.''[20]

Without question this is how Travis had meant to die, saluted by his enemy. However, one persistent report had him ingloriously committing suicide with a single pistol shot to the head.

The battle had lasted only twenty minutes. The sun had still not risen, but the brightening horizon and numerous conflagrations helped illuminate the plaza. It was an absolutely savage arena. Mexican troops streaming over the north wall met with not only gunfire from the barracks and officer quarters bracketing the plaza, but with more friendly fire—this time from Colonel Morales's fourth column at the south end. A dry *acequia* ran from the north to the south through the plaza, and Mexican soldiers jumped down into this natural trench for protection.[24] Later de la

Peña blamed the friendly fire on Santa Anna, stating that the general had "overloaded" the troops with up to seven cartridges apiece. This, de la Peña claimed, sent the Mexican soldiers a message that they should rely on firepower rather than their mainstay, the bayonet.[25]

Despite de la Peña's criticism, Santa Anna had ordered that "the arms, principally the bayonets, should be in perfect order."[4] As the Mexicans began rooting out nests of desperate defenders, the bayonets did indeed become the weapon of choice, giving reach over the giant norteamericanos' butcher knives and clubbed rifles.

Inside the chapel, the battle transcended time for the terrified women and children. Though less than a half hour had passed, Susannah Dickinson believed the battle had consumed more than two hours when her husband came rushing into the baptistery. "Great God, Sue," the shocked artillery captain said, "the Mexicans are inside our walls! All is lost! If they spare you, save my child." He gave Susannah a parting kiss, then drew his sword and returned to the battle.

Colonel Romero, whose column had been ravaged by grapeshot from the high end of the chapel, set to cleaning out the Long Barracks along the east side of the plaza. Down at the south end, Colonel Morales turned the eighteen-pounder around and began blowing apart barricaded doorways and other cannon positions. The friendly fire continued without discipline.

"Our soldiers, some stimulated by courage and others by fury, burst into the quarters where the enemy had entrenched themselves from which issued an infernal fire," said de la Peña. "Behind these came others, who, nearing the doors and blind with fury and smoke, fired their shots against friends and enemies alike, and in this way our losses were most grievous. On the other hand, they turned the enemy's own cannon to bring down the doors to the rooms or the rooms themselves; a horrible carnage took place, and some were trampled to death. The tumult was great, the disorder frightful; it seemed as if the furies had descended upon us. . . . In the midst of this thundering din, there was such confusion that orders could not be understood, although those in command would raise their voices when the opportunity occurred. . . ."

General Cós was finally persuaded that the Mexican soldiers needed to halt their gunfire in order to cut their losses. He ordered a Zapadores bugler named Tamayo to blow the cease-fire, but in vain. The wild shooting continued even after the last defender lay dead. De la Peña estimated that fifty thousand bullets were fired in the space of little more than an hour.[26] That was a gross exaggeration, for each soldier would have had to fire more than twenty-five rounds each. But it helped describe the lunatic gunfire splashing every corner of the plaza.

As the sky lightened, a number of soldiers in the plaza spied a rebel flag hanging from a pole atop the two-story El Cuartel (Long Barracks).[27] Three of the high-spirited Zapadores flung themselves at the objective. All three fell, cut down by gunfire. Then a sub-lieutenant of the same corps, José María Torres, a young impetuous officer, gained the top of the barracks and pulled the flag down. He raised the tricolor of the Zapadores just before a lead ball dropped him, mortally wounded.[28]

Now the cloth symbol of the limestone and adobe symbol had changed hands. The Alamo belonged to Mexico once again.[29]

Much the way Anglo-Americans had overwhelmed Mexican forces in San Antonio in December—fighting room to room, tearing down walls and doors, firing and knifing their way to victory—the Mexican troops now suppressed the Alamo. The bulk of their killing occurred in the long barracks facing the plaza on the east.[30] A honeycomb of loopholes along the barracks façade gave rebel riflemen access to targets in the plaza.[31] One by one, the rooms were blasted with cannonballs and cleared by hand-to-hand combat.

With all clearly lost, a number of rebels then began trying to surrender. "Among the defenders there were thirty or more colonists," de la Peña said. "The rest were pirates, used to defying danger and to disdaining death, and who for that reason fought courageously; their courage, to my way of thinking, merited them the mercy for which, toward the last, some of them pleaded; others not knowing the language, were unable to do so. In fact, when these men noted the loss of their leader and saw that they were being attacked by superior forces, they faltered. Some with an accent hardly intelligible, desperately cried *Mercy, valiant Mexicans;* others poked the points of their bayonets through a hole or a door with a white cloth, the symbol of cease-fire, and some even used their socks."

Trusting these sorry little rags of truce, Mexican troops entered the stony rooms to take prisoners. But among those pleading for mercy stood men determined to kill until they were killed. Treating the white flags as mere bait, they bled the Mexican soldiers with pistols, knives, and bayonets. The result was predictable and savage. "Thus betrayed, our men rekindled their anger," said de la Peña, "and at every moment fresh skirmishes broke out with renewed fury. The order had been given to spare no one but the women and this was carried out, but such carnage was useless and had we prevented it, we would have saved much blood on our part.''

Despite the order to spare the women, at least one woman—Joe claimed she was a Negro—was found shot between two cannons.

It took perhaps twenty minutes to overrun the outer walls, and another infuriating hour to clean out nests of defenders in the old *convento,* which had become a long barracks, and finally the crumbling chapel. Susannah was visited by more dying warriors in the well-protected baptistery of the chapel. Galba Fuqua, one of her teenage friends from Gonzales, appeared in the arched room. A lead ball had shattered both sides of his jaw and he was bleeding from the mouth. He tried to speak but couldn't. Then he held together the broken parts of his jaw and tried again. But no words would come. The bloody, excited boy shook his head in despair and returned to the fight. Almost a half century later, Susannah claimed that Crockett came to her room, fell to his knees, and committed himself to God, then disappeared into the world beyond her cold stone doorway.

For little Enrique Esparza, the battle seemed even longer. He would always remember that it began in darkness and ended in darkness, and through the many decades of the rest of his life, Esparza would translate how that meant the fighting had lasted for a full twenty-four hours.

"The end came suddenly and almost unexpectedly and with a rush," he related in 1907. "It came at night and when all was dark save when there was a gleam of light from the flash and flame of a fired gun. Our men fought hard all day long. Their ammunition was very low. That of many was entirely spent." He, his mother, brothers, and sister huddled in the main room of the chapel, above which his father, Gregorio, manned one of the three cannons on the terrace overlooking the east. His father was shot dead and slumped over his cannon. His mother and baby sister knelt beside him, and Enrique and his brothers clutched her clothing. The traumatized child imagined that he fell asleep for another full night, and that the Mexican army did too, or at least feigned to. But next morning, still in the darkness of his mind, the attack resumed. "Suddenly there was a terrible din. Cannon boomed. Their shot crashed through the doors and windows and the breeches in the walls. Then men rushed in on us. They swarmed among us and over us. They fired on us in vollies. They struck us down with their escopetas. In the dark our men groped and grasped the throats of our foemen and buried their knives into their hearts."[32]

A number of Mexican troops went berserk, and their officers later confessed that they lost control of their army. While Enrique Esparza waited in the chapel beside his father's corpse, soldiers burst in through the entrance. "By my side was an American boy," he said. "He was about my age but larger. As they reached us he rose to his feet. He had been sleeping, but like myself, he had been rudely awakened. As they rushed upon him he stood calmly and across his shoulders drew the blanket on which he had slept. He was unarmed. They slew him where he stood and his corpse fell over me."

In this way, one of Anthony Wolfe's young boys died. Up above, on the artillery terrace, Wolfe grabbed his remaining son, clambered atop the chapel wall, and launched them into space. Some Mexicans claimed he had meant to destroy himself and his son, and that both perished in the fall. Others believed the father and son were trying to escape when they were riddled with bullets.

Three unarmed gunners from one of the artillery crews now tried to take refuge with Susannah in the baptistery. Two were shot. The third, Jacob Walker, a small man who had talked with the young mother about his own wife and four children, suffered a torturous death. "Drunk on blood," as Susannah recalled two months afterward, a group of Mexican soldiers shouldered their way through the archway. They stuck Walker with their bayonets "and lifted him up like a farmer does a bundle of fodder on his pitchfork." Susannah claimed that they raised and lowered Walker several times, while he cried out for death, finally expiring in convulsions.[33]

Across the plaza, Juana Alsbury and her sister, Gertrudis Navarro, huddled in the darkness of their room adjoining the officers' quarters on the west well. Juana peeped through a loophole dug in her wall and saw the Mexican columns surging past on the outside. The sisters listened to the sound of gunfire and struggle swell and then wash past their doorway. It seemed like many hours, perhaps seven or eight, had passed since the battle began. Clutching her infant to her breast, Juana asked her sister to show herself at the door and ask the soldiers not to shoot into their room, since it held only women. "When Señorita Gertrudis opened the door," Juana recalled years later, "she was greeted in offensive language by the soldiers. Her shawl was torn from her shoulders, and she rushed back into the room." At that moment Juana despaired, believing her child was about to become motherless.

"Your money and your husband," a soldier demanded of Gertrudis. The terrified woman said she had neither. Just then a sick rebel, probably a Georgia mercenary named Edwin Mitchell, appeared at Juana's side.[34] Gallantly, but feebly, he tried to defend her from the soldiers, but was bayoneted by her side. No sooner was Mitchell killed than a young

Mexican man being chased by other soldiers grabbed Juana's arm and tried to use her as a shield from his assailants. The soldiers broke his grip and stabbed four or five bayonets into him, and then shot his corpse repeatedly. Momentarily free of the combat outside, the soldiers now took time to loot the room. They broke open Juana's trunk, in which the garrison officers had stored some of their valuables, and took her clothing and silver pesos and a watch belonging to Travis. Distracted by their plunder, the soldiers ignored the sisters for the moment.[35]

Those who missed sticking a live enemy stuck dead ones. Soldiers tamped down fresh rounds and fired into corpses over and over again. Later, officers would deplore the mutilation and pillaging of the dead. The soldiers killed everything they could find, even cornering and dispatching a stray cat, shouting, "It is not a cat, but an American."[36] Pouring through the hospital, they killed all the sick and wounded.

In the south-side room where Bowie had semiquarantined himself, other soldiers found the famous man either dead or dying. One report declared him dead of disease two or three hours before the attack. Others conjured him resurrecting from his cot and firing off a brace of pistols and disemboweling half a dozen Mexicans before succumbing. According to Dr. Sutherland, who later interviewed both Susannah Dickinson and Joe, Bowie was too weak even to lift his head. He was shot repeatedly in the head, and his brains stained the wall until it was replastered. Contradicting herself later, Susannah Dickinson also claimed Bowie had been run through with sabers after shooting two soldiers with pistols. With disdain, Sánchez Navarro observed that "the perverse and braggart Santiago Bowie died like a woman, hidden almost under a mattress." As with Travis, early reports about the fall of the garrison stated that Bowie had put a pistol to his own head and committed suicide.[37]

How many of the terror-stricken rebels turned their weapons against themselves will always remain one of the Alamo's mysteries. At least one man did try to commit suicide, for Susannah Dickinson watched him die. Robert Evans, a tall black-haired Irishman with blue eyes, who had emigrated to Texas after emigrating to New York and then to New Orleans, tried to kill not only himself, but everyone else, including all the women and children in the chapel.[38] He may have been one of the artillery gunners in the chapel or just a nearby rifleman mindful of the end. At any rate Evans could see that the day was lost. In accordance with a pact struck among at least some of the men, Evans grabbed a torch and headed for an antechamber at the side of the chapel, the garrison magazine where the rebels had stored away the several hundred pounds of

Mexican gunpowder captured from General Cós in December. Evans got to within just a few feet of the gunpowder when he was stopped by a Mexican bullet. He died on the floor next to his torch.

Four or five rebels attempted to flee, hopping over the low palisade that Crockett and his men had defended. But by then it was light, and three were quickly intercepted and sabered or lanced to death by cavalry troops patrolling the perimeter. One escapee managed to make his way to the San Antonio River where he tucked himself underneath a wooden bridge to await night. His plan was good, his luck bad. A few hours later a San Antonio woman came down to wash her clothes, saw the fugitive, and informed the army. The man was rousted and killed.[39]

Mexican accounts acknowledged that escapes were attempted, but said that none succeeded. On the other hand, faced with an embarrassing heap of his own dead soldiers strewn around the Alamo's exterior, Santa Anna tried to convince his home audience that many of those bodies were rebels cut down in flight. "In the vicinity are a large number [of dead] which cannot be examined," the President wrote to his government, "and who while trying to escape the bayonets of the infantry fell beneath the sabers of the cavalry whom I had stationed at that spot by design. I can assure you then that there were very few who may have gone to relate the event to their companions."[40]

But apparently a few did escape. Evidence suggests that a red-haired, blue-eyed Arkansas jockey and hunter named Henry Warnell slipped out of the Alamo and straggled across the prairie. Warnell weighed less than 118 pounds, but he was sturdy and savvy by trade. The twenty-four-year-old horseman had expressed a strong preference for fighting in the open, rather than penned up within the Alamo walls. On the final morning, he reportedly put the Alamo behind him. Either before or during the escape, he was badly wounded but made his way to safety. Three months later, according to an affidavit filed by his family (in 1858), Warnell died of his wounds in Dimmit's Landing, or possibly Linnville.

Warnell may, in fact, have been one of two Alamo survivors who seem to have shown up in Nacogdoches in late March. One of them was badly wounded, and they were quoted in the *Arkansas Gazette* that "San Antonio had been retaken by the Mexicans, the garrison put to the sword—that if any others escaped the general massacre besides themselves, they were not aware of it." This was printed on March 29, a week before any other paper received and published Houston's "first" report.[41]

Whether or not Warnell escaped the battle, a number of the besieged did survive it, at least temporarily. Mexican officers rushed among their troops in the Alamo to rescue noncombatants. They seemed to have amazingly precise information about whom they were looking for: On at least two occasions they called for the survivors by name. It was dangerous work. Each room in the Alamo was like a dark cave, possibly holding death or mutilation at the hands of some giant, battle-crazed Anglo-Saxon.

Nevertheless, the officers were genuinely concerned about the women and children. One of these men stepped to the doorway of the baptistery and, unable to see in the gloom, called in with broken English. "Is Mrs. Dickinson here?" Surrounded by mutilated corpses, Dickinson was too frightened to answer. The officer repeated his question. "Is Mrs. Dickinson here? Speak out, for it is a matter of life and death." But when the girl finally stepped from the darkness, several wild soldiers reached forward and one shot her in the right calf. The officer shouted his men back and saved Susannah.[42]

Enrique and his family still clustered by one of the cannons, near the body of his father, Gregorio. "It was pitch dark in the Eastern end of the structure," Enrique said, "and the soldiers of Santa Anna seemed to fear to go there. . . . Santa Anna's men stood still and fired into the darkness and until some one brought lanterns. The last I saw of my father's corpse was when one of them held his lantern above it and over the dead who lay about the cannon he had tended."

Hiding behind the family and the cannon was a Mexican deserter named Brigido Guerrero. He was desperate. His army had returned. He had been caught red-handed in combat against his old comrades. As the siege had progressed, Guerrero had apparently spent much time sweating through this horrifying moment, testing out excuses, praying. Now as the Mexican soldiers came racing up to kill him, he begged for mercy. The soldiers granted him a moment, and Guerrero wove for them an audacious story. The Anglo-Americans had captured him, he explained with Homeric skill, and against his will they had brought him into the Alamo. He had tried to escape, but the Anglo-Americans were too vigilant. He was a prisoner . . . a brother to the Mexican soldiers . . . not a combatant. Unbelievably, Guerrero was believed.

Elsewhere, Travis's young slave Joe crouched among the adobe ruins, listening to Mexican soldiers mopping up room after room. "Are there any Negroes here?" a voice called out in accented English. Joe emerged from his hiding place and said, "Yes, here's one." Immediately two soldiers lunged to kill him, one discharging a barrel of shot at him, the other thrusting with a bayonet. But the officer who had called out, a captain of the roughriding presidial troops named Marcos Barragan,[43] beat the soldiers away with his sword, and took Joe into safekeeping. Only one lead pellet of the buckshot hit Joe, in the side, and the bayonet just scratched him. Miraculously, the young man had weathered the tempest.

Not far away, in equal peril, were Juana Alsbury, her baby, and her sister, Gertrudis Navarro. There were bodies on the dirt floor of their room, and bloody, smoke-stained soldiers feverishly looting Juana's trunk when an officer stepped in from the plaza. He was almost as agitated and overwhelmed as the women he rescued. "How did you come here?" he demanded. "What are you doing here anyhow? Where is the entrance to the fort?" He led the women out of the room. Placing them near one of the cannons that had been turned around to demolish the long barracks' defenses, he instructed them to stay put, they would soon be escorted to Santa Anna. Then he rushed off.

Pockets of defenders continued to resist, and bullets were still buzzing through the air when a second officer approached the shocked and quivering sisters. "What are you doing here?" he said.

Juana replied, "An officer ordered us to remain here, and he would have us sent to the President."

"President! the devil," the officer exploded. "Don't you see they are about to fire that cannon? Leave."

Forlorn, utterly confused, the two women and their baby backpedaled with no destination. Suddenly a voice called to them. "Sister." To Juana's relief, a familiar face took shape from the thick gunsmoke. It was Manuel Perez, a relative or possibly a brother of her first husband. He was a descendant of one of San Antonio's oldest families[44] and had come from town to examine the war zone. Trailing close behind him walked one of James Bowie's female slaves from town. "Don't you know your own brother-in-law?" Perez asked.

Perez put Juana, Gertrudis, and the baby in the slave woman's care, and they were taken to the chapel. There they joined Susannah Dickinson, an old Tejana called Donna Petra, a beautiful young girl named Trinidad Saucedo, and a few other women and children. In all about a dozen noncombatants were spared.

Meanwhile, all across the plaza and in all the rooms, Mexican soldiers circulated among the corpses sticking and resticking the bulky pale Anglo-Saxon bodies with their bayonets, mutilating some, stripping others. Mexican officers later regretted the atrocities. "There were deeds that we refrain from relating because of the sorrow that the account of the events would cause us,'' said General Filisola, who arrived several days after the battle.[45]

At last the sun rolled free and lay upon the eastern prairie. Occasional musket balls still whistled through the complex. But the killing fever abated as units slowly mustered. Some units had nearly ceased to exist. Already soldiers were asking one another what had happened, who was left, who was gone.

Then someone discovered survivors. A half dozen exhausted rebels, among them a fourteen-year-old boy, were hiding in a back room. Troops rushed into the room eager for more slaughter. But a gracious, aging general named Manuel Fernandez Castrillón happened to be present. He called off the wild-eyed troops.

General Castrillón approached the terrified rebels, placed his hand upon his breast, and declared, "Here is a hand and a heart to protect you; come with me to the General-in-Chief, and you shall be saved."[46] Whether or not he spoke English—whether or not the rebels understood Spanish—Castrillón personally guaranteed safety to the captives. A career professional steeped in Old World manners, the general had enough seniority that he could safely chastise his commander and president. As far as he was concerned, these Anglo-Americans had fought as bravely as the Mexican troops. In itself that should earn them asylum. And besides, Mexico was a civilized republic. If nothing else, these and other prisoners of war could be used for labor on public works in Mexico to help defray the expense of the Texas campaign.

Gently General Castrillón led one man, a stooped "venerable-looking" *anciano* (ancient), by the hand as they entered the mission courtyard.[47] The captive's face had gone gray with shock, but his cheeks were still red and his eyes still blue. He was stooped at the waist from a wound or dysentery or maybe just hunger. Castrillón was to learn that his prisoner was a famous comic and sportsman. He had just captured the former congressman David Crockett.

Side by side, the two old men walked out onto the plaza. Hundreds of dead and wounded men sprawled across the two acres of enclosure. The ground was littered with weapons, expended cannonballs, torn uniforms, musket balls, and severed limbs. Men's hair and uniforms had ignited, and between the dense white gunsmoke and smoldering flesh, the air was almost unbreathable. Blood snaked into ruts and depressions in the earth.

Guided by old Castrillón, the prisoners passed among their former friends and comrades. While sunlight stabbed the white and blue gunsmoke, Castrillón and his *anciano* threaded through the Alamo plaza.

Later, Americans would claim there was no surrender, that Crockett
went down like Hercules, clubbing Mexican soldiers into a bony mash at
his feet with the shattered stump of Old Betsy. They would dress him like
Natty Bumpo in buckskins and a raccoon cap, put oaths on his lips and
a dripping Bowie knife in his hands. They would name steamboats,
railroad trains, frontier towns, and a marching song after him. They
would anoint this day, March 6, 1836, the inaugural moment of Manifest
Destiny.

As it was, in the end, shortly after six o'clock in the morning, David
Crockett made a choice. The Go Ahead man quit. He did more than quit.
He lied. He dodged. He denied his role in the fighting.

With his life in the balance, Crockett proceeded to do what he did
best: talk. Like the Mexican deserter in the chapel, he started spinning the
most important tall tale of his life. Crockett wished it understood that he
was a simple traveler who had accidentally gotten swept into the whirlwind of revolution. Fearing that the Mexican army would abuse him for
being a foreigner, Crockett explained, he had taken refuge in the Alamo.
His captor dismissed his story as the fabric of a frightened man, but still
felt it was time to quit killing.

Dressed in an unpretentious field uniform, looking (in Joe's words)
like a Methodist preacher, Santa Anna was surveying the battle scene
when Castrillón presented his grimy, exhausted captives.

"Santa Anna, the august," Castrillón pronounced. "I deliver up to
you six brave prisoners of war."

The general's insolence upset Santa Anna. From the start of this
campaign his staff members had tried to alter his judgment. They had
argued against his overland blitzkrieg upon Béxar, even pressed him to
bypass Béxar.

Santa Anna resented having to fight his own officers as well as the
enemy. Only two days earlier his generals had advised against storming
this decrepit mission, counseling a further wait. But they were wrong,
obviously, for the adobe fortress had crumbled like a dirt clod. And here
was Castrillón opposing him once again. Worse, he was doing it publicly,
in front of the troops.

"Who has given you orders to take prisoners?" Santa Anna demanded. At every level, from red flags to the "Degüello" to written
decrees, Santa Anna had made clear that he would grant no quarter.

The prisoners stood bunched together like so much livestock, only six
feet away from the most powerful man in Mexico. The frontiersman who
had dreamed of becoming President of the United States stood almost

within reach of the President who dreamed of becoming an emperor. Both Crockett and Santa Anna were the same height, about five feet eight or ten inches. Neither spoke the other's language.

Crockett straightened up, perhaps already formulating a speech. He folded his arms across his chest.

What Santa Anna saw was an arrogant mercenary with gunsmoke staining his creased face. He saw a wetback. A slave trader and smuggler. A pirate. A heretic. A quarter of a century earlier, Santa Anna had left men no different from this hanging like fruit from oak and pecan trees by the nearby Medina River or rotting in the turkey and cow shit.

Santa Anna did not look into David Crockett's eyes. "I do not want to see those men living," Santa Anna said. He turned his back on the prisoners. "Shoot them."

What happened next horrified many of the Mexican officers standing near their leader. Among the seven soldiers who later talked about it, several said the order was carried out with musket fire, others that swords were used. But whatever the weapon, the execution was attended by so much wild brutality that nearby officers had to jump out of the way to avoid being injured or killed themselves.

De la Peña was there: "Santa Anna answered Castrillón's intervention in Crockett's behalf with a gesture of indignation and, addressing himself to the sappers, the troops closest to him, ordered his execution. The commanders and officers were outraged at this action and did not support the order, hoping that once the fury of the moment had blown over these men would be spared; but several officers who were around the president and who, perhaps, had not been present during the moment of danger, became noteworthy by an infamous deed, surpassing the soldiers in cruelty. They thrust themselves forward, in order to flatter their commander, and with swords in hand, fell upon these unfortunate, defenseless men just as a tiger leaps upon his prey. Though tortured before they were killed, these unfortunates died without complaining and without humiliating themselves before their torturers. It was rumored that General Sesma was one of them; I will not bear witness to this, for though present, I turned away horrified in order not to witness such a barbarous scene. . . . I confess that the very memory of it makes me tremble and that my ear can still hear the penetrating, doleful sound of the victims."

It was just after eight o'clock. With the loss of some six hundred dead and wounded troops—many of the wounded dying after agonizing days or months without medical care—the Mexican army had overrun approximately 182 mercenaries and revolutionaries. Ever elusive, Santa Anna would report to the Mexican government that his own losses amounted to only 70 killed and 300 wounded, and that enemy dead totaled more than 600. (And matching him for absurdity, Susannah Dickinson would claim the Mexicans lost 1,600—though their total forces in the battle totaled only 1,800.)[48]

Pointing at the scattered heaps of dead and wounded men, Santa Anna expressed his Napoleonic sentiment to Capt. Fernando Urizza. "Much blood has been shed; but the battle is over: it was but a small affair."[36]

Nevertheless, Santa Anna realized the Alamo had cost more lives than could be justified. As Sánchez Navarro blackly observed that day, "It can truly be said that with another such victory as this we'll go to the devil."[23] Even with the loss of six hundred men, Santa Anna still had over five thousand troops in the field. Furthermore, he had predicted control of San Antonio by the beginning of March and it was now the beginning of March. He was on schedule, his army was strong, and within two weeks he would consolidate his domination of western Texas by the capture of Goliad. In terms of strategy, Santa Anna's campaign was intact. But, despite his nonchalance, throwing away hundreds of Mexican lives to take a structure that would have fallen on its own was a serious political wound. Santa Anna's report to Secretary of War Tornel reflected his worries about the political consequences of the battle. As any commander would, he termed the victory a glorious triumph. But he was less than truthful in calling the Alamo ("a mere corral and nothing more" according to his secretary, Ramón Caro[49]) a "Fortress." And he outright lied in presenting the death toll of his troops and of the enemy.

General Filisola was especially critical of the battle, questioning the need to take the Alamo at all since it was surrounded by an army of five thousand or more men. He argued that the rebel garrison could have been starved out, or even persuaded to surrender . . . if surrender had been allowed as an option. "In our opinion all that bloodshed of our soldiers as well as of our enemies was useless," Filisola said, "having as its only objective an inconsiderate, childish and culpable vanity so that it might be proclaimed that Bexar had been reconquered by force of arms and that in the attack many men had died on both sides. As we have already stated, the defenders of the Alamo were ready to surrender with only the condition that their lives should be saved."

What Filisola and other officers failed to appreciate was that their supreme commander's egomania was exacerbated by his dependency upon opium mixed with alcohol. In order to try to make credible his warped judgments, Santa Anna had to become more incredible. This pattern, merely glimpsed in his military decisions in Texas, came to inform garish portions of his later public life. In short, the visionary *caudillo* was mad.

For the moment, though, as the Alamo lay smoking beneath the morning sun, Santa Anna had a victory to savor. The army had been bloodied, with some of the finest units taking the brunt of the losses. But he had crushed into dirt the filibuster spark in San Antonio, and his southern wing under General Urrea was hounding the Anglo-Americans around Goliad. His reconquest of Texas and expulsion of the heretics was on schedule and unobstructed. Twenty-three years had passed since he was last in San Antonio, and now, by repeating the past—by marching along the Camino Real, engaging in battle, and executing filibusters—he appeared to have embraced a secret destiny. His lieutenants might grumble about the death toll, but Santa Anna had just demonstrated to Mexico that he was a magical warrior-king. His victories were Mexico's victories. His greatness was Mexico's greatness.

Shortly after executing the combatants taken prisoner by Castrillón, the gored battalions were assembled in hollow square for a speech. Santa Anna stood before the troops and with great animation lauded them for their courage and thanked them in the name of Mexico. But de la Peña was quick to notice how resentful the soldiers were to their President's lofty words. "The *vivas* were seconded icily, and silence would hardly have been broken if I . . . had not addressed myself to the valiant chasseurs of Aldama, hailing the Republic and them, an act which, carried out in the presence of the commander on whom so much unmerited honor had been bestowed, proved that I never flatter those in power."

Throughout the execution and the speech, the women, children, and Joe were kept under guard in the southwest room of the chapel, across from the baptistery. When Santa Anna finished and retired, the prisoners were marched out through the appalling carnage. Both Susannah Dickinson and Joe saw Crockett lying between the chapel and the two-story barracks building, though the acting San Antonio *alcalde*, Francisco Antonio Ruiz, claimed to find Crockett's remains farther west, possibly closer to the eighteen-pounder.[50] "I . . . even remember seeing his peculiar cap lying by his side," said Dickinson. Since Crockett was never known to wear a coonskin cap, his "peculiar cap" was most likely the visored hat particular to Crockett.[9]

Joe was cut out from the women and children to identify bodies, and the small train of stunned, weeping prisoners was marched past the bodies and debris to the south gate. They were led through the burned, bullet-riddled jacales surrounding the Alamo entrance and over the wooden footbridge to town. Still bunched together, the women and children were confined in the house of Ramón Musquiz, a political chief who had for years been walking the tightrope between faraway Mexican centralism and the realities of an aggressive Anglo-American presence in Texas. He had administered laws as best he could, maintaining his neutrality through the War Dog years and the revolution.[51] In 1835 he had been arrested along with Governor Viesca by General Cós for corrupt government in Coahuila y Tejas,[52] but had escaped and made his way back to San Antonio in time to participate in Cós's surrender to the rebels. Now San Antonio was changing hands again, and Musquiz was again administering civil order. But his loyalty to Santa Anna was suspect, and he was almost as much a prisoner as the others in his house.

None of the women and children had eaten breakfast. Despite the horrifying morning, they were famished. Enrique Esparza's mother began rummaging through Musquiz's house to find food, but when Musquiz came home and found her foraging, he fearfully told her how dangerous it was to leave the prisoners' room. The woman said she didn't care, she was going to feed her family and companions since Santa Anna would not. Musquiz finally admonished her to be quiet and went to his store to fetch them coffee, bread, and meat.

About a half hour after the firing ceased, several of the town fathers—including the acting *alcalde* Francisco Ruiz, the curate of Refugio de la Garza, and Ramón Musquiz—were summoned into the Alamo compound. All night long these gentlemen had been assembled, awaiting directions. They had gathered at a fortified field hospital on Portero Street in the early hours of the morning to help oversee care of the wounded, and when the assault commenced and soldiers began screaming for aid, the town fathers had crossed the bridge to care for them. They had got to within one hundred yards of the Alamo, when in the darkness a party of Mexican chasseurs, probably Colonel Morales's column at the southwest corner, had fired upon them, forcing their retreat back to the field hospital.

Now, as the morning sun played down on the battlefield, Santa Anna sent for the civic leaders to present themselves to him. He asked them to tend the dead. So Ruiz sent off a call to his neighbors to drive in some oxcarts to carry the bodies, and then at Santa Anna's request, walked through the premises with the President and pointed out the three men the Mexicans had heard much about: Travis, Bowie, and Crockett.

Santa Anna had decided that his dead soldiers were to be buried in the consecrated grounds of Campo Santo Cementerio. The rebels, who were heretics and could not rest in consecrated soil, were to be cremated in three pyres. Cremation was considered a final, barbarous insult to the dead. It had disappeared from Western Europe as a burial practice by the sixth century, because it was widely believed that the body needed to be whole in order to resurrect upon the Second Coming.[53] Anglo-Americans would point at Santa Anna's treatment of the Alamo dead as final evidence of his evil.

In order to distinguish the corpses by race and assign each its destination, the faces were to be wiped clean of battle grime. That afternoon one of the Mexican soldiers gained an audience with Santa Anna and presented an unusual request. The soldier's name was Francisco Esparza, and he had an unfortunate brother named Gregorio who had fought with the rebels. With gracious clemency, Santa Anna permitted Francisco to hunt through the bodies and take his brother's to Campo Santo for individual burial.

While the creaking wood-and-rawhide oxcarts slowly trundled bodies downriver to the ford, and through town to mass graves, a company of chasseurs accompanied *Alcalde* Ruiz to the nearby forest to haul back wood for the funeral pyres. As he crossed the river around three o'clock, he was halted by the horrifying sight of dozens and dozens of Mexican bodies drifting in it. The San Antonio River not only anchored all life in the region, it reached out with its *acequias* for many miles around. And now the sacred river was polluted with death. Apparently exhausted by the effort of hauling bodies all the way to the cemetery, soldiers had begun dropping corpses into the water. Ruiz immediately ordered the practice stopped. Then he headed to a field southeast of the Alamo and watched the construction of cremation pyres. Soldiers layered the pyres with wood and kindling, then bodies, then more wood, kindling, and bodies.

On the north side of the Main Plaza, Santa Anna was finishing with more of his ritual labors. He had struck down his enemies. Now he needed to demonstrate his imperial kindness. One by one, he had his prisoners brought in. First came Señora Alsbury with her infant son and her sister, Gertrudis. While his black manservant, Ben, quietly prepared coffee for him in the background, Santa Anna questioned the women about their role in the rebel activities, then gave each of them a blanket and two silver pesos and freed them. The next prisoners were shown in, and the next.

''Where is your husband?'' Santa Anna asked Señora Esparza, who stood surrounded by her frightened children. "He's dead at the Alamo," she answered. Santa Anna asked for the names of other people in her family, and asked if she was aware that Francisco Esparza, Gregorio's brother, was a loyal soldier in the Mexican army. She was. Then, like all of the other women, the Esparza widow received a blanket and two coins and was dismissed. Trailed by her children, she returned to her family's home in San Antonio and wept for many days and nights.

The *caudillo* took extra time in his interview of the blue-eyed teenager Susannah Dickinson, who limped—or was carried—into the room with a gunshot wound in her calf. He was immediately taken with little Angelina, and decided on the spot that he would raise her as his own daughter in Mexico City. Through an interpreter, probably Colonel Almonte, he laid out his plan. The girl would be raised as a virtual princess, the child of Mexico's premier leader. Susannah refused, and Colonel Almonte chivalrously interceded on her behalf. Santa Anna questioned her about the rebel army. After a while, he gave her a blanket and two pesos and dismissed her.

Joe, too, came under special attention. As Travis's slave, he had been very close to the center of events in the Alamo. A modest and candid young man, Joe was very bright ("he related the affair . . . remarkably distinctly for one of his class," a land speculator later complimented him,[54]) and represented a golden source of intelligence to the officers who had already begun poring through papers captured in the battle. Santa Anna interrogated him closely about the state of the rebel army: Were there many American mercenaries participating and were more expected to arrive? When Joe answered that more American citizens were coming to fight, Santa Anna said it didn't matter; if he so chose his army could reach the very Capitol of the United States.[11]

Santa Anna had other good uses to make of Joe. He knew that a prisoner of war was more than a soldier of misfortune: He was a receptacle. He could be filled with illusions and warnings and then set loose to demoralize the enemy. To that end, Joe was treated to a grand review of the Mexican army, and told it numbered eight thousand men. He had seen the wrath of Santa Anna and had looked the dead rebels in the face. Now he was well prepared to spread a message of terror among the colonists and mercenaries over the eastern horizon.

Santa Anna knew also that by sparing and freeing this black slave, he clearly advertised to all slaves in Texas that Mexico was their friend. Escape their master and flee west, and they would enter freedom. (Some even entered the Mexican army.[55]) That was the potent message Anglo-

American slave owners had long dreaded as threatening their entire economic and social construct. The very fact of Joe's survival and release from captivity served notice on all that Southerners held basic and vital in Texas. For years, rumors would continue that Mexican agents were trying to incite slaves on their border.

The afternoon wound down. Troops finished scattering kindling among the pyres. Others buried their dead at Campo Santo. Widows grieved, not only Susannah and Señora Esparza, but the Indian and mestizo women who had followed their men from villages throughout Mexico. In houses, jacales, and tents, in the streets and along the river, wounded soldiers groaned and screamed.

"In fact, the plight of our wounded was quite grievous," de la Peña bitterly declared, "and one could hardly enter the places erroneously called hospitals without trembling with horror. The wailing of the wounded and their just complaints penetrated the innermost recesses of the heart; there was no one to extract a bullet, no one to perform an amputation, and many unfortunates died whom medical science could have saved. General Santa Anna doubtless thought that he could alleviate the sufferings of his victims by appearing frequently among them, smiling at those miserable men who scarcely had the energy to see him, offering them their full pay with one hand but ordering it not to be disbursed with the other. There were many fools who were encouraged by his words, but to mislead them was an insult to their misfortune."

More scandalous than the absence of medical care after the battle was the predatory control of goods which kept even the bare essentials out of the reach of wounded soldiers. Sánchez Navarro observed that the wounded lacked even "mattresses on which to lie or blankets with which to cover themselves, in spite of the fact that on entering Béxar, we took from the enemy the remnants of three or four stores and that one has been set up and called the Government Store, where everything is sold at high price and for cash."

Corrupt officers, among them General Ramírez y Sesma, the quartermaster general Ricardo Dromundo (another of Santa Anna's brothers-in-law), and Santa Anna himself, inflated prices on food and goods to four times their normal rate. *Piloncillo* (sweets) sold for one peso (a day's wage), flour for a peso per pound, a tablet of chocolate for two reales, a measure of corn for three pesos.

The corruption might have been more palatable if the grand *caudillo* had shown his wounded soldiers the barest generosity. But when the general call went out to officers to give up their linen for bandages, Santa

Anna refused.[56] Sánchez Navarro remembered that the President of Mexico grew angry when asked for so much as a single peso.[23]

At last the sun rolled low and touched the western edge of the world. Finally ready, the funeral pyres were lit at five o'clock. Down at Concepción Mission south of town, Pablo Diaz, a Mexican teenager who had emigrated to San Antonio from Monclova with his older brother, witnessed the cremation. "I saw an immense pillar of flame shoot up a short distance to the south and east of the Alamo and the dense smoke from it rise high in the clouds." It was spectacular and substantial, taking two days and nights to burn. Finally on the third day the flame and smoke subsided. "I left my retreat and came forth cautiously," Diaz said. "I noticed that the air was tainted with the terrible odor of many corpses, and I saw thousands of vultures flying over me. As I reached the ford in the river my gaze encountered a terrible sight. The stream was congested with corpses that had been thrown into it. . . . I halted, horrified, and watched the vultures in their revel and shuddered at the sickening sight. Then involuntarily I put my hands before my eyes and turned from the river, which I hesitated to cross. Hurriedly I turned aside and up La Villita Street and went to South Alamo Street. I could not help seeing the corpses which congested the river all around the bend. . . .

"They stayed there many days and until the alcalde [Francisco Ruiz] got a force sufficient to dislodge them and float them down the river. But while this was a gruesome sight, the one I saw later filled me with horror. I went out on the Alameda. It was a broad and spacious irregularly-shaped place and flanked on both sides with huge cottonwood trees, from which it gets its name. . . . Looking eastward, I saw a large crowd gathered. Intuitively I went to the place.

"The crowd was gathered around the smouldering embers and ashes of the fire I had seen from the mission. . . . I did not need to make inquiry. The story was told by the silent witnesses before me. Fragments of flesh, bones and charred wood and ashes revealed it in all its terrible truth. Grease that had exuded from the bodies saturated the earth for several feet beyond the ashes and smouldering mesquite faggots. The odor was more sickening than that from the corpses in the river. I turned my head aside and left the place in shame."[57]

There the remains lay open to the wind and the animals. A year later, Capt. Juan Seguín, the Tejano revolutionary, gathered some of the ashes and bones in a coffin. Placing the coffin in state in the San Fernando Church, he draped it with a Texas Republic flag and set upon that a rifle and sword. On February 25, 1837, a procession of Texas soldiers, local officials, and curious San Antonians walked the remains back across the river. There were three volleys of musket fire and two speeches, and then the ashes were buried by a peach orchard.[58]

A folk tale quickly grew. It was said that the dead rebels became ghosts wielding swords of flame, and that they protected the Alamo from destruction.[59] To this day, the staff and security personnel will not enter certain portions of the Alamo after dark.

= 19 =

THE ALAMO'S FATE remained a mystery to the rebel soldiers in Gonzales for almost five days after the battle was over. Travis had established that he would fire off the eighteen-pounder three times a day, as long as the Alamo held, a distinctive sound which could be heard in Gonzales. But the cannon fire had ceased. The townful of widows (who didn't yet know they were widows) and children listened in vain.

On the afternoon of March 11, Gen. Sam Houston arrived in Gonzales to pull together reinforcements for Travis and the Alamo garrison. At four o'clock that same afternoon, two Tejanos materialized from *ranchos* midway to San Antonio. Andres Barcenas was fleeing Santa Anna's *sorteo* in the company of Anselmo Bergaras, one of Capt. Juan Seguín's men. While resting at a *rancho* the pair had memorized a blood-chilling account of the Alamo's fall from another Tejano who was staying at the *rancho*.[1] The information turned out to be almost as accurate as it was horrifying. The Alamo had fallen; 521 Mexican infantry had been killed, with many wounded; Bowie had died in bed, either by his own hand or the enemy's; Travis had shot or stabbed himself; 7 rebels had surrendered and then been executed; the bodies of the Americans had been burned in a pyre.

Houston promptly arrested the two Tejanos. Some of his men suspected that they were agents sent by Santa Anna to spread confusion with their lies. But Houston's instincts spoke differently. "On my arrival here this afternoon, the following intelligence was received through a Mexican, supposed to be friendly, though his account has been contradicted in some parts by another, who arrived with him. It is therefore only given to you as a rumor, though I fear a melancholy portion of it will be found true. . . . I have little doubt but that the Alamo has fallen—whether above particulars are all true may be questionable."[2] Houston smelled reality, however, and to curb a wild panic in the Anglo-American community, he decided to quarantine the men with their terrible story.

Then Houston wrote a dispatch to Colonel Fannin in Goliad who was still waiting in his stone presidio. Houston finally made up Fannin's mind for him. "Sir: You will, as soon as practicable after the receipt of this order, fall back upon Guadalupe Victoria, with your command, and such artillery as can be brought with expedition. The remainder will be sunk in the river. You will take the necessary measures for the defence [*sic*] of Victoria, and forward one third the number of your effective men to this point [Gonzales], and remain in command until further orders.

"Every facility is to be afforded to women and children who may be desirous of leaving that place. Previous to abandoning Goliad, you will take the necessary measures to blow up that fortress; and do so before leaving its vicinity. The immediate advance of the enemy may be confidently expected, as well as a rise of water. Prompt movements are therefore highly important."[3]

Houston wanted nothing more to do with garrisoned troops "forted up." Instead he had in mind what Santa Anna dreaded most, a guerrilla warfare of the sort Crockett had recommended. "We must not depend on Forts," Houston wrote next day, "the roads and ravines suit us best."[4]

But no Mexican troops speckled the western horizon. There were no refugees from San Antonio. Still, men were beginning to gather at Gonzales the way they had rallied back in September for the Come and Take It cannon fight. There were only a few hundred of them, and as seemed to be the habit of volunteers in this revolution, they had shown up without provisions. Houston's little army had only two days' supply of food, and many of the men were without guns or the ammunition with which to fire them.[5]

On Sunday, March 13, Houston sent Deaf Smith west to hunt up information about the enemy. Within hours the scout came back with all the information Houston could stand. For he had intercepted Susannah Dickinson and her daughter on horseback, along with Ben, Santa Anna's black manservant, who was carrying a proclamation from the President of Mexico to his wayward flock. Plodding along with this trio and hiding in the brush at every noise was Joe, Travis's slave, who had decided life among the Mexican soldiers lacked sufficient attractions. The pathetic survivors of the Alamo introduced Santa Anna's thunderous message into the Anglo-American colonies. No prisoners. No quarter. The revolution was done. Santa Anna was on the march with thousands of soldiers.

"Citizens!" read the proclamation Ben handed to Houston. "A parcel of audacious adventurers, maliciously protected by some inhabitants of a neighboring republic, dared to invade our territory, with an intention of dividing amongst themselves the fertile lands that are contained in the spacious department of Texas; and even had the boldness to entertain the idea of reaching the capital of the Republic. It became necessary to check and chastise such enormous daring. . . . I am pained to find amongst those adventurers the names of some colonists, to whom had been granted repeated benefits, and who had no just motive of complaint against the government of their adopted country. These ungrateful men must also suffer the just punishment that the laws and the public vengeance demand. But if we are bound to punish the criminal, we are not the less compelled to protect the innocent. It is thus that the inhabitants of this country, let their origin be whatever it may, who should not appear to have been implicated in such iniquitous rebellion, shall be respected in their persons and property, provided they come forward and report themselves to the commander of the troops within eight days after they should have arrived in their respective settlements, in order to justify their conduct and to receive a document guaranteeing to them the right of enjoying that which lawfully belongs to them.

"Béxarians! Return to your homes and dedicate yourselves to your domestic duties. Your city and the fortress of the Alamo are already in possession of the Mexican army, composed of your own fellow citizens; and rest assured that no mass of foreigners will ever interrupt your repose, and much less, attack your lives and plunder your property. The supreme government has taken you under its protection, and will seek for your good."[6]

Houston received the news from Deaf Smith between eight and nine o'clock that night. By midnight the rebel army was in retreat along with what remained of the populace of Gonzales. Three cannons had been hastily rolled into the river, and as the marchers worked east into the night the town of Gonzales suddenly leapt into flames. Houston had ordered it razed. The enemy would find nothing but ashes in Gonzales.

But Santa Anna's terrorism worked. No sooner did Houston's army hear the news than men deserted to return home and protect their families. Unlike the mercenaries under Travis and Fannin, many of the soldiers in Houston's patchwork army owned property in Texas, and their first loyalty was to family and hearth. These deserters spread the news of Santa Anna's terrible approach, causing further panic. Houston knew that he would soon have no army this way. "I intend desertion shall not be frequent," he warned, "and I regret to say that I am compelled to regard as deserters all who have left camp without leave; to demand their apprehension; and that, whenever arrested, they be sent to me at headquarters for trial. They have disseminated throughout the frontier such exaggerated reports, that they have proceeded dismay and consternation among the people to a most distressing extent.''[5]

In Washington-on-the-Brazos, the revolutionary delegates were still conducting their bombastic convention. On March 15, they were discussing land issues when a settler arrived with the news that Travis's boys had successfully held the Alamo against Mexican attack, inflicting great loss upon the enemy. This was the first word they had received about the Alamo in many days. But the second word arrived a half hour later in dispatches from Houston. The Alamo was lost.

Andrew Briscoe, one of the convention delegates—a War Dog and friend of Travis's—wrote a letter to the editor of the *Red River Herald,* and his account was quickly copied by newspapers throughout the United States. ''Béxar has fallen! After about an hour's fighting the whole garrison was put to death save the sick and wounded and seven who asked for quarter. All fought desperately until entirely cut down. The rest were coolly murdered. The brave and gallant Travis, in order to save himself from falling into the hands of the enemy, shot himself. Not an individual escaped. . . . Colonels James Bowie and Crockett were among the slain; the first was murdered in his bed in which he had been confined by sickness. The latter fell fighting like a tiger.''[7]

The pond's ripple took weeks to reach the Eastern seaboard. On April 12 the New York *Sun* printed the first news to hit New England, including rumors that Travis and Bowie had committed suicide and that Crockett had surrendered. The tale took on embellishments. The *Louisiana Advertiser* reported that when General Cós entered the Alamo, he forced Joe to identify his dead master, upon which ''Cos drew his sword and mangled his [Travis's] face and limbs with the malignant feeling of a savage.'' When Bowie's body was brought to the pyre, Cós reportedly said that ''he was too brave a man to be burned like a dog, then added *pero no es cosa, échale* [never mind, throw him in].'' The Mexican casualty figures leapt into the thousands.[8]

Naturally, Crockett was not allowed to die an ordinary death. Reported the *Columbian Centinel,* ''CROCKETT was found [within the Alamo] in an angle made by two houses, lying on his back, a frown on his brow, a smile of scorn on his lips—his knife in his hand, a dead Mexican lying across his body, and twenty-two more lying pell-mell before him in the angle. Glory enough this—for one day!''[9]

''Spirits of the mighty, though fallen!'' sang the *Telegraph and Texas Register* with the archaic notes of Sir Walter Scott, ''Honors and rest are with ye: the spark of immortality which animated your forms, shall brighten into a flame, and Texas, the whole world, shall hail ye like the demi-gods of old, as founders of new actions, and as patterns of imitation!"[10]

"By Hercules," Thomas Carlyle responded to news of Bowie's death. "The man was greater than Caesar or Cromwell—nay, nearly equal to Odin or Thor. The Texans ought to build him an altar!"[11]

Not everyone agreed. Well before the Alamo fell, opinions about the rebellion in Texas had hardened largely upon lines that would divide the United States during the Civil War. While Southerners quickly demonized Santa Anna and the Mexican army, Northerners were slow to condemn and, in some cases, actually rationalized the Mexican point of view. "However much our sympathies may be enlisted in favor of the oppressed Texans," a Boston editor wrote in the *Columbian Centinel,* "it cannot be disguised that they have placed themselves in hostile array against their own government. A state of civil war has been produced between the Texans and the Mexican Government, in which it would not be politic, either for the Government or any portion of the people of the United States, to interfere. Should any of our people mingle in the fray, they would be considered in the light of freebooters and pirates, and as such, they would be exposed to capital punishment. So, also, in regard to our nation, should our Government favor the Texans, it would be considered as a breach of the peace with Mexico."[12]

Northern newspapers ranted against the clear violations of U.S. neutrality by mercenaries heading for Texas, condemning Sam Houston and others ("a vile crew of mercenary, hypocritical swindlers [and] artful deceivers") for inviting American citizens to "join the crusade with weapons of war." It was, thundered the New York *Sun,* "a prostitution of national faith and honor. . . . An extensive and well organized gang of swindlers in Texas lands, have raised the cry, and the standard of 'Liberty!' and to the thrilling charm of this glorious word, which stirs the blood of a free people, as the blast of the bugle arouses every nerve of the war-horse, have the generous feelings of our citizens responded in ardent delusion."[13]

Indeed, before it was all over, Northerners would greet Santa Anna as a great man who had been slandered. "SANTA ANNA," cried the *Patriot* of Woonsocket, Rhode Island. "How can we style him a tyrant . . . who opposed the efforts of rebels and used them with deserved severity . . . [who] fought and bled to contravene the efforts of those who wished to . . . substantiate the horrible system of slavery?"[14]

The Mexican media was, of course, ecstatic in their treatment of the conquering *caudillo.* "IMMORTAL GLORY TO THE ILLUSTRIOUS GENERAL SANTA ANNA," shouted *El Nacional,* "ETERNAL PRAISE TO THE INVINCIBLE ARMY OF MEXICO."[15] Much of this good press was a function of the centralists' desire to promote their man. But much also was due to Santa Anna's deliberate deceptions about the number of enemy killed and Mexicans lost. Based on Santa Anna's skewed kill ratio, exuberant Mexican congressmen trampled upon the New Orleans Greys' silk flag, which had been captured at the Alamo and then sent to Mexico City (where it remains today).[15] The federalist papers were less enthusiastic, but it was hard to fault a victor engaged with the Anglo-Saxons. So long as Santa Anna continued winning in Texas, he was assured the vivas of his nation and the relative silence of his critics. And Santa Anna continued winning.

On maps, the strategy for the final thrust to the Sabine River looked like a trident stabbing eastward. The three prongs were composed of General Urrea to the south, General Gaona to the north, and General Ramírez y Sesma in the center. Urrea's southern arm would smash and scatter resistance as far as Brazoria, then head for San Felipe de Austin. Gaona was ordered to take Bastrop along the Camino Real and proceed, eventually, to San Felipe. And Ramírez y Sesma was handed the heart of the colonies, Stephen Austin's little colonial capital, San Felipe. A fourth section under General Andrade would remain in San Antonio, tending the wounded and keeping open the logistics and retreat line.[16]

Less than a week after the Alamo fell, Santa Anna turned his army loose upon the rebels.

Down in the Goliad presidio, Fannin was getting tugged in two different directions. In a closing rescue effort, he had sent Capt. Amon B. King to Refugio to evacuate colonist families. On March 12, Fannin received word that King needed help. But on the same day, he received Houston's correspondence instructing him to abandon the *presidio* and fall back. Torn between Houston's order to retreat and King's plea for help, Fannin became hesitant. "We could not remember ever having seen Fannin, usually so gallant and at times almost rash, so undecided . . ." the young mercenary Herman Ehrenberg said of his commanding officer. ". . . it seemed that one plan after another passed through his head. The large number seemed to confuse him and to hinder him. . . ."[17]

Fannin dispatched Col. William Ward and some of his Georgia Battalion to race south and extract King from his difficulties. Then he waited. But as Houston knew, there was nothing to win by waiting for the tidal wave. General Urrea quickly surrounded Ward and his two hundred men on March 14. That night, under cover of a blinding norther and rainstorm, Ward's band slipped away. Urrea's troops pursued the fleeing Anglo-Americans, killing sixteen and capturing thirty-one.

Urrea's body count was mounting, but so was the number of his prisoners. Soon he had over fifty captive rebels, a sizable body of hostile soldiers who needed to be guarded constantly. Urrea was well aware of Santa Anna's order to execute all prisoners of war, but he quietly refused. Then, on March 16, Urrea captured one of Fannin's messengers who held dispatches exposing Fannin's plan to wait for Ward and King and then abandon Goliad and fall back to Victoria, where the rebels would concentrate.[18] Urrea realized that if he could catch this lamb in mid-retreat, Fannin would be finished. But it would require mobility and speed. And there were the prisoners.

For days, Urrea had been listening to complaints and even receiving petitions from his officers about the prisoners. The division's rapid progress had been exhausting, and the freezing northern weather had sapped them. Urrea's 250 Mayan soldiers, in particular, had suffered. Dropped from their Yucatán jungle into a Texan winter, several had already died in snowstorms. In short, his men were fatigued, and the extra duty of guarding rebels was too much. The officers had pressed Urrea to follow Santa Anna's order and dispense with the pirates. Then, Urrea finally relented. He authorized the execution of thirty mercenaries—after his departure from camp. He determined the remainder of the prisoners to be Mexicans or colonists, and therefore deserving of the benefit of the doubt. These men were ordered to be released. With that he sped off for Goliad.[19]

Goliad—or Fort Defiance—had all the makings of another Alamo siege. The difference was that Fannin could probably have withstood a Mexican assault almost indefinitely, for the fort had been designed as a military stronghold atop a hill. The walls had been strengthened with packed earth to cannonball-proof them, twelve pieces of artillery were mounted, there was a two-hundred-yard "covered way" connecting the presidio with the river. Fannin had over four hundred troops, well-mounted artillery, and abundant food supplies. But Travis's defeat had undermined Fannin's confidence, and Houston's order further subverted Fannin's boast of no retreat. If he was going to retreat, he needed to immediately . . . but he didn't. If he was going to stand and fight, he needed to nerve his men and load his guns . . . but he didn't. Fannin ordered a number of the fort's cannons buried as preparation for a retreat. Then, in the same strange whimsical way he had started and then stopped his relief of the Alamo, Fannin ordered the cannons dug up and re-mounted. It was probably too much to ask for consistency from a commander who did not want to be a commander, and who had joined the Matamoros expedition only to quit. Fannin was perhaps more vulnerable to the wind than any other man in the territory. The result was an even greater debacle than Travis's suicidal stand at the Alamo.

On March 18, a drizzly Friday morning, Fannin's garrison was set to retreat and had already hitched their oxen to the cannon they meant to remove. But when they looked over their walls and spied a small party of Mexican cavalry reconnoitering in the distance, the rebels lost all sight of their priorities. Col. Albert Clinton Horton, a plantation owner and future governor, mounted a small cavalry of his own and sallied out to do battle. The Mexican horsemen retreated, drawing Horton's group toward a larger party of Mexicans who drove him back into the fort. As the Mexicans drifted away, Horton sallied out again. Like puppies chasing one another, the opposing cavalries darted back and forth in full view of the cheering garrison. By the time Horton had returned to the fort, not only were his horses exhausted, but the garrison had forgotten to unhitch, feed, and water the oxen, meaning the retreat had to be postponed.[20] During the day, Fannin once again ordered the cannons buried. And then, once again, he ordered them dug up.

That night another norther rocked the Mexican troops assembling with Urrea to besiege the presidio. The cold, continuous rain soaked the exhausted Mexicans, permitting them no sleep. In the morning a heavy fog coated the land. When Urrea's men finally approached the presidio shortly before noon, they discovered that it was empty. Fannin had packed up and left at nine o'clock that morning, under cover of the fog. In obedience to Houston's instructions, Fannin had destroyed as much of the fort as he could, knocking down houses and walls, spiking cannons (literally driving a spike or nail into the touch hole to disable it) that could not be hauled. All surplus food, including corn and dried meat from seven hundred steers, he collected into the presidio chapel and set afire. Incredibly, the rebels somehow forgot to bring any food with them upon their retreat, so presumably their share went up in smoke too.[21] Once the fog burned off, the towering column of smoke rivaled that of the Alamo pyre.

Undaunted, Urrea immediately set out in pursuit of Fannin's slow-moving army. "I desired to obtain a triumph for our nation on this day," Urrea later confessed, "to celebrate my birthday—pardon my personal pride."[19] Fannin's men seemed intent on handing him the victory, for they were carrying every stick and possession possible to Victoria, and their carts were loaded full. At their first river crossing the banks were so steep that the men had to completely unload and then reload some of the carts to attain the trail, consuming precious time. The oxen were weary, and it became necessary to stop after only a few miles to graze the livestock. Meanwhile, Colonel Horton and his cavalry were galloping about in the rear, scouting the enemy. They reported the Mexicans were still four or five miles distant and disinclined to follow. Fannin's exodus continued, but just two miles farther the oxen seemed ready to collapse. A second, disastrous halt was called on an open field within sight of the sanctuary of Coleto Creek's forest. Fannin's confidence derived from his great contempt for Mexican fighting prowess,[22] and from his belief that four scouts posted in the rear would give an early alert.

Unknown to Fannin, Colonel Horton's scouts had dismounted and were taking a siesta. They awakened just in time to avoid being trampled by the galloping Mexican cavalry. Springing to their saddles, the scouts spurred their horses straight for cover, completely bypassing Fannin's infantrymen. "They now came up at full speed," said Dr. J. H. Barnard, who was with the infantry, "one of them, and one only [young Herman Ehrenberg] joined us. The other three, in the greatest apparent terror, passed about a hundred yards on our right, without even stopping to look at us, and under the strongest appliance of whip and spur, followed by a few hearty curses from our men."

Now aware of its danger, Fannin's column again resumed its tedious advance toward the forest. If they could make it to Coleto Creek they would have both cover and water. Nursing the half-dead oxen along, the infantry patiently pressed along one mile farther. And then, in midafternoon and with the trees of Encinal del Perdido only a half mile ahead, Urrea's cavalry bracketed the column and attacked. Unfortunately for the Anglo-Americans, they were just crossing a low meadow when Fannin decided to make a stand. It was the worst possible place for the garrison to stop. But Fannin's choices had run out.

Through the remainder of the afternoon, the beleaguered garrison fired at will, driving back several Mexican charges. The air was humid almost to the point of rain, which dampened their gunpowder, ruining it. As the afternoon dragged on and the casualties mounted, Ehrenberg and others darted from body to body, searching for weapons loaded with dry powder.[23]

"The balls were whizzing about like bees swarming . . . ," said Abel Morgan of that hot and bloody afternoon. "After a few rounds Cash [a comrade] received a ball in the corner of his head and as he fell he handed me his gun, saying, 'take this, she won't snap [misfire].' My gun had got muckey with powder, and missed fire, and he had noticed it. I took it and kept it the balance of the day. The ball cut the size of it out of his head but did not kill him. In a short time Baker who stood at my right hand, was shot down. He had his thigh broken, and before he was carried into the square he got another ball in the body."[24] Men dropped on every side. A dozen Mexican prisoners took bayonets and dug foxholes for themselves, which took them out of harm's way for the rest of the battle.

Rolling their artillery into position at various corners of the square, the Anglo-Americans slammed grapeshot into the ranks of Mexican soldiers charging with fixed bayonets. Fannin's troops were so certain Colonel Horton would come springing out from the forest that on several occasions they halted their fire lest they hit Horton's men. But Horton did not return until the next day, and by then it was far too late.

The two sides settled in for the ink-black night. Within their hollow square, the rebels suffered enormous discomfort. They had lost seven killed and sixty wounded to the afternoon's musket balls. Fannin himself had been wounded in the thigh ("a musketball penetrated a waterproof coat, a summer coat, trousers, a pocket in the overcoat, but not a silk handkerchief which Fannin found embedded in his body"[23]), and a second ball had broken the cock off his rifle. There was no food and no water. Had they continued to march in their hollow square at the Mexican cavalry's first appearance, the Anglo-Americans could have reached the safety of the trees. Now it was too late. Urrea's initial strike force had been reinforced during the afternoon and now surrounded the rebels' position, blaring away with "incessant" bugle music and shouting out "Sentinel Alerto!"[22] Unknown to Fannin, the Mexicans had nearly run out of ammunition by the end of the day. A mass escape was conceivable that unusually dark night. But Fannin refused to abandon his wounded, and he no longer had the means to transport them. What oxen had not wandered off had been killed by Mexican sharpshooters detailed by Urrea for that very purpose.[25]

All through the night the rebels tightened their defenses, piling up breastworks made of dead horses and oxen, baggage and dirt. Ten miles behind them, in Goliad, lay the best fortress a soldier could have wanted. Now all they could do was scrape earth and dead livestock into a sorry, three-foot-high semblance of a presidio. At last, dawn came, but without Colonel Horton and his troops. Overnight more Mexican soldiers had arrived, bringing with them ammunition and artillery which made the rebel breastworks almost comical. Because the garrison had been caught in a depression, the Mexican artillery "could now reach every nook and cranny of our camp, a circumstance that was not noticed yesterday in the heat of battle."[26]

"The groans of our wounded had now ceased," Ehrenberg reported of that dawn. "They had died either from their wounds or from the cold and wetness of the night; or the rain had somewhat alleviated their pains. Scattered far and near about our camp lay the dead Mexicans, that the Indians either had not found or could not carry away. A few of our men went over to view the dead bodies of the enemies, and not very far away from us they found the banner of the Mexican army under a pile of dead riders and horses and brought it into the camp. But no rejoicing hurrah came over our lips. All knew that the deciding moment, that was to decide over life and death, was soon to strike. The flag was thrown without consideration on the debris of the camp."

Abruptly the Mexicans fired a length of chain at the rebel camp, "which made a wonderful whizzing over our heads." Then the Mexicans sent a second whirling chain across the square.[27] The question of surrender could no longer be postponed. "We whipped them off yesterday," Fannin declared, "and we can do so again to-day." But yesterday the Mexicans had numbered only a few hundred, and now the Anglo-Americans counted over a thousand, including cannons and a hundred pack mules.[28] As usual, the impetuous New Orleans Greys stamped about and postured fiercely, demanding a bloody advance toward the forest "with our guns and Bowie-knives." The Greys howled against surrender. "Citizens, comrades, we now appeal to you. You do not yet know the false character of the Mexicans. You have not yet had enough intercourse with these barbarians to be able to judge them accurately. Believe the Greys; *surrender, capitulation* in Mexican is *to die.* If it shall be *to die,* let us die fighting for Texas, a sacrifice for freedom. With us hundreds of the Mexicans will fall, and possibly we will succeed in breaking through their ranks. . . ."[29] But any such running battle necessarily sacrificed the wounded, and that was out of the question.

While Fannin's men argued and strutted, he gazed across the hasty campground, a panorama of wreckage. Thirst, exhaustion, and Mexican bullets had cut his effective fighting force to two hundred. Dead men and livestock lay among the scattered carts. And the day had just begun. Grimly, Fannin put the question to a vote. The New Orleans Greys and the Alabama Red Rovers wanted to fight on, but the majority ruled, and Fannin ran up a white flag.

Immediately the Mexicans hoisted their own, and a parley commenced in midfield. Urrea sent out three Mexican officers, among them Lt. Col. Juan José Holzinger, a German mercenary who had designed Santa Anna's Manga de Clavo estate, and Col. Juan Morales, who had been the first to get his men inside the Alamo walls a fortnight earlier.[29] There was little to negotiate. The rebels could either surrender or be sliced to pieces by Mexican artillery. Through Holzinger, who spoke fair English, it was communicated that Urrea was empowered to grant no terms. The surrender had to be at discretion, meaning unconditional. Even though they accepted this condition, the rebels acted as if the surrender could be shaped to their specifications. The resulting document was curious. Article 2 provided for the care and treatment of all the wounded; article 3 stated that "all the detachment shall be treated as prisoners of war and placed at the disposal of the Supreme Government."

But Urrea's closing amendment to the surrender nullified these illusions of terms. "When the white flag was raised by the enemy, I ordered their leader to be informed that I could have no other agreement than that they should surrender at discretion, without any other condition, and this was agreed to by the persons stated above; the other petitions which the subscribers of this surrender make will not be granted. I told him this, and they agreed to it, for I must not, nor can I, grant anything else."[30]

Urrea even entered the enemy camp in order to explain the limits of his authority. "If you gentlemen wish to surrender at discretion, the matter is ended," he told Fannin, "otherwise I shall return to my camp and renew the attack."[25] Fannin signed the agreement.

"Well, gentlemen," Colonel Holzinger said as the rebels handed over their guns, "in ten days, liberty and home."

The ferocious New Orleans Greys and Alabama Red Rovers were mortified. "Inwardly deeply humiliated, which showed itself on our faces, we walked up and down in our camp, casting angry looks at Fannin and the others that had voted for the capitulation," wrote Ehrenberg. "Some sat lost in thought with eyes fixed stark on the ground and envied those who had died during the battle. Despair stood on the features of many of the men, who only too well foresaw our fate. Especially one American named Johnson made himself conspicuous because of his anger. Gnashing his teeth, he stamped on the ground. Thick clouds of smoke from his glowing Havana twirled about his head. Like the smoke from a steamboat, cloud after cloud streamed from his mouth, and quicker and quicker they issued forth. Denser and denser did the cloud mass become until it seldom revealed the head, in which now, as it seemed, a terrible plan was being worked up.

"Curiosity had brought many Mexicans into our camp, and in company with the Greys they wandered over the field covered with debris and corpses. Nervously they glanced at the stern grey cannon, which had always been frightful to them, as if they were still afraid of this, although now unarmed, enemy that had driven their dried up soldiers from house to house in San Antonio [in December]. . . ."

Suddenly an explosion lit the misty morning and knocked men to the ground. Terrified horses flew off across the dark green prairie. Just as Robert Evans had tried to do in the final minutes of the Alamo battle, someone had ignited the rebels' powder magazine. "Around the place lay several men wounded, although not severely, and about fifteen yards away from the wagon lay a black body that barely looked like one of a human being. It was still alive but not able to speak. It was burnt coal black like the color of a negro, and it was impossible to tell who the unfortunate one was."[31] A hasty roll call revealed that the dying man was the Havana-smoking Johnson.

At around that moment, Colonel Horton arrived with the reinforcements from Victoria. Including his own cavalry troops, Horton had managed to bring only thirty or forty men back to relieve Fannin.[32] The mounted company reached the scene just in time to see Fannin's surrender. From his timbered vantage point, Horton was aghast. "We stood in astonishment," he said, "and were undecided what to do when suddenly the war-like bugle notes of the Mexicans sounded. No time was to be lost; quickly we had to counsel and just as quickly we were ready. If Fannin had so far forgotten his duty as to surrender, we were obliged to save ourselves for the Republic. . . . Consequently we turned our horses and speedily galloped back to Victoria. . . ."[31]

At two o'clock that afternoon, the rebels were herded back to the Goliad presidio and packed into the burned-out chapel. "Literally stuffed," said Ehrenberg, "as we stood so close man to man that it was possible at the highest for only one-fourth to even sit down. It was well that the inner room of the church had a height of thirty-five to forty feet. If it had been lower, we would have suffocated. As it was, the air remained fairly fresh."[33] It took two more days for carts to carry the Anglo-American wounded (a little over ninety of them) off the battlefield to rejoin their comrades. On Friday, Colonel Ward and his Georgia Battalion—who had been sent south to rescue Captain King—were brought in. After escaping Urrea's encirclement, this group of some 120 men had wandered about for a week trying to reach Victoria, but Urrea had caught them too.

The starving prisoners were given only a little water for the first day, then a steer was driven up and slaughtered. Some roasted their six-ounce portion over little fires made from paneling in the church—including images and *santos,* an act that shocked the religious Mexicans. Others wolfed their beef down raw. The rebels began bartering with Mexican soldiers, swapping their clothing for tortillas. The Mexicans would banter and dicker with the prisoners, justifying their inflated prices by saying, "What good will it [an article of clothing] do you? In a few days you will be shot anyway."[34]

On the fifth morning, Colonel Holzinger offered anyone of Germanic descent among the rebel garrison an opportunity to serve with the Mexican artillery. The offer was scorned. What the rebels did not realize was that behind the scenes, Urrea was laboring to save their lives. He was well aware of Santa Anna's order to shoot all prisoners, already having executed thirty on his way to Goliad. But he believed that the cold-blooded execution of a large body of men would be out of the question, and for that reason had been concentrating prisoners in the presidio.[25] There were now approximately five hundred prisoners at Goliad, including eighty-two fresh mercenaries from New York who had just stepped off the boat at Copano into Mexican arms. These star-crossed New York recruits had already been arrested once by the British for plundering a plantation in the Caribbean. Now they accepted captivity again. Their sole distinction from the rest of the prisoners was that they had not fired a shot in Texas. Urrea directed that the wounded rebels be tended and the healthy ones be put to work rebuilding the destroyed fortifications. The Anglo-American physicians were busy caring for Mexican wounded, and two dozen carpenters had been drafted to build rafts to float Mexican artillery across rivers.

But Santa Anna wanted blood. In a stinging rebuke to Urrea written the moment he received news of their capture, Santa Anna demanded to know why the prisoners had not been shot. "I have been surprised that the circular of the said supreme government has not been fully complied with in this particular; *I therefore order, that you should give immediate effect to the said ordinance in respect to all those foreigners* who have yielded to the force of arms, having had the audacity to come and insult the republic, to devastate with fire and sword, as has been the case in Goliad, causing vast detriment to our citizens; in a word, shedding the precious blood of Mexican citizens, whose only crime has been their fidelity to their country. I trust that, in *reply* to this, you will inform me that *public vengeance has been satisfied* by the punishment of such detestable delinquents."[35]

But Urrea objected to the killings on principle. He confessed great admiration for Fannin ("his manners captivated my affection . . . a gentleman, a man of courage. . . .") and saw nothing to be gained by exterminating these men.[25] As he galloped around the southern prairie scooping up prisoners, Urrea wrote a letter (from Victoria) to Santa Anna recommending clemency.

Even as Santa Anna replied that "I yield to no one, my friend, in tender-heartedness, for I am not aware that I hate any man, and I have never had a thought of avenging even personal injuries," he also rebuked Urrea again.[36] Then he wrote out a final command in triplicate and sent it directly to twenty-eight-year-old Col. José Nicolás Portilla, who was in charge of the prisoners at Goliad. The instruction: Execute the rebels. To be sure the order was followed, Col. José Vicente Miñon—who had stormed the Alamo's south wall alongside Colonel Morales—rode to Goliad by coach to witness the execution.[37]

Colonel Portilla received Santa Anna's directive at seven o'clock on Saturday night. An hour later a second messenger rode in with a completely contradictory message from Urrea which read, in part, "Treat the prisoners well, especially Fannin. Keep them busy rebuilding the town and erecting a fort. Feed them with the cattle you will receive from Refugio."

An impatient and temperamental man, Portilla weighed life and death in his palms. "What a cruel contrast in these opposite instructions!" he complained to his diary. "I spent a restless night."[38] As midnight turned upon Palm Sunday, March 27, Portilla chose which of his higher authorities to obey.

The prisoners awoke to find that a set of cannons aimed at the front gate had been turned around and directed at them. The cannons were apparently heavily packed with grapeshot, for the serious Mexican soldiers standing behind each barrel held burning torches, ready to touch off a point-blank blast "at the first wink." Some sort of move was obviously scheduled, for several companies of raggedly uniformed Mayans stood ready. It was a gray and sultry morning, but in the prisoners' minds they were already rocking homeward on the blue Gulf waters, paroled at last. A few imagined they would be heading deeper into Mexico to labor in mines, but they consoled themselves with the knowledge that punishment would preclude parole, and if there were no parole they would be free to return to Texas someday and fight Mexicans again.

At eight o'clock an officer stepped forward holding orders which he declined to share. The prisoners were excited and curious: Were they marching off to Copano or to Matamoros for their schooner home? Either way, they were homeward bound. The prisoners assembled in a line two-deep and called their roll a last time. Men noted that Fannin was missing, along with all the garrison's physicians and assistants, the wounded, and the 82 New York mercenaries who had landed only a few days before. The prisoners paid no attention to the fact that the Mexican soldiers were carrying no packs or supplies necessary for a long march or even a night out. Shouldering their own knapsacks and what little remained of their belongings, the prisoners marched out through the front entrance of the presidio. Between 425 and 445 of them were divided into three columns, heading in different directions, and guarded on either side by files of small Mexican soldiers. In the distance, cavalry troops swarmed about in small units.

The Greys and a few colonists marched toward Victoria, presuming their destination was an eastern Texas harbor. The young German boy, Herman Ehrenberg, was with this group, and when he turned around to see how close the other two columns were, he saw only the blank prairie. The Georgia Battalion had marched off on one branch of the trail, and Fannin's militia on another. Suddenly, rememering that no quarter had been shown at the Alamo or with captured rebels at San Patricio, Ehrenberg considered the possibility of foul play. His suspicions darted back and forth between hope and fear. He refused to believe the worst. But as a precaution the boy freed himself of his few remaining possessions, letting them slip to the ground and roll away.

Fifteen minutes passed. No one said a word, neither the prisoners nor their flanking guards. The column was ordered to turn left off the Victoria road, which confused the prisoners. A thousand yards away, the San Antonio River snaked through the mesquite and spring grass. Several cavalry troops drew closer, carrying their long, dread lances, and this further confused the men. The prisoners were led toward a man-high mesquite hedge, while the Mexican soldiers formed a double file behind them. A Mexican officer shouted *"Alto!"*

"At that moment we heard the muffled rolling of a musket volley in the distance. Involuntarily we thought of our companions, who had been separated from us and evidently led off in that direction.

"Astonished and confounded we looked at each other, and cast questioning glances first at ourselves and then at the Mexicans. Then another command rang out—'Kneel down!' from the lips of the Mexican officers. Only a few of us understood Spanish and could not nor would not obey the order.

"Meanwhile the Mexican soldiers, who were barely three steps away, had leveled their muskets at our chests and we found ourselves in terrible surprise.

"We still considered it impossible to believe that they were going to shoot us. . . . Only one among us spoke Spanish fluently, whose words seemed incomprehensible to him. In doubt he stared at the commanding officer as if he wanted to read a contradiction of his features of what he had heard. The remainder of us fixed our eyes on him to thrust ourselves on the threatening enemy at the first sound from his lips. But he seemed, as we were, possessed of the unfortunate hope that this order was a naked threat to force us into Mexican service. With threatening gestures and drawn sword the chief of the murderers for the second time commanded in a brusque tone: 'Kneel down!'

"A second volley thundered over to us from another direction, and a confused cry, probably from those who were not immediately killed, accompanied it. This started our comrades out of their stark astonishment which had lasted from five or six seconds. New life animated them, their eyes flashed and they cried out:

" 'Comrades! listen to that crying, it means our brothers, hear their cry! It is their last one! Here is no more hope—the last hour of the Greys has come! Therefore—Comrades!—'

"A terrible cracking interrupted him and then everything was quiet. A thick smoke slowly rolled toward the San Antonio. The blood of my lieutenant was on my clothing and around me quivered my friends. Beside me Mattern and Curtman were fighting with death. I did not see more. I jumped up quickly, concealed by the black smoke of the powder, and rushed down the hedge to the river."[39]

Back in the presidio, the distant gunshots were explained to a startled Dr. Barnard as Mexican troops clearing their guns of damp powder.[40] Beside him, a second surgeon named Dr. John "Jack" Shackleford turned pale. It was he who had drummed up the Alabama Red Rovers—including his son Fortunatas and two nephews—and bankrolled a stand of seventy-five arms. Most of the sixty men of the Red Rovers had been recruited in Courtland, Alabama, an up-and-coming town of three hundred. One third of Courtland's male population had simultaneously caught the war fever and donned the red-dyed linsey-woolsey hunting shirt that was their uniform. Together the bunch had landed at Copano just two months earlier, on January 19. Now, hidden away in Col. Francisco Garay's room, Dr. Shackleford lost his kin. The town of Courtland lost most of its young men.[41]

The wounded rebels had been ordered outside. Those who could not walk were carried. A Mexican officer explained that carts would soon arrive to carry them off to Copano bay. But as volleys of gunfire sounded in the distance, and as soldiers' wives perched upon the walls and pointed at the various massacre sites, the wounded men absorbed the truth.

"When they became convinced from the movements about the fort that they were to be shot," said Joseph Spohn, a survivor, "the greater part of them sat down calmly on their blankets, resolutely awaiting their miserable fate; some turned pale, but not one displayed the least fear or quivering."[42]

Colonel Fannin emerged from his room and demanded to know what was going on. Capt. Carolino Huerta of the Tres Villas battalion directed Fannin to a place near the chapel wall. Limping badly, supported by Spohn, Fannin reached the spot. The Tres Villas officer approached, and Fannin gave him a gold watch which had belonged to his wife. In return, Fannin asked that the captain guarantee his burial. *"Con todas las formalidades necesarias,"* Captain Huerta replied, bowing. Then Fannin gave him a small purse of ten pesos. According to one account, he asked that Captain Huerta not shoot him in the head. Then Fannin sat down on a chair and was blindfolded. At Huerta's command, the firing squad shot Fannin in the head at close range. His body was burned.[42] The wounded were all shot, bayoneted, or sabered. Spohn, Dr. Barnard, and a few other physicians, carpenters, and medical "assistants" were spared, along with the New York contingent which sat outside the fortress wall under peach trees.

A number of men escaped death through the efforts of the so-called Angel of Goliad, Señora Francisca Alavez, the wife of a Mexican officer. Appealing to Col. Francisco Garay, who objected to the executions on principle and spared a body of prisoners, the señora managed to save numerous others. Later, as the army advanced eastward, she sent back messages and provisions to the Anglo-Americans, a remarkable act of humanity. As Dr. Barnard appreciated, "It must be remembered that when she came to Texas she could have considered its people only as *rebels* and *heretics,* the two classes of all others the most odious to the mind of a pious Mexican." The first village Señora Alavez had encountered in Texas was Goliad, a place thoroughly wrecked by Anglo-American occupation, its Hispanic population dispersed. Despite this, the woman showered the prisoners with her compassion.[43] There were other angels too. Some of the women at Matamoros, near the mouth of the Rio Grande, had sent a petition on behalf of a set of prisoners, which post-

poned and eventually canceled their execution. A few wounded Mexican
soldiers at Goliad even saved prisoners by hiding three or four in their
own beds and covering them with their bodies during the massacre.[44]

As at the Alamo, the bodies were stripped and burned. The corpses in
the presidio were carted outside the wall, and when Mexican soldiers
laundered their clothing, it turned the river's skirt red. Four different
pyres were constructed and lit. That night Abel Morgan, who had been
spared as a hospital assistant, saw several Mexican officers unable to eat
their meals because they were weeping.[45] As at the Alamo, the gruesome
crematory piles lay exposed to the elements and carnivores for many
months afterward.

Over in Victoria, General Urrea learned of the massacre several hours
after it had been carried out. Like most of the army's officers—in contrast
to most of the army's regular soldiers—he was profoundly shocked. Over
four hundred unarmed prisoners, well over twice the number of rebels in
the Alamo, had been cut down.

"The cry of horror that the Republic [of Mexico] raised and the
indignation of the civilized world made us tremble and look upon each
other with disdain," said de la Peña. "So many and such cold-blooded
murders tarnished our glory, took away the fruits of victory, and would
prolong the war and make its success doubtful, because it provoked the
enemy and placed him in the difficult dilemma of vanquishing or dying.
What opprobrium, it was said, to appear in the nineteenth century as
barbarous as the Middle Ages! Much like a horde of Hottentots and
assassins."[46]

The adjutant inspector Sánchez Navarro said it more economically.
"Sad day!" he wrote in his diary. "God grant that there may not be
another like it! Would it not be well to save the prisoners for the purpose
of using them if we should some day suffer reverses?"[47]

One small consolation for Urrea was that over a hundred men had
been spared. Skilled laborers were impressed to aid the Mexican advance
toward the Sabine River. The physicians were sent to San Antonio where,
even weeks after the Alamo battle, Mexican wounded in the assault were
in dire need. According to Dr. Barnard some 200 to 300 crippled soldiers
were being quartered in town, and another 300 to 400 had died since
March 6. Barnard and his Anglo-American colleagues found 100
wounded still requiring the most basic of care. "There has been scarcely
a ball cut out as yet, almost every patient carrying the lead he received on
that morning." As Santa Anna's military machine rolled eastward, Mexican officers and townspeople in San Antonio were understandably grate-

ful for the Anglo-Americans' medical attention, treating the physicians with great affection and respect.[48]

After getting shot at, slashed with a Mexican saber, and then shot at some more, the teenager Herman Ehrenberg had escaped into the wilderness. He became the land, the land became him, an agonizing, dreamlike act of communion. For a week of absolute starvation, the boy stumbled about lost. "I stood still to recall the map of the Republic [of Texas] to take my course accordingly," he said. "It took only a few moments and I was ready." But his compass was as imaginary as his mental map. Ehrenberg simply walked on and on, taking his bearings where he could think them up: off a patch of tree moss, from the sun, even from a rainstorm that struck the right side of his face.

Tall undulating prairie grasses swallowed him alive. For mile after mile there was only grass and the sky. "From my feet all around to the cloud layers chasing along the encircling horizon I saw myself as the only living being. No herds of deer grazed here, no gobbling turkeys passed through the prairie, and no song of a bird interrupted the festive quietness of the solitude. During the winter this region must be covered with geese, but they had a month ago undertaken their great journey [northward]. . . . Disregarding the loneliness and filled with dauntless hope I went forward with long steps, constantly and almost unconsciously whistling our favorite march [of the New Orleans Greys]." Like Robinson Crusoe reinventing himself, Ehrenberg draped Spanish moss upon his head to protect himself from the sun. He learned not to sleep in arroyos, which were prone to flash floods. Repeatedly encountering roads, he immediately crossed and abandoned them, fearful of Mexican soldiers. A herd of three hundred mustangs thundered up and considered him, then bolted away. "Meadows and islands of black forests lay about me. Numerous herds of horses, cattle and deer stared at me as I walked past them. Many a flock of turkeys marched around in procession and observed me with misgiving, while the sand grouse trumpeted its monotonous morning march."

Sinking deeper into a visionary frame of mind, Ehrenberg compared his strange odyssey to a trip through the Berlin art museum. "As one hurries through the rooms from one creation to another, so one wanders almost carelessly in the paradise of America from one park to another. . . ." The land and the animals "floated and tumbled about before my gaze." The prairie glowed. He was dying.

On the fifth or sixth day, Ehrenberg caught a small turtle. But he had to discard it, for he had no way to open its shell, no knife or stick. There were not even loose stones upon the dark red soil. He began to see mirages, conjuring up pictures of the ocean upon expanses barren of water. "I threw myself like an insane person on the prairie, buried my face on the earth and broke the hot rays of the sun by covering my head with a handful of grass." He wanted to commit suicide, but lacked the means.

Then one morning a cock crowded. Ehrenberg struggled upright and discovered that he had fallen asleep within a hundred yards of a large plantation. The civilized lines of fences and architecture gave him new vitality, and he walked on, finding more and more plantations. At last selecting one farmhouse to approach, he entered a world of reversals. All the people were gone, and animals were occupying the houses. Chickens and turkeys roosted in the branches of a china tree. Herds of hogs snored in the gardens girdled by fig and peach trees. Inside the house, an albino mule greeted him with braying. In another wealthy home, the wandering man walked into the dining parlor and found the table set and food upon the plates, all of it untouched.

And then, he discovered evidence of human life. "As I searched through the buildings another time for food, I found two names written with charcoal on one of the doors, one of which was the name of my friend, Thomas Camp.

"Up to this time I had the positive conviction that I was the only one to have luckily escaped the massacre. But here the names indicated to me that there were others who had escaped and were already ahead of me to inform the world of the infamous murder at Goliad.

"Enraptured I sank down to thank the great spirit. In the rejoicing of my heart I could have kissed the black lines. . . ."

Rooting around, Ehrenberg turned up a wooden canteen and a gray felt Kentucky hat with a wide brim. In a barn he discovered long strips of dried beef, and draped these over his neck and shoulders. Then he continued on, searching for Sam Houston and his elusive rebel army. Everywhere he went, he beheld evidence that the Anglo-Saxon dream of empire and mission had disintegrated. Ehrenberg meandered through the ghost colonies, borrowing essentials from colonists he'd never met, careful to sign his name as debtor in charcoal upon a wall. The boy never did find Houston's army. Instead—in the third week of his long escape—he walked straight into Mexican captivity once again. By then Santa Anna had determined that the revolutionary Republic of Texas was a dead issue. It almost was.

$=20=$

FROM A DISTANCE it looked like snow, but underhoof it was just white chicken feathers. Each time the long line of Anglo-American refugees heard that the Mexicans were coming just behind them, they would panic and start dumping furniture, bedclothes, and provisions out of their wagons to lighten the load. And chicken feathers would turn the prairies white for hundreds of yards at a stretch as the terrified settlers emptied out their mattresses.[1] They would whip their mules and horses to a frothing gait, then slow down and resume their fatalistic pace. Sometimes they were spurred to panic by thieves, "or devils, rather," who would spook them into a frenzy of dumping their possessions, and then would plunder the goods. Measles, whooping cough, "sore eyes," and other diseases broke out among the teeming fugitives. Bedraggled women and children walked barefoot. Babies silently died. In the absence of the dominant white male, slave men watched over their white households. But alert to their chance, some slaves escaped—and those that didn't hide out in the forests and canebrakes, looting abandoned homes, had to be watched anyway, for many of them were "wild Africans," just recently landed.

As if the land itself were conspiring to cage them in place, Texas flooded. Cold, gray rain fell, turning the roads into slick red-and-black gravy and the rivers into frantic choke points. The lowlands filled with water. Livestock drowned. One ox sank to its head in a bog and was simply left behind, still alive.[2] The bloated corpses of domestic animals bobbed out to sea.

Filled to the tops of their banks, the rivers demanded solutions of all those crossing: a dangerous fording, a rickety wooden bridge that was under water, ferrymen who gouged their pick of desperate customers. The bayous waited with quicksand, mosquitoes, and other nuisances. Having just gotten his family across one bayou, a refugee named Mr. King swam back to fetch his horses. "He had gotten nearly across with them, when a large alligator appeared. Mrs. King first saw it above water and screamed. The alligator struck her husband with its tail and he went under water. There were several men present, and they fired their guns at the animal, but it did no good. It was not in their power to rescue Mr.King.''[3] Like a succubus, Texas had drawn them deep into a dream, and now would not let them loose from the nightmare.

"The desolation of the country through which we passed beggars description," said Noah Smithwick, one of the rearguard scouts. "Houses were standing open, the beds unmade, the breakfast things still on the tables, pans of milk moulding in the dairies. There were cribs full of corn, smoke houses full of bacon, yards full of chickens that ran after us for food, nests of eggs in every fence corner, young corn and garden truck rejoicing in the rain, cattle cropping the luxuriant grass, hogs, fat and lazy, wallowing in the mud, all abandoned. Forlorn dogs roamed around the deserted homes, their doleful howls adding to the general sense of desolation. Hungry cats ran mewing to meet us, rubbing their sides against our legs in token of welcome.''[4]

Among the thousands of refugees streaming back to their homeland through the rain and mud, across rivers and bayous, were the grim Gonzales widows. Isaac Millsaps's blind wife rode with her six children. Sidney Gaston Kellogg, who had lost her brother, husband, and ex-husband all in the same day at the Alamo, gave birth to John Kellogg, Jr., as the exodus pulled her up the Camino Real. Now widowed for a second time, Esther Berry House Floyd whipped on the team pulling a sturdy wooden cart with her four children and an elderly slave couple piled in back.[5] Elizabeth, the petite Dutch wife of James George, was watched over by the crippled help, Rowe, who would soon marry her.[6]

Robert Hancock Hunter, a twenty-three-year-old settler boy who was rangering with one of the rearguard patrols, described what happened when a set of Gonzales widows caught up. "The Capt ast them, which way are you going. We are trying to git a way from the Mexicans, (there husbands was kild in the Alamo). The Capt ast them if they had no weapons. They said, yes, our horses was out on the prire, & we could not finde them, & we left our supper on the table, & we took what little clothing we could carry & our children & left. The Capt had his own waggon & team. Colonel Knight and White of San Felipe [had] put 2 large tobacco boxes in our waggon & the Capt told Leutienant McCallister to throw them boxes out of the waggon & give room for those women & children. [McCallister replied] Hell Capt that tobacco was given to the company. I was sitting on the waggon toung, & the Capt said to me Bob give me that ax, & I give it to him. The boxes was too large for one man to handle, so he took the ax & chopt the boxes to peaces, & throw it out on the ground & cald his men to come & git there tobacco. They took what they wanted. A bout this time General Houstons army come a long, & the Capt haled them, Boys dont you want some tobacco. They holloid out yes. Here help yourselves, & they took all the tobacco. That gave room for the women & children, so we got them all a bord.''[7]

The refugees were a pathetic, muddy lot, and a number of wealthy Southern ladies absolutely refused to deal with them. Among these well-appointed belles was the wife of a prominent local slave runner, Colonel Fannin. Midway through a pleasure cruise along the Gulf, Mrs. Fannin did not yet realize that she had just been widowed by the events at Goliad. When a party of sick and hungry women and children boarded the same sailing vessel, Mrs. Fannin refused to share food with them or even recognize them. Her behavior shocked one of the refugees—a colonist's wife who was herself a lady and happened to be carrying two thousand dollars stitched into her corset. ''I had always praised the great courtesy of the southern people,'' said Mary Helm, ''and never in my life had reason to think different till *now*. I had realized that I could not get a smile from any of the company in the vessel [i.e., Mrs. Fannin and her traveling companions].''[8] Jaws clenched, Mary Helm kept to her strata in the boat's social hierarchy, tending the sick and searching for food.

It was not only women and children who were fleeing. On March 17, two days after word of the Alamo's fall came, the revolutionary convention adjourned and dispersed ''with haste and in confusion. A general confusion seems to have seized them,'' said William Gray, the land speculator. ''Their families are exposed and defenseless, and thousands are moving off to the east. . . . The families of this place [Washington-on-the-Brazos], and storekeepers, are packing up and moving. I had sent some clothes to be washed by a woman who occupied a shed at the end of town. I went this morning to get them, and found the place deserted. . . . But in their haste and panic they had not forgot to be honest. My clothes were washed and neatly tied up, and placed in an adjoining office, whence I got them.''[9] With his clean laundry in hand, Gray resigned himself to the fact that political and legislative matters of Republic were postponed until it was certain there would even be a Republic.

Convention delegates, land speculators, and other VIPs all joined in the undignified business of scattering for safety. Vice President Lorenzo de Zavala rode a little mule. Ex–Lt. Gov. James Robinson's wife found herself ''afoot'' after her horse was pressed into military service and, mad as a wet hen, warned one and all that she would be ''durned'' if she did not confiscate the first horse to come down the road. She was not the only dignitary eating humble pie. A number of delegates were on foot, along with a respectable English capitalist who had been negotiating to loan the two-week-old nation $5 million.[9] The brand-new Cabinet traveled in a body. One night William Gray slept on the floor and shared a blanket with the secretary of war. The secretary of the navy and attorney general shared a blanket next to them, but "the President and Vice-President were accommodated with beds."[10] Elsewhere, obediently trailing along in the unhappy mass, walked the old priest and young presidio officer whom Fannin had several weeks earlier forwarded to convention members as Mexican spies. "They are alone and unguarded," observed Gray, "very little like prisoners."[9]

As they fled, the irrepressible Go Ahead men continued swapping, wrangling, and jawboning about the land. Gray never missed an opportunity to talk about his land loan with Cabinet members, and he was constantly being approached by men wanting to sell him real estate . . . now going at bargain rates. Everywhere Gray rode, men pointed at plots of prairie or river or forest and described how they had meant for the empty land to bear a town, a farm, a business, a mill, a landing. One of the last landmarks Gray passed before reaching the Sabine River was the remains of an earlier dream. This was an old slaving station that had been part of Jean Laffite's—and James Bowie's—slave-running network. Now it was a shelter for cows.[11]

At the river crossings, thousands of despairing souls prayed for ferrymen to get them over. "The horrors of crossing the Trinity are beyond my power to describe," said Dilue Rose Harris, who at the time was just eleven years old. "One of my little sisters was very sick, and the ferryman said that those families that had sick children should cross first. When our party got to the boat the water broke over the banks above where we were and ran around us. We were several hours surrounded by water. Our family was the last to get to the boat. We left more than five hundred people on the west bank. Driftwood covered the water as far as we could see. The sick child was in convulsions. It required eight men to manage the boat." A few days later the baby died and was buried at Liberty.

What propelled this exodus of Anglo-Americans from Texas was fear fueled by rumor, rumor fired by execution. No one knew what Santa Anna's limits were. A horrifying body of atrocity propaganda sprang to life. It was said that, forced by Santa Anna, Mexican women had sold poisoned food to the Alamo garrison, which had weakened the rebels and killed Bowie.[12] The stories turned graphic and savage, demonizing the enemy. Benjamin Harrison, the thirty-year-old son of General (later President) William Henry Harrison, was said to have been captured by Urrea. According to the tale, Mexican soldiers tied him up, castrated and disemboweled him, and let him die by inches.[13] In fact, Harrison was a captive of Urrea, though he enjoyed the comforts of a guest. "He was entertained in the General's [Urrea's] tent, and was permitted to return to the United States on his parole. The General, on his departure, gave him a fine riding horse, $100, a cloak, and also permission to bring off an American prisoner as a servant. . . . Colonel Garay conducted him away from the Mexican camp, and at parting presented him with his sword."[14] Despite Harrison's return from the dead, the stories of a handful of escapees from the Goliad massacre escalated the horror. Before the propaganda ran its course, a Mexican soldier supposedly described the *real* death of James Bowie. According to this ghastly version, Bowie was still alive when the crematory pyres had been lit. The invalid rebel had insulted his captors "in excellent Castilian," which drove them to spread-eagle Bowie, split his mouth open, and cut out his tongue. Then the writhing hero had been thrown alive into the flames.[15] By the time this sort of wild and gory exaggeration reached the United States, the papers were reporting that Texas's "sunny plains and fertile fields, the monuments of *American* enterprise and industry, are by a despot's hands strewn with the mangled bodies of our butchered *female* relatives and friends, and whitening with the bones of their murdered children; and their blood is still fresh on the Spanish knife, and Mexican bayonet. . . ."[16]

The realities were quite bad enough, as some of the old-timers in Texas already knew. Noah Smithwick, a blacksmith and combat veteran of Bowie's Concepción Battle, told of one old Texas hand in his rearguard patrol who was scared white even without the propaganda. "[He] had been through several revolutions, from which he had derived a holy horror of Spanish methods of warfare, and he so worked upon the natural timidity of our commanding officer, that he saw a Mexican soldier in every bush. He actually tore up his commission, lest it be found on him, and condemn him to certain death."[17]

Lashed along by terror, the Army of the Republic of Texas was in full flight along with the rest of the colonies. Starting with 374 volunteers at Gonzales, Houston picked up another 125 by the time he withdrew to Peach Creek . . . but 25 promptly deserted upon hearing of the fall of the Alamo.[18] Houston determined to make a stand at the Colorado River, but when news arrived of the capture and extermination of Fannin's command, he packed up his army and made a beeline eastward toward Louisiana.

"The enemy are laughing you to scorn," the provisional Texas president David Burnet howled at his commander in chief. "You must fight them. You must retreat no farther. The country expects you to fight. The salvation of the country depends on you doing so." Burnet was not alone. Houston's officers and men also found the retreat humiliating and continually agitated for combat.

But, like Santa Anna, the big general with his saber tied on with a piece of buckskin kept his own counsel, weaving strategy from his intuitions and spurning even the appearance of consensual leadership.[19] "While the General either for want of his customary excitement [Houston supposedly gave up alcohol for the duration of the campaign] or as some say from the effect of opium is in a condition between sleeping and walking which amounts nearly to a constant state of insanity."[20] At night the sleepwalking general read from Swift's *Gulliver's Travels* and Caesar's *Commentaries*.

But discontent came second nature to frontier volunteers and Houston largely ignored it. His soldiers obeyed, but only barely. A mulligan stew of insubordinate and violent privates and opportunistic officers, his army was no different from the other Anglo-American armies patched together for this revolution. One soldier complained that Houston's army was less organized than an election riot. "There are too many men in this army, Sir, who have an eye to office after the war is over and who have more regard to their own interests, than to the welfare of Texas. These individuals appear to have joined the army for no other reason than to gain popularity by the most-fawning and obsequious conduct towards all around them, carrying favors with the most disaffected by the most gross abuse of those at the head of affairs, and finally sparing no means however base to advance themselves."[20]

With their leaders incessantly locked in squabbles, the troops simply tagged along without any drilling or training. Most of their free time was spent in trying to keep dry and fill their bellies. At their level, insubordination seemed to be limited to issues of subsistence, as Robert Hunter colorfully enunciated. "The Boys went up a bout a half mile up the river to Mr Beasins house. He had a smoke house full of fine bacon. General Houston had it garded, & only one man there, we told him that we wanted some bacon. He said well you cant git it. We said, why you. He said that Houston had it garded. We said by you a lone. He said there is 10 of us.

Where is the balance of your men [we asked]. They have gon be hinde
that hill to git a shot at them Mexicans. Well we want some bacon, & we
are going to have it. He said, I cant keep you from it. There was 5 of us,
& we got down & broke the door down, got us a middlen a peace & cut
each one in 2 peaces, & tide them to geather. . . .''[7]

Houston wisely ignored this kind of disobedience, realizing that the
Mexicans would loot whatever his men did not. The more serious problem by far was desertion, for men saw nothing wrong with abandoning
the retreating army in order to protect their families. Hundreds of young,
single men who had come to Texas for land turned tail and ran, ignoring
every call for assistance. Houston saved his powder for an Andrew
Jackson–style killing that would straighten up the whole army all at once.
His chance came when two deserters were brought up before courts-
martial. Each was condemned to be shot in front of the whole army, and
two graves were dug. The first deserter was brought out. ''The hole Army
was marched out to the ground, & the grave was dug & a coffin was there,
& the Army was formed in a half circle a round the grave. The man was
blindfolded, & made to kneel on the ground by the coffin, & there 12 men
to shoot him. The officer gave command, he said present arms, take ame.
Just at that moment, Colonel Hockley was coming in a lope from camp,
holloing, halt, halt, halt, & the officer said order arms. Colonel Hockley
rode up and said Lieutenant here is repreave.''[7] The entire execution had
been staged, of course. But its message was clear. There would be obedience or there would be death.

Given desertion, hunger, and disease, Houston's army resembled
more a tottering skeleton than a fighting force. On the west bank of the
Brazos River, Houston halted for rest and training. It was a good idea but
a bad location. ''Should the river rise much higher we shall be compelled
to seek some more elevated position,'' wrote one soldier. ''Even now we
are under the necessity of swimming to reach the prairie, and are almost
flooded in our encampment.'' The camp's water supply was a stagnant
pool used for washing clothes, watering livestock, and dumping sewage
and cattle guts. Of nine hundred men, fully three hundred were sick and
out of commission. There was not a barrel of flour to be found in camp,
and some of the men had no firearms at all.[20] Discipline was nonexistent.

As the Mexicans advanced, Houston retreated, drawing louder yelps
from President Burnet. ''Have we so far forgotten our wonted boasts of
Superior prowess,'' he taunted, ''as to turn our *backs* to an equal number
of a foe that has given us every imaginable incentive to action, vigorous

prompt daring action. . . . A further retreat without a fight, would be infinitely disastrous . . . the country demanding a fight—situation *mortifying.*[21]

In turn, Houston demanded that Burnet and his government quit running. "For Heaven's sake, do not drop back again with the seat of government!" he said. "Your removal to Harrisburg has done more to increase the panic in the country than anything else that has occurred in Texas, except the fall of the Alamo."[22]

No matter who had laid the egg, the indignant rebel army felt like a chased chicken. They ran from Gonzales to the Colorado, then to San Felipe and up to Groce's Ferry, getting madder with every step and agitating to turn and bleed the Mexican army. Houston ignored them. "Had I consulted the wishes of all," he complained, "I should have been like the ass between two stacks of hay. Some wished me to go below, others above." Houston let his army take bets on which turn of the compass he would make, though it was crystal clear to a handful what Houston actually had in mind.

Just as Travis had tried to suck the rebel army west to San Antonio, Houston was trying to tug the U.S. Army across the Sabine River from Louisiana. By retreating close enough to the border where he hoped to involve General Gaines's men, Houston was, in effect, leading Santa Anna into a gigantic ambush.

It was President Jackson who had set up the ambush. He wanted Texas, but he didn't want an international war. In order to insert U.S. troops into Mexican territory and at the same time adhere to the law, he needed loopholes. He needed loyal and opportunistic men whose actions he could, if need be, disavow. He had them. Sam Houston was already in place. And one of the most impetuous and aggressive officers available to Jackson, Gen. Edmund Gaines, was transferring combat veterans—red-hot from fighting a brutal guerrilla war with the Seminoles in Florida—to Fort Jessup on the western edge of Louisiana. Gaines's written instructions were to maintain U.S. neutrality and keep the Indians from joining the fray. Gaines more than understood. Hot pursuit of Indian renegades covered all bases: International law allowed it, Congress could not reject it, and the frontiersmen reveled in it.

Gaines was the perfect tool for Jackson's plans. Together, he and Jackson had successfully used the hot-pursuit gambit in Florida in 1818. From experience, Jackson knew Gaines's wild penchant for galloping into situations with minimal orders. If, as seemed likely, Gaines caused an international scene, Jackson could always deny accountability. Gaines knew the game well. In addition, Gaines was intimate with the Texas situation, for his cousin James Gaines was one of the oldest War Dogs west of the Sabine, having filibustered as early as 1813 and participated in the Fredonian Rebellion in 1826. The two aging cousins kept in close contact through the Texas Revolution, and so Gen. Edmund Gaines was well informed and ready to project a U.S. military presence. And by early April Gaines was in place at Fort Jessup.[23]

One month after the Alamo fell, on April 7, Houston wrote from his Brazos camp, "Don't get scared at Nacogdoches. Remember old Hickory claims Nachez as 'neutral Territory.' "[24] What this cryptic remark referred to was Jackson's "belief" that an old, semiformal no-man's-land between the Sabine River and the Neches River could be freely entered by U.S. troops without violating any international treaties, despite the fact that Colonel Almonte had clarified Mexican sovereignty over this allegedly neutral strip in 1834.

The Jacksonian players saw an opportunity to lure Santa Anna into the region of disputed legal status, and there crush him. Then the Jackson administration could point at territorial ambiguities; Gaines could withdraw his troops; Texas could be Anglo-American.[25]

General Gaines wasted no time in preparing an invasion force. He called upon the governors of Louisiana, Mississippi, Alabama, and Tennessee to each deliver two to three battalions of militiamen. "The war in Texas, which has of late assumed a sanguinary and savage aspect, has induced the President of the United States to require a considerable augmentation of the regular force to be concentrated upon this section of the national frontier, to which my attention has been particularly directed."[26]

Caretaking the national border was one thing, crossing it was another. Jackson's orders (through Secretary of War Cass) had pointed out that "public considerations demand the exercise of great discretion and experience,"[27] and Gaines realized the need to justify any trespass. As he carefully explained to the governors ordered to raise troops for him, the Indian situation was highly volatile. A Mexican agent named Manuel Flores had reportedly passed up the Red River Valley and whipped the Caddo Indians into a homicidal frenzy. It was—Gaines said—his fear that the Caddos attacking Anglo-Americans in Texas would spill across the Sabine and attack Americans in Louisiana. "These facts and circumstances present to me the important question," he said, "whether I am to sit still and suffer these movements to be so far matured as to place the white settlements on both sides of the line wholly within the power of these savages; or whether I ought not instantly to prepare the means for protecting the frontier settlements, and, if necessary, compelling the Indians to return to their own homes and hunting grounds."[26] In other words, Gaines intended to mask his invasion as a preemptive strike upon the Indians. If U.S. troops happened to encounter the Mexican army, which was after all allegedly stirring up the Indians, then Gaines would "inflict summary punishment on such of the enemy by whom they [American frontier settlements] are now menaced, as may teach them to respect us, and in future to pay more regard than they seem now disposed to pay to our rights and treaties."[28]

Gaines's stratagem was transparent, and one dyspeptic administration official later complained about it. "I have no doubt [it] was intended by Gaines to get troops there [the Sabine River] who at once went over to the Texan army."[29] The governor of Louisiana was also skeptical. Upon receiving the general's call for militia troops, he decided that Gaines was being duped by Texas land speculators . . . and he refused to raise troops for such a venture. The governors of Alabama and Mississippi also declined to forward militiamen.[30]

However, Secretary of War Cass authorized General Gaines to advance into Texas as far as Nacogdoches, that is, no farther than the Neches River. This was precisely the Jacksonian interpretation that Houston predicted. By the time Gaines received this written authority to trespass (issued April 25), the revolution was over and Gaines had acted anyway. As Jackson intended, and Houston and a few others anticipated, the general had readied the 3rd and 6th Regiments of U.S. infantry to invade Mexico.

Inside Texas men were carefully leaking alarms to Gaines, providing him with appropriate excuses for his preemptive strike. The most prominent of these Cassandras was John T. Mason. Mason was a Jackson political appointee (secretary of the territory of Michigan, 1830–31), who had resigned government service to work as a confidential agent of the Galveston Bay and Texas Land Company,[31] the grand real estate scheme that included land development by slaves purchased in Bermuda, the construction of hotels and warehouses in Texas, and the proposal to buy Texas from Mexico for $10 million.[32] Now, as Santa Anna's army was sweeping the real estate empire right off the map, Mason wrote to General Gaines, pleading for military aid.

Mason knew that Gaines could not simply march into Mexican territory, and so he invented a horrifying scenario to justify U.S. military intervention.[33]

On April 13, Mason wrote that a tremendous bloodbath was about to occur. A huge, demonic assembly of Indians and Mexicans was poised and ready to slaughter defenseless thousands of refugees who were now trapped on the west bank of the flooded Sabine River. "The expectation is that, at this moment, Nacogdoches is occupied by the Indians and Mexicans; and, if they pursue the families on their flight, all must be massacred, without instantaneous relief." Mason breathlessly begged that General Gaines immediately send five hundred troops into Texas, adding that provisions would be purchased and furnished to the soldiers from his own or rebel funds. "With your immediate cooperation, thousands of lives can be saved; without your aid, all are liable to be destroyed, and may now be past the hope of relief."[34]

A day later, at two o'clock in the morning,[35] Gaines received a mysterious letter signed only with the initials F.B.S. (possibly written by John Mason). "Nacogdoches has been abandoned, and by this hour, probably is in ruins. A detachment of the Mexican army has, by an extraordinary movement, been united with the Indians of the north, whom, it is reported, are 1500 strong, and unless timely succor is obtained the country will be overrun, and the depredations and horrors which were so lately enacted in Florida [by the Seminoles] will now be removed on the western border of our happy land."[36] Toward further buttressing the case for intervention, a deposition was obtained from a Tejano named Miguel Cortinez. In this statement, Cortinez described how his brother—allegedly a Mexican agent—had incited the Cherokee nation to kill and plunder in Nacogdoches. Cortinez said that when he asked the Cherokee chief if that was his intention, the chief replied that he would join the Mexicans against the Anglo-Americans "and fight while a man of his tribe remained."[37]

With his cover story sufficiently documented by this flurry of reports, General Gaines then issued orders to march for the Sabine River. On April 14 thirteen companies of U.S. troops embarked from Fort Jessup for the invasion. They took with them two fieldpieces, plus thirty-five rounds of ammunition and twelve days' supplies for each soldier. As Gaines set out, he was confident that, once the governors sent their militiamen, he would soon have seven thousand to eight thousand troops on hand. "I cannot state positively what Genl Gaines may do," said Samuel Carson, a former U.S. congressman from North Carolina, a plantation owner, and a land speculator. "But one thing I think I may say that should he be satisfied of the fact, that the Mexicans have incited any Indians who are under the control of the U States to commit depredations on either side of the line he will doubtless view it as a violation of the

Treaty . . . and be assured that he will maintain the honor of his country and punish the agressor be him whome he may. . . . It is only necessary then to satisfy Genl Gaines of the facts, in which case be assured he will act with energy and efficiency. The proofs will I have no doubt be abundant by the time he reaches Sabean [River] in which case he will cross and move upon the agressors."[35]

As General Gaines and his thirteen companies approached the Sabine River, they saw abundant evidence that Anglo-Americans were fleeing Texas. But they saw no proof at all of an Indian uprising. To the contrary, the Indians were terrified of the Anglo-American uprising. A U.S. Army lieutenant, J. Bonnell, rode up the Red River Valley to assess the Indian problem—and found none. Manuel Flores had indeed passed among the Caddo Indians, urging them to fight, but not only had the Caddo refused to enter into the revolution, they had fled to the prairie, convinced the Anglo-Americans meant to kill *them*. Lieutenant Bonnell was hard-pressed even to find any Caddos, locating only a handful of women and children and a warrior or two. A Caddo chief told Bonnell, "Tell General Gaines, the great chief, that even if the Caddoes should see the Spaniards (Mexicans) and Americans (white inhabitants of Texas) fighting, they would only look on, but take no part on either side."[38]

Nacogdoches was empty. Neither Mexicans nor Indians rampaged in its deserted streets.[39] There was no bloodbath upon the Sabine. Gaines was able to learn of the death of just one white man, an Indian trader.[40] Perched on the banks of the Sabine River, General Gaines had almost crossed his Rubicon, but not quite. Lieutenant Bonnell's report scotched the invasion, ruining the excited propaganda and fabrications of Mason, Carson, and F.B.S. Hot pursuit no longer held credence. The Indians were not just peaceful, they were in hiding.

On April 20, realizing that he could not justify the use of state militia troops to their governors, General Gaines suspended his call for militiamen. Just the same he held his position on the Sabine, waiting for an opening to cross "the supposed line" between the United States and Mexico. What he saw—the heartrending tatters of the Texas dream—chilled his blood. Hundreds of Anglo-American women and children streamed past his encampment with tales of hardship, agony, and loss. But in itself their plight was not just grounds for crossing the international border.

In his report to the secretary of war, Gaines downplayed Lieutenant Bonnell's report, emphasizing that the lieutenant had confirmed that a Mexican agent had tried to talk the Indians into violence, and treating the

Indian threat as kinetic. Despite the Caddos' words of peace, Gaines represented that the Caddo tribe was possibly joining up with the Comanches and Cherokees to attack Anglo-Americans. By keeping a large force of professional soldiers poised to strike, Gaines said, any such Indian horde would be intimidated, and if they were not, then Gaines's force could promptly punish them. "Even should everything appear to be settled and quiet when the mounted force [of U.S. soldiers] arrives . . . a well-regulated movement of such a force as I shall then have, added to that of the third and sixth infantry, upon the late threatened and panic-stricken frontier, would produce a moral effect upon the Indians and inhabitants, as well as upon the troops, giving them a knowledge of the topography and military resources of this important section of the national frontier. . . ."[40]

In short, even after General Gaines lost his ability to justify invading Mexico, he did not pull back from a potentially incendiary situation.

One thing General Gaines did not mention in his report was that a number of his troops were already "deserting" into Texas. According to one report, some two hundred troops ended up in the rebel army. In fact, General Gaines was lending soldiers to General Houston. These so-called deserters did not bother to change out of their American uniforms, and when hostilities wrapped up, most "deserted" back to General Gaines's command[41] though a number decided life was easier in the Texas army, and refused to go back to regular duty.[42] A few months later, Gaines would go ahead and occupy Nacogdoches with a cavalry squadron and six companies of infantry—324 men total. The action naturally outraged Mexican authorities, but the troops would remain in Texas until December.

In Houston's opinion his army could fight once and once only. Until then, his men were better off baiting the Mexicans into deep eastern Texas. The farther the Mexicans marched, the longer their supply line stretched, the more exhausted they became, and the closer they got to General Gaines.

When the news of Fannin's capture first reached Santa Anna, the Mexican general all but declared the campaign over. By then, Santa Anna had seen the Alamo reduced to smoking ruins and Gonzales in ashes. The only rebels any of his army had encountered were amateur soldiers, badly clothed, badly disciplined, badly led. The colonists and squatters were nowhere to be seen, thoroughly scattered and hightailing it for the U.S. border. Texas was purged. All that remained to be done was the mop-up, and that certainly didn't require the presence of a heroic *caudillo*. Now more than ever, Mexico needed its president, for Miguel Barragán, the *ad interim* president Santa Anna had left in place, had died on March 1. The political situation back home worried him.[43] He had no illusions about the limits of his influence a thousand miles from the center of power. Under the new *ad interim* president, the expedition was sent a decree that specifically contradicted Santa Anna's policy of no quarter. It spared any prisoner of war captured in Texas (except for military and civil leaders of the revolution) from capital punishment, and exiled all "rebel colonists" who did not throw themselves on the mercy of the Mexican government.[44] In short, the new *ad interim* president nullified Santa Anna's most basic tenet: terror. It was decidedly time for Santa Anna to return.

But a number of his generals cautioned that the revolution was not over.[45] A few even dared to warn about a Mexican defeat. And there was another extenuating factor for Santa Anna to consider. With nothing but one long string of triumphs to show for himself, General Urrea was stealing Santa Anna's thunder.[46] Feathers ruffled, the peacock staff and their megalomaniac commander steeled themselves for a campaign all the way to the Sabine River. On March 31, Santa Anna's private coach rolled westward to carry his beautiful Tejano "wife" to points south. The *caudillo* himself shoved east for the Louisiana border.[47]

By late March the Mexican army had run out of supplies and Santa Anna directed that the various generals feed their troops from whatever they could plunder.[48] There was much to plunder. As the Mexican army passed into the Anglo-American colonies, they entered a virtual land of Oz filled with bluebonnets and Indian paintbrush, astounding wealth and strange machines and marvels. Since the Aztec days, Mexicans had loved their flowers, valuing a rare bouquet almost more than gold.[44] For months the Mexican soldiers had labored through regions scoured by northers, where even the winter pasturage had been burned off by Travis and others. But now, as spring blossomed, eastern Texas opened to them like a bizarre paradise.

"On the 7th [of April] we started our march at eight o'clock in the morning, and after a small wooded area, we passed through some prairies so beautiful that I lack words to describe them," recorded Colonel de la Peña, who dismounted for the sheer joy of walking through the fields. "It was all a field of lilies and poppies of an exquisite and unique variety, not only in their varied colors but also because of the forms nature had given them. The soul expanded, and it is difficult to explain the joy that it felt in its enchantment. . . . Being at the head of a sapper unit and extraordinarily affected by what my eyes admired, and seized by an enthusiasm bordering on insanity, I called to the soldiers to shoot me, that I might be buried in this vast garden. . . ."[49]

The astonished Mexicans found corn a yard high, fat cattle so domesticated they rushed up in search of their owners, and loyal dogs sitting in front of their masters' doors. The hogs were as large as six-month-old calves, and the barns were full of ginned and carded cotton. On April 15 soldiers lined the bank to watch a steamboat (the *Yellowstone*) moving downriver, "dumbfounded by the sight of a machine so totally unfamiliar and unexpected."[49]

Most of the Mexicans had never seen Anglo-American farms, and even the fence construction was mystifying and wonderful to them. Running as deep as 170 feet, the wells had reinforced walls and came equipped with perfectly made wooden buckets. The soldiers found machinery, nails, iron bars, peach orchards, china, wagons, and plows. Some of the houses held wine in cellars, fine furniture, clocks, and smokehouses with hams. Soldiers and camp followers cut open bales of cotton waiting for transport, and slept on thick soft wads. The women spread the white cotton loose on the black and red riverbanks so that when they emerged from bathing, their feet would not get muddy.

The army pillaged with giddy abandon. When Urrea's southern wing joined the main column, they set up an impromptu marketplace and offered for sale exotic booty that included candle wax, white sugar, bitter chocolate, cigars at a peso a box, crystal, fine hats, and tailored clothes. Up north General Gaona's men plundered Bastrop. But General Ramírez y Sesma, whose troops spearheaded the drive through the heart of the colonies, collected the lion's share of goods, which caused jealousy and resentment. Soldiers dubbed Ramírez y Sesma's quarters the customhouse for the liquor, hardware, clocks, mirrors, and goods stored there. Officers catching up with this advance column noted, with envy, that common troops and their women possessed gilded pitchers and shining crystal. Repeatedly soldiers got drunk on the liquor left behind by the colonists. (To Houston's disgust, it was reported that a barrel of gin and one of wine had been poisoned with arsenic and left for the Mexicans; the barrels were destroyed.[50]) Drunken companies became insubordinate, soldiers brawled and even killed one another.[51]

As the expedition passed farther east, they confiscated goods, burned homes that Houston's army had not yet burned, and liberated Negro slaves.[52] General Urrea was gratified to find a variety of colonists awaiting his arrival. Branded "Tories" by the rebels, these colonists were, above all, anxious to preserve their holdings, and eagerly assured Urrea of their loyalty to Mexico. At Victoria, the colonists presented the general with six enemy prisoners.[53] At Brazoria, he received intelligence about rebel movements and recruits ready to fight against Houston because he and his army were considered adventurers.[54] River after river, town after town, the Mexican army rolled through the colonies.

Everywhere they went, the army found evidence of the rebels. But except for erasing the largely mercenary bands under Travis and Fannin, the Mexicans found very few rebels. One day General Urrea's division came to a complete halt just west of Matagorda. With a bodyguard of cavalry troops, Urrea galloped to the head of the column to discover the cause of the delay. As he raced past young Herman Ehrenberg (who had just been captured a second time), Urrea called out with a laugh, "The Texans, my little Prussian!" Hours later, scouts returned to declare that all was safe and the army advanced once again. Only later did Ehrenberg learn that the column had been fooled by a scarecrow set up by the rebels on the flat roof of a house and armed with a musket.[55] As April stretched out that straw sentinel seemed to be the sum total of resistance left in Texas.

When Santa Anna had constructed his initial trident thrust into eastern Texas, he assigned himself as a behind-the-lines commander. But as the annoying news of Urrea's victories poured into headquarters in San Antonio, Santa Anna apparently had second thoughts about overseeing the action. In the world of *personalismo,* glory translated as power. So in the first week of April, Santa Anna joined the central column of his army and took over the vanguard. He raced for San Felipe de Austin, then jumped on toward Columbia, Brazoria, and finally, Harrisburg. Santa Anna had reason for speed. According to reports, the rebel government and Houston's army were not far distant. There was a chance Santa Anna could sever the revolution's spine in one bold move.[56]

At the head of some seven hundred infantry and fifty cavalry troops streamlined for speed—their women and children left behind, and the men carrying only their bedrolls and trail provisions—Santa Anna rushed forward. He ordered General Cós to bring up five hundred more soldiers at the first opportunity and sprinted day and night.[56] But upon entering Harrisburg the night of April 15, he found the town on fire and deserted except for three printers putting to bed the latest edition of the *Telegraph and Texas Register.*[57] They candidly informed Santa Anna that Houston was up north at Groce's Crossing with eight hundred men and two cannons, and that the rebel president, vice president, and other Cabinet members were due east at New Washington.[58]

Santa Anna arrested the printers, threw their printing press into the river, and finished burning Harrisburg to the ground. Then he sent Colonel Almonte and the cavalry dashing Gulfward to catch the rebel leadership at New Washington. With literally just a minute to spare, President Burnet and his rebel Cabinet escaped capture. Almonte and the cavalry galloped up just as the revolutionary government hastily rowed away from the dock. The little boat was still within musket range when Almonte saw Mrs. Burnet on board, and he forbade his troops to open fire on a woman. So Santa Anna's rapid grab for the rebel ringleaders produced nothing but a fistful of air.

Santa Anna now determined to intercept the rebel army and finish the chase once and for all. Local colonists let the Mexican president know where Houston was and where he was heading. The Mexican general set off for the Trinity River by way of Lynchburg, for a change one step ahead of the retreating enemy. Houston could come to him this time.[58]

The Which Way Tree marked the fork at which Houston had to decide: left toward Nacogdoches and the protective shadow of the U.S. eagle, or right toward Harrisburg and a lot more than a donnybrook. Houston knew from captured Mexican couriers and documents where Santa Anna was going. He estimated that there were only 500 soldiers with their *presidente,* with 1,000 reinforcements massed just forty miles behind. In fact Santa Anna had 750 troops, roughly equivalent to Houston's effective fighting force. But Houston's army lusted for battle. His officers—particularly men fresh from the United States like Sidney Sherman and Mirabeau Buonaparte Lamar (who later became president of Texas)—wanted hot, glorious combat. By the time his army reached the Which Way Tree, it was fundamentally a mutiny waiting to happen.[59] Essentially Houston could choose between having an army or not, for his men meant to go Harrisburg-way and savage Santa Anna's bunch. To great cheers, he chose the right-hand path.

Trailing to their rear was a party of refugees which included a pioneer woman named Mrs. Mann. Promised that the army was going toward Nacogdoches and the Sabine River, Mrs. Mann had loaned her oxen to Houston's army to haul two six-pounders dubbed the Twin Sisters. Now Mrs. Mann realized that she'd been double-crossed. According to Pvt. Robert Hunter, "She rode up to the general & said, general you tole me a d——m lie, you said that you was going on the Nacogdoches road. Sir I want my oxen. Well Mrs Mann we cant spare them [said Houston]. We cant git our cannon a long with out them. I dont care d——m for your

cannon, I want my oxen. She had a pare of holster pistols on her saddle
pummel & a very large knife on her saddle. She turned a round to the
oxen, & jumpt down with knife & cut the raw hide tug that the chane was
tide with. The log chane hook was broke & it was tide with raw hide. No
body said a word. She jumpt on her horse with whipin hand, & away she
went in a lope with her oxen." When the huge wagon master rode after
her to fetch back the oxen, Houston warned him Mrs. Mann would fight.
The wagon master yelled back, "damn her fighting," words eaten when
he angrily returned hours later with his shirt torn to "baby rags" and
without the oxen.[60]

Once Houston committed himself, morale soared. The Go Ahead men
reached a cold killing pitch when they passed through Harrisburg and
found just charcoal and smoke. The rebel rearguard had reduced Gonzales, San Bernard, and San Felipe to the same sorry state, but Harrisburg
had been largely destroyed by Mexican hands and it made the rebels mad.
In addition, several survivors of the Goliad massacre had joined the army
with their barbarous tales of treachery and death. And Houston made sure
his troops knew about the possessions of the Alamo garrison that Santa
Anna's men now had. "A Mexican prisoner was brought into camp,"
one rebel recalled. "He was a copper colored boy, eighteen years old. I
was present when Gen Houston questioned him, through an interpreter; &
heard him state that he was one of the men who handled the 'Gaut-
dam-yees' [God Damn ye's—a favorite Anglo-American expression] in
the Alamo; that every butcher knife, pocket knife, pistol, handkerchief,
watch, & every dollar, upon the bodies of the slain Texians, was appropriated by the soldiers, & that he obtained an excellent pocket knife,
which he took from the pocket of a dead man."[61] On April 18, the scout
Deaf Smith captured Capt. Miguel Bachillar, a special courier on his way
to Santa Anna's column. Captain Bachillar's dispatches were in deerskin
saddlebags bearing the name "W. B. Travis."[62] A pocketknife, a pair of
saddlebags, the Goliad survivors: These artifacts fed the fire of rebel
vengeance.[63]

The rebel army fought with the muddy Texan road, virtually clawing
their way closer to the enemy. The wagons bogged down repeatedly and
had to be unloaded and hand-carried empty across flooded areas. Remarkably, the army covered fifty-five backbreaking miles in just two and
a half days, much of it on empty stomachs and little sleep. "This morning
we are in preparation to meet Santa Anna," Houston wrote. "It is the
only chance of saving Texas. . . . We go to conquer. It is wisdom growing out of necessity to meet the enemy now; every consideration enforces

it. No previous occasion would justify it. The troops are in fine spirits, and now is the time for action."[64]

Houston's army crossed two more bayous by raft, swimming, and bridge to gain the sea-level plain known as San Jacinto. Houston left behind his sick men and the army's baggage under guard, along with Captain Bachillar, the hapless Mexican courier. The captain had already endured Deaf Smith's "trading" his ragged pants and coats and worn-out brogans for the Mexican's braided leather uniform, bead-banded sombrero, and fine shoes and socks.[65] Now he was chained to a tree and teased like an animal. "He was the liveles [liveliest] sort of fellow," one rebel said. "All next day we had a heap fun with him. Every one that could taulk Spanish was around him, develing him."[60]

Houston's army now nestled into the northern tip of a virtual island. Upon the map, his choice for a battlefield looked like a prescription for suicide. To one side stretched Buffalo Bayou, some three hundred feet wide and fifteen to thirty feet deep. To the other side, the San Jacinto River blocked retreat. And just opposite the army lay a placid marshy blot called Peggy Lake. Surrounded on three sides by a full-scale swamp, Houston hid his men in a forest of live oak dripping gray Spanish moss. Santa Anna had meant to catch him here. Instead, he caught Santa Anna.

A few hours later, the Mexican vanguard arrived from New Washington, eight miles south, where the revolutionary Cabinet members had rowed to sanctuary. On his way to cut off the rebels at Lynch's Ferry, Santa Anna suddenly found himself cut off at Lynch's Ferry. One of Napoleon's prime maxims was that "a general should say to himself many times a day: If the hostile army were to make its appearance on my front, on my right, on my left, what should I do?"[66] The enemy was on Santa Anna's front, buried among the live oaks, giant magnolias, rhododendrons, and hyacinths, so that it was impossible to read their numbers. With no apparent plan, the Mexican general half-heartedly probed the rebel position. In terms of Napoleonic instincts, Santa Anna flunked.

Shortly before noon, the Twin Sisters started dueling with the sole Mexican cannon, a brass nine-pounder with the inscriptions "El Volcán" and "Violati Fulmina Regis" (the strength of royal lightning).[67] There were few casualties on either side, though Colonel Neill's hip was shattered by a lead ball, putting him out of action. On the Mexican side, Capt. Fernando Urizza was wounded by grapeshot, which killed the horse beneath him.[68] Over the next four hours, El Volcán's carriage was damaged, and as the Mexican cavalry drew it back to safety, Col. Sidney

Sherman sallied out from the woods. Sherman had equipped fifty-two Kentuckian mercenaries from his own pocket and had arrived in Texas waving a flag with a half-naked Liberty proclaiming Liberty or Death. Now Sherman galloped forth to grab El Volcán, but failed miserably, losing two men and several horses in the foolish skirmish. Worse, he nearly triggered a general attack by the Mexicans, which prompted an infuriated Houston to take away Sherman's command of the cavalry and give it to Mirabeau Lamar. Though his troops clamored to burst out onto the field and tackle the enemy, Houston kept them bottled tight in the woods, biding his time.

The Mexicans withdrew to about three fourths of a mile away, placing their backs to Peggy Lake in one of the worst battle positions conceivable. "The camping ground of His Excellency's selection was, in all respects, against military rules. Any youngster would have done better. . . . What ground had we to retreat upon in case of a reverse?" Colonel Delgado asked himself. "From sad experience, I answered—None!" When Delgado raised the issue of their camp placement with General Castrillón, the answer was despairing and impassioned. "What can I do, my friend?" Castrillón replied. "I know it well, but I cannot help it. You know that nothing avails here against the caprice, arbitrary will and ignorance of that man [Santa Anna]."[68]

The Mexican soldiers spent the rest of the afternoon and all night fashioning a five-foot-high breastwork of packs, baggage, sacks of beans and hard bread, branches, and dirt. Bracing for an Alamo-hour attack before dawn the next morning, April 21, the Mexican soldiers readied for Houston's onslaught. They waited. But not a rebel appeared.

At nine o'clock, General Cós arrived in Santa Anna's encampment at the head of four hundred reinforcements and a *caballada* of pack mules. But to his *caudillo's* supreme irritation, Cós showed up with green recruits, not select combat veterans. Later, with bitter hindsight, Santa Anna would insist that he had specified veteran troops, though he hadn't. "As is well known," he said, "such recruits contribute little in sustaining a battle, but cause the very grave evil of introducing disorder with their irregular operations among tried veterans, especially in a surprise."[69]

The sun curved up and through its zenith, and still the rebels didn't make a sound from their forest fortress. Cós's men had marched hard to cross Vince's Bridge and join the advance column, and Santa Anna ordered them to stack their arms and go to sleep. His own troops were exhausted from a long night of defensive preparations. With their midday meal in belly, the Mexican army scanned the green woods one more time, and then retired for a siesta. A fairy tale would grow that a beautiful mulatto girl named Emily Morgan—the Yellow Rose of Texas—lay down with Santa Anna in his silk field tent and stole his consciousness. More likely the seductress was the warm sun, a full stomach, and a nip of opium. At any rate, Santa Anna slept, and his army slept around him. Three quarters of a mile of blank hog-bed prairie separated the two armies. No one in his right mind would try to cross that exposed stretch in the full glare of sunlight.

Habituated to a four o'clock reveille, Houston's army had risen long before dawn, spoiling to fight. For six weeks, Houston himself had slept no more than three hours per night. But on the morning of the greatest battle of his life, the Go Ahead general lay dreaming mystical stratagems, his head pillowed upon a coil of rope. To his men's bafflement, he slept until the sun had drawn its arc in the bright blue sky. When he opened his eyes and looked up, he saw an eagle—his totem eagle—drifting high overhead. "The sun of Austerlitz had risen again," he told himself, referring to the most decisive of Napoleon's victories.[70] He lifted up from the ground. It was time to fight.

When the rebels saw the tiny string of dots that was General Cós and his reinforcements approaching Santa Anna's camp, there was murmuring that Houston had missed his chance, the Mexican army was massing. Deaf Smith rode in, remarking, "A hot time is preparing for us—the enemy is increasing."[62] But Houston calmed his troops, declaring the reinforcements only a sham, and inviting the men not to believe their own eyes. Later Houston would tell Santa Anna that he had purposely waited for Cós's addition before attacking, because there was no sense taking two bites of the same cherry.[70] Nevertheless, Houston sent Deaf Smith and a handful of mounted men racing for Vince's Bridge to burn or chop it down.

As the morning dragged and the rebels stewed, Col. John Wharton—one of the Wharton brothers and a War Dog—circulated from campfire to campfire, electrifying the men with war talk. "Boys," he preached, "there is no other word to-day but fight, fight! Now is the time!" When Houston heard of Wharton's rabble-rousing, he grimly accepted that his soldiers would not be held back any longer. "Fight," he told Wharton, "and be damned."[62]

At three-thirty in the afternoon, while Santa Anna still slept, the rebel army assembled. The center column was flanked by a left and right wing, and the cavalry deployed left on the San Jacinto River side. At four o'clock, the army quietly trundled their Twin Sisters artillery out onto the prairie, advancing through grass and sunshine. When they were partway across the field, Deaf Smith wheeled up with ax in hand, announcing that Vince's Bridge had been destroyed. There would be no more Mexican reinforcements and Santa Anna's men could not retreat. But the rebels would not be able to retreat either. This contest was for all or nothing. The rebels went ahead.

With one of those fantastic oversights that sometimes inform history, the Mexicans failed to set pickets out. Not a single scout circled in the field to sound the alarm against precisely this kind of brash assault. Some of the Mexican soldiers were rooting through a nearby woods for tree boughs to construct shelters and fires. Most were asleep in camp. The cavalry horses had been unsaddled and were being lazily ridden bareback to and from the river. As if ghosts, the rebels walked upright and invisible through the open field.[68]

The files of rebels fanned sideways into a line two-deep and nearly a thousand yards long. The Twin Sisters were bullied along in the center of the ragged formation. As they walked—over on the left flank Colonel Sherman's regiment was trotting at double time—the men held their fire with a discipline remarkable for volunteers. Their martial field band was sorely limited in both numbers and repertoire. There was only a drummer and a fifer, and the one tune they knew was a popular and risqué love ballad called "Come to the Bower."

> "Will you come to the bow'r I have shaded for you?
> Our bed shall be roses all spangled with dew.
> There under the bow'r on roses you'll lie
> With a blush on your cheek but a smile in your eye!"

Back and forth across the front of the line, Houston rode his white stallion Saracen. The bare-breasted Liberty flag led them forward, its flagstaff topped with the dainty white glove of a Kentucky lieutenant's sweetheart. Sir Walter Scott could not have drawn a more clarified picture of the Anglo-Saxon spirit.

Within two hundred yards of the Mexican camp, Houston ordered the Twin Sisters spun about. The two cannons were loaded with chopped horseshoes, and when they were ignited, the scrap-iron razor cut the sleeping Mexicans. Closing fast now, the Go Ahead warriors fired at will. Like wild animals, they snapped the chain of command and got on with the business of slaughter.

"We were all firing as rapidly as we could," said Pvt. Alfonso Steele, whose regiment targeted General Cós's new arrivals. "And as soon as we fired every man went to reloading, and he who first got his gun reloaded moved on, not waiting for orders. I got my gun loaded and rushed on into the timber and fired again. When the second volley was poured into them in that timber they broke and ran. As soon as I got my gun loaded again I ran on a little in front of our men and threw up my gun to shoot, when I was shot down. Dave Rusk was standing by me when I was shot. He told some of the men to stay with me, but I told him, 'No, take them on.'

"One of our own men in passing asked me if he could take my pistol, but by this time I was bleeding at the nose and mouth so I couldn't speak; so he just stooped down and got it and went on."[71]

The rebels descended like demons from the Mexican breastwork, and one Mexican survivor attributed their ferocity to corn whiskey, for they fought with drunken abandon.[17] The camp erupted into chaos. "The utmost confusion prevailed," said Colonel Delgado, who stood upon ammunition crates to survey the scene. "General Castrillón shouted on one side; on another, Colonel Almonte was giving orders; some cried out to commence firing; others, to lie down and avoid grapeshot. Among the latter was His Excellency.

"Then, already, I saw our men flying in small groups, terrified, and sheltering themselves behind large trees. I endeavored to force some of them to fight, but all efforts were in vain—the evil was beyond remedy; they were a bewildered and panic-stricken herd."[68]

The heartbeat of Mexican defense was the single nine-pounder, El Volcán. Five times it blasted grapeshot and minié balls among the rebels.[67] Some of the Mexican soldiers rushed to their breastwork and snapped off a volley or two. Five balls punched into Saracen's white side, dropping the horse beneath Houston's rein. Houston mounted a second horse, but this one too fell to Mexican gunfire. A musket ball struck Houston in his Achilles' heel, shattering his right ankle. He slung himself into the saddle of a third horse.

Eight miles away, Robert Hancock Hunter was guarding his prisoner, Captain Bachillar. He could hear the sound of battle very clearly. "A bout 3 oclock in the evening, we hered a cannon fire, & a nother & a nother, three fired in sussesston & stopt. About 2 minutes a nother fired, & the little twin sisters commenced. They popt like popcorn in a oven, & we could here the small arms very plane. Our prisiner was the livelest fellow you ever seen while the cannon was firing. As soon as the big gun stopt, he becum sulkey & would not talk. We wanted to know what was the matter. It was a long time before he would talk, & he said that Sant Anna was whipt. How do you know [we asked]. [The prisoner replied] I dont here his guns."[60] He was right.

One of the Twin Sisters gouged a hole through the slapdash breast-work, and the rebels streamed into the camp, howling and shouting "Remember Goliad! Remember the Alamo!" "Old Jimmie Curtice had a son-in-law, Wash Cottle, slain in the Alamo, whom he swore to avenge," said one soldier. San Jacinto gave him the opportunity and he made the most of it. "The boys said he clubbed his rifle and sailed in, in Donnybrook fair style, accompanying each blow with 'Alamo! You killed Wash Cottle!' "[17]

"Meeting no resistance," Colonel Delgado said, "[the rebels] dashed, lightning-like upon our deserted camp. Then I saw His Excellency running about in the utmost excitement wringing his hands, and unable to give an order. General Castrillón was stretched on the ground, wounded in the leg. Colonel Trevino was killed, and Colonel Marcial Aguirre was severely injured. . . .

"Everything being lost, I went—leading my horse, which I could not mount, because the firing had rendered him restless and fractious—to join our men, still hoping that we might be able to defend ourselves, or to retire under the shelter of night. This, however, could not be done. It is a known fact, that Mexican soldiers, once demoralized, cannot be controlled, unless they are thoroughly inured to war.

"On the left, and about a musket-shot distance from our camp, was a small grove, on the bay shore. Our disbanded herd rushed for it, to obtain shelter from the horrid slaughter carried on all over the prairie by the blood-thirsty usurpers. Unfortunately, we met, on our way, an obstacle difficult to overcome. It was a bayou, not very wide, but rather deep. . . . It was there that the greatest carnage took place."[68]

Exercising his presidential prerogative, Santa Anna "accepted" Col. Juan Bringas's horse and cut loose of the immediate disaster. Over in the bayou, Colonel Almonte swam and urged his men to safety, pulling with his left hand while he held his saber above the water with his right. Those who stayed in camp were shot, clubbed, or knifed to death.

By Houston's own calculation, from the first shot to the capture of the Mexican camp, the battle lasted just eighteen minutes. After that the Mexicans broke, dropping their weapons and running away. Along the bayou and all across the prairie, Mexicans fell to their knees, pleading, "Me no

Alamo,'' and begging to surrender. Wounded men clutched at the rebels' ankles and prayed for mercy. But the butchery had only just begun.

What followed was one of the great war atrocities in U.S. history, a slaughter that went on for hours, with rebel officers completely unable to corral their berserk troops. Over the next few hours as many Mexicans— most of them unarmed—were killed as Anglo-Americans in the entire revolution. The final body count was 9 Anglo-Americans killed or mortally wounded versus some 630 Mexicans killed. As one rebel captain put it, ''Such slaughter on one side and almost miraculous preservation on the other have never been heard of since the invention of gunpowder.''[72]

The rebel secretary of war, Thomas Jefferson Rusk, saw the wounded General Castrillón cornered upon an ammunition crate, a statuesque figure in the crazed vortex. One of Castrillón's men had urged him to flee, but the general replied, ''I've never showed my back, I'm too old to do it now.'' Determined to save this general who stood scowling with his arms folded, Rusk ordered his troops to cease fire. He even knocked aside some of the rifle barrels. Unaware that Castrillón was the officer who had temporarily saved Crockett and a handful of other prisoners at the Alamo, the rebels shot him down.

When Wharton similarly tried to halt the slaughter, a soldier answered, ''Colonel Wharton, if Jesus Christ were to come down from heaven and order me to quit shooting Santanistas, I wouldn't do it, sir!'' According to one eyewitness, when the man stepped back and cocked his rifle at the officer's chest, ''Wharton very discreetly (I always thought) turned his horse and left.''[73]

Houston was equally impotent. With his wounded leg draped over the saddle pommel of his third horse, he tried repeatedly to bring order to the victory. He ordered the drum to beat a retreat, and when that didn't work, bellowed out, ''Parade, men, parade!'' No one listened. At last he shouted, ''Gentlemen! gentlemen! gentlemen!'' There was a momentary pause around him. ''Gentlemen,'' he said, ''I applaud your bravery, but damn your manners!'' Then he rode off, leaving the men to their blood feast.[62] ''Boys,'' shouted one of Houston's captains, ''you know how to take prisoners, take them with the butt of your guns, club guns, & remember the Alamo, remember Labaher [La Bahía, or Goliad], & club guns right & left, & nock their god damn brains out.''[60] They didn't need a lecture. Bragged another soldier, ''We obeyed no command but the impulse of our own feelings. We came, we saw, we conquered.''[72]

A rebel physician tracked one Mexican officer into the marsh and found the man bogged and helpless, desperate to surrender. "Supposing myself alone, I extended my left hand to raise him up, but was surprised to hear a voice behind me saying: 'Oh! I know him; he is Col Bertrand, of San Antonio de Béxar. General Terán made him Colonel.' This was said by one Sánchez, a Mexican, in Capt. Seguín's Company, composed of some thirty Mexicans fighting on our side. He had scarcely done speaking when I observed three others coming up with levelled guns. I cried out to them: 'Don't shoot, don't shoot; I have taken him prisoner.' These words were hardly spoken, when bang goes a gun, the ball entering the forehead of poor Bertrand, and my hands and clothes are spattered with his brains, as he falls dead at my feet. Then comes up Col. Forbes; he searches his pockets, in one of which he finds a fine gold snuff-box, saying: 'This I will take to Houston.' "[62]

Back in front of the breastworks, still bleeding from his wounds, Private Steele saw two terrified Mexicans running through the grass. "When they got in about twenty steps of us they saw us and threw up their hands and began to 'jabber' something. I said to the fellow with me, 'Shoot one of them Mexicans.' He said, 'I can't do it; they want to surrender.' I said, 'I don't want any more prisoners; hand me my gun (which was lying where I had fallen) and I shot one of them down; the other ran off."[71]

Elsewhere Stephen Austin's cousin, Sgt. Moses Bryan, came across a young Mexican drummer boy lying on his face. One of Colonel Sherman's mercenaries pricked the boy with a bayonet point, and the boy grabbed the man's legs crying out, *"Ave María Purísima! Per Dios, salva mi vida!"* ("Hail Mary most pure! For God's sake, save my life!"). "I begged the man to spare him, both of his legs being broken already," Sergeant Bryan said. "The man looked at me and put his hand on his pistol, so I passed on. Just as I did so, he blew out the boy's brains."[73]

Some of the most cold-blooded slaughter centered at Peggy Lake, a few hundred yards south of the camp. There a large mass of Mexicans rushed into the twenty-foot-deep water, forming an organic bridge of horses and men, dead and living. When the rebels caught scent of this frenzied bottleneck, they took position along the bank and conducted a turkey shoot. Pvt. William Foster Young said it all: "I sat there [on the bayou shore] and shot them until my ammunition gave out. Then I turned the butt end of my musket and started knocking them in the head."[73] The rebels killed almost anything that moved. Blinded and bleeding, Private Steele was seated on a Mexican corpse when some of his comrades approached, bayoneting all the enemy wounded. Mistaking Steele for a Mexican, they started to lunge for him, too, but an officer recognized the teenager and intervened.[71]

Finally Colonel Almonte managed to gather four hundred soldiers together and make a mass surrender. Sickened by the atrocities, Secretary of War Rusk took personal charge of the prisoners, and his first act was to move them away from the berserkers lining the bayou. As the body of prisoners crossed toward camp, Houston cried out in despair, thinking the enemy had rallied or that Mexican reinforcements had arrived. "All is lost!" he anguished, "My God, all is lost!" Reflecting back on that day, he later confessed that a hundred disciplined soldiers could have rubbed his mad dog army from existence.

The blood frenzy eased only when darkness stole the rebels' vision. There were some 730 prisoners, over 200 of them wounded. The wounded Mexicans would be denied medical treatment for three full days after the battle.[68] One immediate effect would be the death of dozens of soldiers who otherwise might have recovered. In the longer run, the neglect led to an outbreak of cholera among the prisoners.[74] Their suffering would extend for months as they were held on the oyster shell and sand banks of Galveston and ever so slowly repatriated or "taken in" by Anglo-American families as virtual slaves.

The prisoners' first night was terrible, long on fear and hunger, and all too close to God. "After having kept us sitting about an hour and a half, they marched us into the woods, where we saw an immense fire, made up of a huge pile of wood, even whole trees being used," said Colonel Delgado. "I and several of my companions were silly enough to believe that we were about to be burnt alive, in retaliation for those who had been burnt in the Alamo. We should have considered it an act of mercy to be shot first. Oh! the bitter and cruel moment! However, we felt considerably relieved when they placed us around the fire to warm ourselves and to dry our wet clothes. We were surrounded by twenty-five or thirty sentinels. You should have seen those men, or rather, phantoms, converted into moving armories—some wore two, three, and even four braces of pistols; a cloth bag, of very respectable size, filled with bullets; a powderhorn; a saber or a bowie-knife besides a rifle, musket, or carbine. Everyone of them had in his hand a burning candle. I wonder where they obtained so many of them, for the heat of their hands and the breeze melted them very fast; and yet, that illumination was kept up the whole night. Was this display of light intended to prevent us from attempting an escape? The fools! Where could we go in that vast country, unknown to us, intersected by large rivers and forests, where wild beasts and hunger, and where they themselves would destroy us?"[68]

Seven miles off, another Mexican officer was enduring his own dark night of the soul. He had been chased by the rebel cavalry all the way to what remained of Vince's Bridge, and there had been unsaddled and had lost his horse. Hiding in a thicket of small pines, he slipped his pursuers and changed his costume. Alone in the Texas wilds, he meditated upon all the ways his life had reached an end. Next day, a search party scouring the plain for Santa Anna scooped him up. Joel Robison, who could speak Spanish, interrogated the prisoner who was dressed commonly enough in white linen pants and a blue trooper's jacket . . . but with red worsted slippers and a silk shirt buttoned with diamond studs. He was a cavalry-man, the prisoner said, and Santa Anna had escaped to Thompson's Pass farther south. Trotting at the point of a lance, the prisoner covered two or three miles back toward camp, but finally complained he could go no farther on foot. Robison's partner argued for finishing him with a lead ball. But Robison gave the prisoner a hand up and ferried him on the rump of his horse. As they rode they chatted. The prisoner asked if it was Houston who had commanded at the battle and what the body and pris-oner count was. He was, naturally enough, very keen to know what the rebels planned to do with their prisoners. When Robison told him that Houston's force had amounted to six or seven hundred, the prisoner insisted such a figure had to be a gross underestimate. Nearing camp, the prisoner was further sobered by the grisly corpses on the battlefield. Not until they approached the motley throng of prisoners did Robison learn who it was he really carried on the back of his horse. In unison, every Mexican officer rose to his feet, and the troops called out, "El Presi-dente." Santa Anna had returned to his army.[75]

Now revealed, Santa Anna requested an audience with his military counterpart. The Anglo-Americans had been hounding Colonel Almonte and General Cós unmercifully, demanding a list of all the captured of-ficers. Throughout the morning, the victors had labored to discover if Santa Anna was among their battle-shocked captives. Now—at two o'clock in the afternoon—he appeared. Every rebel anticipated a bloody reckoning.

Houston was lying propped beneath an oak tree, dozing and grunting in considerable pain with his shattered ankle. "I am Gen. Antonio López de Santa Anna, President of Mexico, Commander-in-Chief of the Army of Operations," the prisoner announced himself, "and I put myself at the disposition of the brave Gen. Houston. I wish to be treated as a General should be when a prisoner of war.''

Houston woke up and lifted up on one elbow. He was courteous, even friendly. "Gen. Santa Anna!" he said. "Ah, indeed! Take a seat, General; I am glad to see you; take a seat."[76] Santa Anna sat on a black box nearby, and with the help of three different interpreters, the two generals got down to the business of victory and defeat. All around them crowded the hairy, wild-eyed rebels, waiting for the word to take Santa Anna off to one side for a killing. The word never came.

Later, in trying to explain why Santa Anna was spared, a rumor grew that the frightened Mexican *caudillo* flashed a Masonic distress signal to his captors, and that it was recognized and respected.[77] Only a conspiracy or mystical solidarity could seem to answer the baffling question of why Houston spared his prisoner. But opium was more likely the explanation. Houston's physician at San Jacinto was John C. Hunt, and he was sedating his heroic patient with opium. Waking from an opiated nap, Houston appeared mellow and forgiving. Terrified by the smell of death just beyond camp, nervous, hungry, and sleep-deprived, Santa Anna requested a bit of relief also. He asked for some opium, and Dr. Hunt handed him some.[78]

Captor and captive quickly drove to the heart of the matter. Santa Anna wished to live. Houston wished Texas. Santa Anna proposed to end the war by sending his army home. In return, he would be liberated.

Houston demurred, stating that only the civil government of the Republic of Texas could negotiate such matters.

Santa Anna had no authority to negotiate either, but that didn't stop him. Without a blush or a pause, the president of Mexico replied—with sterling understatement—that he had an aversion to civil governments. Surely, he implied, the two generals could arrive at an arrangement. Houston continued to balk. Santa Anna flattered him, saying that Houston had been born to an extraordinary destiny. One proof was that he had just captured the Napoleon of the West.

Houston asked how Santa Anna justified his conduct at the Alamo and Goliad. Santa Anna responded that the battle of the Alamo fit all rules of war, and that he was unaware of any special terms of capitulation at Goliad. However, he offered to make an example of General Urrea once he returned to Mexico City.[79]

Houston never raised his voice. Like two gentlemen discussing a lady, they sat beneath the oak tree and chatted through the languid afternoon, shaping the future of two nations. Pleasantly teased by their hits of opium, the Anglo-Saxon chieftain and the Hispanic *caudillo* set up the continental chessboard in positions that would still be playing out a century and a half later.

Houston feared that the Mexican army—under the more competent leadership of Filisola, Urrea, and others—might still attack him. He had won the battle, but his men were exhausted, and twenty-five hundred enemy troops were concentrating a scant two to three days away, with another thousand gathered at San Antonio. Houston had no illusions. His army had won yesterday's battle through sheer, bloodthirsty luck. Now, on the day after victory, his army was closer than ever to defeat. Very simply, Houston could not afford to fight even a single battle more. With no time to spare, Houston leisurely probed Santa Anna. Would General Filisola surrender the remainder of the army at Santa Anna's order? Even with his head on the chopping block, Santa Anna thought not. But Santa Anna believed Filisola would withdraw from Texas if ordered to do so. The order was sent.

Less than a month later, the oak tree dialogue was formalized in two treaties, one public, the other private. But even before the Mexican government heard about these so-called Treaties of Velasco, it declared null and void any act or negotiation Santa Anna undertook while still a prisoner of the Anglo-Americans. International law was on the Mexican government's side: Actions under the duress of captivity were never accepted as binding. Nevertheless, Santa Anna solemnly signed the treaties on May 14. The ink in his signature was worth more than his promises, and the Anglo-American leaders knew it. But the ambiguities growing out of Texan, and later U.S., claims based on the bastard Velasco Treaties would fester for nearly a decade. Ultimately Houston's tête-à-tête with Santa Anna would culminate in the first U.S. intervention in Central America, the invasion of Mexico.

Later that afternoon, Ramón Caro, Santa Anna's personal secretary, was escorted out onto the battlefield to retrieve some essentials for his general's comfort and state business: a silk tent, a folding cot, a trunkful of clothing, and Caro's *escritoire* (portable writing table). The overrun Mexican camp devastated Caro. The naked, blackening bodies of fifty Mexican soldiers lay strewn about the breastwork, among them that of General Castrillón.[80] The rebels had spent their day profitably, stripping the dead and hunting for silver. One rebel had been seen pulling out the teeth of dead Mexicans and collecting them in a tin bucket, explaining that they were worth five dollars apiece to him.[81]

Over near Peggy Lake, men probed for treasure. "It was said that

Sant Annas money chest was throwed in there," said Robert Hunter, "& a passel of us Boys went & cut out some poles 6 or 7 feet long, probed down to finde the money & we could not finde bottom, & got some poles 10 or 12 feet long. We could feel the ded horses, & I expect men, but no bottom, & we gave it up. That laggune was full of men & horses for a bout 20 or 30 feet up & down it, & non of them ever got out."[60]

Capt. Juan Seguín did manage to locate the war chest, which when first inventoried was said to hold twelve thousand pesos. By the time various officers finished "counting," the amount was only seven thousand pesos. This was divided up, with each soldier receiving approximately eleven dollars, which he could use to purchase Mexican plunder, everything from Mexican ponchos and muskets to saddles, horses, and the officers' camp ware. The rebels howled at Santa Anna's aristocracy, ridiculed his china, silver tea urns, cut-glass tumblers and decanters, and silk underwear, failing to remember that George Washington's camp gear had included a hinged walnut cot and silver toothbrush and tongue scraper.[82] Some of the rebel officers like Colonel Forbes and Colonel Sherman were so charmed with some of the more elegant paraphernalia that they simply stole them . . . a fact much resented by the soldiers.

Houston's army and prisoners remained camped upon the San Jacinto plain. On the night Filisola started pulling the Mexican army back toward Mexico, Colonel de la Peña sighted a brilliant aurora borealis in the direction of the battlefield. Some of the soldiers deduced that the illumination came from the intense flames of a cremation of their fallen comrades. It didn't.[83] The Mexican dead were neither burned nor buried. They simply bloated under the sun, and at night wolves and coyotes screamed and feasted. Confirming their own low opinion of the enemy, the Anglo-Americans remarked on how carnivores quickly stripped the dead horses to the bone, but seemed repelled by the Mexican bodies . . . "presumably because of the peppery condition of the flesh."[17] The stench finally became unbreathable.

On the third day, a hard-bitten Scotch-Irish widow named Peggy McCormick dropped in on Houston. She wanted him to clean up after himself. "Take them dead Mexicans off my league," she demanded. "They haunt me the longest day I live." Houston told her no, that it was up to Santa Anna to bury them, but that Santa Anna would not because this had been a massacre, not a battle.[60] The widow insisted.

"Madam," Houston protested, hiding a grin, "your land will be famed in history as the classic spot upon which the glorious victory of San Jacinto was gained. Here was born, in the throes of revolution, and amid the strife of contending legions, the infant of Texas independence! Here the latest scourge of mankind, the arrogantly self-styled Napoleon of the West met his fate!''

"To the devil with your glorious history," Mrs. McCormick snapped. "Take off your stinking Mexicans."[84]

But there the bodies lay, turning to skeletons which grazing cattle chewed for their salt. The locals complained that it ruined their milk, and finally dug a trench and threw in some of the remains. But for years afterward, steamboats passing up the San Jacinto would stop nearby and curious tourists would wander among the ghastly bones and tell one another stories about Santa Anna's apocalypse and the birth of Texas.

=21=

FROM BALTIMORE SOUTH the dogwoods blossomed with snow-white petals and the red bud trees showed pink. It was a season of hope and beauty, a time for renewal. But in his White House office, the gaunt hickory wand of a man who was called King Andrew saw only death and ruin, and for that he cursed Congress. He had—cautiously, and urging caution—authorized General Gaines to cross the Mexican border with U.S. troops and proceed as far as Nacogdoches, but when Congress learned of it a firestorm of protest ignited, led by the man whom Jackson had supplanted as President, John Quincy Adams. When Jackson requested money for volunteers, in case General Gaines's troops needed reinforcing, Congress howled, rejecting any movement that might force a duel of eagles. Clearly, the United States was not ready to make war on Mexico . . . not directly, not yet. His hands tied, Jackson was furious. Even as he watched, Texas was sliding through his fingers like so much sweet creek water. News had reached Washington, D.C. that the Alamo had fallen, and then that Goliad, too, was gone. The Anglo-American frontline had held the Mexican advance no better than a spiderweb catching gusts of prairie wind. By mid-May, as Jackson hungrily waited for the next dispatch, there was little reason to hope Houston or any other Anglo-Americans still remained in Texas.

And then the word came. On May 16 a bright young captain from General Gaines's staff, Ethan Allen Hitchcock, rode into the capital, bearing a wallet of documents fresh from the battlefield. Jackson immediately received him. "I am not sure that I ever saw a man more delighted," the weary soldier wrote of his President. "If there had been a vacancy in the dragoons at that time I think he would have given it to me on the spot."[1]

Observing Jackson's demand for secrecy, General Gaines had sent Hitchcock to convey verbally the more covert details of his operations. "[Captain Hitchcock's] discriminating mind and perfect integrity and honor will enable him to communicate more fully than my present delicate health (much impaired by a succession of bad colds) will allow me to write, the facts and circumstances connected with this interesting subject, the opinions and wishes of the inhabitants of the eastern border of Texas, together with the late occurrences, and present state of my command."[2]

Besides his intelligence report, the captain presented two documents, one a letter from the Texan secretary of war to General Gaines, the other a scrap of paper bearing words of uncertain authorship. Jackson instantly identified the hand. "Yes! that's his writing! I know it well!" the old warrior enthused. "That's his writing! That's Sam Houston's writing! There can be no doubt of the truth of what he states!" What the scrap proclaimed was victory. Texas was conquered.

"Then [Jackson] ordered a map," Hitchcock remembered, "got down over it, and looked in vain for the unknown rivulet called San Jacinto. He passed his finger excitedly over the map in search of the name, saying: 'It must be there! No, it must be over there!' moving his finger round but finally giving up the search."

Old Hickory was not alone. All through the states and territories people futilely combed their maps as the San Jacinto story cascaded from city to city, newspaper to newspaper. What mattered about Texas had always been less its parts and places than its promise of furtherance. Texas meant a perpetuation of the Anglo-Saxon mission. Until this moment Texas had figured in the American mind almost exclusively as an abstraction, not a geography, not soil and sky. All of Washington celebrated, for San Jacinto vindicated the Alamo and Goliad in a way that transcended ordinary life. When Aaron Burr, the ancient, dying traitor who had reached for Texas (but then had been betrayed), learned of Houston's astounding victory, he whispered bitterly, "I was thirty years too soon."[3]

On the day he learned of San Jacinto, even John Quincy Adams could not help but pause and marvel: "There was glorious news from Texas," he wrote, "transmitted in handbills—that Santa Anna had been defeated and taken by Houston, and shot, with all his officers."[4]

Not everyone in the capital was elated, however.[5]

It was one thing to marvel at two ex-congressmen's fantastic adventures in a faraway land, quite another to embrace and endorse the invasion of another country. A little more than a week after Captain Hitchcock reined his horse to a halt at the White House steps, Adams stood in Congress and violently denounced the Texas Revolution and U.S. complicity in it, proclaiming that it invigorated Southern slavocracy. In what he termed the most hazardous speech of his life, Adams castigated the Jackson administration for its efforts to lend military support to the Texas rebels, charging the President with flirting with a war with Mexico. He chided U.S. arrogance, warning that Mexico was better able to overrun the American border than vice versa.[6] Adams's speech sobered his colleagues. A giddy rush to recognize the Texan republic's independence— an act that would have struck Mexico as second only to a declaration of war—cooled. It was finally decided that any such recognition should wait until all the facts were in, and until the new nation could demonstrate a working system of government. Nevertheless, on July 4, Congress voted money to send a U.S. minister to Texas.[7]

At best, Texan independence had been gained through the use of American mercenaries, American arms, and American money, all of them illegal under American neutrality laws. At worst, the President himself had been covertly involved. Only because he turned south instead of north at the Which Way Tree, thereby choosing to fight Santa Anna without General Gaines's direct intervention, did Houston avoid exposing the larger conspiracy. The miracle of San Jacinto lay as much in Jackson's lucky escape from an international war as in Houston's lucky victory.

In order to rationalize, if not sanction, the Anglo-American seizure of Texas, Anglo-Americans needed to be bewitched. They needed an artificial history that would present piracy as heroism, wrong as right, aggression as defense. The battle cry "Manifest Destiny" had not yet been uttered, not those words anyway, and the imperialistic ethic did not yet fit, not comfortably. What the United States required was a sanctifying epic, a propaganda that would shout Go Ahead all through the streets and forests and fields. Texas provided. By plucking heroes and martyrs from the still-smoking ash of its battlefields, by copying the colors of Old Glory, the Lone Star bastard declared itself worthy. By dressing itself in tales of glory, Anglo-Saxonism could redeem itself of all sins of trespass. Texas spoke to Americans: With the golden sun as their compass, the Anglo-Saxon crusaders could never lose their way.

Details were still hazy when Sam Houston arrived fresh from San Jacinto and gave Americans their first view of the patriot-warrior cult that Texas was hawking. Houston's ankle wound had worsened, and in early May he started for New Orleans for medical treatment. But the hero of San Jacinto practically died trying to find passage on a ship. Ever feuding, members of the interim government refused to allow Houston to travel with them, and he had to scrape up a ride on a small trading vessel named the *Flora*. When the *Flora* came steaming into New Orleans, a band struck up and the waiting crowd roared its welcome to the hero.[8] After a week of watching Houston lie semicomatose on the open deck, the steam packet's captain had judged him near death. But when Houston heard the crowd, he rose to the occasion, literally ascending from his death bed. The vision of this giant, stinking, hatless Achilles with his harrowing wound struck the crowd still. Houston surveyed the horrified crowd, then dropped in a faint.[9] Surgeons would remove twenty pieces of shattered bone from Houston's ankle, and he would limp the rest of his life.

Soon, Houston returned to Texas, where he was to play out the role of founding father of the castaway republic, a role Crockett and Travis and Fannin and others had coveted. In the remainder of his lifetime, Houston would serve twice as president of the Texas republic.

On February 28, 1845, the United States Congress adopted a joint resolution offering the Republic of Texas statehood. Texan politicians coyly took until October to say yes, and it took until December for the news to reach Washington.

On February 19, 1846—almost exactly one decade after the Alamo siege—Sam Houston opened his arms in front of the log capitol building in Austin. As the Lone Star flag of the Texas Republic descended for the last time, he embraced its cloth. The United States had finally added Texas to the Union. Houston would serve as its senator for almost fourteen years, and then as its governor.

To the end, he believed that Mexico should belong to the United States. Near the sunset of his life, as the Civil War loomed, Houston actively envisioned leading ten thousand Texas Rangers, supported by Indians and Mexicans, to conquer Mexico and establish a protectorate with himself as the ruler.[10] He went so far as to sponsor a bill in the U.S. Senate in early 1858 to establish a protectorate over Mexico, but Congress voted him down. Changing saddles a year later, the senator-governor tried to raise support for his quixotic filibustering invasion by approaching the commander of the eighth U.S. military district at San Antonio, a colonel by the name of Robert E. Lee. Lee had other wars to fight though, as did Houston's mythical "ten thousand Texas Rangers." Seventy-five thousand Texans donned the gray, and Houston was deposed as governor. In 1863, Houston would expire with the words "Texas, Texas" upon his lips.[11]

*   *   *

Treating his personal defeat as a national defeat, Santa Anna exchanged Texas for his life. In his treaty with the rebels, he ordered the Mexican army to remove west of the Rio Grande, to repatriate all prisoners, and to return all confiscated property. When his officers learned of their commander's extraordinary—and extralegal—arrangements, they were revolted.[12] Calling Santa Anna contemptible, de la Peña expressed the common sentiment. "Anyone else in [Santa Anna's] position and circumstances would have blown out his brains before signing his own disgrace, for there is no greater degradation."[13]

Urrea and others urged General Filisola, who had taken over command of the army, to attack the rebels and rescue their captive comrades. "There is no doubt that we should have returned to restore the honor of our arms and to avenge the blood of our comrades; we were in a better position than ever to give battle and to end the campaign with a glorious and decisive action," said de la Peña. "All prospects favored us: number and discipline, but above all, justice. Before retreating we should at least have tried to find our commander in chief; an effort should have been made to rescue him if he were still alive, even if only for the honor of the nation, for he was after all its first magistrate."[14]

But General Filisola was a psychological orphan, an Italian who had joined the Spanish army and then abandoned it to become a Mexican "revolutionary." He soldiered not from any sense of patriotism, but because it was all he knew. Filisola was industrious and widely admired for his integrity, but he was a military automaton, strictly mindful of the chain of command. It was for that very reason Santa Anna had chosen him for his second in command. Now, given the choice between his *caudillo* and Mexico, Filisola chose as Santa Anna knew he would. He ordered a retreat.

Filisola was denounced as a despicable buffoon, and officers railed against the retreat.[14] But the army retreated. Watched from a distance by a handful of Anglo-American scouts, the Mexicans turned their backs on the Sabine River and marched through the veil of rain. The bayous, rivers, and arroyos swelled with water. The road disappeared and soldiers fanned out at random, each finding his own best way. Wounded men dragged themselves along on crutches or fell from jarring wagons. Mud hobbled the army, on some days limiting its movement to a few miles. Artillery got stuck to the axle, and de la Peña had to shuck his boots when he dismounted and sank to his knees in mud. The steady downpour saturated firewood, and what little food the soldiers ate was cold. The hungry troops took to bending mulberry trees and stripping them of their half-ripe fruit.[15] When the rains finally ceased, the army was caught in midprairie. Suddenly the soldiers and their families faced bony thirst all over again. It was no wonder that men began to fantasize that their campfires at night were the lights of their hometown plazas. Even as they struggled with the elements and tried to comprehend their baffling defeat, the army received word from Mexico City that a special legion of honor had been approved for the Texas veterans.[15] The unhappy officers greeted the news with grim humor.

As the dispirited expedition approached Goliad and San Antonio, Filisola obediently began to return goods to the colonists. He started by handing over his coachman, a Negro slave who had fled to promises of Mexican liberation. (A Mexican officer rescued the miserable man from Anglo-American custody by disguising him as a soldier and sending him to Matamoros.[16]) Elsewhere, angry Mexican officers chose to destroy confiscated items rather than turn them back to the Anglo-Americans. At Goliad the army passed the gruesome remains of Fannin's command. There, the residents, who had suffered devastation at the rebels' hands, insulted the Mexican army for their cowardice. "We were obliged to offer explanations without denying their charges," said de la Peña, "lest we appear ashamed of something of which we are guilty."

Tejano refugees began joining the army on its departure, relating tales of how the Anglo-Americans were forcing them off their ranches, out of Texas . . . "one of them was riding bareback, unmistakable proof that he had scarcely had time to flee."[17] It was a portent of the racism and land theft that would mark the shift from Mexican control to Anglo-American control.

Following almost on the heels of the Mexican retreat came the victors' advance. News of Houston's triumph sliced through the long trail of fleeing Anglo-Americans, halting their desperate exodus in midstride. "Towards sunset, a woman on the outskirts of the camp began to clap her hands and shout 'Hallelujah! Hallelujah!' " said one refugee. "Those about her thought her mad, but following her wild gestures, they saw one of the Hardings, of Liberty, riding for life towards the camp, his horse covered with foam, and he was waving his hat and shouting, 'San Jacinto! San Jacinto! The Mexicans are whipped and Santa Anna a prisoner!' The scene that followed beggars description. People embraced, laughed and wept and prayed, all in one breath. As the moon rose over the vast, flower decked prairie, the soft southern wind carried peace to tired hearts and grateful slumber."[18]

In one wretched, disease-infested camp after another, an energetic courier named McDermot spread the news with a unique flair. "He was an Irishman and had been an actor," remembered Dilue Rose Harris, who was eleven years old at the time. "He stayed with us that night and told various incidents of the battle. There was not much sleeping during the night. Mr. McDermot said that he had not slept in a week. He not only told various incidents of the retreat of the Texas army, but acted them. The first time that mother laughed after the death of my little sister was at his description of General Houston's helping to get a cannon out of a bog."[19]

All along the eastern border of Texas and across the river in Louisiana refugees reversed their course, following their own tracks and ruts back to what was left of their homes. They passed through a landscape littered with corpses and burned plantations. The Stafford plantation—once consisting of a sugar mill, cotton gin, blacksmith shop, gristmill, slave quarters, and main house—was now marked by nothing more than a crib containing a thousand bushels of corn. Here and there, anywhere it seemed, the dead lay unburied and anonymous, wherever lead or disease or hunger had dropped them. Fannin's men lay beneath the sky in the ash heaps; what was left of Travis and Bowie and Crockett and the Alamo garrison blew with the spring winds. It was a sobering landscape. "The first thing that we saw on the other side [of the river] were a few unrecognizable and mouldering corpses," said one soldier.[20] Dilue Rose Harris crossed the San Jacinto battlefield near dusk, "a grewsome [*sic*] sight. We camped that night on the prairie, and could hear the wolves howl and bark as they devoured the dead."[19]

Settlers returned to find their homes ransacked and burned. Dilue Rose and her family were lucky. Their house had been spared the torch, though the door had been torn off by Mexican soldiers searching for eggs. "As soon as it was light enough for us to see we went to the house," she recalled, "and the first thing we saw was the hogs running out. Father's bookcase lay on the ground broken open, his books, medicines, and other things scattered on the ground, and the hogs sleeping on them . . . there was one big hog that would not go out till father shot at him. Then we children began picking up the books. We could not find those that Colonel Travis gave us. . . ." The first thing the girl's father did—regardless of the pillaged household, and worse, regardless of the Sabbath—was to observe one of the most sacred rituals of the Anglo-Saxon frontier. He hitched up the oxen, snaked them out into the bottom, and plowed for the corn crop. Once upon a time David Crockett had done the same, striking his seed into the earth even before he built a roof over his head. All across

Texas, resilient Anglo-Americans set themselves in similar order. Bit by bit, they fastened their grip upon the land.

Texas boomed and busted all at once. The Anglo-American population exploded and new towns sprouted from the black and red dirt. Just a month after the revolution, the city of Houston was born on a piece of paper, then transferred piecemeal upon the land. "The sidewalks are only marked out," a foreigner observed, "and the finished buildings have considerable gaps between them . . . the docks still obstructed by enormous tree trunks; stumps of great Southern pines [have] been left standing in the street."[21] By 1839 Houston boasted a population of three thousand (all but forty of them men), and sixty-five places of business (forty-seven of them saloons or gambling houses).[22] Log cabins were thrown up, "and in there pell mell they crammed Senators, Representatives and civil servants who were only too happy to have a roof over their heads and to procure at the price of gold, not beds, but sacks of woodshavings, into which they inserted themselves for the night as in the sheath of a sword. What a race!" marveled the foreigner. "What can the Mexicans do against men of this kidney!"[23]

The new republicans were not only men of kidney, but also wild imagination. As if they could shape their geography at whim, ambitious politicians considered making the Pacific Ocean their western boundary. On second thought they grandly decided that the Rio Grande would suffice, a claim that had no basis in Spanish or Mexican history. Even then, their imagined nation contained 375,000 square miles, an area roughly equal to the size of the original thirteen colonies. At first count only thirty thousand Anglo-Americans occupied this vast area, mainly spread through the southeastern river country. It was a wispy presence, especially when compared to eight million Mexicans.

The new landlords of Texas were by no means secure in their holdings. Just because General Filisola had withdrawn across the Rio Grande did not mean Mexico had ceded the territory. To the contrary, through the first and only decade of the Texas republic's existence, Mexico kept troops poised along the Rio Grande, ready to reassert her sovereignty over the rebellious territory. Despite Texan efforts to negotiate a secret deal with Santa Anna (for recognition of Texan independence), Mexico refused to concede an inch of the territory. This unwavering hostility made it necessary—though not desirable—for Texas to maintain a force of American mercenaries.[24] It was a neat balancing act. Texas needed to garrison mercenaries it didn't want in order to secure itself from an enemy it couldn't afford to reveal, for any possibility of war with Mexico diminished Texas' union with the United States.

The truth of the matter was that the Republic of Texas was never meant to stand on its own two feet. The so-called Texas Revolution was designed only to wrench a huge chunk of Mexican territory free of Mexican control long enough for the United States to annex it. Annexation would bring to Texas the protection of the U.S. Army and Navy, in addition to solving the difficulties of financing frontier development projects.[25] In the republic's first national election on September 5, 1836, Texans unanimously declared their desire to be annexed to the United States rather than risk the independence for which they had supposedly fought. On December 22, 1836, Old Hickory answered the anxious Texans.

In a written message to Congress, the White House flatly rejected the Texan request for annexation. The Presidential message signed by Jackson emphasized the sensitivity of foreign relations. "Upon the issue of this threatened invasion [by Mexico], the independence of Texas may be considered as suspended. . . ," said the message. "Prudence, therefore, seems to dictate that we should still stand aloof, and maintain our present attitude, if not until Mexico itself, or one of the great foreign powers, shall recognize the independence of the new government [of Texas], at least until the lapse of time, or the course of events shall have proved, beyond cavil or dispute, the ability of the people of that country to maintain their separate sovereignty, and to uphold the government constituted by them."[26] In short, the Texans were told to prove themselves.

The message shocked everyone, from the Texan minister to the United States, William H. Wharton (one of the original War Dogs), to John Quincy Adams, who wrote that Jackson had completely reversed his spirit. In fact, Jackson never wrote the message bearing his signature. From November 1836 until the time he handed over power to his successor, Martin Van Buren, Jackson was desperately ill in the White House. It was Secretary of State John Forsyth, probably along with President-elect Van Buren, who penned the cautious and diplomatically astute rejection of Texas annexation. Their reasons for turning Texas away from the front door were simple: The United States could not afford a war with Mexico, and the upcoming Van Buren administration could not afford a war with Congress.[26] And so Texas braced against the Mexican invasion—which never came.

For Jackson—who had almost singlehandedly authored the policy of taking what Latin America would not give—turning Texas away from the Union was particularly galling. The Old Chief retired from the White House, but not from his fight to gain Texas. From his beloved Hermitage in Tennessee, Jackson loudly championed annexation, even recommending that Presidential candidate Henry Clay be lashed for his opposition. Meanwhile, disease, old wounds, and medical cures whittled down the sticklike warrior. Toward the end, Jackson was literally rotting; the skin below his waist needed to be bound to the bone by wrappings. In 1845, shortly after Congress voted to accept Texas, Jackson finally succumbed. Sam Houston rushed to Jackson's sickbed, but death beat him by half an hour. Just before they lowered Old Hickory's body into the earth, a household parrot began flapping madly and railing and cursing at the mourners.

Through the ten years of the Republic, Anglo-Americans shaped Texas in the image of their fatherland. It was not an easy metamorphosis. For one thing, the giddy promise of fortunes built on land speculation never saw fulfillment. Denied U.S. annexation, Texas lands represented a risky investment in danger of Mexican repossession. More important, the bottom fell out of land speculation.[27] In 1836 Jackson clamped down on paper money, declaring that only silver or gold, or bank notes based on them, would be accepted in payment for public lands. That action, and a depression in Britain which dropped cotton prices, collapsed the American economy. The Panic of 1837 was on. Building operations ceased. Canals and roads were left unfinished. Banks failed. Unemployment rocketed, and hunger riots broke out in eastern cities. And land speculation died in its tracks. Public land sales for the entire year of 1837 brought in only $1 million, the equivalent of a fortnight's sales in the previous year.[28]

Just the same, Anglo-American settlers poured into Texas. Among those seeking new "situations" came husband-hunting widows, large numbers of physicians, lawyers, printers, and footloose young men with or without weapons.[29] Many returned home after a quick look at the prospects: There were already abundant numbers of physicians and lawyers, and widows were cautioned against landing there with high hopes. A number of would-be mercenaries from Kentucky and Tennessee were disgusted to find Texan military and political opportunities well picked over.[30] Emigrants arrived to be victimized by "vast numbers" of forged land titles.[31] The bottom lands most richly suited to cotton farming were largely gone, and it would take the savage Texas Rangers many years with their Colt revolvers to drive the Comanches back from other desirable real estate. Despite these and other adversities, more and more settlers crossed the Sabine or put ashore at Gulf ports. They drove deeper and deeper into Texas, building their roads (and later their turnpikes) upon the migration paths of rapidly vanishing buffalo herds.[32] By 1850, Texas's population numbered over 210,000; by 1860, over 600,000.[33] Of this number, 182,000 were Negro slaves, and they were worth more than the land itself. Of equal note, the 1860 census could find only 12,000 Hispanics in all of what was once Hispanic domain. On top of that, the Texas state census listed Tejanos as foreigners who had been born outside the United States.[34]

If there was one victim of the Texas Revolution, it was the Tejano. For decades after Houston gloriously bearded the Mexican lion at San Jacinto, Anglo-Saxon supremacy raged against the Hispanic residents of Texas. The *1840 Emigrant's Guide* described Tejanos as "far inferior to Anglo-Americans, or any class of Europeans . . . mostly illiterate and vacant of ambition . . . cowardly and incompetent." Their dialect of Spanish was said to differ from Castilian Spanish "as far as does the rude dialect of a plantation negro from the style of Addison." The *Guide's* author took consolation in predicting that all vestiges of these decadent people would "soon be swallowed up and lost, and the Anglo-Texians give character and complexion to the whole nation."[35]

In November 1836, shortly after resigning from the vice-presidency of Texas, the Hispanic politician and intellectual Lorenzo de Zavala fell from a boat into the chill waters of Buffalo Bayou. Within days he contracted pneumonia and died, and his family buried him opposite the San Jacinto battleground, still littered with the skeletons of his fellow Mexicans.[36] Zavala was lucky, for he didn't live to see the extent to which Texas independence excluded Tejanos. The utopian democracy and capitalism that he had envisioned for an independent Texas became viciously racist, devouring every Hispanic to the Rio Grande.

The Tejanos of Nacogdoches were plundered, robbed, killed, and turned out of their homes by norteamericano adventurers, and their numbers plummeted from over 650 in 1834 to 170 in 1850. Anglo-Americans reentered Victoria and accused resident Tejanos of collaborating with the enemy. Overnight laws appeared that permitted the mayor—an Anglo-American—to order the arrest of any person suspected of spying, and every Tejano was suspect. Every Tejano had to obtain a passport within twelve hours of entering town, and none could leave without notifying the authorities. Any person deemed to lack visible means of support was legally expelled.[37] Goliad was virtually depopulated.

A small resistance movement sprang up, with some of the same Tejanos who had fought against Santa Anna in the Texas Revolution now fighting against their Anglo-American liberators. Manuel Flores, who had conspicuously fought the Mexican army at San Jacinto and served in the new Texas army for another year afterward, became disenchanted with all the talk of getting annexed by the United States. He had fought for independence, not American dominion, and soon joined the Cordova Rebellion, which aimed to incite Texas Indians (particularly Sam Houston's Cherokee allies, whose treaty with the Texas government had just been repudiated) into an alliance with Mexican guerrillas. The rebellion was crushed, and Flores was killed in 1838 when Texas Rangers raided the guerrilla camp along the San Gabriel River.[38]

No hero of the Texas Revolution came to a more tragic end than Capt. Juan Seguín, the square-jawed Tejano who had dashed through the Alamo siege line to summon aid for Travis. By the time he gathered help, the Alamo had fallen, and so Seguín formed a rear guard to protect the Anglo-American retreat. It was through prisoners of Seguín and his Tejano company that Houston learned of Santa Anna's presence, intelligence that led directly to the San Jacinto battle. He and his troops distinguished themselves in the battle, and Seguín was the man who reported finding Santa Anna's war chest containing over twelve thousand dollars in silver pesos. After the revolution the energetic soldier was promoted to lieutenant colonel of the Texan army and sent to occupy San Antonio. Seguín buried the ashes and bones of Travis, Crockett, Bowie, and all the other Alamo defenders in a ceremony that surpassed the burial of Fannin's men for reverence and martial dignity. In short, Seguín was faithful to the revolution in every way.

By 1837, however, he had begun to see disturbing cracks in the revolutionary wall. The cry for annexation by the United States was unsettling enough, but when, a year after the Alamo battle, Gen. Felix Huston commanded Seguín to raze San Antonio and relocate its citizens east of the Brazos River, Seguín refused. A month later he was ordered to seize horses from San Antonio citizens for military use. He knew from personal experience how much the Béxarenos had already suffered, for he had returned to find his own ranch despoiled by Mexicans and Anglo-Americans alike. Seguín started to recognize that his power had limits and a price. More and more it became apparent that he was being used and that his people were being victimized.

"In those evil days, San Antonio was swarming with adventurers from every quarter of the globe . . . bad men, fugitives from their coun-

try, who found in this land an open field for their criminal designs,"
Seguín wrote. "At every hour of the day and night, my countrymen ran
to me for protection against the assaults or exactions of those adventurers.
Some times, by persuasion, I prevailed on them to desist; some times,
also, force had to be resorted to. How could I have done otherwise? Were
not the victims my own countrymen, friends and associates? Could I
leave them defenceless [sic], exposed to the assaults of foreigners, who
on the pretext that they were Mexicans, treated them worse than
brutes?"[39] One of the worst of these grasping Anglo-Saxons was a gun-
smith named Goodman who demanded Tejano property and terrorized
Béxarenos, beating them bloody and burning their ranchos. Goodman
and other Anglo-Americans resentful of Seguín's power finally trumped
up charges that the Tejano soldier was collaborating with the Mexican
army. Seguín requested a court of inquiry to clear his name, but his
commanding officer—an Anglo-American—answered that there were no
grounds for inquiry.

Realizing that he was a marked man, Seguín went underground,
hiding on various ranchos until at last deciding to fortify his own rancho
and make a stand. Friends, family members, and supporters gathered, in
all about one hundred people, to repel a Texas army company that was
descending the San Antonio River, burning Tejano farms and ranches
along the way. "Hardly a day elapsed without receiving notice that a
party was preparing to attack me," Seguín said of his besieged ranch.
"We were constantly kept under arms. Several parties came in sight, but,
probably seeing that we were prepared to receive them, refrained from
attacking."[40]

Travis's Alamo battle was playing out all over again, except that this
time it was Anglo-Americans who were massing to overwhelm a handful
of Hispanics with their backs against the wall. Wisely deciding against a
last stand, Seguín dispersed his followers and fled to Mexico. "I had to
leave Texas, abandon all, for which I had fought and spent my fortune,
to become a wanderer," he said. "I resolved to seek a refuge amongst my
enemies, braving all dangers. . . . I left Béxar without any engagements
towards Texas; my services paid by persecutions, exiled and deprived of
my privileges as a Texan citizen, I was in this country a being out of the
pale of society, and when she could not protect the rights of her citizens,
they were privileged to seek protection elsewhere. I had been tried by a
rabble, condemned without a hearing, and consequently was at liberty to
provide for my own safety."

By this time Santa Anna was back in power. When he heard that his old enemy had crossed the border and was in Mexican hands, he decided, instead of shooting Seguín outright, to allow the Tejano to prove his loyalty to Mexico. In September 1842, Gen. Adrian Woll, who had fought Seguín at the Alamo, led a military raid on San Antonio. The hapless Seguín was ordered to lead a squadron of Mexican soldiers into the main square of his hometown, a neat piece of propaganda. In a single dramatic instant, his presence announced to every Tejano that Seguín had broken ties with the Anglo-American "revolution," that Santa Anna was merciful to his wayward children, and that Mexico was the *patria*. When Seguín and the Mexican army withdrew past the Rio Grande nine days later, a number of Tejano families filed along in search of sanctuary. Seguín, a man considered a traitor by the two nations he had tried to serve, returned to Texas after the Mexican War.

Like a Gulf hurricane, Anglo-Americans surged across the map, consolidating their hold upon Texas. The threat of Mexican invasion spurred them to ever greater heights of folly, racism, and violence. "Are there not freemen enough in Texas," challenged the *Telegraph and Texas Register,* "to rise and at once crush the abject race, whom, like the musquetoe [sic], it is easier to kill, than endure its annoying buzz?"[41] The contempt for Tejanos and their life-style accelerated. Protestant Anglo-Saxons camping in and around the old missions along the San Antonio showed their scorn for Catholicism by practicing their marksmanship on religious statues and vandalizing the chapels.[42] The phrase "cutting the patching," which referred originally to trimming the cotton cloth that bedded a muzzle-loader's ball, during the Texas Republic years came to connote "still following the trade—killing Mexicans."[43]

More waves of mercenaries and adventurers arrived from the United States with visions of Spanish booty and señoritas. The self-styled commander of this next wave of largely Southern recruits was Felix Huston, described by one of his followers as "ambitious as Cortez. . . . It was his thoughts by day and his dreams at night to march a conquering army into the 'Hall of the Montezumas.' During intervals at drill . . . he would pour floods of burning eloquence and arouse passions by allusions to the tropical beauties of the land far beyond the Rio Grande."[44] Equally fervid, Sam Houston wrote a letter to Santa Anna: "Most Excellent Sir, Ere the banner of Mexico shall . . . float on the banks of the Sabine, the Texan standard of the single star, borne by the Anglo-Saxon race, shall display its bright folds in liberty's triumph on the Isthmus of Darien."[45] Right up to the American annexation of Texas and the U.S. military invasion of

Mexico a few months later, Texans and other adventurers barked for conquest.[46]

The last messenger from the Alamo had been a boy named Ben Highsmith. In the ensuing years Highsmith became a Texas Ranger, and when the stars came out he would pass around the campfire his whetstone for men to sharpen their knives with. Three inches long and half as wide, the finger of stone had a deep groove worn in the middle from where Sam Houston and James Bowie and Buck Travis and Ben Milam and Deaf Smith and others had supposedly put an edge on their steel.[47] In effect every Anglo-American in Texas sharpened his knife on that touchstone.

When General Andrade had received his orders in 1836 to pull back to the Rio Grande, he had directed his men to destroy the Alamo. One of the captive physicians sent to tend Mexican wounded, Dr. J. H. Barnard, watched the destruction work. "They are now as busy as bees, soldiers, convicts and all, tearing down the walls, etc."[48] A few days later, a large fire blazed in what was left of the structure. "As soon as they had fairly left, Dr. Shackelford and myself, accompanied by Senor Reriz [Ruiz] and some other of the citizens, walked over to see the state in which they [had] left it," Dr. Barnard said. "We found the fire proceeding from a church [the Alamo chapel], where a platform had been built extending from the great door to the top of the wall on the back side for the purpose of taking up the artillery to the top of the church. This was made of wood, and was too far consumed for any attempt to be made to extinguish it. The walls of the church being built of solid masonry, of course would be but little injured by the fire. The Alamo was completely dismantled, all the single walls were leveled, the fessee [fosse] filled up, and the pickets torn up and burnt. All the artillery and ammunition that could not be carried off were thrown in the river."

What remained of the Alamo whistled in the blue northers and baked under the August sun, slowly collapsing into a pile of memories. "When I first saw the Alamo, in 1845 . . . it was a veritable ruin," one Texan recalled of his boyhood, "partly from the destruction caused by the battle, but mostly from its long abandonment as the abode of man. No doors or windows shut out the sunshine or storm; millions of bats inhabited the crevices in the walls and flat dirt roofs, and in the twilight the bats would pour forth in myriads. It was a meeting place for owls; weeds and grass grew from the walls, and even the cacti plant decorated the tumbledown roof of the old building that flanked the church. . . . In the south wall [of the chapel] was a breach near the ground, said to have been made by Santa Anna's cannon. We boys could run up the embankment to the outer wall and on to the roof of the convent building—it was a famous playground."[49]

Increasingly the Alamo became a receptable of fancy and lore. Just a year after the Alamo fell, an Arkansas boy named James Nichols found local Tejanos hawking souvenirs of the famous battle. "While thare I found a Mexican with old Davy Crockets gun and it was broak off at the bretch and it was a very noted gun. The naked barrel weighed 18 pounds with a plate of silver let into the barrel just behind the hind sight with the name Davy Crockette ingraved on it and another plate near the bretch with Drue Lane make ingraved on it, and thare was a young man with us claimed to be a son of Davy Crocketts baught the gun and carried it off home." Tejano entrepreneurs quickly learned which of the Anglo-Saxon "martyrs" appealed to early-day tourists. Around 1840, Nichols returned to San Antonio and this time "found Crocketts cap mad out of a rackoon skin with the hair pulled out leaving only the fur and with a fox tail hanging down behind, also his shot pouch mad of panter-skin with the tail for a flap. I told Father about it and he wrote to Bob Crockette, Memphis, Tennessee, but never got an answer, and I saw them once after that but I could not buy them."[50]

Every so often the Alamo would disgorge further artifacts. During the Mexican War, the interior of the chapel was cleared of debris to make room for U.S. Army supplies.[51] In the process two or three skeletons surfaced from deep inside the ramp, along with rotting fur caps and buckskin trappings.[52] Other skeletons appeared in 1878. Cannons that had been spiked and buried by General Andrade's retreating troops were resurrected to lie, like beached corpses, beneath the now-famous arch or "hump" added—for no good reason—on top of the chapel façade by the U.S. military. Limestone from the battered walls was carved into tobacco pipes or quaint crucifixes by enterprising locals and sold like religious relics to Anglo-American visitors. Tejano "guides" escorted early tourists through the ruins, pointing out the alleged sites of Crockett and Bowie's last stands. When the real blood and brain stains faded, local guides pointed at fresher marks left by meat the U.S. Army hung near the walls.[53]

Elderly Tejanas made a small cottage industry out of spinning tales about the Anglo-Saxon heroes. "On going to the Alamo to make sketches," related a British artist in 1843, "an old Mexican woman kindly brought me out a small chair and table. She had lived near the 'Alamo' from a child and had known nearly all those who had fallen in the wars. 'Yes sir,' said she. 'I knew them all. Poor Travis! What a tiger Santa Anna must have been. I shed many a tear during that siege. He can have no peace.' "[54] The Homer of these tale-telling crones was Madam Candaleria who lived to ripe old age. With a pet Chihuahua upon her lap, she daily regaled listeners with her recollections of the siege and the deaths of the great James Bowie and David Crockett.[55]

The ultimate Alamo souvenirs were the handful of people who had survived the siege. Several were messengers who had been lucky enough to ride out before the Mexicans attacked. There was Ben Highsmith with his famous whetstone, who took a musket ball in the leg during the Mexican War, but recovered and fathered thirteen children in Bastrop.[56] Dr. Sutherland, who was one of the first messengers to leave the Alamo, practiced medicine and landed a postmaster job, wrote an account of the battle, and died at the age of seventy-five.[57] John Smith, El Colorado, entered local politics, serving as mayor of San Antonio three times before entering the state senate.

By far the most mysterious figure was the Frenchman, Louis "Moses" Rose. Except for one or two anonymous survivors of the battle itself, Rose was the final white man to slip loose of the Mexican noose. After rejecting Travis's invitation to step across the line and fight to the death, Rose had jumped the Alamo wall and fled through the prairie. By the time he reached the Anglo-American colonies weeks later, Rose was nearly dead, his legs filled with prickly pear cactus thorns. "My God!" exclaimed a settler who knew him. "Rose, is this you, or is it your ghost?" With a pair of forceps, the settler and his wife painstakingly extracted from Rose's legs scores of thorns, "some of them an inch and a half in length, each of which drew out a lump of flesh and was followed by a stream of blood. Salve was applied to his sores and they soon began to heal."[58]

For the rest of his life Rose was questioned as to why he hadn't stayed and fought with Travis and the boys. His reply was always, "By God, I wasn't ready to die." After the revolution the illiterate mercenary settled in Nacogdoches and opened a notoriously bad meat store, verbally and sometimes physically abusing customers who complained. Part of his ill-treatment of customers may have stemmed from their ill-treatment of him, for he was branded a deserter and a Judas. He made no secret of his flight from the Alamo, and Texans made no secret of their contempt for him. His first name was insultingly feminized to "Luesa," and when someone made a drunken attempt on his life, no charges were filed against the known assailant. According to a relative, Rose never received the bounty of land granted to each soldier who had carried a gun in the revolution.[59] Nevertheless, Rose was considered a credible enough witness to the Alamo siege to testify in the claims brought on behalf of six other rebels under Travis and Bowie.[60]

Eventually the lame pariah drifted out of Texas into Louisiana where he died in 1850. The quasi-religious dimensions of his "cowardice" at the Alamo and his betrayal of the Anglo-Saxon cause continued well into the twentieth century. In 1975, it was reported that Moses Rose's grave had been located in an overgrown pine brake near Logansport, Louisiana. No marker identified the spot, but researchers found a bed of yucca cactus growing among the pines. Since yucca are not indigenous to Louisiana, it was reasoned that some of the old thorns in Rose's legs must have grown out of his corpse.[61] If so, it would have been miraculous indeed, for thorns are not seeds, just spiny bits of armor.

Another unhappy survivor of the Alamo was the sole English-speaking male to live through both the siege and Mexican capture. This was Joe, the twenty-four-year-old slave of young Colonel Travis. After "escaping" Mexican captivity, Joe had accompanied Susannah Dickinson, her daughter, and Santa Anna's own black servant to Gonzales and points east. For a brief time the young, well-spoken black man was treated respectfully by the most powerful Anglo-Americans in Texas, among them Sam Houston, President David Burnet, and other members of the Texas Cabinet. But soon enough Joe was returned to his life of servitude as part of Travis's estate. That estate had numerous claims against it by everyone from Travis's landlady to Noah Smithwick, the blacksmith. The estate's executor put Joe to work planting cotton and marking cattle, and hired him out at a dollar a day. Bridling at this unrelenting labor, Joe made a break for freedom. A year to the day after the San Jacinto battle, Joe and several Mexicans—probably prisoners captured in the revolution—mounted two of the executor's horses and rode off into the night. A reward of fifty dollars for the Alamo survivor apparently brought results, for a year later Joe was again working off Travis's debts.[62] After that, the young slave simply vanished from all records, one more character lost in the maze called Texas.

But no one was more lost than Susannah Dickinson, the black-haired teenage beauty from Tennessee. After witnessing the nightmarish slaughter of nearly every man she knew in Texas—her husband, her friends and neighbors from Gonzales—the girl was turned loose to reckon her own destination. Like Joe, she stepped from Mexican captivity into the rapt attention of the Anglo-American army. Like Joe, when her information was exhausted, Susannah was essentially discarded. The assumption was that someone would care for her. Certainly Texas did not. During the next two decades neither Susannah nor her daughter, Angelina, the so-called Babe of the Alamo, received a penny of state aid even though they were destitute.[63] Deeply traumatized by the Alamo violence, Susannah became a virtual model of self-destruction, marrying four more times and sinking into nymphomania and prostitution in the city named for Sam Houston. Her second husband beat her until she miscarried. (Susannah gained one of the first divorces granted in Texas.[64]) Husband three died of "digestive fever," a euphemism for alcoholism.[65] And husband four divorced Susannah on grounds of adultery (the Baptist pastor who converted Susannah declared her "a great bundle of untamed passions").

The Babe of the Alamo, Angelina, grew up desperately seeking the attention of men. Married at age sixteen, Angelina soon took other men to bed. Divorce followed, and then prostitution. A few years after the Civil War, Angelina died of a hemorrhaging uterus. The prodigal mother survived her prodigal daughter by more than another decade.

Susannah's fifth husband was a steady, dignified German emigrant who was so taken by Susannah's cabbage, bacon, and corn bread that "he just up and married her."[66] This time marriage took for the wild Tennessee woman, and she sold her league of land, "fled" Houston and its wicked temptations, and set up a cabinet-making business. The couple's peach orchard became recognized as one of the best in central Texas, and Susannah devoted herself to raising her grandchildren. Every now and then the Alamo would trespass upon her tranquility like an unwanted vagabond husband, and to the end of his days her German husband was jealous and resentful of what the Alamo meant to her. Over the years Susannah granted interviews about the siege and battle. "As she conversed," one journalist recalled, "she seemed at times to stop as if in a sudden reverie or dream, and I fancied I saw almost a wild light dancing in her eyes for a moment."[67] Like Moses Rose, she was sometimes called upon to clear up a bounty claim by testifying to the presence of one or another individual at the Alamo.

In 1878, a nationally touring play called *Davy Crockett* (wrapped around the Sir Walter Scott story of Lochinvar) finally came to Austin for a onetime performance. Susannah was invited to the theater as a guest of honor. Like Crockett before her, the now obese woman was thrilled by the attention. But like the canebrake congressman himself, Susannah seemed bewildered by the Go Ahead force of the staged fiction.[67] It had been one thing to survive Mexican bayonets that chill red dawn; it was something else again to resist this assault called legend. Susannah surrendered to the beautiful Anglo-Saxon illusion. Gilded and tricked out, padded with gunsmoke and painted with blood, reshaped in the image of its mythmakers, the Alamo battle strode into future memory as an affirmation of conquest. Just so, after many years of suffering, the whore Susannah regained her innocence.

Of all the men and women who reached for Texas, Santa Anna came closest to gaining for himself a life of fantasy. He remained, arguably, the most fascinating character of them all.

Though passions were still running hot in favor of lynching or shooting the elegant *presidente,* rebel leaders managed to hold their men at bay for over a month after his captivity. Santa Anna was quietly placed aboard the armed schooner *Invincible* for his return to Veracruz, and on June 1 all seemed well. Santa Anna even went so far as to write a bizarre farewell to the Texan army which had hosted him. "My friends! I have been a witness of your courage in the field of battle, and know you to be generous. Rely with confidence on my sincerity, and you shall never have cause to regret the kindness shown me. In returning to my native land, I beg you to receive the sincere thanks of your grateful friend. Farewell!"[68]

Unfortunately, a storm delayed the *Invincible's* departure by two days, which almost spelled the end for Santa Anna, for the winds did not delay the steamboat *Oceana's* arrival with two hundred and fifty mercenaries fresh from the United States. Upset that they'd missed the doings at San Jacinto, the *Oceana's* contingent instantly began howling for Santa Anna's blood. "Gen'l Santa Anna had better be executed twenty times if it could be done that often," threatened one of the rabble's leaders, Memucan Hunt. "We had better undergo campaign and campaign than allow him to be the cause of a rupture and violence between the people and the Govt."[69] Though the mercenaries had just set foot on Texas soil and were in no position to speak of themselves as "the people," much less to bully the government of Texas, they outnumbered the Texas Cabinet members. Another mercenary leader, Thomas Jefferson Green, boarded the *Invincible* to take over the prisoner. Convinced that he was about to be torn limb from limb, Santa Anna tried to overdose himself with opium, and his captors found him alternately raving and weeping like a child. He was chained and set in a rowboat for transfer to the *Oceana,* and during the short ride he was compelled to wave a Texas flag to the beachside mob. In that way, the Texas government's bid for early peace with Mexico was completely shattered.

Santa Anna's degradation continued. For the next six months he and several of his officers, including Colonel Almonte—the future Mexican minister to the United States—were confined and abused. Santa Anna was chained to an oak tree for fifty-two straight days, and he was shackled with a ball and chain. A drunken Anglo-American nearly assassinated him by firing a pistol through an open window. At least three times more he attempted suicide, once by eating fruit in the belief, popular at the time, that fruit carried cholera.[70] His stomach was pumped, and the doctor who "saved" his life was later rewarded when Santa Anna spared the doctor's son from execution after another Texan filibuster into Mexico.[71] At long last, the miserable prisoner of war was repatriated. But in order to go south, he first had to travel north through the very country where relatives of executed Texans lived. On November 30, 1836, Santa Anna rode horseback across the San Jacinto plain, and paused wordlessly to contemplate the unburied bones of his soldiers.[72]

To his enormous surprise and relief, the norteamericanos not only respected Santa Anna's safety, they actually received him as a visiting statesman. Santa Anna met with General Gaines one day, and in Maryland he spent an amiable hour with the great American general Winfield Scott.[73] The Kentucky state legislature paid a visit to the captive general, and northern newspapers hailed him. In Washington, in January 1837, Santa Anna found himself the subject of curiosity, a sort of Napoleonic exile from his own government (which had replaced and repudiated him). Congressmen and officials shared thoughts with him, and wealthy land speculators from New York and Philadelphia, seeking to play both sides of the Texas game just in case, communicated their best wishes.[74]

The highlight of Santa Anna's whirlwind visit to the city he'd once threatened to decorate with the Mexican flag was a White House dinner with Old Hickory. Though Santa Anna no longer held power in Mexico, there was little doubt that he soon would again, and so Jackson laid an exploratory offer upon the table. Toward hastening a possible annexation of the territory, Jackson proposed cashing Mexico out of Texas for $3.5 million, money that Jackson privately termed "hush money."[75] Santa Anna was not yet in a position to earn the quitclaim, but the offer delighted him. The Mexican chargé d'affaires in Washington had coldly ignored his former *presidente* as if he were a leper, but the most powerful man in the United States had treated Santa Anna as an equal. The self-styled Napoleon of the West began to sense that his fall from grace was not permanent.

As a final gesture of diplomatic meddling, Jackson arranged for the U.S. frigate *Pioneer* to sail his Mexican guest back to Veracruz. A U.S. military officer, Lt. J. Tattnall, officially escorted the disgraced *caudillo* ashore. Upon news of Santa Anna's coming, a huge crowd had clustered on the Veracruz breakwater, including several Mexican regiments of uncertain loyalties. The moment was tensely dramatic, with neither the *caudillo* nor his people sure of their choreography. Arm in arm, the magical tyrant and his crisply uniformed U.S. escort stepped from barge to wharf and walked forward. "There ensued a profound silence in the multitude of late so vociferous and swayed by conflicting emotions. As they approached the soldiery, a change appeared to come over their thoughts and purposes. The salute was given, the band struck up, the colors drooped amidst the most enthusiastic vivas from soldiers, citizens and rabble."[76] Santa Anna was home. Foxlike, he retired to his hacienda near Jalapa to bide time and dream.

The times were ripe for a creative mind. Mexico was boiling with discontent, its deficit having ballooned from 3 million pesos in 1835 to 17 million pesos in 1838.[77] Conservatives and liberals rocked in and out of power, and *pronunciamientos* rained upon the masses. Mexico City seethed with ambitious factions, knotted with incoherent causes, intrigues, and backstabbing. "The cannon directed against the palace kill people in their beds, in streets, entirely out of that direction, while this ball, intended for the citadel, takes its flight to San Cosme!" recorded a woman living through these turbulent times. "Both parties seem to be *fighting the city* instead of each other; and this manner of firing from behind parapets, and from the tops of houses and steeples, is decidedly safer for the soldiers than the inhabitants."[78] During yet another revolution, the same woman observed, "The soldiers in the day-time amuse themselves by insulting each other from the roofs of the houses and convents. Yesterday, one of the president's party singled out a soldier in the citadel, shot him, and then began to dance the *Enanos*, and in the midst of a step, *he* was shot, and rolled over, dead."[79]

But no matter how bloody and complicated Mexico's sufferings, no one of vision forgot Texas.

"The loss of Texas will inevitably result in the loss of New Mexico and the Californias," Secretary of War Tornel predicted. "Little by little our territory will be absorbed, until only an insignificant part is left to us. Our destiny will be similar to the sad lot of Poland [that is, annexation to Russia]. Our national existence, acquired at the cost of so much blood, recognized after so many difficulties, would end like those weak meteors

which, from time to time, shine fitfully in the firmament and disappear.''[80]
One way or another, Mexico wanted Texas back in her fold.

Three years after the Alamo fell, Santa Anna climbed back into the saddle of power. In a ridiculous action known as *"Guerra de los Pasteles"* or the Pastry War, France sought to punish Mexico over unpaid debts (prominent among them, a thousand pesos' worth of damage to a French emigrant's pastry shop). A French blockade of Mexican ports in 1838 finally culminated in a hit-and-run attack on Veracruz. Forewarned, Santa Anna had descended from his Jalapa estate to orchestrate a proper Mexican defense. Early one December morning, a French special forces squad raided the coastal town, failing to capture Santa Anna only because he fled nearly naked. Quickly donning his dignity, Santa Anna mounted a counterattack and chased after the retreating French soldiers. A French eight-pounder coughed out a blast of grapeshot. Santa Anna lost his lower left leg and very nearly his life. Santa Anna had the presence of mind to wring pathos from his pain. He invented a wild battle account in which he claimed well over a hundred enemy casualties (in fact, there were sixty-eight). *"We conquered, yes, we conquered,"* he wrote. "Mexican arms secured a glorious victory in the plaza; and the flag of Mexico remained triumphant: I was wounded in this last effort and probably this will be the last victory that I shall offer my native land. . . . May all Mexicans, forgetting my political mistakes, not deny me the only title which I wish to leave my children; that of a 'good Mexican.' ''[81]

Santa Anna recovered, though his amputation was crude and left a painful two-inch stick of bone extending below the flesh.[82] Three months after the Pastry War collapsed, the hero of Veracruz was carried into Mexico City upon a litter and installed as acting president. Before long he was, once again, the reigning dictator. By 1842 his powers were so extensive that he was able to command a state funeral for his amputated leg, complete with bodyguard, church officials, brightly caparisoned cadets from the military academy on Chapultepec hill, and Cabinet ministers and the diplomatic corps.[83] It was but one lavish gesture among many, including statues, busts, and paintings of the grand *caudillo* (who was secretly called the "Immortal Three-Fourths" in reference to his leg[84]), a new national theater named El Gran Teatro de Santa Anna, and extraordinary graft and corruption. A wicked back street skit sprang up in which cemetery spirits petitioned their underworld congress not to accept Santa Anna's dead leg lest it be infected with revolutionary tendencies: the result, they feared, would be a tyranny by a disembodied bone.[85]

It was during this period that the United States finally blessed Mexico with a halfway tolerant minister, Waddy Thompson. After a long string of scoundrels and meddlers, Thompson brought a refreshing professionalism to American diplomacy in Mexico. He found Santa Anna curious, and his brand of rule distasteful. But he refused to condemn Mexican politics. "I ride my own gentle and well-trained horse with a light bridle," he decided, "but it is no reason why my neighbor, whose horse is wild and intractable, should do the same."[86]

Now that he was back in power, Santa Anna could have acted to "sell" Texas, clearing the way for U.S. annexation. Instead he erected a statue of himself pointing north toward Texas (some wags insisted toward the National Treasury) and talked of war. But his extravagant spending left no money for roads, much less war, and in 1844, another coup dropped Santa Anna from office. A hostile mob jammed through the streets of Mexico City, and to Santa Anna's horror, displayed his leg bone dug out from its cenotaph. The statue pointing toward Texas was pulled down and dragged through the streets along with the leg, and El Gran Teatro de Santa Anna was spared devastation only by a hasty name change to the Teatro Nacional.[87] Santa Anna escaped the same rough treatment by fleeing into the night. A band of Indians recognized their one-legged leader and took him captive. As it turned out, the Indians had a grotesque sense of humor. Rather than turn him in to the authorities for a reward, they decided to cook him alive and present him to the nation as a giant tamale. A huge cauldron of water was set to boil, chiles and spices were solicited from village huts, and banana leaves were brought in from the jungle for a wrapping. If not for the intervention of a local priest who held out the Host and backed the Indians away, Santa Anna would have died an agonizing death.[88]

The 1844 coup was followed by a year-long exile in Havana. Santa Anna might never have been heard of again if not for the Mexican War. But when hostilities broke out and American forces invaded his homeland, the Mexican fox managed to return to his people by offering to the Americans to negotiate a peace settlement. The Americans slipped him through their blockade back into Mexico . . . and Santa Anna promptly marshaled a twenty-thousand-man army to oppose the U.S. invasion. Grateful Mexicans elected him president once again and he applied himself to defending the patria with every means available. By any measure, the conflict was one-sided and barbaric, one of the low points in American history.

The Mexican War was widely opposed by U.S. citizens including Ulysses Grant ("I had a horror of the Mexican War . . . only I had not the moral courage to resign''[89]), Ralph Waldo Emerson, Robert E. Lee, Daniel Webster, Henry Clay, John Quincy Adams, and Henry David Thoreau, who was imprisoned for his refusal to pay taxes that would support a war of aggression.[90] Congressman Abraham Lincoln challenged the U.S. administration with ''spot resolutions,'' which demanded to know one spot of American soil on which American blood had been shed by Mexicans.[91] One spot offered by President Polk was the strip of land between the Rio Grande and the Nueces River, the hotly contested region that represented the difference between how the United States wanted Texas to look on the map and how Mexico had always perceived it.[92] Polk blockaded the Mexican port of Matamoros, inserted troops along the Rio Grande, and generally provoked a reaction . . . then invaded.

No one enjoyed the war more than Texans and Southern ''volunteers,'' who plundered, murdered, and raped their way through Mexico. ''How much they seem to enjoy acts of violence too!'' wrote U. S. Grant. ''I would not pretend to guess the number of murders that have been committed upon the persons of poor Mexicans and our soldiers, since we have been here, but the number would startle you.'' Another soldier destined to be a Civil War general, George Meade, tried to hide his eyes from the racism rampant in the Manifest Destiny killers from Texas. ''They have killed five or six innocent people walking in the streets, for no other object than their own amusement. . . . They rob and steal the cattle and corn of the poor farmers, and in fact act more like a body of hostile Indians than civilized Whites.'' One seventeen-year-old regular rode into a town just visited by Southern volunteers and found a Mexican they had shot and scalped, but left still alive. The regulars galloped after the berserk volunteers and finally reached them at a cave at the end of a ravine. ''Climbing over the rocks we reached the entrance, and as soon as we could see in the comparative darkness a horrid sight was before us. The cave was full of our volunteers yelling like fiends, while on the rocky floor lay over twenty Mexicans, dead and dying in pools of blood. Women and children were clinging to the knees of the murderers shrieking for mercy. . . . Most of the butchered Mexicans had been scalped; only three men were found unharmed. A rough crucifix was fastened to a rock, and some irreverent wretch had crowned the image with a bloody scalp. A sickening smell filled the place.''[93]

Anglo-Saxon racism reached such heights—with even Mexican priests and nuns suffering the frenzied abuse—that a number of Irish immigrants and disgusted Anglo-Americans deserted to the Mexican side and formed the 250-man San Patricio Corps. (When captured, 50 of these defectors were hanged, and others were branded with a *D* for deserter and whipped.) In one resonant atrocity, Texas Rangers—disparaged as "packs of human bloodhounds"—surrounded a rancho near Agua Fria. "The place was surrounded, the doors forced in, and all the males capable of bearing arms were dragged out, tied to a post and shot! . . . Thirty-six Mexicans were shot at this place, a half hour given for the horrified survivors, women and children, to remove their little household goods, then the torch was applied to the houses, and by the light of the conflagration the ferocious Tejanos rode off to fresh scenes of blood."[94] When General Scott protested their atrocities, the Rangers mocked him, calling him "Old Fuss and Feathers." Gen. Zachary Taylor finally refused to accept any more Texan volunteers, but the barbaric freewheeling Texas Rangers stayed on.

In the end, the war lasted a little less than two years and cost twelve thousand to fifteen thousand lives. Mexico was knocked to the dirt and dismembered.[95]

Once again, Santa Anna was packed off to exile, this time for five years in Jamaica and Colombia. But again the crazy moon of Mexican politics changed direction and he was brought back and given command. In 1853 he dispensed with the democratic trappings of office and declared himself absolute dictator. He modestly declined the title of Emperor, which had been Augustín de Iturbide's aristocratic touch. But while Iturbide had limited himself to being addressed as His Highness, it became Santa Anna's pleasure to be called "Su Alteza Serenisima" or His Most Serene Highness.[96]

Every now and then the bizarre aging *caudillo* was reminded of Texas. Some of his officers from that faraway campaign still knocked about: Urrea, who had turned liberal on him and attempted a coup; Nicolás de la Portilla, the lieutenant colonel at Goliad who had carried out the order to execute Fannin's men, and who was now a brigadier general;[97] Almonte, with whom he had shared chains and an oak tree after San Jacinto, and who was now a minister to France where men were conspiring to place a European monarch on the throne of Mexico.[98] Others, like de la Peña or Filisola, were dead, Filisola of cholera and de la Peña probably of the same, certainly poor and forgotten. And then there were the nameless ones, men who had survived the massacre at San Jacinto and managed, one way or another, to return to their quiet lives in Mexico. They did not even need to speak for their *caudillo* to see them, for they proudly wore a gold ring in their left earlobes as a mark of honor.[99]

In 1855 Santa Anna fell from power once again. The ship that sailed him into exile this time carried the name *Iturbide,* after the Napoleonic dreamer whom Santa Anna had himself helped to exile decades ago. Santa Anna drifted about the Caribbean for the next twenty years, fitful, scheming, despairing upon his tropical Elbas. He never again entered Texas, but at the age of seventy-two he returned to the United States, took up headquarters on Staten Island, and tried to mount a filibustering expedition against Maximilian, the French emperor of Mexico. His fortune rapidly disappeared into the pockets of American swindlers, and after a year the bitter *caudillo* entered his fifth and final exile.[100]

In 1874 the mists parted and Santa Anna stepped forth one last time. The train—there was now a train—pulled into the brand-new Buenavista station in Mexico City, and an eighty-year-old man with quivering hands, a wooden peg leg, and eyesight clenched with cataracts cautiously stood. After so many years spent in the tropics, the high air felt chilly and the old hero requested a military greatcoat for cover. All that could be found was a woolen shawl. Anticipating a public greeting outside the train station, Santa Anna declined. But aside from a few family friends, no one noticed the eagle's frail descent. He did not yet seem to grasp that his return from exile merely pronounced his transparency. Mexico no longer feared him.

Two more years of life remained to the now penniless *caudillo.* During that time, he rejected surgery for his cataracts. "No," he said, "I do not wish to see; leave me sunk in darkness, I am more tranquil this way." With his waistcoat stained with spilled chili, the ancient tyrant waited in the sunshine by his doorway for the final invisibility.

Then one day a miracle happened. Like an angel, "an old man of the people" arrived at the house of Vergara No. 6. The two *ancianos* sat down, and Santa Anna listened. His guest was a faithful and anonymous warrior who had fought under him at Tampico and Veracruz, and he was bearing a gift. A story and a box. Long, long ago, during the coup of 1844, when rioters had tipped over the president's statue and defiled his buried leg, this nameless soldier had followed along, biding his time. Finally the mob had dispersed, leaving the leg in the street. Reverently, the simple soldier and his wife had hidden the treasure and waited. Now thirty years had passed and there was no more need to wait.

Santa Anna opened the box. Inside lay the bones of his missing leg. Overjoyed by this incredible offering, he broke down and wept. His grotesque duty done, the old *carbón* stood to leave. Santa Anna cried out that there should be gold or a military promotion to reward such faithfulness. But alas there was nothing. At a loss, he nearly allowed the soldier to slide away. But then Santa Anna stood and reached out. He opened his arms and embraced the soldier and kissed him upon the forehead. "I do for you that which is done for a good son," he declared with traces of his old presidential timbre.

The two old men held each other. And for a moment—a rare moment—the prodigal *caudillo* was embraced by Mexico. But it was a last embrace. When Santa Anna finally closed his eyes upon the dream in 1876, Mexico closed her eyes upon him. Buried without honors, scarcely noticed, he left simple testimony to his thunderous odyssey: a skeleton, curiously complete.

NOTES

The following abbreviations have been used:
DRTL—The Daughters of the Republic of Texas History Research Library, San Antonio
PTR—Papers of the Texas Revolution, 1835–1836, ed. John Jenkins, 10 vols. (Austin: Presidential Press, 1973)
SWHQ—Southwestern Historical Quarterly

CHAPTER 1

1. Burke Davis, *Old Hickory* (New York: Dial Press, 1977), p. 234.
2. Allan Nevins et al., *A Pocket History of the United States* (New York: Pocket Books, 1981), p. 165.
3. Nineteenth-century European scholars decided—just in time for Manifest Destiny—that Anglo-Saxons were a genetically democratic tribe and that westward motion was racially inevitable. For a full discussion of this phenomenon, see Reginald Horsman, *Race and Manifest Destiny: The Origins of American Racial Anglo-Saxonism* (Cambridge: Harvard University Press, 1981).
4. The term Manifest Destiny was coined in 1845 by a New York newspaper editor named John L. O'Sullivan, but as early as 1839 he was writing that "the nation of many nations is destined to manifest to mankind the excellence of divine principles; to establish on earth the noblest temple ever dedicated to the worship of the most High." Norman A. Graebner, *Empire on the Pacific* (New York: Ronald Press Co., 1955), p. 17. Interestingly, this consummate expansionist—like many before and after him—had land investments in Latin America. William H. Goetzmann, *When the Eagle Screamed* (New York: John Wiley & Sons, 1966), pp. 76–77.
5. This helter-skelter vanguard breed was predominantly Scotch-Irish, a combination born when seventeenth-century England shipped its armed, dissident Scots by the thousands away from their border across to Northern Ireland. The Scottish exiles formed Dublin and the Ulster counties, but soaring rents and the English suppression of their woolen goods inspired a second exodus, this time to America. For more on the background of Scotch-Irish frontier people, see T. R. Fehrenbach, *Lone Star* (New York: American Legacy Press, 1983); Arthur S. Link et al., *The American People: A History* (Arlington Heights, Illinois: AHM

Publishing, 1981), vol. 1, p. 257; Frederick Merk, *History of the Westward Movement* (New York: Alfred A. Knopf, 1978), pp. 49–50; and James Oakes, *The Ruling Race* (New York: Alfred A. Knopf, 1982), p. 16.

6. James C. Curtis, *Andrew Jackson and the Search for Vindication* (Boston: Little, Brown and Company, 1976), pp. 93–94.

7. Edward Pessen, *Jacksonian America* (Homewood: Dorsey Press, 1978), p. 181.

8. Ibid., pp. 319–21, 195.

9. David Crockett, *A Narrative of the Life of David Crockett* (Lincoln: University of Nebraska Press, 1987), pp. 210–11.

10. In 1817 Jackson invested in a land company that bought a vast territory below the Muscle Shoals of the Tennessee River. Collusive bidding assured that no one submitted a bid higher than two dollars per acre for cotton land that sold shortly after at forty times that price. Pessen, *Jacksonian America,* p. 177. See also Oakes, *Ruling Race,* p. 63.

11. Albert Katz Weinberg, *Manifest Destiny* (Gloucester: Peter Smith, 1958), p. 32.

12. George Lockhart Rives, *The United States and Mexico, 1821–1848* (New York: Charles Scribner's Sons, 1913), vol. 1, pp. 24–25.

13. W. H. Timmons, *The Anglo-American Advance into Texas, 1810–1830* (Boston: American Press, 1981), p. 33.

14. Gene Brack, *Mexico Views Manifest Destiny, 1821–1846* (Albuquerque: University of New Mexico Press, 1975), pp. 47–48.

15. Ironically, the darkest American beliefs derived from a Spanish Dominican missionary, a priest named Bartolomé de Las Casas who had penned this continent's first yellow journalism in the sixteenth century in an effort to undermine the autonomy of the conquistadores. His exaggerations spread among Spain's many European enemies and laid the foundation for the so-called Black Legend. The English government found it particularly useful in whipping up public hatred of the enemy; before each new war with Spain, it reissued translations of de Las Casas's work. Naturally, the propaganda found passage to the English colonies in America. Charles Gibson, ed., *The Black Legend* (New York: Alfred A. Knopf, 1971), p. 73.

16. Mary S. Helm, *Scraps of Early Texas History* (Austin: B. R. Warner & Co., 1884), p. 4.

17. Though the Spanish kept the coastlines and borders of New Spain sealed tight, artifacts did leak back and forth across the border. Silver pesos—many defaced with hammer blows to wipe away the king's profile (and later the Mexican eagle), or cut into pieces of eight, or bits—circulated as legal tender in the United States.

18. Rives, *U.S. and Mexico,* vol. 1, p. 167.

19. Rumors flew among the Mexicans regarding the purchase terms. According to one, the United States was offering a $12 million "loan" to Mexico, with

Texas to be pledged as security; Mexico would default and Texas would drop into the American palm. In fact, Secretary of State Henry Clay's top offer—made through Poinsett—was the mere $1 million. Adding insult to injury, he brazenly pointed out that by ridding herself of Texas, Mexico City would suddenly be located in the very center of Mexico. For some reason this struck him as being desirable, or at least symmetrical, to the Mexican mind. Furthermore, Clay said the sale would automatically rid Mexico of her Comanche problem, for Comanches were Texan Indians: no Texas, no Comanches. He also helpfully proposed that Mexico simply hand half of Texas over to the United States. Timmons, *Anglo-American Advance*, p. 31–32.

20.   Pronounced Tay-has, the place-name was spelled with a *j*, but in older Spanish spellings the *j* was often interchanged with an *x*, and Anglo-Americans hardened the pronunciation of Texas.

21.   Marilyn McAdams Sibley, *Travelers in Texas, 1761–1860* (Austin: University of Texas Press, 1967), p. 176.

22.   Andrew Anthony Tijerina, "Tejanos and Texas: The Native Mexicans of Texas, 1820–1850" (Ph.D. diss., University of Texas at Austin, 1977), p. 8.

23.   Knitted together with a long spiderweb of *acequias* or irrigation canals, San Antonio anchored a long riverside string of secularized missions, one of which loomed across a footbridge east of town. This crumbling behemoth was the Mission San Antonio de Valero, later called the Alamo. It had been built as a walled pueblo to house Coauhuiltecan Indians while they were being Christianized and to protect them from predatory Comanches. But plans for its glorious three-story chapel with twin bell towers had been scuttled when the domed roof collapsed in the mid-1700s. For more on the colonial missions of San Antonio, see Marion A. Habig, *The Alamo Chain of Missions: A History of San Antonio* (Chicago: Franciscan Herald Press, 1968).

24.   José María Sánchez, "A Trip to Texas in 1828," *SWHQ* (April 1926), p. 258.

25.   Eugene C. Barker, *Mexico and Texas, 1821–1835* (Dallas: P. L. Turner Co., 1928), p. 53.

26.   For decades Spain and Mexico had been aware of the Anglo-Saxon trespassers, but for budgetary reasons they had been forced to ignore them. Calling the westward movement of Americans "an eruption," the governor of Spanish Louisiana had pleaded for help as early as 1796. Abraham P. Nastair, *Borderland in Retreat* (Albuquerque: University of New Mexico Press, 1976), p. 99. Another Louisiana governor depicted them as insects, and a bishop spoke of them as wild animals who fled at the sight of their fellow creatures.

27.   Sánchez, "A Trip to Texas," p. 281.

28.   The Spanish term *pelinegro*, meaning "black sheep," was corrupted by Tejano slang into the pejorative *pelegrino*, meaning an Anglo-American immigrant. Arnoldo De León, *The Tejano Community, 1836–1900* (Albuquerque: University of New Mexico Press, 1982), p. 136. Indeed, the Anglo-Americans' own countrymen called this westward moving flock of black sheep "the perspiration of the eastern States." Harriet Martineau, *Society in America* (Gloucester: Peter Smith, 1968), p. 180.

29. Tijerina, "Tejanos and Texas," pp. 284–85.

30. Jean Louis Berlandier, *The Indians of Texas in 1830* (Washington, D.C.: Smithsonian Institution Press, 1969), p. 61.

31. Terán told his government that Texas could produce enough food to feed all of Mexico. A civil servant named Tadeo Ortiz calculated that Texas could produce more cotton annually than the entire United States, with ample acreage left for cattle and other crops. Juan Almonte, who served under Santa Anna, also toured Texas and reached similar conclusions.

32. Alexis de Tocqueville, *Journey to America* (New Haven: Yale University Press, 1960), p. 118.

33. Poinsett helped obtain charters for Masonic lodges practicing the York rite. The conservative Escoses (practicing the Scots rite), among them Santa Anna, did not appreciate Poinsett's destabilizing contribution. The Yorkinos (Yorkmen) did not dare acknowledge the American influence, which left Poinsett with precious few public allies. Rives, *U.S. and Mexico,* vol. 1, pp. 163–65.

34. Ibid., pp. 243–44.

35. Richard R. Stenberg, "Jackson, Anthony Butler, and Texas," *Southwest Social Science Quarterly* (December 1932), pp. 274–80. Butler offered the same amount to another Mexican, Lorenzo de Zavala, a Texan land speculator like himself, and a future vice president of the Republic of Texas.

36. Sam Houston had once bludgeoned a fellow congressman in the streets of Washington with a hickory walking cane (cut from the grounds of Jackson's Hermitage). Jackson had threatened the life of his secretary of war. Lawyers beat, gouged, knifed, and shot one another. Courtroom order was sometimes obtained at gunpoint.

37. Stenberg, "Jackson, Anthony Butler, and Texas," p. 270.

38. William Bollaert, *William Bollaert's Texas* (Norman: University of Oklahoma Press, 1956), p. 257.

CHAPTER 2

1. Two generations earlier, in Daniel Boone's day, such hasty exits from the law or bankruptcy or marriage had read "Gone to Kentucky" or "Gone to hell or Kentucky." Everett Dick, *The Dixie Frontier* (New York: Capricorn Books, 1964), pp. 13–14.

2. James Lockhart et al., *Early Latin America* (Cambridge: Cambridge University Press, 1983), p. 60.

3. Frederic Gaillardet, *Sketches of Early Texas and Louisiana* (Austin: University of Texas Press, 1966), p. 59.

4. David Holman, *Buckskin and Homespun* (Austin: Wind River Press, 1979), p. 84.

5. G. L. Rives, *The United States and Mexico, 1821–1848* (New York: Charles Scribner's Sons, 1913), vol. 1, p. 290.

6. Gaillardet, *Sketches of Early Texas*, p. 59.

7. Nancy Nichols Barker, *The French Legation in Texas* (Austin: Texas State Historical Association, 1971), p. 65.

8. Marquis James, *The Raven* (St. Simon: Mockingbird Books, 1981), p. 133.

9. Holman, *Buckskin*, p. 3.

10. James, *The Raven*, p. 255.

11. Ibid., pp. 140–42. Houston's lawyer during this scandal was Francis Scott Key. Llerena B. Friend, *Sam Houston* (Austin: University of Texas Press, 1985), p. 31.

12. James, *The Raven*, p. 19.

13. David Crockett, *A Narrative of the Life of David Crockett* (Lincoln: University of Nebraska Press, 1987), pp. 88–90.

14. James, *The Raven*, pp. 73–74.

15. Houston also formulated a boozy vision of forging an Indian confederation along the Rocky Mountains and establishing himself as their white savior-king.

16. By contrast, the national per capita consumption of pure alcohol in 1850 was 2.1 gallons. Arthur S. Link, et al., *The American People* (Arlington Heights: AHM Publishing Company, 1981), vol. 1, p. 383.

17. W. J. Rorabaugh, *The Alcoholic Republic* (New York: Oxford University Press, 1979), pp. 15–20.

18. This was apparently an Osage word, not Cherokee. See Jack Gregory et al., *Sam Houston with the Cherokees, 1829–1833* (Austin: University of Texas Press, 1967).

19. Richard R. Stenberg, "The Texas Schemes of Jackson and Houston, 1829–1836," *Southwestern Social Science Quarterly* (December 1934), p. 240.

20. J. Frank Dobie, "James Bowie, Big Dealer," *SWHQ* (January 1957), p. 349.

21. A New York land syndicate acquired title from the venal Coahuila y Tejas legislature for more than 6,250,000 acres, the Mason grant. While serving as Jackson's minister to Mexico, Anthony Butler was simultaneously moonlighting for another land syndicate, the New York–based Galveston Bay and Texas Land Company. This unscrupulous company offered 7.5 million acres of land scrip at one to ten cents per acre, suckering hundreds or thousands to Texas with useless "titles" in hand. (Mexican land grants were nontransferable.) The Nashville Company did the same thing with the Sterling Robertson grant.

22. Stenberg, "The Texas Schemes of Jackson and Houston," p. 244.

23. Dobie, "James Bowie, Big Dealer," pp. 338–39.

24. Harris Gaylord Warren, *The Sword Was Their Passport* (Baton Rouge: Louisiana State University Press, 1943), pp. 96–100.

25. The Laffites stayed out of the actual fighting themselves. Nevertheless, this gave Spain and Mexico one more reason to equate filibusters with pirates.

26. Later on a "freedom train" sprang up among Tejanos in Texas, channeling escaped slaves to freedom in Mexico.

27. Dobie, "James Bowie, Big Dealer," pp. 339–40.

28. Andrew Forest Muir, ed., *Texas in 1837* (Austin: University of Texas Press, 1958), p. 94.

29. Elizabeth May Morey, "Attitude of the Citizens of San Fernando Toward Independence Movements in New Spain, 1811–1813" (Master's thesis, University of Texas at Austin, 1930), pp. 8–10.

30. Herman Ehrenberg, "Texas und Seine Revolution," trans. E. W. Bartholomae (Master's thesis, University of Texas, ca. 1925), p. 115.

31. Ferdinand Roemer, *Texas* (San Antonio: Standard Press, 1935), p. 134.

32. The land fraud that brought Bowie to the U.S. Supreme Court's attention in 1833 began when the Louisiana Territory came under U.S. possession in 1803. The United States had sworn to honor all of the old Franco-Spanish titles, but the documents that had not been lost, stolen, or eaten by bugs often defied legal or literal interpretation. The Bowie brothers quietly went to work within the chaos. First they created a fictional old man and called him Bernardo Sampayreac. They outfitted him with a magnificent—equally fictional—grant of land from the Spanish governor of Louisiana and dated it 1783. Then they had old Sampayreac convey to the Bowies his supposed 60,000 arpents of Arkansas land (roughly 2,450,000 acres or 3,812½ square miles)! The Bowies, in turn, sold off a major portion of Arkansas to eager buyers. When the buyers pressed for confirmation of title in the Superior Court of Arkansas, they learned of certain peculiarities with their purchases. By the end of 1827, 131 claims lay before the court, but while the court fumbled documents and rulings, some based on bribed witnesses, the audacious Bowies managed to sell off another forty-four grants. It took four more years for the court to rule that the Spanish grants had been forgeries. By then the Bowies had cheated over a hundred ranking men of the community. In 1833 the U.S. Supreme Court ruled that the Bowies' land deals had been worth less even than fool's gold. For more on this remarkable fraud, see Edward S. Sears, "The Low Down on Jim Bowie," *From Hell to Breakfast* (Dallas: Southern Methodist University Press, 1944).

33. On his way back through Nacogdoches, Bowie stopped just long enough to apply for a quarter league of land on the Laffites' old base camp, Galveston Island. It was perfectly situated for sea trade, which to Bowie meant ideal for the smuggling trade. On his application, he declared 109 dependents. The dependents were slaves he intended to sell to Anglo-American settlers in Texas or to sneak into the United States through his established methods. Dobie, "James Bowie, Big Dealer," p. 344.

34. They rode north in search of old Spanish mines near the desolate San Saba Mission, but all they found was a desperate battle between Bowie's half dozen and 150 Indians.

35. Pat Ireland Nixon, *The Medical Story of Early Texas: 1528–1853* (San Antonio: Mollie Bennett Lupe Memorial Fund, 1946), p. 138.

36. There is no baptismal record in the San Fernando Church in San Antonio for any child of James Bowie or Ursula Veramendi. Furthermore, records of the deaths of the Veramendis in Monclova do not mention children. *Burials of Santiago Apostolo Church of Monclova, Mexico, September 6–14, 1833,* trans. John Ogdon Leal (San Antonio: Mormon Genealogy Library). Nor does a relative's letter describing the deaths mention children (Jose Antonio Navarro, letter to Samuel Williams, September 26, 1833). A Texas State Supreme Court ruling of 1883 stated that Bowie's wife died leaving no children. Texas State Supreme Court, "Marco Veramendi v. J. H. Hutchins et al.," *Cases Argued and Decided in the Supreme Court of the State of Texas* (1883), vol. 48, p. 547. Apparently the myth of the two children originated when Amelia Williams inserted them into the published version of her Ph.D. dissertation (Bernice Strong, letter to L. Tuffly Ellis, DRTL, June 14, 1984). In 1944, this lack of evidence for any children was pointed out by C. L. Douglas in *James Bowie: The Life of a Bravo* (Dallas: Banks Upshaw and Co., 1944), p. 214.

37. Sears, "The Low Down on Jim Bowie," p. 196.

38. Archie P. McDonald, *Travis* (Austin: Jenkins Publishing Co., 1976), pp. 25–26. "Elder Travis," Buck's uncle Alex, was converted during the Second Great Awakening. He turned into a homemade preacher who ministered and made peace in the community.

39. Ibid., pp. 52–55.

40. Ruby Mixon, "William Barret Travis: His Life and Letters" (Master's thesis, University of Texas, 1930), p. 298.

41. One of the disappointed victims of the Galveston Bay and Land Company land fraud wrote an account. This nameless man saw what young Travis saw—a land seething with Go Ahead men. "At the inn [in San Felipe de Austin, where Travis eventually settled], I found twenty or thirty men who had come from different quarters in pursuit of places to settle," he recorded. "These persons, commonly called land-hunters, were almost all from the United States, and generally from the South Western States. . . . Among these strangers I found a number of very intelligent men: but I learnt that a portion of them had fled from justice, or as they chose to call it, from law, in their own country. It is a well known fact that a considerable proportion of our countrymen who are found in Texas, are of this character. I saw at the breakfast table one morning, among those who were seated with me, four murderers who had sought safety in this country, and a gentleman assured me, that on one occasion, he had set [*sic*] down with eleven." Andrew Forest Muir, ed., *Texas in 1837* (Austin: University of Texas Press, 1958), pp. 214–15.

42. William Barret Travis, *Diary of William Barret Travis* (Waco: Texian Press, 1966), p. 15.

43. *"Chingaba"* was Travis's version of a term used to describe the relationship between Cortez and an Indian woman (La Chingada) who translated for his expedition and thereby helped open Mexico to savage and humiliating European conquest. For a full discussion of the word *chingar* (*chingaba, Chingada,* and so on) and its unusual texture in the Mexican language, see Alan Riding, *Distant Neighbors* (New York: Alfred A. Knopf, 1985), p. 18; and Octavio Paz, *The Labyrinth of Solitude* (New York: Grove Press, 1985), pp. 73–88.

44. Rebecca Cummings gave Travis a lock of hair and the cat's eye ring which he took with him to the Alamo. In exchange, Travis gave her a brooch, a kiss, and a twenty-five-cent bottle of mercury for her venereal disease.

45. From the POISINDEX SUBSTANCE IDENTIFICATION, vol. 59 (Micromedex Inc., 1974–1989).

46. Travis, *Diary of William Barret Travis,* p. 24n. 36.

47. Scott's novels were America's first best-sellers; five hundred thousand volumes of the Waverly series came off American presses in one decade. Rollin G. Osterweis, *Romanticism and Nationalism in the Old South* (Gloucester: Peter Smith, 1964), pp. 41–43. Ladies and gentlemen imitated Scott characters. Barges, steamboats, and stagecoaches were christened after Scott characters. The library shelves of Mississippi steamboats consisted almost exclusively of Scott novels. James Oakes, *The Ruling Race: A History of American Slaveholders* (New York: Alfred A. Knopf, 1982), pp. 160–161. By 1832, *Rob Roy,* Scott's Robin Hood novel, had seen thirty productions as a play. Osterweis, *Romanticism and Nationalism,* p. 163.

48. From Virginia to Texas, Dixieland knights mounted on Kentucky thoroughbreds and frontier mustangs staged medieval jousts, tricking themselves out with makeshift helmets and wooden lances. All across the South country courthouses sprouted fake battlements and castle towers. The "Southron" gentry became so affected that a disgusted Mark Twain even blamed the Civil War upon "the Sir Walter disease." Ibid., pp. 99, 49–50.

49. Paulding became one of the first popular voices to glorify America's westward mission through what he called the "wise white man," who "wheresoever he goes, to whatever region of the earth, whether east or west, north or south, carries with him his destiny, which is to civilize the world, and rule it afterwards." Richard Drinnon, *Facing West* (New York: Meridian Press, 1980), p. 126.

50. Among these War Dogs was Travis's close friend "Three-Legged Willie" Williamson, who came to Texas in his early twenties, practiced law, edited several newspapers, and later served in the state legislature. Another youthful War Dog was Moseley Baker, a resident of North Carolina, a lawyer, newspaper editor, and speaker of the state house in Alabama. After cheating the State Bank of Alabama of $26,700, he fled to New Orleans, where he was apprehended, but then escaped to Texas in 1832–33, sneaking past an arrest reward for $2,000. Paul C. Boethel, *Colonel Amasa Turner* (Austin: Von Boeckmann-Jones, 1963), pp. 5–6. As one of the leaders of the War Party, Baker lost no time in fiercely calling for Texas Independence. He later incorporated the Texas Railroad, Navigation and Banking Company and served in the state congress. Another of this tiny, aggressive fraternity of Go Ahead lawyers was Green B. Jameson, a Kentuckian, who was two years older than Travis. He practiced law until the rebellion finally broke out, then joined James Bowie and became the chief engineer at the Alamo. The Wharton brothers, John and William, were also young lawyers active in the War Party. They moved to Texas from Tennessee, agitated for secession from Mexico, and later served in the Texas congress. These and others, many of them bound by Masonic ties, were the young men Stephen Austin denounced as "demagogues, pettyfoggers, visionary speculators and schemers" who were "forever damning those [like himself] who are in office merely because they are in office." Andrew Anthony Tijerina, "Tejanos and Texas: The Native Mexicans of Texas, 1820–1850" (Ph.D. diss., University of Texas at Austin, 1977), pp. 307–308. To this sort of criticism, John Wharton raised a drink to "The Austins—may their bones burn in hell!" Mary D. Boddie, "Thunder on the Brazos" (unpublished, ca. 1979), p. 136. A last-minute War Dog, Mirabeau Lamar came to Texas from Georgia in 1835 after losing a congressional bid based upon a platform of Georgia's secession. With that failure, he crossed the international border and within months—possibly days—was laboring for the secession of Texas from Mexico. He was a bright, quirky lawyer, who wrote poems and later became President of Texas. His opinion of the Anglo-Americans in Texas was rather low. "I attended one of their meetings held in Washington [Texas]," he wrote, "where I mingled in the discussion. The meeting was all confusion; the people knew nothing of what they had assembled for & retired as ignorant as they came; they are damnd [*sic*] stupid & easily ruled by Demagogues & factions." Mirabeau Lamar, "Mirabeau B. Lamar's Texas Journal," *SWHQ* (October 1980), p. 321.

51.   Eugene C. Barker, *Mexico and Texas, 1821–1835* (Dallas: P. L. Turner Co., 1928), p. 57.

52.   The acting president Anastasio Bustamente had led an expedition of his own to Nacogdoches in 1827 to suppress a badly conceived revolt called the Fredonian Rebellion. Waving a homemade flag, bearing a homemade constitution, the rebels had declared a republic of Fredonia. But even before Bustamente arrived, the rebellion had been suppressed by Stephen Austin and the Anglo-American colonists themselves, and the rebels had fled to the United States.

53.   Barker, *Mexico and Texas,* p. 59.

54.   Tijerina, "Tejanos and Texas," p. 89.

55.   In his diary, the War Dog Travis made not a single mention of government leaders in Mexico, and further wrote, "as for my opinion, it is worth but little, as I pay little attention to politics." Travis, *Diary of William Barret Travis,* p. 95.

56.   Full responsibility and management of education lay with the local *ayuntamiento* (town council). Tijerina, "Tejanos and Texas," p. 123. San Antonio de Béxar, a relatively destitute Tejano town, managed to lead the state in students per population, a feat accomplished through taxes they levied upon themselves.

57. *A Visit to Texas* (Austin: Steck Co., 1952), pp. 257–58.

58. In 1822 thirty-seven Negroes had been executed in Charleston, South Carolina, because of the rumor of an insurrection. And in 1831 the slave Nat Turner had actually led a small "army" of black rebels on a killing spree in southern Virginia.

59. Boddie, "Thunder on the Brazos," pp. 46–47.

60. Martha Anne Turner, *William Barret Travis: His Sword and His Pen* (Waco: Texian Press, 1972), p. 30.

61. In a few short years these same War Dogs would be seething to have Santa Anna's blood. But in 1832 they viewed him as a useful foil for their ambitions, and the battle cry that went up at Velasco was "Long Live Santa Anna."

CHAPTER 3

1. Hidalgo spoke his Otomi Indian parishioners' language and illegally established two industries—winemaking and silk culture—to benefit his flock in the town of Dolores. Though he conspired with *criollos* to overthrow the *peninsulares* and ultimately the king, he depended upon Indian and mestizo support. The revolt was set for December 1810 at a large regional fair, but in mid-September the royalists learned of the plot and swiftly scooped up several of the conspirators. On September 16, barely ahead of arrest, Hidalgo summoned parishioners with the church bell and issued his everlasting *Grito de Dolores*.

2. Hidalgo's college nickname had been *El Zorro*, the Fox, for his sharp intelligence. Hugh M. Hamill, Jr., *The Hidalgo Revolt* (Gainesville: University of Florida Press, 1966), p. 60.

3. John Lynch, *The Spanish American Revolutions* (New York: W. W. Norton and Co., 1973), p. 298.

4. Frances Toor, *A Treasury of Mexican Folkways* (New York: Bonzanza Books, 1985), pp. 174–76.

5. Hamill, *The Hidalgo Revolt*, p. 156.

6. It was future president Anastasio Bustamente who finally removed the head for Christian burial in 1821. John Anthony Caruso, *The Liberators of Mexico* (Gloucester: Peter Smith, 1967), p. 205.

7. Morelos actively solicited *criollo* support for the war because Hidalgo's Indian rabble had fulfilled every *criollo*'s nightmare of a French-style reign of terror.

8. The Inquisition had stipulated that if the civil court spared Morelos's life, he be banished to an African garrison for life and made to recite the seven penitential psalms every Friday until he died.

9. Wilbert H. Timmons, *Morelos—Priest, Soldier, Statesman of Mexico* (El Paso: Texas Western Press, 1963), pp. 160–67.

10. Arthur S. Link, et al., *The American People: A History* (Arlington Heights: AHM Publishing, Co., 1981), p. 201.

11. Lynch, *The Spanish American Revolutions,* p. 327. The bloodbath and devastation reached deep north, even into Texas. Royalist troops executed San Antonio men, imprisoned and raped their women, and crushed the town's economy. Soldiers who "did not seem to be other than devils" simply preyed on the citizens. Indians ringed the suffering town, stealing almost every military horse and murdering Mexicans on the street. Crops could not be planted, or if planted, could not be harvested for fear of the Comanches. San Antonians were reduced to foraging in the countryside for deer, turkeys, and other food. Antonio Menchaca, *Memoirs of Antonio Menchaca* (San Antonio: Yanaguana Society, 1937), pp. 16–18.

12. "Foreign assistance" came in the form of ruinous loans from British bankers (by 1827 not even Britain would lend Mexico money) and the sale by equally ruinous *agiotistas* (traffickers) of government notes, which mortgaged future income from customs houses. Stanley Green, *The Mexican Republic* (Pittsburgh: University of Pittsburgh Press, 1987), pp. 150–53.

13. In 1825 Mexico City boasted 150,000 citizens, only a slightly smaller number than those in New York City. Guadalajara was larger than Baltimore, Puebla larger than Boston, and Guanajuato's population equaled that of New Orleans.

14. George Lockhart Rives, *The United States and Mexico, 1821–1848* (New York: Charles Scribner's Sons, 1913), vol. 1, pp. 51–53.

15. Ibid., vol. 2, pp. 101–2.

16. During his Inquisition hearings in 1815, Morelos was accused of sending his illegitimate son to a Protestant country. Morelos pleaded guilty to the charge, but pointed out that the boy was being educated in a Catholic school.

17. Guerrero later became president of Mexico and abolished slavery in 1829. A special exemption was granted the Texan colonists who had screamed that abolition equaled confiscation of their property.

18. David J. Weber, *The Mexican Frontier* (Albuquerque: University of New Mexico Press, 1982), p. 178.

19. *Gazette of Louisville,* 29 December 1836.

20. Helen Willits Harris, "Almonte's Inspection of Texas in 1834," *SWHQ* (January 1938), pp. 198–99.

21. Anonymous letter to unknown recipient, *PTR,* #3538.

22. Juan N. Almonte, "Statistical Report on Texas," *SWHQ* (January 1925), p. 211.

23. Harris, "Almonte's Inspection of Texas in 1834," p. 210.

24. Because they formed a majority in Texas, but only a ninth of the total in the combined state of Coahuila y Tejas, the Anglo-Americans were agitating for separate statehood.

25. Weber, *The Mexican Frontier,* p. 141.

26. Mexico had opened the floodgate of Anglo-American immigration, and by 1830 it was apparent that she had to close it. One thing was certain; using Americans to buffer Mexico from Americans was, as James Madison had put it, like inviting Gauls to defend Rome. Frederick Merk, *History of the Westward Movement* (New York: Alfred A. Knopf, 1978), pp. 137–38. Austin compared Mexico's task to building a dam of straw.

27. Weber, *The Mexican Frontier*, p. 176.

28. The influential Menchaca family of San Antonio ran herds of cattle east, and received slaves, tobacco, French fabrics, and other contraband in exchange. Alicia Vidaurreta Tjarks, "Comparative Demographic Analysis of Texas, 1777–1793," in David J. Weber, *New Spain's Far Northern Frontier* (Albuquerque: University of New Mexico Press, 1979), p. 169, fn. 48.

29. Weber, *The Mexican Frontier*, p. 141.

30. Green, *The Mexican Republic*, p. 136.

31. *A Visit to Texas* (Austin: Steck Co., 1952), pp. 197–98.

32. Harris, "Almonte's Inspection of Texas," p. 207.

33. G. K. Feathersonhaugh, quoted in Rollin G. Osterweis, *Romanticism and Nationalism in the Old South* (Gloucester: Peter Smith, 1964), pp. 181–82.

34. See Benjamin Lundy, *The War in Texas* (Philadelphia, 1837).

35. Harris, "Almonte's Inspection of Texas," pp. 203–5. Almonte was not the first to suggest an Indian buffer against the United States; in 1805 the Spanish governor of Texas had invited Kickapoos exiled from Wisconsin to settle east Texas to block Anglo-American entry. Jean Louis Berlandier, *The Indians of Texas in 1830* (Washington, D.C.: Smithsonian Institution Press, 1969), p. 10.

36. Almonte estimated that the Brazos department, the hotbed of rebel activity, contained eight hundred men capable of bearing arms; the Nacogdoches area, nine hundred. In the Hispanic section, around San Antonio, he counted only three hundred. Harris, "Almonte's Inspection of Texas," pp. 202–10.

CHAPTER 4

1. These conventions were a direct link to a widespread political reform movement calling for amendment of state constitutions restricting poor, unlanded free whites from voting. In Virginia, North Carolina, Mississippi, Tennessee, and other states, constitutions were amended to make politics more representative. Fletcher M. Green, "Democracy in the Old South," in Patrick Gerster and Nicholas Cords, *Myth and Southern History* (Chicago: Rand McNally College Publishing Co., 1974), pp. 84–85.

2. David J. Weber, "Scarce More than Apes: Historical Roots of Anglo-American Stereotypes of Mexicans," in Weber, ed., *New Spain's Far Northern Frontier* (Albuquerque: University of New Mexico Press, 1979), pp. 297–98.

3. Williamson, Address at San Felipe (June 22, 1835), *PTR*, #329.

4. Ugartechea, Letter to Tenorio, *PTR*, #277.

5. In *Waverly*, an educated but naïve young English lord was propelled into the

Highlands, a strange, harsh, beautiful country peopled with immensely hardy, illiterate fighters who loved two things in life: drinking and battling. Young Waverly's visit coincided with the Jacobite Rebellion, Scotland's uprising against English tariffs and English government. The revolt began with a single cannon shot.

6. Ruby Mixon, "William Barret Travis: His Life and Letters" (Master's thesis, University of Texas, 1930), pp. 130–45.

7. "They have always been on one side; the right side," Travis wrote. "They have never barked up the wrong tree, and I hope, never will. God grant that all Texas men stand as firm as Harrisburg in 'the hour that will try men's souls.' " Ibid., p. 160.

8. Travis, letter to Briscoe, *PTR, #564.*

9. Austin, letter to Holley, *PTR, #534.*

10. Austin, circular to committee, *PTR, #651.*

11. They dubbed it the Come and Take It flag, or the Old Cannon flag.

12. Noah Smithwick, *The Evolution of a State or Recollections of Old Texas Days* (Austin: University of Texas Press, 1983), pp. 74–75.

13. Palmer had participated in the bald and futile Fredonian Revolt land grab a few years earlier, which marked him as a radical even among the War Dogs. James T. De Shields, *Tall Men with Long Rifles* (San Antonio: Naylor Co., 1935), pp. 11–12.

14. Smithwick, *Evolution of a State,* p. 71.

15. De Shields, *Tall Men,* p. 17.

16. "In fine," one of the happy victors concluded in his brisk account of the battle, "the Anglo-American spirit appears in every thing we do; quick, intelligent, and comprehensive; and while such men are fighting for their rights, they may possibly be overpowered by numbers, but, *if whipped, they won't stay whipped."* Macomb, letter to unknown, *PTR, #757.*

CHAPTER 5

1. Herman Ehrenberg, translated by E. W. Bartholomae, "Texas und Seine Revolution" (Thesis, University of Texas, ca. 1925), pp. 41–42.

2. Samuel Maverick, *Samuel Maverick, Texan* (San Antonio: 1952), p. 30.

3. Karle Wilson Baker, "Trailing the New Orleans Greys," *SWHQ* (April 1937), p. 215.

4. Over the next half year—even as the Greys were being slaughtered in a wholesale execution ordered by Santa Anna—pro-Texas rallies continued across the United States, sparking a circuslike electricity. Two-foot-high broadsides suddenly sprouted on lampposts or on storefronts in cities and towns throughout the South and along the Eastern seaboard.

5. Ehrenberg, "Texas," p. 12.

6. Claude Elliott, "Alabama and the Texas Revolution," *SWHQ* (50, no. 3), pp. 322–23.

7.   Rollin G. Osterweis, *Romanticism and Nationalism in the Old South* (Gloucester: Peter Smith, 1964), p. 200.

8.   Everett Dick, *The Dixie Frontier* (New York: Capricorn Books, 1964), pp. 268–69.

9.   During the Mexican War the volunteers horrified the regulars with their acid racism and unbelievable atrocities. Volunteers raped, plundered, and murdered, "fighting over their poor victims like dogs." John K. Mahon, *History of the Militia and the National Guard* (New York: Greenwood Press, 1968), p. 93.

10.   Drawing upon his own volunteer days under Andrew Jackson in the Creek War, he said, "When regular troops were living bountifully, the militia were in a state of starvation." James Atkins Shackford, *David Crockett* (Chapel Hill: University of North Carolina Press, 1986), pp. 114–15.

11.   Houston, letter to Parker, *PTR*, #757.

12.   Eugene Barker, "The Texan Revolutionary Army," *Texas State Historical Association* (April 1906), p. 256.

13.   Between 1830 and 1836, the value of real estate throughout America rose 150 percent. Roy M. Robbins, *Our Landed Heritage* (Gloucester: Peter Smith, 1960), pp. 59–60. On their opening days, U.S. land offices in new territories were typically flooded with hundreds of men from all across the United States. In fierce, fast bidding their best lands would disappear in hours.

14.   In November a group of New York land speculators staged a number of save-Texas rallies in New York City. The New York *Courier and Enquirer* called the rebels "a set of frontiersmen styling themselves Texians or Texonians," and warned that the driving force behind their revolution was a party of land speculators. Just the same, several thousand dollars were pledged and a number of volunteers signed up to fight the Mexicans. James E. Winston, "New York and the Independence of Texas," *SWHQ* (April 1915), pp. 370–74.

15.   Andrew Forest Muir, ed., *Texas in 1837: An Anonymous, Contemporary Narrative* (Austin: University of Texas Press, 1958), p. 72.

16.   In Victoria, two young Southerners heard the clap-clapping of hands around a corner and figured it was Negro slaves patting out a juba dance. But instead of merry dancers, they found a Mexican woman on her knees by a fire, patting out tortillas. Noah Smithwick, *The Evolution of a State or Recollections of Old Texas Days* (Austin: University of Texas Press, 1983), pp. 9–10.

17.   Maverick, *Samuel Maverick*, p. 16.

18.   Ehrenberg, "Texas," p. 137.

19.   Ibid., p. 60.

20.   Eli Mercer, letter to Austin, *PTR*, #831.

21.   Smithwick, *Evolution of a State*, pp. 76–80.

22.   James T. De Shields, *Tall Men with Long Rifles* (San Antonio: Naylor Printing Company, 1935), p. 40.

23.   James W. Pohl et al., "The Military History of the Texas Revolution: An Overview," *SWHQ* (January 1986), p. 275.

24. But Dr. Anson Jones, a future president of Texas, found the consultation's resolutions hypocritical.

25. Ehrenberg, "Texas," pp. 66–71.

26. Ibid., pp. 75–82; see also George Erath's account, Sam Houston Dixon et al., *The Heroes of San Jacinto* (Houston: Anson Jones press, 1932), p. 167; and Alfred Kelso's account, in Dixon, *Heroes,* p. 213.

27. George L. Rives, *The United States and Mexico, 1821–1848* (New York: Charles Scribner's Sons, 1913), vol. 1, p. 298.

28. Insubordination was not infrequent in Anglo-American frontier militias. David Crockett once boasted that he had led a mutiny against Andrew Jackson during the Creek War (he hadn't, though a mutiny did occur). And in 1842, Texan troops mustering to fight the Mexican army experienced hilarious chaos. "From the time of the first assembling of the troops until their departure," described one contemporary, "there was much confusion, arising out of a want of provisions and ammunition, but, above all, from the insubordination and ambitious pretentions of various persons in the army." Ibid., vol. 1, p. 490.

29. Ehrenberg, "Texas," pp. 90–91.

30. De Shields, *Tall Men,* pp. 61–63.

31. "Being within thirty feet of him when he fell, I believe myself competent to give a correct statement of the facts as I saw them," Creed Taylor later related. "Milam, Johnson, Cook, Morris, Karnes, York, and other leaders had assembled at the Verimendi house to formulate plans for the final assault. Milam carried a small field glass (a present to him by General Austin). With this glass, and while standing in the front yard of the building, Milam was viewing the Mexican stronghold on the Plaza. At this moment a shot rang out and Milam fell, the ball piercing his head. . . . One of those present in the yard called attention to the fact that at the report of the shot he saw a white puff of smoke arising from the branches of a large Cypress tree that stood on the margin of the river. At this announcement all eyes were turned in the direction of that tree, the outline of a man was seen, several rifle shots rang out and the corpse of the daring sharp-shooter crashed down through the branches and rolled into the river." Ibid., p. 65.

32. Lois Garver, "Benjamin Rush Milam," *SWHQ* (October 1934), p. 197.

33. "I never heard a single order during the whole siege," Ehrenberg observed. Perhaps because no one would have obeyed an order.

34. Vicente Filisola, *The History of the War in Texas* (Austin: Eakin Press, 1985–87), vol. 2, pp. 93–96.

35. Rives, *U.S. and Mexico,* vol. 1, p. 302.

36. Ehrenberg, "Texas," p. 110.

CHAPTER 6

1. The U.S. government was careful not to offend Spain with visible aid to the revolutionary movement. For one thing Spain had been an ally and had fought

British troops during the American Revolution. For another, a number of delicate treaties between the United States and Spain were pending. But a covert federal agent—a U.S. special agent and consular officer named William Shaler—was apparently authorized to assist Gutiérrez. Shaler contributed money to Gutiérrez's embryonic army, published propaganda for it, and accompanied the invaders into Texas as an observer, writing letters directly to President James Monroe. Ted Schwarz, *Forgotten Battlefield of the First Texan Revolution* (Austin: Eakin Press, 1985), pp. 10–11.

2. According to the Spanish vice-consul in New Orleans, U.S. agents paid money to the American "rebels" and armed and clothed them from government warehouses and the federal arsenal.

3. Ibid., pp. 22–23.

4. Harris Gaylord Warren, *The Sword Was Their Passport* (Baton Rouge: Louisiana State University Press: 1943), p. 44.

5. The Kempers promptly collected a gang of thirty river pirates, squatters, and frontier drifters from Georgia, Kentucky, and Tennessee, and returned to "revolutionize" West Florida. Proclaiming "Floridean freedom," they wrote a declaration of independence ("For a people to be free it is sufficient that they will it . . .") and made a flag with seven blue and white stripes and two stars. Isaac J. Cox, *The West Florida Controversy* (Gloucester: Peter Smith, 1967), pp. 154–56. The few Anglo-American settlers in Florida who had earlier bothered to take an oath of loyalty to Spain now renounced it and joined the Kemper "rebels" in halfheartedly attacking a Spanish fort at Grand Pre. The attempt failed and the Kempers were routed. But they returned in 1810.

6. Broadsides appeared on posts and walls. Newspapers editorialized: "There is no American heart that does not beat in unison with the people of Florida. . . ." Ibid., pp. 355–56. At the diplomatic level, the Spanish government appealed to the U.S. State Department to prevent Americans from joining the "insurrection." The State Department assured Spain that neutrality would be strictly upheld, then occupied West Florida with U.S. Army troops.

7. He had—reluctantly—returned several escaped black slaves to American authorities, but had championed six U.S. Army deserters requesting to settle in eastern Texas. He had followed a policy of live-and-let-live with Anglo-American squatters.

8. Felix D. Almaraz, Jr., *Tragic Cavalier* (Austin: University of Texas Press, 1971), p. 54.

9. Schwarz, *Forgotten Battlefield*, pp. 38–39. One royalist officer swore to destroy the filibusters by fire and blood and cursed that "in Hell shalt thou be put, thy body burnt and thy ashes scattered." Ibid., p. 48. This is precisely what happened to Anglo-American filibusters in 1836.

10. In addition, there was a leadership crisis. The Tejano contingent under Miguel Menchaca had expressed differences with a new army leader named José Alvarez de Toledo, a Cuban-born royalist-turned-rebel. The power struggle between the local and the outsider turned into a mutiny that threw the battle plan into chaos. The result was that major chunks of the filibuster army fled, leaving the Americans and Tejanos to cast themselves upon the royalist breastworks nestled along the edge of a thick forest.

11. Schwarz, *Forgotten Battlefield*, p. 108.

12. Wilfrid Hardy Callcott, *Santa Anna* (Hamden: Archon Books, 1964), p. 37; and John Anthony Caruso, *The Liberators of Mexico* (Gloucester: Peter Smith, 1967), p. 267.

13. Antonio López de Santa Anna, *The Eagle* (Austin: Pemberton Press, 1967), p. 245.

14. Oakah L. Jones, Jr., *Santa Anna* (New York: Twayne Publishers, 1968), p. 24. There was nothing unusual about Santa Anna's interest. West Point cadets studied Napoleonic warfare as early as 1817, and American generals scoured Napoleon's maxims.

15. Robert B. Holtman, *The Napoleonic Revolution* (Philadelphia: J. B. Lippincott Co., 1967), p. 51.

16. There were many similarities between Napoleon and Santa Anna. Both were born in obscurity, both were quarrelsome and domineering in school. Both attended prestigious military academies, both achieved the rank of second lieutenant at the tender age of sixteen. Both reached manhood fighting in civil wars. Both joined with republican forces to defeat royalist forces: Napoleon at Toulon in 1793, Santa Anna at Veracruz in 1821. Neither had the patience to rule in peacetime, consequently each prosecuted battle after battle, war after war. Each became a tyrant.

17. The king's share of the spoils became a traditional fifth, thus the "quinto real" or royal fifth.

18. James Lockhart et al., *Early Latin America* (Cambridge: Cambridge University Press, 1983), pp. 79–80.

19. When Cortez killed the Aztec king, he replaced the Indian monarch with the Spanish king. But when the Mexican revolution "killed" the Spanish king, the king stayed dead.

20. Gene Brack, *Mexico Views Manifest Destiny* (Albuquerque: University of New Mexico Press, 1975), p. 54.

21. Stanley C. Green, *The Mexican Republic* (Pittsburgh: University of Pittsburgh Press, 1987), p. 39.

22. Callcott, *Santa Anna*, pp. 74–78.

23. As Santa Anna set out for the Tampico battle, an old veteran of Napoleonic wars had caught his sleeve and said, "This campaign may do for you what Napoleon's Egyptian campaign accomplished for him."

24. Vicente Filisola, *The History of the War in Texas* (Austin: Eakin Press, 1985–87), vol. 2, p. 234.

25. Jones, *Santa Anna*, p. 45.

26. Callcott, *Santa Anna*, pp. 185–86.

27. Ibid., pp. 68–69; and Jones, *Santa Anna,* p. 48.

28. Eduard Harkort, *In Mexican Prisons* (College Station: Texas A&M Press, 1986), p. 79.

29. Ibid., pp. 58–59.

30. Santa Anna, *The Eagle,* p. xii.

31. Frances Calderon de la Barca, *Life in Mexico* (Berkeley: University of California Press, 1982), p. 510. Another time, the U.S. minister predicted an upcoming coup by noting that when Santa Anna's cock was killed in the ring, public applause became ominously enthusiastic. Callcott, *Santa Anna,* p. 185.

32. Ibid., p. 154.

33. North of the border, the *Niles' Weekly Register* caustically viewed the situation as an abomination. "The curse of heroism is upon Mexico," it reported. "It now appears that *General* Santa Anna, late one of the loudest bawlers for liberty and now president of the miscalled republic, is in the exercise of power which a constitutional *king* would not venture upon. He has rallied round him an army of *priests*—a great army of leeches, shouting for the preservation of *'our holy religion'* that they may fleece their flocks!—and their miserable dupes, an ignorant people, bellow out 'down with the heretics.' " Jones, *Santa Anna,* p. 58.

34. In the late 1820s, Jalisco boasted 11,200 militia soldiers; Yucatán, 18,000; and Zacatecas, over 17,000. Green, *The Mexican Republic,* pp. 186–87, 201–2.

35. Miguel A. Sánchez Lamego, "The Battle of Zacatecas," *Texana* 7, no. 3 (1969), p. 192.

36. Harkort, *In Mexican Prisons,* p. 172n. 19.

37. Callcott, *Santa Anna,* pp. 115–19.

38. Among the officers serving Santa Anna in both the Zacatecas campaign and the Texas campaign were José Maria Romero, Ventura Mora, Juan Arago, Adrian Woll, Eugenio Tolsa, Joaquín Ramírez y Sesma, and José Urrea. See Sánchez Lamego, "The Battle of Zacatecas," pp. 194–95.

39. Austin, letter to Holley, *PTR,* #534.

40. Joseph Milton Nance, *After San Jacinto* (Austin: University of Texas Press, 1963), p. 19.

41. Ricard G. Santos, *Santa Anna's Campaign Against Texas* (Salisbury: Documentary Publications, 1968), p. 2.

42. After the British bankers' experience with Mexico in the mid-1820s, foreign lenders kept away from the destitute nation.

43. The Church charged 5 percent interest; the national pawnshop, Monte de Piedad, took an average of forty-two thousand pawns annually, and charged 6.25 percent interest. See also Green, *The Mexican Republic,* p. 114.

44. On top of that, the port of Tampico was closed due to an attack by the American-financed rebel General José María Mexia, meaning the nation had one less customhouse to draw from.

45. Antonio López de Santa Anna, "Manifesto Relative to His Operations in

the Texas Campaign and His Capture," in Carlos Eduardo Castañeda, *The Mexican Side of the Texan Revolution by the Chief Mexican Participants* (Austin: Graphic Ideas Inc., 1970), p. 10.

46. George L. Rives, *The United States and Mexico, 1821–1848* (New York: Charles Scribner's Sons, 1913), vol. 1, p. 320.

47. Callcott, *Santa Anna*, p. 127.

48. Ramón Martinez Caro, in Castañeda, *The Mexican Side*, p. 101.

49. Filisola, *The History of the War in Texas*, vol. 2, pp. 126–29.

50. Ibid., pp. 110–11.

51. A Mexican officer, who had just returned with General Cós from the humbling defeat in Béxar, answered that the Anglo-Americans would fire not one but a million shots. Castrillón laughed. Santos, *Santa Anna's Campaign*, p. 44.

52. Callcott, *Santa Anna*, p. 126.

53. Holtman, *The Napoleonic Revolution*, p. 41.

54. Santa Anna, "Manifesto," in Castañeda, *The Mexican Side*, p. 7.

CHAPTER 7

1. James Atkins Shackford, *David Crockett* (Chapel Hill: University of North Carolina Press, 1986), p. 213.

2. David Crockett, *A Narrative of the Life of David Crockett* (Lincoln: University of Nebraska Press, 1987), pp. 161–69.

3. The leatherstocking was the ultimate superhero. Boone's 1784 biography by John Filson was reprinted, plundered, revamped, and virtually memorized. James Fenimore Cooper and James Kirke Paulding struck gold with similar Western heroes padding ever westward in quiet moccasins.

4. Shackford, *David Crockett*, pp. 134–36.

5. Paul Andrew Hutton, "Introduction," Crockett, *A Narrative of the Life*, p. xx.

6. Shackford, *David Crockett*, pp. 124–25.

7. Frederick S. Voss, "Portraying an American Original: The Likenesses of Davy Crockett," *SWHQ* (April 1988): 471–73.

8. One night Crockett came face to face with an image of his elusive Davy. *The Lion of the West* had come to Washington for a benefit performance, and Crockett went to see himself depicted. Though the playwright Paulding insisted that Col. Nimrod Wildfire had nothing to do with Crockett, on this night actor James Hackett strode onstage, paused, turned to Crockett's reserved booth, and bowed to his maker. Crockett stood and bowed back to his image. Together, they brought the house down.

9. A year after the suspicious biography Crockett published his own autobiography, which was at least partially ghostwritten by a Whig congressman and friend, Thomas Chilton. In 1835 he fixed his name to two more Whig-written books (*Col. Crockett's Tour to the North and Down East* and *Life of Martin Van Buren*).

10. Michael Lofaro, "The Hidden 'Hero' of the Nashville Crockett Almanacs," in Michael Lofaro, *Davy Crockett* (Knoxville: University of Tennessee Press, 1985), p. 60.

11. Catherine L. Albanese, "Davy Crockett and the Wild Man; or, the Metaphysics of the *Longue Duree*," in Lofaro, *Davy Crockett*, pp. 86–88.

12. Long before the Rio Grande River became linked with the term *wetback*, the Sabine and Red River of Louisiana and Arkansas marked the international border. The men and women crossing toward hope of a better life all crossed west in Mexico. In 1835–36 almost all the wetbacks were white Anglo-Americans trespassing on Mexican soil.

13. Crockett, letter to his family, *PTR*, #1739.

14. Crockett, *A Narrative*, p. 124.

15. The Jacksonian-Whig feud had migrated west along with the Anglo-Americans and Crockett wanted an exit clause from any Jacksonian regime. Shackford, *David Crockett*, pp. 217–21.

CHAPTER 8

1. Arnoldo De León, *The Tejano Community, 1836–1900* (Albuquerque: University of New Mexico Press, 1982), p. 12.

2. By land—through Natchitoches and Nacogdoches—the journey could take two or three times longer.

3. Mary S. Helm, *Scraps of Early Texas History* (Austin: B. R. Warner & Co., 1884), pp. 48–53.

4. Eugene Barker, "Finances of the Texas Revolution," *Political Science Quarterly* (December 1904), pp. 630–34.

5. Walter Lord, "Myths and Realities of the Alamo," in *The Republic of Texas*, ed. Stephen B. Oates (Palo Alto: American West Pub. Co., 1968), p. 25.

6. Barker, "Finances of the Texas Revolution," p. 622.

7. Jerry J. Gaddy, comp., *Texas in Revolt* (Fort Collins: Old Army Press, 1983), pp. 14–15.

8. The Neutrality Act had had an early test in 1806 when thirty-six American filibusters en route to South America were captured by a Spanish fleet and turned over to the United States for prosecution. The men were tried. Their jury declared them innocent. Charles G. Fenwick, *The Neutrality Laws of the United States* (Washington, D.C.: Carnegie Endowment, 1913), pp. 17–40.

9. George L. Rives, *The United States and Mexico, 1821–1848* (New York: Charles Scribner's Sons, 1913), vol. 1, pp. 368–71.

10. Marquis James, *The Raven* (Saint Simon: Mockingbird Books, 1981), p. 218.

11. Hobart Huson, "Reporting Texas" (unpublished, copy in DRTL), p. 148.

12. Joseph Milton Nance, *After San Jacinto* (Austin: University of Texas Press, 1963), p. 25.

13. Eugene Barker, "The Texas Revolutionary Army," *Quarterly of the Texas State Historical Association* (April 1906), p. 237.

14. James Pohl and Stephen L. Hardin, "The Military History of the Texas Revolution," *SWHQ* (January 1986), p. 271.

15. Houston, letter to Smith, *PTR, #1955*.

16. The thieving began in early November when a band of volunteers from the Ayish Bayou near the Louisiana border entered Gonzales a month after the Gonzales cannon fight. Many of the town's men had joined the rebels besieging San Antonio. On the night of November 2, the Ayish Bayou "troops" rousted all the women and children from their cabins and ransacked the town, stealing money and clothing, turning their horses loose in the cornfields, and nearly beating to death a man named L. Smither: "After goind to Bead thiy Enterd the house twice by bursting Evry door and window and coming in crowds and dragd me into the Streats and beat my head to a poltice and would have kild me in the most torturing manner for now caws on earth." Smither, letter to Austin, *PTR, #1087*.

17. James T. De Shields, *Tall Men with Long Rifles* (San Antonio: Naylor Printing Company, 1935), p. 72.

18. Kathryn Stoner O'Connor, *The Presidio La Bahia del Espiritu Santa de Zuniga, 1721–1846.* (Austin: Von-Boeckmann-Jones Co., 1984), pp. 126–27.

19. For example, see William R. Carey, letter to his family, *PTR, #1762*.

20. Ruby Cumby Smith, "James W. Fannin, Jr., in the Texas Revolution," *SWHQ* vol. 23, no. 3 (1919), p. 199.

21. Barker, "The Texas Revolutionary Army," p. 238.

22. Rives, *U.S. and Mexico,* vol. 1, pp. 304–5.

23. Houston, letter to Bowie, *PTR, #1510*.

24. Thomson and Clements, letter to Smith, *PTR, #2073*.

25. Houston, address to soldiers, *PTR, #1791*.

26. Johnson, address to General Council, *PTR, #1956*.

27. Neill, letter to Houston, *PTR, #1783*.

28. Houston, letter to Smith, *PTR, #1813*.

29. Jameson, letter to Houston, *PTR, #1831*.

30. Ironically, Seguín still serves the Anglo-American myth of the Texas Revolution. Apologists point to him as proof that Tejanos actively supported the rebels. He did, but he bitterly regretted it.

31. As a young lawyer Bonham was once imprisoned for three months for thrashing a man who insulted his client—a Southern belle—before the judge and jury, then threatening to pull the nose of the judge who reprimanded him. For the length of his stay, Bonham enjoyed regular visits from the local ladies who fed their hero "upon the fat of the land and decorated his cell with flowers."

32. Bowie, letter to Smith, *PTR, #1989*.

33. Travis, letter to Austin, *PTR, #1107*.

34. Travis, letter to Austin, *PTR,* #1214.

35. Travis's Morning Report, *PTR,* #1306.

36. Travis, letter to General Council, *PTR,* #1382.

37. Travis, letter to Robinson, *PTR,* #1529.

38. Smith, letter to Travis, *PTR,* #1605.

39. John K. Mahon, *History of the Militia and the National Guard* (New York: Macmillan Publishing Company, 1983), pp. 82–84.

40. Travis, letter to Smith. William C. Binkley, ed., *Official Correspondence of the Texas Revolution* (Baton Rouge: Louisiana State University Press, 1952), vol. 1, pp. 352–53.

41. In Nacogdoches the same thing happened to a company of Kentucky volunteers. Local election judges ruled them ineligible, "which caused an angry excitement," according to one witness. "The company was drawn up with loaded rifles, and the First Lieutenant, Woods, swore that the men should vote, or he would riddle the door of the Stone House, where the election was held, with rifle balls. . . . They were all day under arms, and frequently marched to and fro, with drum and fife, before the door of the Hustings—a shameful spectacle." William F. Gray, *From Virginia to Texas, 1835* (Houston: The Fletcher Young Publishing Company, 1965), pp. 89–90.

42. Pollard, letter to Smith, *PTR,* #2080.

43. Neill et al., Memorial to the Convention, *PTR,* #2021.

44. Travis, letter to Smith, *PTR,* #2074.

45. Baugh, letter to Smith, *PTR,* #2076.

46. Travis, letter to Smith, *PTR,* #2084.

47. Baugh, letter to Smith, *PTR,* #2076.

48. Travis and Bowie, letter to Smith, *PTR,* #2094.

CHAPTER 9

1. William Gray, *From Virginia to Texas, 1835* (Houston: The Fletcher Young Publishing Company, 1965), p. 103.

2. The Cloud Family Newsletter, vol. 2, no. 2, p. 16. In the DRTL.

3. For more on the Revolutionary War genealogy of Anglo-Americans at the Alamo, see Bicentennial Project, *The Alamo Heroes and Their Revolutionary Ancestors* (San Antonio: 1976).

4. John Sutherland, *The Fall of the Alamo* (San Antonio: Naylor Press, 1936), pp. 11–12.

5. Transcript of Daniel Cloud letter, in the DRTL.

6. One of Autry's daughters had married a wealthy plantation owner, Mr. Smith, who now brought the bankrupt family under his roof while Autry chased rainbows. Mary Autry Greer, "Major M. Autry," a transcript of a letter, in the DRTL.

7. Micajah Autry, letter to his wife, *PTR,* #1398.

8. Autry's journey included the perils of starvation and of smallpox. But, he reported, "I fear the Tavern bills a great deal worse. Such charges were never heard of. . . ." Autry, letter to his wife, *PTR*, #1462.

9. Antonio Menchaca, *Memoirs of Antonio Menchaca* (San Antonio: Yanaguana Society, 1937), p. 22.

10. Sutherland, *Fall of the Alamo,* pp. 11–12.

11. Herman Ehrenberg, "Texas und Seine Revolution," translated by E. W. Bartholomae (Thesis, University of Texas, ca. 1925), p. 31.

12. Menchaca, *Memoirs,* pp. 22–23.

CHAPTER 10

1. In the following two years, Filisola pacified Central America from Guatemala to El Salvador in the name of Mexico, and then took it upon himself to grant independence to Central America—an unauthorized move which almost ended his career. In 1829 he fought the Spanish invasion at Tampico, and in 1831 he became an *empresario* with the right to settle six hundred non-U.S. families in far northeastern Texas. He never fulfilled the terms of his grant. Stephen Austin met Filisola in 1833 and liked him, describing the soldier as a "blunt, honest, candid and prompt soldier. He has been over thirty years in service . . . and what is rather uncommon, he has not made a fortune. . . . He is the friend of farming and agricultural interests—a decided enemy of smugglers and lawyers, for he thinks they demoralize the community by placing temptations before weak or avaricious persons." James M. Day, *Evacuation of Texas* (Waco: Texian Press, 1965), p. vi.

2. Castrillón served as Santa Anna's "agent" as early as 1822. John Anthony Caruso, *The Liberators of Mexico* (Gloucester: Peter Smith, 1967), p. 269.

3. A German mercenary named Eduard Harkort shared a dungeon cell in the infamous Perote Prison with Castrillón. "He was tall and strong and, with his curly hair, he towered over everyone—a true Roman type. He was well bred, educated, and quick. . . . He was from Havana. His sonorous voice led all conversations and discussions; almost all of his suggestions were well received. . . . He was at times impetuous and unjust, but otherwise pleasant in social intercourse. The whole group gave him the appropriate respect. Eduard Harkort, *In Mexican Prisons* (College Station: Texas A&M University Press, 1986), p. 94.

4. Harkort called him "extremely impetuous and temperamental, with a rather fierce-looking and coarse physiognomy. He exaggerated everything, going from one extreme to the other, but free of any arrogance. . . . He was impatient and easily enraged."

5. He was a popular man in the remoter sections of north-central Mexico, serving as governor of Durango and later getting elected a senator. Within two years after the Texas campaign, Urrea attempted a Santanista-style coup of his own, taking control of Sonora and Sinaloa states for a brief time. At the end of his federalist revolt, in June 1839, Urrea would finally surrender to his former commander, Santa Anna, only to escape, be recaptured, escape again, and be recaptured again. George L. Rives, *The United States and Mexico, 1821–1848* (New York: Charles Scribner's Sons, 1913), vol. 1, pp. 435, and 450–51.

6. Miguel A. Sánchez Lamego, *Treinta Contra Cuatrocientos* (Mexico: Editorial Militar Mexicana, 1966), p. 52.

7. He was part of a new crop of officers who were too young to have served under the Spanish regime in Mexico, but just old enough to be serving under generals (like Santa Anna) who had.

8. In Carmen Perry's introduction to José Enrique de la Peña, *With Santa Anna in Texas* (College Station: Texas A&M Press, 1983), pp. xii–xiii.

9. Admiral Porter came with U.S. minister Joel Poinsett's recommendation and received twelve thousand dollars annually plus perquisites. Rives, *U.S. and Mexico,* vol. 1, p. 93.

10. De la Peña, *With Santa Anna,* p. 6.

11. Rives, *U.S. and Mexico,* vol. 1, p. 94.

12. It was a concept that President Monroe's administration had considered for the U.S. Army in the 1820s, an alternative to a large, expensive standing army.

13. Rives, *U.S. and Mexico,* vol. 1, p. 54.

14. Under Spanish rule, an intricate terminology had grown to categorize every possible mixture of races: *peninsular* or *gachupin* (a European-born pure-blooded Spaniard), *criollo* (an American-born pure-blooded Spaniard), *mestizo* (Spanish and Indian), *mulato* (or mule, a Spanish and African), *lobo* (Indian and African), and combinations of all the above. Not until the twentieth century did the term *mestizo* lose its pejorative sense, at which point Mexico began to honor its mixed heritage.

15. Vicente Filisola, *The History of the War in Texas* (Austin: Eakin Press, 1985–87), vol. 2, p. 130.

16. "The soldiers of the Mexican army are generally collected by sending out *recruiting* detachments into the mountains, where they hunt the Indians in their dens and caverns, and bring them in chains to Mexico. There is scarcely a day that droves of these miserable and more than half-naked wretches are not seen thus chained together and marching through the streets to the barracks, where they are scoured and then dressed in a uniform made of linen cloth or of serge. . . ." Waddy Thompson, *Recollections of Mexico* (New York: Wiley and Putnam, 1846), pp. 172–73.

17. De la Peña, *With Santa Anna,* pp. 8–9.

18. Ibid., pp. 20–21.

19. Ibid., pp. 30 and 8.

20. Miguel A. Sánchez Lamego, *El Soldado Mexicano, 1837–1848* (Mexico City: Editions Nieto-Brown-Herfter, 1958), p. 60.

21. "They are . . . wholly unaccustomed to labor or exercise of any sort, and as a conclusive proof of their inferiority to our own Indians, I will mention the fact that frequent incursions are made far into the interior of Mexico by marauding bands of Comanches . . . and of all our western tribes the Comanches are the most cowardly. . . ." Thompson, *Recollections*, p. 172.

22. Nelson Reed, *The Caste Wars of Yucatán* (Stanford: Stanford University Press, 1964), p. 22.

23. Ibid., p. 27.

24. De la Peña, *With Santa Anna*, p. 68.

25. Reed, *The Caste Wars*, p. 27.

26. Frances Toor, *A Treasury of Mexican Folkways* (New York: Bonanza Books, 1985), pp. 82–83 and 157.

27. Ibid., pp. 28–29.

28. Reed, *The Caste Wars*, pp. 77–78.

29. Frances Calderon de la Barca, *Life in Mexico* (Berkeley: University of California Press, 1982), pp. 275–76.

30. They left gifts behind the column of death in the ancient Palace and claimed to see splendid ghosts dancing in the courtyard. Those not making the pilgrimage sacrificed turkeys in the mountain caves and Zapotec women took dough animals to a sacred wall.

31. Toor, *Treasury of Mexican Folkways*, pp. 192–93.

32. Harkort, *In Mexican Prisons*, p. 43.

33. Filisola, *History of the War*, vol. 2, pp. 132–33.

34. Ibid., p. 152. When bags of corn accidentally ripped, soldiers and women would immediately cluster "like chickens in order to pick up the last grain."

35. De la Peña, *With Santa Anna*, pp. 114–15.

36. Filisola, *History of the War*, vol. 2, pp. 161–62.

37. By the march's end, a single tortilla cost two reales (a real was one eighth of a peso, or one piece of eight: Two reales equaled two "bits," or twenty-five cents American). Ibid., p. 62.

38. De la Peña, *With Santa Anna*, p. 19.

39. Ibid., p. 60.

40. Filisola, *History of the War*, vol. 2, pp. 112–13, 153.

41. Ramón Caro, "A True Account of the First Texas Campaign and the Events Subsequent to the Battle of San Jacinto," in Carlos Eduardo Castañeda, *The Mexican Side of the Texan Revolution* (Austin: Graphic Ideas Incorporated, 1970), pp. 102–103. "It may be said that the army marched trusting in the favor of Divine Providence," General Filisola commented, "and Saint Peter does not always order things so that they may heal with his shadow."

42. Sánchez Lamego, *El Soldado Mexicano*, p. 59.

43. Filisola, *History of the War*, vol. 2, p. 153.

44. "A number of officers, many sergeants and many more corporals and soldiers, because of the method of getting them into the army and the corruption there, took with them women and children, others their parents, others younger brothers and sisters, and others finally their girl friends or lovers," said General

Filisola, "and therefore scarcities mounted since all of these had to subsist in that wilderness on the scarce and bad rations of the soldiers." Ibid., p. 164.

45. De la Peña, *With Santa Anna*, p. 22.

46. Filisola, *History of the War*, vol. 2, pp. 124–25n.

47. De la Peña, *With Santa Anna*, p. 190.

48. The American wife of a Spanish minister described a typical set of *soldaderas* following yet another of Santa Anna's armies (in 1841). "The sick followed on asses," Frances Calderon de la Barca said, "and amongst them various masculine women, with *sarapes* or *mangas* and large straw hats, tied down the coloured handkerchiefs, mounted on mules or horses. The sumpter mules followed, carrying provisions, camp-beds, etc.: and various Indian women trotted on foot in the rear, carrying their husbands' boots and clothes. There was certainly no beauty amongst these feminine followers of the camp, especially amongst the mounted Amazons, who looked like very ugly men in a semi-female disguise." Calderon, *Life in Mexico*, pp. 433–34.

49. Sánchez Lamego, *El Soldado Mexicano*, p. 57.

50. Thompson, *Recollections*, p. 173.

51. Guillermo Prieto's account, in Wilfrid Hardy Callcott, *Santa Anna* (Hamden: Archon Books, 1964), p. 154.

52. The Prussian army had conducted tests that demonstrated that volley firing almost literally could not hit the side of a barn; against a ten-foot-square target at 120 yards, a platoon using volley firing scored only 47 percent of the time. But Frederick the Great had decreed that firepower won battles and had gone so far as to ban soldiers from aiming their guns. Michael Glover, *The Napoleonic Wars* (New York: Hippocrene Books, 1978), pp. 10–17.

53. De la Peña, *With Santa Anna*, p. 13.

54. José Juan Sánchez Navarro, "A Mexican View of the Texas War," *The Library Chronicle* vol. 4, no. 2; pp. 60–61.

55. Filisola, *History of the War*, vol. 2, pp. 152–53.

56. De la Peña, *With Santa Anna*, pp. 9–19.

57. Filisola wondered if his commander's mysterious behavior was the result of "some strange suggestion of the treachery of our hidden adversaries, or [was] because of chance, or because of the effect of some physical infirmity. . . ." Filisola, *History of the War*, vol. 1, p. 145.

58. De la Peña, *With Santa Anna*, p. 24.

59. Francisco Becerra, *A Mexican Sergeant's Recollections of the Alamo and San Jacinto* (Austin: Jenkins Pub. Co., 1980), pp. 16–17.

60. Filisola, *History of the War*, vol. 2, pp. 146–48.

61. Richard G. Santos, *Santa Anna's Campaign Against Texas, 1835–1836* (Salisbury: Documentary Publications, ca. 1968), p. 12.

62. John C. Gunn, *Gunn's Domestic Medicine* (Knoxville: University of Tennessee Press, 1986), pp. 401–4.

63. George M. Dolson's letter, in Thomas Lawrence Connelly, ed., "Did

David Crockett Surrender at the Alamo?'' *Journal of Southern History* (August 1960), p. 372.

64. Sam Houston Dixon and Louis Wiltz Kemp, *The Heroes of San Jacinto* (Houston: Anson Jones Press, 1932), p. 241.

65. Callcott, *Santa Anna,* p. 37.

66. De la Peña, *With Santa Anna,* p. 93.

67. They passed through Querétaro, famed for its pear and apple wines, where the thick cloth for military uniforms was manufactured. They passed through mountainous Guanajuato, treading the highway of revolution and counterrevolution, where the priest Hidalgo's rabble had massacred Spanish loyalists, where the great silver mines set still flooded from sabotage, and crossed one plain strewn with thousands of crosses marking revolutionary victims. Jean Louis Berlandier, *Journey to Texas During the Years 1826–1834* (Austin: Texas State Historical Association, 1980), vol. 1, pp. 186, 85–86.

68. Ibid., pp. 210–11.

69. Not long before, Saltillo's principal crop had been wheat, which they sold to coastal villages and southern mining towns. But for the last number of years, American flour smuggled through Texas had hurt their market. Ibid., p. 231.

70. The day Santa Anna reached San Antonio, General Gaona was just arriving at Presidio de Rio Grande two hundred miles behind. Filisola, *History of the War,* vol. 2, p. 147.

71. Ibid., p. 102.

72. Ibid., p. 159.

73. Berlandier, *Journey to Mexico,* vol. 1, p. 264.

74. James W. Pohl and Stephen L. Hardin, "The Military History of the Texas Revolution," *SWHQ* (January 1986), p. 278.

75. It was a common practice in this region to post messages to a tall tree, along with a dead buzzard to advertise its location. Berlandier, *Journey to Mexico,* p. 279.

76. De la Peña, *With Santa Anna,* p. 33.

77. Filisola, *History of the War,* vol. 2, pp. 120–23. The pre-Columbian folklore of various Mexican tribes spoke of an afterlife journey in which dead souls traversed hardships little different from those met upon the Camino Real to Texas, with a river to ford, hot plains to cross, and roads spiked with thorns and brambles. Toor, *Treasury of Mexican Folkways,* p. 163.

78. Filisola, *History of the War,* vol. 2, pp. 260, 114–19.

79. De la Peña, *With Santa Anna,* pp. 26–29.

80. Filisola, *History of the War,* vol. 2, pp. 158–59.

81. "There were very few places where the brigades made camp that did not see small crosses for little ones and rough sticks that the piety of the soldiers had placed on the graves of their unfortunate companions who had died." Ibid., p. 165.

CHAPTER 11

1. New Orleans Notice, *PTR, #2207.*

2. Hall, address to the Public, *PTR, #2206.*

3. Fannin, letter to Robinson, *PTR, #2037.*

4. Travis, letter to Grimes, *PTR, #2235.*

5. Fannin, letter to Robinson, *PTR, #2142.*

6. John Sutherland, *The Fall of the Alamo* (San Antonio: Naylor Press, 1936), pp. 11–12.

7. Travis, letter to Vaughan, *PTR, #2135.*

8. Fannin, letter to Robinson, *PTR, #2109.*

9. Jameson also proposed less drastic revisions: "... to square the Alamo and erect a large redoubt at each corner supported by Bastions & leave a ditch all around full of water. when [*sic*] squared in that way four cannon[s] & fewer men would do more effective service than twenty pieces of artillery does or can do in the way they are now mounted. ..." Jameson, letter to Robinson, *PTR, #2110.*

10. Sutherland, *Fall of the Alamo,* pp. 12–13.

11. Royall, letter to Houston, *PTR, #2121.*

12. Juan N. Almonte, "The Private Journal of Juan Nepomuceno Almonte," reprint from *SWHQ* (July 1944), p. 7.

13. José María Rodriguez, *Rodriguez Memoirs of Early Texas* (San Antonio: Standard Printing Co., 1961), p. 8.

14. Sutherland, *Fall of the Alamo,* pp. 15–16.

15. From this same tower in 1813, a party of curious boys with binoculars had watched the glint and flash of the Battle of the Medina and heard the booming of cannons.

16. Frederick Charles Chabot, *With the Makers of San Antonio* (San Antonio: privately published, 1937), p. 274.

17. Vicente Filisola, *The History of the War in Texas* (Austin: Eakin Press, 1985–87), vol. 2, p. 150.

18. During the past autumn, Dimmitt had served as a captain and with Ben Milam had captured Goliad. But Dimmitt's Go Ahead impulsiveness—he had framed his own Declaration of Independence seventy-two days before the rebels declared theirs; the council suppressed his declaration as premature—led to his resignation.

19. Sutherland, *Fall of the Alamo,* pp. 19–20.

20. Travis and Bowie, letter to Fannin, *PTR, #2161.*

21. J. M. Morphis, *History of Texas* (New York: United States Pub. Co., 1875), p. 174.

22. Travis, letter to Ponton, *PTR, #2163.*

23. Sutherland left at the Alamo his seventeen-year-old nephew, William Sutherland, a medical student. The September before, the boy had shown up in

San Antonio to take residence in the home of José Antonio Navarro, the local land commissioner, and learn Spanish. After the rebels captured San Antonio, William joined Travis's regular cavalry.

24. Bowie, letter to Santa Anna, *PTR, #2156.*
25. Almonte, "Private Journal," p. 8.
26. Batres, letter to Bowie, *PTR, #2158.*
27. Travis, letter to Houston, *PTR, #2177.*
28. Almonte, "Private Journal, p. 8.
29. Travis, letter to Houston, *PTR, #2177.*

CHAPTER 12

1. Frederick Charles Chabot, *With the Makers of San Antonio* (San Antonio: privately published, 1937), p. 157.
2. Enrique Esparza's account to Charles Merrit Barnes, San Antonio *Express,* 12 May 1907.
3. José Enrique de la Peña, *With Santa Anna in Texas* (College Station: Texas A&M University Press, 1975), p. 38.
4. José María Rodriguez, *Rodriguez Memoirs of Early Texas* (San Antonio: Standard Press, 1935), pp. 8–9.
5. The word *presidio* derives from the Latin *praesidium,* meaning a garrisoned place, generally a garrison presiding over a military district. The term entered Spanish usage in 1570 when it was applied to forts in Morocco and the hostile Indian frontier of northern Mexico. Max L. Moorehead, *The Presidio* (Norman: University of Oklahoma Press, 1975), p. 34.
6. John Sutherland, *The Fall of the Alamo* (San Antonio: Naylor Press, 1936), p. 22.
7. Michael Glover, *The Napoleonic Wars* (New York: Hippocrene Books, 1978), p. 14.
8. Travis, letter to the Convention, *PTR, #2234.*
9. Juan N. Almonte, "The Private Journal of Juan Nepomuceno Almonte," reprint from *SWHQ* (July 1944), p. 8.
10. Vicente Filisola, *The History of the War in Texas* (Austin: Eakin Press, 1985–87), vol. 2, p. 84.
11. Dennis Hart Mahan, *A Complete Treatise on Field Fortification* (New York: Macmillan Pub. Co., 1968), p. 30.
12. James E. Ivey, "Mission to Fortress" (unpublished), pp. 23–24. Copy in the DRTL.
13. There were other weak points, particularly a palisade or barricade of vertical stakes that ran diagonally between the chapel to the hospital. It was this position that Travis assigned Crockett and "his" twelve boys to defend.
14. The Mexican army watched the rebels pile dirt against the north parapet. "It was noted that they were working incessantly on opening up a ditch on the

inside of the parapet with the intention of enlarging it and giving more resistance against our artillery,'' Filisola said.

15. Filisola, *History of the War,* vol. 2, p. 171.

16. *Curanderos* were valued by Mexican communities for their work with the sick, the wounded, and the insane, but often they lived in intentional obscurity. While their gifts of healing were highly personal, the *curanderos* typically accepted their talents modestly as a gift from God which would be lost if abused. Ari Kiev, *Curanderismo* (New York: Free Press, 1968), pp. 22–32. Señora Candaleria would not have attached a special title to herself, and probably wouldn't even have identified herself as a *curandera*.

17. Sometimes they exorcised *aguajque* (Aztec for ''air spirits'') or purged the *ojo* (evil eye) or countered the effects of a *nagual* (shapeshifting sorcerer).

18. Through this technique, a patient might be diagnosed as suffering from *tristeza* (sadness over some loss)—as in the death of one's wife—or from *espanto* (fright or bad conscience).

19. William Corner, *San Antonio de Bexar* (San Antonio: Bainbridge and Corner, 1890), pp. 117–18.

20. Frances A. Toor, *A Treasury of Mexican Folkways* (New York: Bonanza Books, 1985), pp. 145–52.

21. Juana Alsbury, in ''Mrs. Horace A. Alsbury,'' *John S. Ford Papers,* Texas University Archives, pp. 121–22.

22. Sentinels and gunfire restricted the numbers of visitors, but through the very last night civilians exited the Alamo.

23. Chester Newell, *History of the Revolution in Texas* (New York: Arno Press, 1973), pp. 207–8.

24. M. L. Crimmins, ''American Powder's Part in Winning Texas Independence,'' *SWHQ* (July 1948), p. 107.

25. Travis, letter to the Convention, *PTR, #*2234.

26. Travis, letter to the public, *PTR, #*2168.

27. In this and another communiqué, Travis claimed the Mexicans called for an unconditional surrender, at which point he fired his cannon. In fact the sequence of documents (Bowie's letter to the Mexicans, and their reply to him) shows that Travis fired first, at which point the Mexicans declared the rebels' only hope for clemency was immediate surrender. But for Travis to admit firing first, even before a parley, would be for him to admit being impetuous and overly passionate.

28. Martin, letter to Barrett, *PTR, #*1553.

29. Travis, letter to Houston, *PTR, #*2177.

30. Ramón Caro, ''A True Account of the First Texas Campaign,'' in Carlos Eduardo Castañeda, *The Mexican Side of the Texan Revolution* (Austin: Graphic Ideas Incorporated, 1970), p. 104.

31. J. M. Morphis, *History of Texas from Its Discovery and Settlement* (New York: United States Publishing Company, 1875), p. 175.

CHAPTER 13

1. James T. De Shields, *Tall Men with Long Rifles* (San Antonio: Naylor Printing Company, 1935), pp. 163–64.

2. Men affectionately named and tended their hunting guns and proved their starch through the ability to "cut the center" at barbecues and muster day target shoots. The ornithologist John Audubon had the chance to visit Daniel Boone in his dotage and watched the sainted old man "bark" squirrels to earth. Everett Dick, *The Dixie Frontier* (New York: Capricorn Books, 1964), p. 143.

3. Thomas Dionysius Clark, *The Rampaging Frontier* (Indianapolis: Bobbs-Merrill Co., 1939), pp. 31–33.

4. Austin, circular to the Committee, *PTR, #745.*

5. Noah Smithwick, *The Evolution of a State or Recollections of Old Texas Days* (Austin: University of Texas Press, 1983), p. 8.

6. "Our guns no a count, little dobble barrels shot guns," said one rebel. "I had a Harperferry yauger. The lock was tide on with buck skin strings, & the Mexicans had fine muskets." James W. Pohl and Stephen L. Hardin, "Military History of the Texas Revolution," *SWHQ* (January 1986), p. 282.

7. Shotguns were scorned by the country lads entering the frontier, and Washington Irving commented on "the lads of the West holding 'shotguns,' as they call the double-barrel guns, in great contempt . . . and the rifle the only fire-arm worthy of a hunter." Washington Irving, *A Tour on the Prairies* (Oklahoma City: Harlow Pub. Co., 1955), p. 45. The rebels looked down upon muskets, too. "The musket was such a contemptible weapon in the eyes of the volunteers that even the man who carried it fell heir to its contempt," said New Orleans Grey Herman Ehrenberg. "In our opinion as well as that of the inhabitants of the Free States of North America it was fit only for hirelings." Herman Ehrenberg, "Texas und Seine Revolution," translated by E. W. Bartholomae (Thesis, University of Texas, ca. 1925), p. 230.

8. The British lost 2,036 men; the Americans 8 killed, 13 wounded. Besides American grapeshot, there were several reasons for the British defeat, including a failure to observe tactics, the swiftness of the river, and bad decision making. But American marksmanship took all the credit. In fact, the dawn battlefield was so dark and smoky that riflemen could barely see to aim.

9. John William Ward, *Andrew Jackson* (New York: Oxford University Press, 1981), pp. 20–21.

10. Amelia W. Williams, "A Critical Study," *SWHQ* (January 1934), p. 271.

11. Juan N. Almonte, "The Private Journal of Juan Nepomuceno Almonte," reprint from *SWHQ* (July 1944), p. 10.

12. Travis, letter to Houston, *PTR, #2177.*

13. Bonham, letter to Houston, *PTR, #1355.*

14. Almonte, "Private Journal," p. 10; Vicente Filisola, *The History of the War in Texas* (Austin: Eakin Press, 1985–87), vol. 2, p. 171.

15. Travis, letter to the Convention, *PTR, #2234.*

CHAPTER 14

1. Situated on a hilltop that overlooked the grassy countryside for miles around, Goliad commanded the road connecting San Antonio to the sea and gave whoever occupied it a monopoly of landing sites upon the coast. The rebels' capture of Goliad early in October had cut General Cós off from any possible reinforcement via nearby Copano Bay and thereby dropped San Antonio into rebel hands.

2. Juan N. Almonte, "The Private Journal of Juan Nepomuceno Almonte," reprint from *SWHQ* (July 1944), p. 9.

3. Fannin, letter to Robinson, *PTR*, #2173.

4. Brooks, letter to his mother, *PTR*, #2218; and letter to his father, *PTR*, #2171.

5. Fannin, letter to Robinson, *PTR*, #2182.

6. Urrea, letter to Santa Anna, *PTR*, #2192.

7. Thomas, letter to his father, *PTR*, #2291.

8. Fannin, letter to James Robinson, *PTR*, #2146.

9. Ferguson, letter to his brother, *PTR*, #2219.

10. Fannin, letter to Robinson, *PTR*, #2146.

11. Fannin, letter to Mims, *PTR*, #2195.

12. Brooks, letter to his mother, *PTR*, #2218.

13. Duval, letter to his father, *PTR*, #2279.

14. Fannin, letter to Mims, *PTR*, #2195.

15. Smith, circular to the public, *PTR*, #2189.

16. William Gray, *From Virginia to Texas, 1835* (Houston: The Fletcher Young Publishing Company, 1965), p. 119.

17. Much later, Sherman would erect a one-room log cabin on a bluff near the site of his massacre and call it Mount Vernon.

18. Gray, *From Virginia to Texas,* p. 158–59.

19. Ibid., p. 108.

20. Ibid., pp. 120–21.

21. George L. Rives, *The United States and Mexico, 1821–1848* (New York: Charles Scribner's Sons, 1913), vol. 1, pp. 311, 303.

22. Gray, *From Virginia to Texas,* pp. 124–25.

23. Houston, letter to Collinsworth, *PTR*, #2313.

24. Gray, *From Virginia to Texas,* pp. 126–27.

25. Among people offering land for sale, Antonio Navarro offered five leagues of land (22,140 acres), Francisco Ruiz wanted to sell four leagues (17,752 acres), and Lorenzo de Zavala wished to liquidate eleven leagues (48,708 acres). Ibid., p. 128.

26. Texas Loan, *PTR*, #2510.

27. Constitution of the Republic of Texas, *PTR*, #2347.

28. Gray, *From Virginia to Texas,* pp. 130–32.

29. Travis, letter to the Convention, *PTR*, #2234.

CHAPTER 15

1. Green, letter to Burnley, *PTR,* #2296; and letter to Coleman and Ward, *PTR,* #2297.
2. George L. Rives, *The United States and Mexico, 1821–1848* (New York: Charles Scribner's Sons, 1913), vol. 1, p. 372.
3. For years, runaway slaves and renegade Indians regularly fled to Spanish east Florida to take sanctuary from their pursuers. When Spain refused to sell Florida in 1817, General Gaines received orders authorizing hot pursuit of Indian renegades. Shortly after, General Jackson, who had actively encouraged land speculators to invest in real estate around Pensacola, took over Gaines's command of the southern branch of the U.S. Army. At the head of two thousand men, Jackson crossed the Spanish border, chased Seminoles, and captured the Spanish fort at St. Marks. He dropped the Spanish flag, raised Old Glory, and executed two British subjects, breaching not only international law, but also Gaines's original orders, which specified that Spanish forts were *not* to be attacked. He went on to seize Pensacola. Robert Remini, *Andrew Jackson* (New York: Harper & Row Pub., 1969), pp. 76–86.
4. Cass, letter to Gaines, *PTR,* #1895.
5. Monasterio, letter to Butler, *PTR,* #2323.
6. Butler, letter to Monasterio, *PTR,* #2325.
7. Gaines, letter to Cass, *PTR,* #2473.

CHAPTER 16

1. Juan N. Almonte, "The Private Journal of Juan Nepomuceno Almonte," reprint from *SWHQ* (July 1944), p. 7.
2. Richard G. Santos, *Santa Anna's Campaign Against Texas, 1835–1836* (Salisbury: Documentary Publications, ca. 1968), p. 81.
3. José Enrique de la Peña, *With Santa Anna in Texas* (College Station: Texas A&M University Press, 1975), p. 57.
4. Ibid., p. 79.
5. Vicente Filisola, *The History of the War in Texas* (Austin: Eakin Press, 1985–87), vol. 2, p. 147.
6. Santa Anna, letter to Tornel, *PTR,* #2116.
7. Filisola, *History of the War,* vol. 2, pp. 189–92.
8. De la Peña, *With Santa Anna,* pp. 81–82.
9. Santa Anna fantasized settling Texas with military colonies "such as those established by Russia in Siberia, by England in East India, and even by Spain itself in this country. . . ." Santa Anna, letter to Ramírez y Sesma, *PTR,* #1402.
10. Santa Anna, letter to Tornel, *PTR,* #2116.
11. De la Peña, *With Santa Anna,* p. 99.
12. Santa Anna, letter to Ramírez y Sesma, *PTR,* #1402. A circular issued on December 30 defined the problem—foreigners—and declared the solution—

death. "1st. All foreigners who may land in any port of the republic or who enter it armed and for the purpose of attacking our territory shall be treated and punished as pirates, since they are not subjects of any nation at war with the republic nor do they militate under any recognized flag. 2nd. Foreigners who introduce arms and munitions by land or by sea at any point of the territory now in rebellion against the government of the nation for the purpose of placing such supplies in the hands of its enemies shall be treated and punished likewise." De la Peña, *With Santa Anna,* p. 83.

13. Santa Anna, letter to Ramírez y Sesma, *PTR,* #2204.

14. De la Peña, *With Santa Anna,* p. 83.

15. George L. Rives, *The United States and Mexico, 1821–1848* (New York: Charles Scribner's Sons, 1913), vol. 1, p. 158; John Anthony Caruso, *The Liberators of Mexico* (Gloucester: Peter Smith, 1967), p. 120.

16. Richard Drinnon, *Facing West* (New York: Meridian Press, 1980), p. 111. The *Baltimore Gazette* reminded readers of the Jackson precedent. Regarding Santa Anna's order to execute mercenaries and rebels, it said, "There has never perhaps been a sounder article of international law . . . than that which constitutes a high and capital crime for an individual to levy war upon a government . . . this is the article on which General Jackson relied, when he hung Ambrister and Arbuthnot, when we were at peace with Great Britain." Jerry J. Gaddy, comp., *Texas in Revolt* (Fort Collins: Old Army Press, 1983), p. 18.

17. There were other precedents to consider, especially the practice of paroling prisoners of war after gaining their pledge not to bear arms against their captors. Guided by this principle, the Anglo-Americans had released General Cós in December, and the French would spare another of Santa Anna's generals, Antonio Gaona, at Veracruz in 1838. Rives, *U.S. and Mexico,* vol. 1, p. 439.

18. Filisola, *History of the War,* vol. 2, p. 180.

19. Ibid., p. 198.

20. De la Peña, *With Santa Anna,* p. 44.

21. Francisco Becerra, *A Mexican Sergeant's Recollections of the Alamo and San Jacinto* (Austin: Jenkins Publishing Company, 1980), pp. 25–26.

22. Alicia Viadaurreta Tjarks, "Comparative Demographic Analysis of Texas, 1777–1793" in David J. Weber, *New Spain's Far Northern Frontier* (Albuquerque: University of New Mexico Press, 1979), p. 150.

23. Ramón Caro, "A True Account," in Carlos Eduardo Castañeda, *The Mexican Side of the Texan Revolution* (Austin: Graphic Ideas Incorporated, 1970), p. 110.

24. Santa Anna, "Manifesto," in Castañeda, *The Mexican Side,* p. 13.

25. De la Peña, *With Santa Anna,* pp. 42–45.

26. Captain Fernando Urizza, "Urizza's Account of the Alamo Massacre," in *The Texas Almanac, 1857–1873,* comp. James Day (Waco: Texian Press, 1967), p. 173.

CHAPTER 17

1. José Enrique de la Peña, *With Santa Anna in Texas* (College Station: Texas A&M University Press, 1975), p. 36.
2. John Sutherland, *The Fall of the Alamo* (San Antonio: Naylor Press, 1936), pp. 25–26.
3. Cummings, letter to his father, *PTR, #2088.*
4. Martha Anne Turner, *William Barret Travis* (Waco: Texian Press, 1972), pp. 276–77.
5. Travis wrote: "The spirits of my men are still high although they have had much to depress them . . ." Letter to the Convention, *PTR, #2234.*
6. But Mexican officers were convinced the rebels had very explicitly targeted their president, for artillery fire had struck Santa Anna's headquarters and snipers had reached for him when he had reconnoitered on horseback.
7. Sutherland, *Fall of the Alamo*, p. 31.
8. Travis, letter to Ayres, *PTR, #2233.*
9. Sutherland, *Fall of the Alamo*, p. 36.
10. Juan N. Almonte, "The Private Journal of Juan Nepomuceno Almonte," reprint from *SWHQ* (July 1944), pp. 11–12.
11. De la Peña, *With Santa Anna*, pp. 44–45.
12. Vicente Filisola, *The History of the War in Texas* (Austin: Eakin Press, 1985–87), vol. 2, p. 176.
13. For a wonderful glimpse at how Alamo historians excavate and debate facts of the battle, see Steven G. Kellman, "The Yellow Rose of Texas," *Journal of American Culture* (Summer 1982), pp. 45–48, and the rebutting letters between Kevin R. Young and Philip Haythornthwaite (donated by Young to DRTL, in the Moses Rose file).
14. Rose claimed that Travis scratched his ritual line on March 3. But on that same night John Smith crawled through the Mexican encirclement to bring more help, and Smith never mentioned Travis's line. Nor did the final messenger to leave the Alamo on March 5, a sixteen-year-old boy named James L. Allen, who rode to Fannin with still another plea. Walter Lord, "Myths and Realities of the Alamo," Stephen B. Oates, ed. *The Republic of Texas* (Palo Alto: American West Publishing Company, 1968), p. 23. That would seem to place the drawing of the line on March 5, sometime after Allen left, by which time the situation had grown unbearably desperate.
15. David Crockett, *A Narrative of the Life of David Crockett* (Lincoln: University of Nebraska Press, 1987), p. 74.
16. George L. Rives, *The United States and Mexico, 1821–1848* (New York: Charles Scribner's Sons, 1913), vol. 1, p. 298n.
17. W. P. Zuber, "An Escape from the Alamo," in James Day, comp., *The Texas Almanac, 1857–1873* (Waco: Texian Press, 1967), pp. 691–96.

CHAPTER 18

1. Dilue Rose Harris, "The Reminiscences of Mrs. Dilue Harris," *SWHQ* (1901), p. 161.

2. A few head would continue to graze along Mustang and Chocolate Bayous, and some took sanctuary with ranch cattle into the next decade.

3. Bicentennial Project, *The Alamo Heroes and Their Revolutionary Ancestors* (San Antonio: 1976), p. 48; also from letter from Mrs. Clifford Lewis III, in the Lewis file of the DRTL Defender files.

4. José Enrique de la Peña, *With Santa Anna in Texas* (College Station: Texas A&M University Press, 1975), pp. 62–63.

5. Ibid., pp. 40–45.

6. Santa Anna Order, *PTR*, #2248.

7. James E. Ivey, "Mission to Fortress: The Defenses of the Alamo" (unpublished ms. in the DRTL), p. 22.

8. Ibid., pp. 28–29.

9. Eric von Schmidt, "The Alamo Remembered—From a Painter's Point of View," *Smithsonian* (March 1986), p. 65.

10. See Dennis Hart Mahan, *A Complete Treatise on Field Fortification* (New York: Greenwood Press, 1968), p. 144, for a description of precisely this kind of pre-dawn attack.

11. Joe's account, in the Frankfort *Commonwealth*, 25 May 1836.

12. Robert B. Holtman, *The Napoleonic Revolution* (Philadelphia: J. B. Lippincott Company, 1967), p. 52.

13. De la Peña, *With Santa Anna*, pp. 46–47.

14. Richard G. Santos, *Santa Anna's Campaign Against Texas, 1835–1836* (Salisbury: Documentary Publications, ca. 1968), p. 36.

15. Sánchez Navarro, "A Mexican View of the Texas War," *The Library Chronicle*, vol. 4, no. 2, p. 73.

16. Vicente Filisola, *The History of the War in Texas* (Austin: Eakin Press, 1985–87), vol. 2, pp. 177–178; and Sánchez Navarro, "A Mexican View," p. 72.

17. Tom W. Glaser, "Victory or Death," in Susan Prendergast Schoelwer, ed. *Alamo Images* (Dallas: DeGolyer Library and Southern Methodist University Press, 1985), p. 83.

18. Filisola later criticized the Alamo defense as second-rate. Filisola, *History of the War*, vol. 2, pp. 178–79.

19. Lester R. Dillon, Jr., "American Artillery in the Mexican War, 1846–1848," *Military History*, vol. 11, no. 1, p. 25n.

20. De la Peña, *With Santa Anna*, pp. 48–50.

21. Sánchez Navarro, "A Mexican View," p. 73.

22. Decimation—the loss of one out of every ten men—was a normal formula for the breakdown of morale and for certain retreat. Glaser, "Victory or Death,"

p. 97. Even if a conservative sum of three hundred were lost outside the north wall, the casualty rate for the seventeen hundred troops of the combined first, second, third, and fifth columns approached almost one in five, or twice the decimation formula.

23. Sánchez Navarro, "A Mexican View," pp. 62–64.

24. Colonel Morales stopped his men from firing on their own troops, but other Mexicans continued killing Mexicans.

25. For years to come, European-style assaults would continue to use musket fire to demoralize the enemy, while depending on the bayonet to carry the charge.

26. De la Peña, *With Santa Anna,* pp. 50–51.

27. Time has obscured whether it was a Mexican tricolor with the number 1824 (for the federalist Constitution of 1824), or a five-dollar flag Travis had brought with him to the Alamo, or the sky-blue battalion flag brought from New Orleans by the Greys and captured at the Alamo.

28. Like many of the Mexican casualties, he did not die until after the battle was over. Miguel A. Sánchez Lamego, *The Siege and Taking of the Alamo* (Santa Fe: Blue Feather Press, 1968), p. 38.

29. Only a few brief hours later, Santa Anna would send the captured flag of the New Orleans Greys to Mexico City as proof of U.S. involvement in the rebellion. It remains there to the present, a trophy of what Mexico called the War with Texas.

30. There the garrison had arranged its second line of defense, digging trenches in the dirt floors of their rooms, reinforcing some of the doors, building semi-circular barricades of rawhide "curtains" and rammed earth within other doorways.

31. Reuben M. Potter, *The Fall of the Alamo,* Charles Grosvenor, ed. (Hillsdale: Otterden Press, 1977), pp. 14–15.

32. Enrique Esparza, "The Alamo's Only Survivor," San Antonio *Express,* 12 May 1907.

33. J. M. Morphis, *History of Texas* (New York: United States Publishing Company, 1875), p. 176; San Antonio *Express,* 27 April 1881; and mentioned in William Parker letter, *PTR,* #2923.

34. Edwin Mitchell's brother Warren was soon to die at Goliad.

35. Juana Alsbury, "Mrs. Alsbury's Recollections of the Alamo," in John Ford Papers (Texas University Archives), pp. 122–23.

36. Fernando Urizza, "Urizza's Account of the Alamo Massacre," James Day, comp., *Texas Almanac, 1857–1873* (Waco: Texian Press, 1967), pp. 173–74.

37. J. Frank Dobie, "James Bowie, Big Dealer," *SWHQ* (January 1957), p. 352; John Sutherland, *The Fall of the Alamo* (San Antonio: Naylor Press, 1936), p. 40; Morphis, *History of Texas,* p. 177; and Houston, letter to H. Raguet, *PTR,* #2314.

38. Bicentennial Project, *The Alamo Heroes,* p. 30.

39. Potter, *Fall of the Alamo,* pp. 36–38.

40. Filisola, *History of the War,* vol. 2, p. 181.

41. If the wounded survivor was Warnell, it makes sense that he would have ended up in Nacogdoches. For some time before the autumn uprising, Warnell had worked for Gen. Edward Burleson in or around Mina (current Bastrop), which was only eighty miles east along the Camino Real. Warnell would logically have sought refuge there, and once there might have decided to continue farther along the road to reach a larger population center, Nacogdoches, and greater safety. Wherever it was Warnell died, General Burleson administered the dead soldier's estate.

42. Susannah Dickinson, interviewed by Dean Richardson of St. Marks Episcopal Church circa 1842, in Mary Maverick, *Memoirs of Mary A. Maverick* (San Antonio: Alamo Printing Co., 1921), pp. 135–36; and Morphis, *History of Texas,* p. 176.

43. De la Peña, *With Santa Anna,* p. 116.

44. Frederick Charles Chabot, *With the Makers of San Antonio* (San Antonio: privately published, 1937), pp. 94–95.

45. Filisola, *History of the War,* vol. 2, p. 179.

46. From Dolson letter, in Thomas Lawrence Connelly, "Did David Crockett Surrender at the Alamo," *Journal of Southern History* (August 1960), pp. 369–76; and Dan Kilgore, *How Did Davy Die* (College Station: Texas A&M University Press, 1978), pp. 36–37.

47. Kilgore, *How Did Davy Die,* p. 23.

48. For an excellent table comparing casualty figures with their sources, see Santos, *Santa Anna's Campaign,* p. 79.

49. Ramón Caro, "A True Account," in Carlos Eduardo Castañeda, *The Mexican Side of the Texan Revolution* (Austin: Graphic Ideas Incorporated, 1970), p. 103.

50. Francis Antonio Ruiz, "Fall of the Alamo, and Massacre of Travis and His Brave Associates," in James Day, comp., *Texas Almanac, 1857–1873* (Waco: Texian Press, 1967), pp. 356–57.

51. Musquiz's neutrality resembled a careful dance. On the one hand, toward avoiding "some commotions" with slave-owning Anglo-Americans, Musquiz had declined to publish an antislavery decree in 1829. On the other hand, he had disapproved an Anglo-American "peace" convention in 1832.

52. George L. Rives, *The United States and Mexico, 1821–1846* (New York: Charles Scribner's Sons, 1913), vol. 1, pp. 184–85, 266.

53. Glaser, "Victory or Death," pp. 97–98. Not until 1866 would cremation be reintroduced to the United States.

54. William F. Gray, *From Virginia to Texas, 1835* (Houston: The Fletcher Young Publishing Company, 1965), pp. 136–37.

55. De la Peña, *With Santa Anna,* p. 179n.

56. Ibid., pp. 61–62.

57. Pablo Diaz interviewed by Charles Merritt Barnes, "The Alamo Bones," San Antonio *Express,* 1 July 1906.

58. Account from Columbia, Texas *Telegraph,* 28 March 1837.

59. Adina de Zavala, *History and Legends of the Alamo* (San Antonio: privately printed, 1917), pp. 55–56.

CHAPTER 19

1. Deposition of Barcenas and Bergaras, *PTR,* #2292.

2. Houston, letter to Fannin, *PTR,* #2303.

3. Houston, letter to Fannin, *PTR,* #2301.

4. Houston, letter to Dimmitt, *PTR,* #2307.

5. Houston, letter to Collinsworth, *PTR,* #2328.

6. Santa Anna, circular to the public, *PTR,* #2266.

7. Briscoe, letter to editor, *PTR,* #2501.

8. Hobart Huson, comp., "Reporting Texas," in the DRTL, pp. 81–82.

9. *Columbian Centinel,* 11 May 1836.

10. Paul Andrew Hutton, "Introduction," in Susan Prendergast Schoelwer, *Alamo Images* (Dallas: DeGolyer Library and Southern Methodist University Press, 1985), p. 5.

11. Paul I. Wellman, *The Iron Mistress* (Garden City, N.Y.: Doubleday, 1951).

12. *Columbian Centinel,* 2 March 1836.

13. Benjamin Lundy, *The War in Texas* (Upper Saddle River: Gregg Press, 1970), pp. 32–33.

14. Marquis James, *The Raven* (St. Simon: Mockingbird Books, 1981), p. 228.

15. Michael P. Costeloe, "The Mexican Press of 1836 and the Battle of the Alamo," *SWHQ* (April 1988), pp. 536–39.

16. Vicente Filisola, *The History of the War in Texas* (Austin: Eakin Press, 1985–87), vol. 2, p. 188.

17. Herman Ehrenberg, "Texas und Seine Revolution" (Thesis, University of Texas, ca. 1925), p. 173.

18. Fannin, letter to Horton, *PTR,* #2319; and letter to White, *PTR,* #2320.

19. José Urrea, "Diary of the Military Operations of the Division Which Under His Command Campaigned in Texas," in Carlos Eduardo Castañeda, *The Mexican Side of the Texas Revolution* (Austin: Graphic Ideas Incorporated, 1970), pp. 226–230.

20. Joseph H. Barnard, *A Composite of Known Versions of the Journal of Dr. Joseph H. Barnard* (Refugio: n.p., 1949), pp. 19–20.

21. Kathryn Stoner O'Connor, *The Presidio La Bahia del Espiritu Santu de Zuniga, 1721–1846* (Austin: Von Boeckmann-Jones, 1984), p. 128.

22. Barnard, *Journal,* pp. 22–24.

23. Ehrenberg, "Texas," p. 169.

24. Abel Morgan, *An Account of the Battle of Goliad and Fanning's Massacre* (Paducah; n.p., 1847), pp. 5–7.

25. Urrea, "Diary," p. 234.

26. Ehrenberg, "Texas," p. 173.

27. Morgan, *An Account,* p. 8.

28. Barnard, *Journal,* pp. 25–26.

29. Ehrenberg, "Texas," pp. 174–76, 246.

30. Fannin's surrender terms, *PTR, #*2377.

31. Ehrenberg, "Texas," pp. 177–80.

32. Far from finding hundreds of volunteers mustering in Victoria, he had ridden into a town almost barren of people.

33. Ehrenberg, "Texas," pp. 184–85.

34. Ibid., p. 193.

35. Santa Anna, letter to Urrea, *PTR, #*2408.

36. George L. Rives, *The United States and Mexico, 1821–1848* (New York: Charles Scribner's Sons, 1913), vol. 1, p. 333n.

37. José Enrique de la Peña, *With Santa Anna in Texas* (College Station: Texas A&M University Press, 1975), pp. 85–86.

38. Urrea, "Diary," p. 244n.

39. Ehrenberg, "Texas," pp. 196–203.

40. Barnard, *Journal,* p. 32.

41. Ibid., p. 32; and Kevin Young, *Texas Forgotten Heroes* (Goliad: Goliad County Historical Commission, 1986), p. 5.

42. Joseph H. Spohn's account, in O'Connor, *The Presidio La Bahia,* pp. 142–145; De la Peña, *With Santa Anna,* p. 90.

43. Barnard, *Journal,* pp. 34–35.

44. De la Peña, *With Santa Anna,* p. 92.

45. Morgan, *An Account,* pp. 12–13.

46. De la Peña, *With Santa Anna,* p. 92.

47. José Juan Sánchez Navarro, "A Mexican View of the Texas War," *The Library Chronicle* vol. 4, no. 2; p. 62.

48. Barnard, *Journal,* pp. 38–39.

CHAPTER 20

1. Four of the better accounts of the Runaway Scrape are: Harris, "The Reminiscences of Mrs. Dilue Rose Harris"; William F. Gray, *From Virginia to Texas, 1835* (Houston: The Fletcher Young Publishing Company, 1965); Helm, *Scraps from Texas History;* and Ann Raney Coleman, *Victorian Lady on the Texas Frontier,* C. Richard King, ed. (Norman: University of Oklahoma Press, 1971).

2. Gray, *From Virginia to Texas,* p. 169.

3. Harris, "The Reminiscences," p. 169.

4. Noah Smithwick, *The Evolution of a State or Recollections of Old Texas Days* (Austin: University of Texas Press, 1983), p. 90.

5. From the Dolphin Ward Floyd file in the DRTL, Defenders Collection; also, Robert Hancock Hunter, *The Narrative of Robert Hancock Hunter* (Austin: Encino Press, 1966), pp. 21–23.

6. From the transcript of a letter by family members James and Jonathon Brown, June 11, 1945, in James George file in DRTL, Defenders Collection.

7. Hunter, *Narrative,* pp. 11–13.

8. Mary S. Helm, *Scraps of Early Texas History* (Austin: B. R. Warner & Company, 1884), pp. 13–14.

9. Gray, *From Virginia to Texas,* pp. 134–35.

10. Ibid., p. 144.

11. Ibid., p. 170.

12. Herman Ehrenberg, "Texas und Seine Revolution" (Thesis, University of Texas, ca. 1925), pp. 160–61.

13. Hobart Huson, comp., "Reporting Texas," in the DRTL, p. 100.

14. Gray, *From Virginia to Texas,* p. 162.

15. J. Frank Dobie, "James Bowie, Big Dealer," *SWHQ* (January 1957), p. 352.

16. Huson, "Reporting Texas," p. 95.

17. Smithwick, *Evolution of a State,* p. 91.

18. Sam Houston, "Campaign of 1836, and Its Termination in the Battle of San Jacinto," in James M. Day, comp., *The Texas Almanac, 1857–1873* (Waco: Texian Press, 1967), p. 271.

19. Houston, letter to Rusk, *PTR, #2475.*

20. Perry, letter to Potter, *PTR, #2676.*

21. Burnet, letter to Rusk, *PTR, #2724.*

22. Houston, letter to Rusk, *PTR, #2475.*

23. Gaines, letter to Cass, *PTR, #2638.*

24. Houston, letter to Raguet, *PTR, #2623.*

25. As Santa Anna drew closer, informed rebels took more and more consolation in Gaines's close presence. "Genl Gains [*sic*] left here [New Orleans] last evening to take command of 1200 men at Fort Jessup," said Henry Austin, a lawyer, land speculator, and cousin of Stephen Austin. "Rumor says he said he was going to Texas to command the army so soon as I raise Money. . . ." Austin, letter to Holley, *PTR, #2460.*

26. Gaines, letter to the Governors, *PTR, #2639.*

27. Cass, letter to Gaines, *PTR, #1895.*

28. Gaines, letter to Cass, *PTR, #2638.*

29. Amos Kendall, Postmaster General, in Joseph Milton Nance, *After San Jacinto* (Austin: University of Texas Press, 1963), p. 25.

30. George L. Rives, *The United States and Mexico, 1821–1848* (New York: Charles Scribner's Sons, 1913), vol. 1, p. 375. Ten years later, Gaines would again call up state militiamen for an invasion of Mexico. The difference was that by 1846, the old patriot was considered a liability; he was relieved of command and sent north (vol. 2, pp. 248–49).

31. Walter Prescott Webb, ed., *The Handbook of Texas* (Austin: Texas State Historical Association, 1952), vol. 2, p. 154. Around the same time Mason took employment with the land company, Sam Houston was also being considered for a role as company agent; after the revolution, Houston was reportedly employed as an attorney for the company.

32. Ibid., vol. 1, p. 663.

33. Though by treaty the United States was bound to prevent Indians in the United States from warring in Mexico, Mason said that if the Indians in Texas rose up, then Indians in the United States would too. Mason, letter to Gaines, *PTR*, #2529.

34. Mason, letter to Gaines, *PTR*, #2747.

35. Carson, letter to Burnet, *PTR*, #2755.

36. Green, letter to Bowie, *PTR*, #2671.

37. Deposition of Cortinez, *PTR*, #2726.

38. Bonnell, letter to Gaines, *PTR*, #2804.

39. Quitman, letter to Houston, *PTR*, #2775.

40. Gaines, letter to the secretary of war, *PTR*, #2807.

41. Smithwick, *Evolution of a State*, p. 93.

42. When Gaines sent a U.S. army officer to fetch the troops back to regular duty, Houston shrugged and reckoned that the men could go if they wished, but he lacked authority to send them back. Benjamin Lundy, *The War in Texas* (Upper Saddle River: Gregg Press, 1970), p. 29n.

43. Juan N. Almonte, "The Private Journal of Juan Nepomuceno Almonte," reprint from *SWHQ* (July 1944), p. 15.

44. Tornel, decree, *PTR*, #2763.

45. José Juan Sánchez Navarro, *La Guerra de Tejas*, ed. Carlos Sánchez Navarro (Mexico City: Editorial Polis, 1938), pp. 155–56.

46. " 'Urrea does everything,' [Santa Anna and his other generals] would cry out, 'he alone has the glory, while we just sit watching his victories.' " José Enrique de la Peña, *With Santa Anna in Texas* (College Station: Texas A&M University Press, 1975), p. 81.

47. Ramón Caro, "A True Account," in Carlos Eduardo Castañeda, *The Mexican Side of the Texan Revolution* (Austin: Graphic Ideas Incorporated, 1970), p. 110.

48. Vicente Filisola, *The History of the War in Texas* (Austin: Eakin Press, 1985–87), vol. 2, pp. 210–11.

49. José Enrique de la Peña, *With Santa Anna in Texas* (College Station: Texas A&M University Press, 1975), pp. 102–105.

50. Houston, "Campaign of 1836," *Texas Almanac*, p. 270.

51. De la Peña, *With Santa Anna*, pp. 99–126; and Filisola, *History of the War*, vol. 2, p. 207.

52. For example, on April 14 Urrea liberated fourteen Negro slaves and their families. José Urrea, "Diary," in Castañeda, *The Mexican Side*, p. 246.

53. Vicente Filisola, "Representation to the Supreme Government with Notes on His Operations as General-in-Chief of the Army of Texas," in Castañeda, *The Mexican Side*, p. 238.

54. Ibid., pp. 250–51.

55. Ehrenberg, "Texas," pp. 283–84.

56. Santa Anna, letter to Filisola, *PTR*, #2749.

57. The *Telegraph and Texas Register* was owned and edited by Gail Borden, who would go on to invent condensed milk.

58. Santa Anna, "Manifesto," in Castañeda, *The Mexican Side*, p. 74–75.

59. At one point, Houston averted Lamar and Sherman's coup attempts by pegging notices to hickory trees near their tents, threatening to fill them with mutineers. N. D. Labadie, "San Jacinto Campaign," in James Day, comp., *Texas Almanac*, p. 150.

60. Hunter, *Narrative*, pp. 14–16.

61. James L. Haley, *Texas* (Garden City, N.Y.: Doubleday & Co., 1985), p. 71.

62. Labadie, "San Jacinto Campaign," *Texas Almanac*, pp. 162–64.

63. Santa Anna later complained that the captured documents gave Houston an intelligence windfall, claiming it led to his defeat. Santa Anna, "Manifesto," in Castañeda, *The Mexican Side*, p. 31.

64. Houston, letter to Raguet, *PTR*, #2801.

65. Transcript of Moses Austin Bryan letter to Cordelia Fisk, May 26, 1880, in DRTL.

66. Robert B. Holtman, *The Napoleonic Revolution* (Philadelphia: J. B. Lippincott Company, 1967), p. 48.

67. Anonymous letter to unknown, *PTR*, #2949.

68. Delgado, "Mexican Account," in James Day, comp., *Texas Almanac*, pp. 616–17.

69. Santa Anna, "General Santa Anna's Official Report," *The Battle of San Jacinto* (Houston: Union National Bank, 1936), p. 31.

70. Marquis James, *The Raven* (St. Simon: Mockingbird Books, 1981), p. 206.

71. Alfonso Steele, *The Biography of Alfonso Steele* (n.p., n.d.), p. 5.

72. Huson, "Reporting Texas," pp. 128–29.

73. David Nevin, *The Texans* (New York: Time-Life Books, 1975), pp. 139–41.

74. Sylvia Van Voast Ferris, *Scalpels and Sabers* (Austin: Eakin Press, 1985), p. 75.

75. "Account of the Capture of Santa Anna," in James Day, comp., *Texas Almanac*, p. 243; and Filisola, *History of the War*, pp. 225–26.

76. Moses Austin Bryan, letter to General S. Sherman, July 1, 1859, in *The Battle of San Jacinto* (Houston: Union National Bank, 1936), p. 32.

77. Wilfrid Hardy Callcott, *Santa Anna* (Hamden: Archon Books, 1964), p. 139.

78. Sam Houston Dixon and Louis Wiltz Kemp, *The Heroes of San Jacinto* (Houston: Anson Jones Press, 1932), p. 241.

79. Houston, "The 1836 Campaign," *Texas Almanac*, pp. 288–89.

80. Caro, "A True Account," p. 127.

81. R. B. Blake, *Sidelights of San Jacinto* (Austin: Texas Highway Dept., n.d.), vol. 2, p. 14.

82. Keith C. Wilbur, *Revolutionary Medicine* (Chester: Globe Pequot Press, 1980), pp. 52–53.

83. De la Peña, *With Santa Anna*, p. 124.

84. John J. Linn, *Reminiscences of Fifty Years in Texas* (New York: D. & J. Sadlier & Co., 1883), p. 264.

CHAPTER 21

1. George L. Rives, *The United States and Mexico, 1821–1848* (New York: Charles Scribner's Sons, 1913), vol. 1, pp. 385–86.

2. Gaines, letter to the secretary of war, *PTR*, #3016.

3. Marquis James, *The Raven* (St. Simon: Mockingbird Books, 1981), p. 219.

4. John Quincy Adams, *Memoirs of John Quincy Adams* (Philadelphia: J. B. Lippincott & Co., 1876), vol. 9, p. 282.

5. "Never have I seen greater surprise, nor more indecent joy than that which the news produced in these people, who believed it implicitly as an article of faith without stopping to examine its origin, circumstances and the numerous contradictions," said the shocked Mexican minister to the United States, Manuel Gorostiza. "Men and women, large and small, educated and ignorant, all congratulated each other as though their own salvations were involved, and they all felt that now they could freely express their own hatred of Mexico. On that day nothing else was talked of in the Senate and certainly the expressions employed were not those due to the decorum and gravity of that body." Wilfrid Hardy Callcott, *Santa Anna* (Hamden: Archon Books, 1964), pp. 147–48.

6. Adams, *Memoirs*, vol. 9, p. 289; Rives, *U.S. and Mexico*, vol. 1, p. 388.

7. Rives, *U.S. and Mexico*, vol. 1, p. 387–88. Anglo-Americans labored to justify the seizure of territory from a sovereign nation. Stephen Austin begged the issue. What was occurring in Texas was "a national war in reality . . . a national war sub rosa. This will not do; this state of the matter can not, ought [not] to continue. Make it at once and above board and boldly what it is in fact, a national war in defense of national rights, interests and principles and of Americans." Austin, letter to Jackson, *PTR*, #2764.

8. On the Senate floor, Thomas Hart Benton went so far as to compare Sam Houston to Mark Antony.

9. James, *Raven,* pp. 214–15.

10. According to Houston's plan, he would subjugate Mexico once and for all, expand U.S. territory, prevent the brewing Civil War, and possibly become president of the United States.

11. Rollin G. Osterweis, *Romanticism and Nationalism in the Old South* (Gloucester: Peter Smith, 1964), pp. 183–84.

12. Mexican losses in the Siege of Béxar, the Alamo siege, the Coleto Creek fight with Fannin, and the San Jacinto debacle totaled fourteen hundred or more, double the number of Anglo-American mortalities. By far the worst of the Mexican casualties had occurred under the direct command of Santa Anna, and his capture was seen as a blessing in disguise by some Mexican officers. José Enrique de la Peña, *With Santa Anna in Texas* (College Station: Texas A&M University Press, 1975), p. 161.

13. Ibid., p. 178.

14. Ibid., pp. 134–40.

15. Ibid., pp. 171–74.

16. Ibid., p. 179n.

17. Ibid., p. 185.

18. T. R. Fehrenbach, *Lone Star* (New York: American Legacy Press, 1983), p. 234.

19. Dilue Rose Harris, "The Reminiscences of Mrs. Dilue Harris," *Texas State Historical Association* (January 1901), pp. 168–77.

20. Herman Ehrenberg, "Texas und Seine Revolution" (Thesis, University of Texas, ca. 1925), pp. 336–37.

21. Frederic Leclerc, *Texas and Its Revolution* (Houston: Anson Jones Press, 1950), p. 27.

22. Edward Stiff, *The Texan Emigrant* (Cincinnati: George Conclin, 1840).

23. Nancy Nichols Barker, ed., *The French Legation in Texas* (Austin: Texas State Historical Association, 1971), p. 69.

24. James Winston, "Kentucky and the Independence of Texas," *SWHQ* (July 1912), p. 50.

25. The Republic started out $1.25 million in debt, and within five years was $7 million in debt. David Eason Wood, "Economic Development of Texas, 1820–1860," (Master's thesis, 1940).

26. Rives, *U.S. and Mexico,* vol. 1, pp. 394–97.

27. In the United States, public land sales had risen from $2 million in 1830 to $24 million in 1836.

28. Arthur S. Link et al., *The American People* (Arlington Heights: AHM Publishing Company, 1981), pp. 339–40.

29. Andrew Forest Muir, *Texas in 1837* (Austin: University of Texas Press, 1958), pp. 165–67.

30. A number of mercenaries returned home complaining that the Texan masses were animated by a desire to plunder, that the Cabinet was corrupt and imbecile, and that the Texas army was full up with mercenaries. Winston, "Kentucky," pp. 45–46; and James Winston, "Virginia and the Independence of Texas," *SWHQ* (January 1913), p. 277n.

31. Anonymous, *Texas in 1840, Or the Emigrant's Guide to the New Republic* (New York: Arno Press, 1973), p. 268.

32. Wood, "Economic Development," p. 34.

33. Marilyn McAdams Sibley, *Travelers in Texas* (Austin: University of Texas Press, 1967), p. 93.

34. T. R. Fehrenback, *Lone Star* (New York: American Legacy Press, 1983), pp. 287–88.

35. Anonymous, *Texas in 1840*, pp. 227–28.

36. Lorenzo de Zavala, *Journey to the United States* (Austin: Shoal Creek Publishers, 1980), p. xvi.

37. These and other refugees from the Anglo-American takeover found sanctuary at the nearby Carlos Rancho. But in 1842, maddened by a mini-invasion of San Antonio by the Mexican army, local Texans razed the ranch. The refugees were expelled from Texas. Arnoldo De León, *They Called Them Greasers* (Austin: University of Texas Press, 1983), pp. 77–78.

38. Ruben Rendon Lozano, *Viva Tejas* (San Antonio: Alamo Press, 1985), p. 43.

39. Juan Seguín, "Personal Memoirs of John N. Seguín from the Year 1834," in *Northern Mexico on the Verge of the United States Invasion*, ed. David J. Weber (New York: Arno Press, 1976), p. 19.

40. Seguín, "Personal Memoirs," pp. 25–27.

41. Joseph Milton Nance, *After San Jacinto* (Austin: University of Texas Press, 1963), p. 29.

42. John Russell Bartlett, *Personal Narrative of Explorations and Incidents in Texas, New Mexico, California, Sonora, and Chihuahua* (New York: D. Appleton, 1854), pp. 42–43.

43. Charles Spurlin, "Camp Life of Texas Volunteers in the Mexican War," *Military History of Texas and the Southwest*, vol. 15, no. 4, p. 43.

44. James, *Raven*, pp. 223–24.

45. Ibid., p. 266.

46. In 1841 and 1842, small armies of War Dogs attacked Mier and moved on Santa Fe, only to be captured and either shot or imprisoned in Perote Prison, above Santa Anna's beloved Jalapa.

47. Andrew J. Sowell, *Early Settlers and Indian Fighters* (Austin: Ben C. Jones, 1900), p. 31.

48. Barnard, *Journal*, pp. 43–45.

49. Donald E. Everett, *San Antonio* (San Antonio: Trinity University Press, 1979), p. 18.

50. James Wilson Nichols, *Now You Hear My Horn* (Austin: University of Texas Press, 1967), pp. 13–14.

51. Kevin Young, "Major Babbitt and the Alamo Hump," *Military Images* (July/August 1984), pp. 16–17.

52. William Corner, *San Antonio de Béxar* (San Antonio: Bainbridge and Corner, 1890), p. 11.

53. Susan Prendergast Schoelwer, "Search for the Alamo," ed. Schoelwer *Alamo Images* (Dallas: DeGolyer Library and Southern Methodist University Press, 1985), p. 41.

54. William Bollaert, *William Bollaert's Texas* (Norman: University of Oklahoma Press, 1956), pp. 223–24.

55. Corner, *San Antonio,* pp. 117–19.

56. Sowell, *Early Settlers,* p. 30; and Webb, *Texas Handbook,* vol. 1, pp. 808–9.

57. Walter Prescott Webb, *The Texas Handbook* (Austin: University of Texas Press, 1952), vol. 2, pp. 691–92.

58. W. P. Zuber, "An Escape from the Alamo," in James M. Day, comp., *The Texas Almanac, 1857–1873* (Waco: Texian Press, 1967), p. 696.

59. Steven G. Kellman, "The Yellow Rose of Texas," *Journal of American Culture* (Summer 1982), pp. 45–48; L. P. Teer, "Was There a Coward at the Alamo?" *Frontier Times* (October/November 1965); pp. 14–16, 54–55.

60. R. B. Blake, "A Vindication of Rose and His Story," in *In the Shadow of History,* ed. Frank Dobie et al., vol. 15 of the *Texas Folklore Society Publications* (Austin: Texas Folklore Society, 1939), pp. 27–41.

61. Sarah Colletti, "Found: Alamo Traitor's Grave," *The Shreveport Times,* 25 May 1975.

62. "$50 Dollar Reward," *Telegraph and Texas Register,* 26 May 1837. It was said that one of Travis's slaves walked from Texas back to Alabama, supposedly even swimming the Mississippi River and breasting his way through other hazards, to carry news of his master's death at the Alamo. This probably was not Joe, however.

63. Richard King, *Susanna Dickinson* (Austin: Shoal Creek Publishers, 1976), pp. 80–83.

64. Ibid., pp. 57–58.

65. Ibid., pp. 63–65.

66. Ibid., pp. 74–75.

67. Ibid., pp. 107–9.

68. Santa Anna, address to the Texan army, *PTR,* #3251.

69. Hunt, letter to the Texan government, *PTR,* #3273.

70. Sylvia Van Voast Ferris, *Scalpels and Sabers* (Austin: Eakin Press, 1985), p. 75.

71. Kenneth Reuben Durham, *Santa Anna: Prisoner of War in Texas* (Paris: Wright Press, 1986), p. 59.

72. Ibid., p. 71.

73. Scott was being court-martialed for his misconduct in a Florida campaign. A decade later, Santa Anna would be facing Scott in the Mexican War. Oakah L. Jones, *Santa Anna* (New York: Twayne Publishers, 1968), p. 74.

74. Juan N. Almonte, "The Private Journal of Juan Nepomuceno Almonte," reprint from *SWHQ* (July 1944), p. 15.

75. James, *Raven*, p. 228.

76. Callcott, *Santa Anna*, p. 151.

77. Gene Brack, *Mexico Views Manifest Destiny* (Albuquerque: University of New Mexico Press, 1975), p. 97.

78. Frances Calderon de la Barca, *Life in Mexico* (Berkeley: University of California Press, 1982), p. 243.

79. Ibid., p. 426.

80. José María Tornel, "Relations Between Texas, the United States of America, and the Mexican Republic," in Carlos Eduardo Castañeda, *The Mexican Side of the Texan Revolution* (Austin: Graphic Ideas Incorporated, 1970), p. 380. Mexican concerns were not imaginary. The *New Orleans Bee* had called for the complete elimination of the nation of Mexico and her inferior people. Brack, *Mexico Views*, p. 82.

81. Callcott, *Santa Anna*, pp. 154–60.

82. Jones, *Santa Anna*, p. 79.

83. Lesley Byrd Sympson, "Santa Anna's Leg," in *Mexico: From Independence to Revolution*, ed. W. Dirk Raat (Lincoln: University of Nebraska Press, 1982), pp. 60–83; also, Rives, *U.S. and Mexico*, vol. 1, p. 460.

84. Callcott, *Santa Anna*, p. 269.

85. Ibid., p. 186–87.

86. Waddy Thompson, *Recollections of Mexico* (New York: Wiley & Putnam, 1846), p. 60.

87. Callcott, *Santa Anna*, pp. 207–8.

88. Ibid., pp. 212–14.

89. Rodolfo Acuña, *Occupied America* (New York: Harper & Row, 1981), p. 12.

90. José Agustin Balserio et al., *The Americas Look at Each Other* (Coral Gables: University of Miami Press, 1969), p. 51.

91. Link et al., *The American People*, p. 359.

92. The sole grounds for calling the Rio Grande an international boundary was Santa Anna's signature upon the Treaties of Velasco, which he had signed under duress after his capture at San Jacinto ten years earlier, a signature that the Mexican government had instantly disavowed. In fact, so far as Mexico was concerned, all of Texas to the Sabine River still belonged to Mexico.

93. Acuña, *Occupied America*, pp. 15–17.

94. Samuel E. Chamberlain, *My Confessions* (New York: Harper & Row, 1956), pp. 176–77.

95.   It was a curious fact that while Mexico lost 40 percent of her territory in the surrender terms, she sacrificed less than 1 percent of her population. With all of the conquered nation to pick from, the United States took only the least populated regions in northern Mexico. The reason: Southern expansionists did not want to have to extend citizenship privileges upon a whole new set of colored people. Richard Slotkin, *The Fatal Environment* (New York: Atheneum, 1985), pp. 185–87.

96.   Jones, *Santa Anna,* p. 129.

97.   Rives, *U.S. and Mexico,* vol. 2, p. 65; Eduard Harkort, *In Mexican Prisons* (College Station: Texas A&M University Press, 1986), pp. 147–48n.

98.   Webb, *Texas Handbook,* vol. 1, p. 35.

99.   Thomas J. Green, *Journal of the Texian Expedition Against Mier* (New York: Arno Press, 1973), p. 200; and Calderon, *Life in Mexico,* pp. 431–32.

100.   But before he left, Santa Anna made one further, lasting contribution to American heritage besides Mexican land. He had contracted a young American interpreter named James Adams to serve as his secretary while on Staten Island. During that winter, Adams had frequently watched his employer cut and chew slices from some tropical vegetable called "chicle," a sort of substitute for tobacco. Adams persuaded Santa Anna to leave his supply of chicle, to which he added a sweetener and a sugar coat. The result was Chiclets Gum and a fortune for its "inventor." Jones, *Santa Anna,* p. 145.

BIBLIOGRAPHY

PRIMARY SOURCES

UNPUBLISHED MANUSCRIPTS

Bryan, Moses Austin. Transcript of a letter to Cordelia Fisk, May 26, 1880. The Daughters of the Republic of Texas History Research Library, San Antonio.

Huson, Hobart, comp. "Reporting Texas." In the DRTL.

Navarro, José Antonio. Letter to Samuel Williams, September 26, 1833. Translated by John Ogden Leal. The Daughters of the Republic of Texas History Research Library, San Antonio.

CONTEMPORARY NEWSPAPERS

Austin, Texas, *Daily Statesman*

Boston, Massachusetts, *Columbian Centinel*

Boston, Massachusetts, *Daily Centinel and Gazette*

Cincinnati, Ohio, *Republican and Commercial Register*

Columbia, Texas, *Telegraph*

Dover, New Hampshire, *Dover Gazette and Stafford Advertiser*

Fort Worth, Texas, *Fort Worth Gazette*

Frankfort, Kentucky, *Commonwealth*

New York, New York, *The New York Sun*

New York, New York, *The New Yorker*

Manufacturers and Farmers Journal

Mexico City, Mexico, *El Mosquito Mexicano*

Philadelphia, Pennsylvania, *The United States Gazette*

San Antonio, Texas, *Daily Light*

San Antonio, Texas, *Express*

San Felipe de Austin and Columbia, Texas, *Telegraph and Texas Register*

GOVERNMENT DOCUMENTS

Adjutant general's letter concerning the Alamo, 1875–1878. "Testimony of Mrs. Hanning Touching the Alamo Massacre," September 23, 1876. Texas State Archives.

Baptismal records of San Fernando Church, San Antonio, June 24–July 26,

1828. Translated copy at the Daughters of the Republic of Texas History Research Library, San Antonio.

Burials of Santiago Apostolo Church of Monclova, Mexico, September 6–14, 1833. The Daughters of the Republic of Texas History Research Library, San Antonio.

Marriage records of San Fernando Church, San Antonio, January 9–May 12, 1831. Translated copy at the Daughters of the Republic of Texas History Research Library, San Antonio.

Muster rolls. New Orleans Greys at Quintana, October 26, 1835. Archives of adjutant general's office. Copy at the Daughters of the Republic of Texas History Research Library, San Antonio.

Texas State Supreme Court. "Marco Veramendi v. J. H. Hutchins et al." *Cases Argued and Decided in the Supreme Court of the State of Texas,* vol. 48 (1883): 547.

BOOKS AND ARTICLES

Adams, John Quincy. *Memoirs of John Quincy Adams.* Edited by Charles Francis Adams, vol. 9. Philadelphia: J. B. Lippincott Company, 1876.

Almonte, Juan N. "The Private Journal of Juan Nepomuceno Almonte, February 1–April 16, 1836." Reprint from *Southwestern Historical Quarterly* 48, no. 1 (July 1944).

———. "Statistical Report on Texas." *Southwestern Historical Quarterly* 28, no. 3 (January 1925).

Alsbury, Juana. "Mrs. Alsbury's Recollections of the Alamo." An interview, in the *John S. Ford Papers,* pp. 122–24. Texas University Archives.

Austin, Stephen Fuller. *Fugitive Letters: Stephen F. Austin to David G. Burnet.* Compiled by Jacqueline Beretta Tomerlin. San Antonio: Trinity University Press, 1981.

Barnard, Joseph H. *A Composite of Known Versions of the Journal of Dr. Joseph H. Barnard.* Edited by Hobart Huson. Refugio, Tex.: n.p., 1949.

Bartlett, Jon Russell. *Personal Narrative of Explorations and Incidents in Texas, New Mexico, California, Sonora and Chihuahua.* New York: D. Appleton, 1854.

Becerra, Francisco. *A Mexican Sergeant's Recollections of the Alamo and San Jacinto . . . As Told to John S. Ford in 1875.* Austin: Jenkins Publishing Company, 1980.

Berlandier, Jean Louis. *The Indians of Texas in 1830.* Edited by John C. Ewers. Translated by Patricia Reading Leclercq. Washington, D.C.: Smithsonian Institution Press, 1969.

———. *Journey to Mexico During the Years 1826–1834.* 2 vols. Austin: Texas State Historical Association, 1980.

Binkley, William Campbell, ed. *Official Correspondence of the Texas Revolution.* 2 vols. New York: D. Appleton-Century Company, 1936.

Blake, R. B., ed. *Sidelights on the Battle of San Jacinto.* 2 vols. Austin: Texas Highway Dept., n.d.

Bollaert, William. *William Bollaert's Texas.* Edited by W. Eugene Hollon and Ruth Lapham Butler. Norman: University of Oklahoma Press, 1956.

Calderon de la Barca, Frances. *Life in Mexico.* Berkeley: University of California Press, 1982.

Castañeda, Carlos Eduardo. *The Mexican Side of the Texan Revolution by the Chief Mexican Participants.* Austin: Graphic Ideas Incorporated, 1970.

Chabot, Frederick Charles, ed. *Texas Letters.* San Antonio: Yanaguana Society, 1940.

Chamberlain, Samuel E. *My Confessions.* New York: Harper & Row, 1956.

Chevalier, Michel. *Society, Manners and Politics in the United States.* Garden City, N.Y.: Doubleday & Company, 1961.

Clopper, Joseph Chambers. "J. C. Clopper's Journal and Book of Memoranda for 1828." *Texas Historical Association Quarterly,* vol. 13 (1909–1910).

Coleman, Ann Raney. *Victorian Lady on the Texas Frontier.* Edited by C. Richard King. Norman: University of Oklahoma Press, 1971.

Crockett, David. *An Account of Colonel Crockett's Tour to the North and Down East, Etc.* Philadelphia: E. L. Carey and A. Hart, 1835.

———. *Col. Crockett's Exploits and Adventures in Texas.* Philadelphia: T. K. and P. G. Collins, 1836.

———. *A Narrative of the Life of David Crockett of the State of Tennessee, Written by Himself.* Introduction by Paul Andrew Hutton. Lincoln: University of Nebraska Press, 1987.

Day, James M., comp. *The Texas Almanac, 1857–1873.* Waco: Texian Press, 1967.

De la Peña, José Enrique. *With Santa Anna in Texas: A Personal Narrative of the Revolution.* Edited and translated by Carmen Perry. College Station, Tex.: Texas A&M University Press, 1975.

De Shields, James T. *Tall Men with Long Rifles: The Glamorous Story of the Texas Revolution As Told by Captain Creed Taylor.* San Antonio: Naylor Printing Company, 1935.

de Tocqueville, Alexis. *Journey to America.* Edited by J. P. Mayor. Translated by George Lawrence. New Haven: Yale University Press, 1960.

Duval, J. C. *Early Times in Texas.* Austin: H.P.N. Gammel & Co., 1892.

Ehrenberg, Herman. *With Milam and Fannin: Adventures of a German Boy in the Texas Revolution.* Edited by Henry Smith. Dallas: Tardy Publishing Company, 1935.

———. "Texas und Seine Revolution." Translated by E. W. Bartholomae. Thesis, University of Texas, ca. 1925. This is a more tangled translation of *With Milam and Fannin* but contains more material.

Elfer, Maurice. *Madam Candelaria: Unsung Heroine of the Alamo.* Houston: Rein Company, 1933.

Filisola, General Vicente. *Evacuation of Texas*. Waco: Texian Press, 1965.
————. *The History of the War in Texas*. Translated by Wallace Woolsey. 2 vols. Austin: Eakin Press, 1985–87.
Flint, Timothy. *Recollections of the Last Ten Years*. Boston, 1826.
Gaddy, Jerry J., comp. *Texas in Revolt: Contemporary Newspaper Accounts of the Texas Revolution*. Fort Collins, Colo.: Old Army Press, 1983.
Gaillardet, Frederic. *Sketches of Early Texas and Louisiana*. Translated by James L. Shepherd III. Austin: University of Texas Press, 1966.
Gray, William F. *From Virginia to Texas, 1835*. Houston: The Fletcher Young Publishing Company, 1965.
Green, Thomas J. *Journal of the Texian Expedition Against Mier*. New York, Arno Press, 1973.
Gunn, John C. *Gunn's Domestic Medicine: A Facsimile of the First Edition*. Knoxville: University of Tennessee Press, 1986.
Harkort, Eduard. *In Mexican Prisons: The Journal of Eduard Harkort, 1832–1834*. Edited and translated by Louis E. Brister. College Station: Texas A&M University Press, 1986.
Harris, Dilue Rose. "The Reminiscences of Mrs. Dilue Harris." *Texas State Historical Association* vol. 4, no. 3 (January 1901).
Helm, Mary S. *Scraps of Early Texas History*. Austin: B. R. Warner & Company, 1884.
Holley, Mary Austin. *Texas*. Lexington, Ky.: J. Clarke & Company, 1836.
Hunter, Robert Hancock. *The Narrative of Robert Hancock Hunter*. Edited by William D. Wittliff. Austin: Encino Press, 1966.
Irving, Washington. *A Tour on the Prairies*. Oklahoma City: Harlow Publishing Corporation, 1955.
Jenkins, John H., ed. *The Papers of the Texas Revolution, 1835–1836*. 10 vols. Austin: Presidial Press, 1973.
Lamar, Mirabeau B. "Mirabeau B. Lamar's Texas Journal." *Southwestern Historical Quarterly* vol. 64, no. 2 (October 1980) and no. 3 (January 1981).
Leclerc, Frederic. *Texas and Its Revolution*. Houston: Anson Jones Press, 1950.
Leutenegger, Benedict, ed. and trans. *Inventory of the Mission San Antonio de Valero: 1772*. Austin: Texas Historical Commission, 1977.
Linn, John J. *Reminiscences of Fifty Years in Texas*. New York: D.&J. Sadlier & Company, 1883.
Lundy, Benjamin. *The War in Texas*. Upper Saddle River, N.J.: Gregg Press, 1970.
Mahan, Dennis Hart. *A Complete Treatise on Field Fortification*. New York: Greenwood Press, 1968.
Martineau, Harriet. *Society in America*. Gloucester: Peter Smith, 1968.
Maverick, Mary A. *Memoirs of Mary A. Maverick*. Edited by Rena Maverick Green. San Antonio: Alamo Printing Company, 1921.

Maverick, Samuel. *Samuel Maverick, Texan: 1803–1870*. Edited by Rena Maverick Green. San Antonio: 1952.

Meine, Franklin J., ed. *The Crockett Almanacks: Nashville Series, 1835–1838*. Chicago: Caxton Club, 1955.

Menchaca, Antonio. *Memoirs of Antonio Menchaca*. San Antonio: Yanaguana Society, 1937.

Miller, Thomas Lloyd. *Bounty and Donation Land Grants of Texas, 1835–1888*. Austin: University of Texas Press, 1968.

Morgan, Abel. *An Account of the Battle of Goliad and Fannin's Massacre*. Paducah, Ky: n.p., 1847.

Muir, Andrew Forest, ed. *Texas in 1837: An Anonymous, Contemporary Narrative*. Austin: University of Texas Press, 1958.

Navarro, José Antonio. *The Diary of José Antonio Navarro*. Edited by Maria I. Calderon. San Antonio: 1983.

Nichols, James Wilson. *Now You Hear My Horn*. Edited by Catherine W. McDowell. Austin: University of Texas Press, 1967.

Nunez, Felix. "Fall of the Alamo." *The Fort Worth Gazette*, 12 July 1889.

Olmstead, Frederick Law. *Journey Through Texas*. New York: Dix, Edwards and Company, 1857.

Ortega y Gasca, Felipe de. *Contemporary Perspectives of the Old Spanish Missions of San Antonio*. San Antonio: Institute for Intercultural Studies and Research, 1979.

Parker, A. A. *Trip to the West and Texas*. Concord, N.H.: White and Fisher, 1835.

Pike, Zebulon Montgomery. *The Southwestern Expedition*. Edited by Milo Milton Quaife. Chicago: Lakeside Press, 1925.

Pourade, Richard F. *The Sign of the Eagle: A View of Mexico, 1830–1855*. San Diego: Copley Press, 1970.

Rodriguez, José María. *Rodriguez Memoirs of Early Texas*. San Antonio: Standard Printing Company, 1961.

Roemer, Ferdinand. *Texas*. Translated by Oswald Mueller. San Antonio: Standard Press, 1935.

Ruiz, José Francisco. *Report on the Indian Tribes of Texas in 1828*. Edited by John C. Ewers. Translated by Georgette Dorn. New Haven: Yale Library, 1972.

Sánches, José María. "A Trip to Texas in 1828." *Southwestern Historical Quarterly* vol. 29, no. 4 (April 1926).

Sánchez Navarro, José Juan. *La Guerra de Tejas: Memorias de un soldado*. Edited by Carlos Sánchez Navarro. Mexico City: Editorial Polis, 1938.

————. "A Mexican View of the Texas War: Memoirs of a Veteran of the Two Battles of the Alamo." *The Library Chronicle* vol. 4, no. 2.

Santa Anna, Antonio López de. *The Eagle*. Edited by Ann Fears Crawford. Austin: Pemberton Press, 1967.

Seguín, Juan N. *Personal Memoirs of John N. Seguin, From the Year 1834 to the Retreat of General Woll from the City of San Antonio 1842.* San Antonio: Ledger Book and Job Office, 1858.

Smithwick, Noah. *The Evolution of a State or Recollections of Old Texas Days.* Austin: University of Texas Press, 1983.

Steele, Alfonso. *Biography of Private Alfonso Steele.* n.p., n.d. In the DRTL.

Stephens, John Lloyd. *Incidents of Travel in Yucatan.* Vol. 2. Norman: University of Oklahoma Press, 1962.

Sterne, Adolphus. *Hurrah for Texas!* Edited by Archie P. McDonald. Waco: Texian Press, 1969.

Stiff, Edward. *The Texan Emigrant: 1692–1840.* Cincinnati: George Conclin, 1840.

Sutherland, John. *The Fall of the Alamo.* San Antonio: Naylor Press, 1936.

Texas in 1840, or the Emigrants' Guide to the New Republic. New York: Arno Press, 1973.

Thompson, Waddy. *Recollections of Mexico.* New York: Wiley & Putnam, 1846.

Travis, William Barret. *Diary of William Barret Travis: August 30, 1833–June 26, 1834.* Edited by Robert E. Davis. Waco: Texian Press, 1966.

Trollope, Francis. *Domestic Manners of the Americans.* Edited by Donald Smalley. New York: Vintage Books, 1949.

A Visit to Texas. Austin: Steck Co., 1952.

Weber, David J., ed. *Foreigners in Their Native Land: Historical Roots of the Mexican Americans.* Albuquerque: University of New Mexico Press, 1973.

———, ed. *Northern Mexico on the Eve of the United States Invasion: Rare Imprints Concerning California, Arizona, New Mexico and Texas, 1821–1846.* New York: Arno Press, 1976.

———, ed. *Troubles in Texas, 1832: A Tejano Viewpoint from San Antonio.* Translated by Conchita Hassell Winn and David Weber. Dallas: Wind River Press, 1983.

White, Gifford. *1830 Citizens of Texas.* Austin: Eakin Press, 1983.

Zavala, Lorenzo de. *Journey to the United States of North America.* Edited and translated by Wallace Woolsey. Austin: Shoal Creek Publishers, 1980.

Zuber, William Physik. *My Eighty Years in Texas.* Edited by Janis Boyle Mayfield. Austin: University of Texas Press, 1971.

SECONDARY SOURCES

Acuña, Rodolfo. *Occupied America: A History of Chicanos.* New York: Harper & Row, 1981.

Almaraz, Felix D., Jr. *Tragic Cavalier: Governor Manuel Salcedo of Texas, 1808–1813.* Austin: University of Texas Press, 1971.

Anderson, John Q. *Texas Folk Medicine: 1,333 Cures, Remedies, Preventives, and Health Practices.* Austin: Encino Press, 1970.

Baker, Karle Wilson. "Trailing the New Orleans Greys." *Southwest Review* vol. 22, no. 3 (April 1937).

Balserio, José Agustin, and Muna Munoz Lee. *The Americas Look at Each Other*. Coral Gables: University of Miami Press, 1969.

Bancroft, Hubert Howe. *History of Texas and the North Mexican States*. San Francisco: A. L. Bancroft and Company, 1889.

Bannon, John Francis. *The Spanish Borderlands Frontier, 1513–1821*. New York: Holt, Rinehart and Winston, 1970.

Barker, Eugene C. "Finances of the Texas Revolution." *Political Science Quarterly* vol. 19, no. 4 (December 1904).

———. "Land Speculation as a Cause of the Texas Revolution." *Southwestern Historical Quarterly* vol. 10, no. 1 (July 1906).

———. *Life of Stephen F. Austin*. Austin: University of Texas Press, 1985.

———. *Mexico and Texas, 1821–1835*. Dallas: P. L. Turner Co., 1928.

———. "The San Jacinto Campaign." *Quarterly of the Texas State Historical Association* vol. 4, no. 4 (April 1901).

———. "The Tampico Expedition." *Quarterly of the Texas State Historical Association*, vol. 6 (1902–3).

———. "The Texas Revolutionary Army." *Quarterly of the Texas State Historical Association*, vol. 9, no. 4 (April 1906).

Barker, Nancy Nichols. *The French Legation in Texas*. Austin: Texas State Historical Association, 1971.

Barnes, Charles Merritt. *Combats and Conquests of Immortal Heroes*. San Antonio: Guessaz and Ferlet Company, 1910.

Barnes, Thomas C., Thomas H. Naylor, and Charles W. Polzer. *Northern New Spain: A Research Guide*. Tucson: University of Arizona Press, 1981.

Baugh, Virgil E. *Rendezvous at the Alamo: Highlights in the Lives of Bowie, Crockett, and Travis*. Lincoln: University of Nebraska Press, 1985.

Bicentennial Project. *The Alamo Heroes and Their Revolutionary Ancestors*. San Antonio: 1976.

Binkley, William Campbell. *The Expansionist Movement in Texas, 1836–1850*. Berkeley: University of California Press, 1925.

———. *New Spain and the Anglo-American West: Historical Contributions Presented to Herbert Eugene Bolton*. Los Angeles: privately printed, 1932.

———. *The Texas Revolution*. Baton Rouge: Louisiana State University Press, 1952.

Blake, R. B. "A Vindication of Rose and His Story." In *The Shadow of History*, edited by Frank Dobie, Mody C. Boatright, and Harry H. Ransom. Austin: Texas Folk-lore Society, 1939.

Boddie, Mary D. "Thunder on the Brazos: The Outbreak of the Texas Revolution at Fort Velasco, June 26, 1832." Unpublished, ca. 1979. In DRTL.

Boethel, Paul C. *Colonel Amasa Turner, The Gentleman from Lavaca, and Other Captains at San Jacinto*. Austin: Von Boeckmann-Jones, 1963.

Bonham, Milledge L., Jr. "James Butler Bonham: A Consistent Rebel." *Southwestern Historical Quarterly* vol. 35, no. 2 (October 1931).

Brack, Gene. *Mexico Views Manifest Destiny, 1821–1846: An Essay on the Origins of the Mexican War*. Albuquerque: University of New Mexico Press, 1975.

Bradfield, Jane. *RX Take One Cannon; The Gonzalez Come and Take It Cannon of October, 1835*. Shiner, Tex.: Patrick J. Wagner Research and Publishing Co., 1981.

Bradley, Willo Mae Robinson. *The Runaway Scrape of the Texas Revolution*. Stephenville, Tex.: 1983. In DRTL.

Brogan, Evelyn. *James Bowie: A Hero of the Alamo*. San Antonio: Theodore Kunzman, 1922.

Brown, James, and Jonathon Brown. "Notes on James George and Elizabeth George." Letter to Leila Jeffrey, June 11, 1945. In the James George File, Defenders Collection, the Daughters of the Republic of Texas History Research Library, San Antonio.

Buck, Samuel M. *Yanaguana's Successors: The Story of the Canary Islanders' Immigration into Texas in the Eighteenth Century*. Privately published, 1980.

Burke, James Wakefield. *David Crockett: Man Behind the Myth*. Austin: Eakin Press, 1984.

Burkhalter, Lois Wood. *Gideon Lincecum, 1793–1874*. Austin: University of Texas Press, 1965.

Caballero, Romeo Flores. *Counterrevolution: The Role of the Spaniards in the Independence of Mexico, 1804–38*. Translated by Jaime E. Rodriguez. Lincoln: University of Nebraska Press, 1974.

Callcott, Wilfrid Hardy. *Church and State in Mexico, 1822–1857*. Durham, N.C.: Duke University Press, 1926.

———. *Santa Anna: The Story of an Enigma Who Once Was Mexico*. Hamden, Conn.: Archon Books, 1964.

Campbell, T. N. "Journey to Mexico During the Years 1826–1834: A Review." *Southwestern Historical Quarterly* vol. 86, no. 3 (January 1983).

Canales, J. T., ed. *Bits of Texas History in the Melting Pot of America*. Brownsville, Tex.: n.p., 1950.

Caruso, John Anthony. *The Liberators of Mexico*. Gloucester: Peter Smith, 1967.

Castañeda, Carlos Eduardo. *Our Catholic Heritage in Texas, 1519–1836*. Vol. 6 of *The Fight for Freedom*. Austin: Von Boeckmann-Jones, 1936.

Chabot, Frederick Charles. *The Alamo: Altar of Texas Liberty*. San Antonio: Naylor Printing Company, 1931.

———. *The Alamo: Mission, Fortress and Shrine*. San Antonio: The Leake Company, 1935.

———. *With the Makers of San Antonio*. San Antonio: privately published, 1937.

Clark, Thomas Dionysius. *The Rampaging Frontier: Manners and Humor of Pioneer Days in the South and Middle West*. Indianapolis: Bobbs-Merrill, 1939.

Colletti, Sarah. "Found: Alamo Traitor's Grave." *The Shreveport Times*, 25 May 1975.

Connelly, Thomas Lawrence. "Did David Crockett Surrender at the Alamo? A Contemporary Letter." *Journal of Southern History* vol. 26, no. 3 (August 1960).

Connor, Seymour V. *Battles of Texas*. Waco: Texian Press, 1967.

————. *Texas: A History*. Arlington Heights, Ill.: AHM Publishing Company, 1971.

————, and Odie B. Faulk. *North America Divided: The Mexican War, 1846–1848*. New York: Oxford University Press, 1971.

Corner, William. *San Antonio de Bexar: A Guide and History*. San Antonio: Bainbridge and Corner, 1890.

Cortada, James W. *Two Nations over Time: Spain and the U.S., 1776–1976*. Westport, Conn.: Greenwood Press, 1978.

Costeloe, Michael P. "The Mexican Press of 1836 and the Battle of the Alamo." *Southwestern Historical Quarterly* vol. 91, no. 4 (April 1988).

Cox, Isaac J. *The West Florida Controversy, 1798–1813*. Gloucester: Peter Smith, 1967.

Crawford, Ann Fears, and Crystal Sasse Ragsdale. *Women in Texas: Their Lives, Their Experiences, Their Accomplishments*. Burnet, Tex.: Eakin Press, 1982.

Crimmins, M. L. "American Powder's Part in Winning Texas Independence." *Southwestern Historical Quarterly* vol. 52, no. 1 (July 1948).

Crook, Elizabeth. "Notes on the Texas Revolution: A Day by Day Account." Unpublished, kindly loaned to the author.

Crow, John A. *The Epic of Latin America*. Berkeley: University of California Press, 1980.

Cruz, Gilberto Rafael, and James Arthur Irby, eds. *Texas Bibliography: A Manual on History Research Materials*. Austin: Eakin Press, 1982.

Curilla, Richard. "The Degüello." *Alamo Lore and Myth Organization* vol. 3, no. 3 (September 1981).

Curtis, Gregory. "Forgery Texas Style." *Texas Monthly* (March 1989).

Curtis, James C. *Andrew Jackson and the Search for Vindication*. Boston: Little, Brown and Company, 1976.

Daughters of the Republic of Texas, comp. *The Alamo Long Barrack Museum: Convento, Fortress, Museum*. Dallas: Taylor Publishing Company, 1986.

Davenport, Harbert. "The Men of Goliad." *Southwestern Historical Quarterly* vol. 48, no. 1 (July 1939).

Davis, Burke. *Old Hickory: A Life of Andrew Jackson*. New York: Dial Press, 1977.

Davis, James E. *Frontier America 1800–1840: A Comparative Demographic Analysis of the Settlement Process*. Glendale, Calif.: Arthur H. Clark Company, 1977.

Davis, John. "The Texas Revolution: A Day by Day Account." Unpublished, kindly loaned to the author.

Day, James M. *Black Beans and Goose Quills*. Waco: Texian Press, 1970.

De León, Arnoldo. *The Mexican Image in Nineteenth-Century Texas*. Boston: American Press, 1982.

———. *The Tejano Community, 1836–1900*. Albuquerque: University of New Mexico Press, 1982.

———. "Tejanos and the Texas War for Independence: Historiography's Judgment." *New Mexico Historical Review* vol. 61 (April 1986).

———. *They Called Them Greasers: Anglo Attitudes Towards Mexicans in Texas, 1821–1900*. Austin: University of Texas Press, 1983.

De Onis, José. *The United States As Seen by Spanish American Writers: 1776–1890*. New York: Gordian Press, 1975.

Devereaux, Linda Ericson. *Tales from the Old Stone Fort*. Lufkin, Tex.: Pineywood Printing, 1976.

De Voto, Bernard. *The Year of Decision: 1846*. Boston: Little, Brown and Company, 1943.

Dick, Everett. *The Dixie Frontier: A Social History of the Southern Frontier*. New York: Capricorn Books, 1964.

Dillon, Lester R., Jr. "American Artillery in the Mexican War, 1846–1847." *Military History* vol. 11, no. 1.

Dixon, Sam Houston, and Louis Wiltz Kemp. *The Heroes of San Jacinto*. Houston: Anson Jones Press, 1932.

Dobie, J. Frank. "James Bowie, Big Dealer." *Southwestern Historical Quarterly* vol. 60, no. 3 (January 1957).

———. "Rose and His Story of the Alamo." In *The Shadow of History*, edited by J. Frank Dobie, Mody C. Boatright, and Harry H. Ransom. Austin: Texas Folk-lore Society, 1939.

"Document Reveals Possible Survivor of Alamo Massacre." In the *Victoria Advocate*, 18 July 1985. Copy in the Henry Warnell File, Defenders Collection, the Daughters of the Republic of Texas History Research Library, San Antonio.

Douglas, C. L. *James Bowie: The Life of a Bravo*. Dallas: Banks Upshaw and Company, 1944.

Downey, Fairfax. *The Sound of Guns*. New York: D. McKay Company, 1956.

Drinnon, Richard. *Facing West: The Metaphysics of Indian-Hating and Empire-Building*. New York: Meridian Press, 1980.

Dufour, Charles L. *The Mexican War: A Compact History, 1846–1848*. New York: Hawthorn Books, 1968.

Durham, Kenneth Reuben. *Santa Anna: Prisoner of War in Texas*. Paris, Tex.: Wright Press, 1986.

Eaton, Jack D. *Excavations at the Alamo Shrine (Mission San Antonio de Valero)*. San Antonio: Center for Archaeological Research, University of Texas, 1980.

Elliott, Claude. "Alabama and the Texas Revolution." *Southwestern Historical Quarterly* vol. 50, no. 3 (January 1947).

Espy, Jacqueline Runnels. "Notes on Eliel Melton." Letter to Mrs. Boyd, January 27, 1964. In the Eliel Melton File, the Daughters of the Republic of Texas History Research Library, San Antonio.

Everett, Donald E. *San Antonio Legacy*. San Antonio: Trinity University Press, 1979.

Exley, Jo Ella Powell, ed. *Texas Tears and Texas Sunshine*. College Station, Tex.: Texas A&M University Press, 1985.

Fehrenbach, T. R. *Lone Star: A History of Texas and Texans*. New York: American Legacy Press, 1983.

Fenwick, Charles G. *The Neutrality Laws of the United States*. Washington, D.C.: Carnegie Endowment for International Peace, 1913.

Ferris, Sylvia Van Voast. *Scalpels and Sabers: Nineteenth-Century Medicine in Texas*. Austin: Eakin Press, 1985.

Flynn, Jean. *Remember Goliad: James W. Fannin*. Austin: Eakin Press, 1984.

Fox, Anne A., Feris A. Bass, Jr., and Thomas R. Hester. *The Archaeology and History of Alamo Plaza*. San Antonio: Center for Archaeological Research, University of Texas, 1976.

Fox, Daniel E. *Traces of Texas History, Archaeological Evidence of the Past 450 Years*. San Antonio: Corona Publishing Company, 1983.

Friend, Llerena B. *Sam Houston: The Great Designer*. Austin: University of Texas Press, 1985.

Fuqua, Don L. "Notes on Galba Fuqua." Letter to Lois Lentz, October 29, 1975. In the Galba Fuqua File, the Daughters of the Republic of Texas History Research Library, San Antonio.

Garrison, George Pierce. *Texas: A Contest of Civilizations*. Boston, New York: Houghton, Mifflin and Company, 1903.

Garver, Lois. "Benjamin Milam." *Southwestern Historical Quarterly* vol. 38, nos. 2 and 3 (1934).

Gatell, Frank Otto, and John M. McFaul, eds. *Jacksonian America, 1815–1840: New Society, Changing Politics*. Englewood Cliffs, N.J.: Prentice-Hall, 1970.

Gerster, Patrick, and Nicholas Cords. *Myth and Southern History*. Chicago: Rand McNally Publishing Company, 1974.

Gibson, Charles, ed. *The Black Legend: Anti-Spanish Attitudes in the Old World and the New*. New York: Alfred A. Knopf, 1971.

Gilbert, Randal B. "Arms for Revolution and the Republic." *Military History of Texas and the Southwest* vol. 9, no. 3.

Glover, Michael. *The Napoleonic Wars: An Illustrated History: 1792–1815.* New York: Hippocrene Books, 1978.

Goetzmann, William H. *When the Eagle Screamed: The Romantic Horizon in American Diplomacy, 1800–1860.* New York: John Wiley & Sons, 1966.

Goldwert, Marvin. *History As Neurosis: Paternalism and Machismo in Spanish America.* Lanham, Md.: University Press of America, 1980.

Graebner, Norman A. *Empire on the Pacific: A Study in American Continental Expansion.* New York: Ronald Press Company, 1955.

———, ed. *Manifest Destiny.* Indianapolis: Bobbs-Merrill, 1968.

Green, Michael Robert. "Activo Batallon de Tres Villas, February-April, 1836." *Military History of Texas and the Southwest* vol. 14, no. 1.

———. "El Soldado Mexicano, 1832–1836." *Military History of Texas and the Southwest* vol. 13, no. 1.

———. "To The People of Texas & All Americans In the World." *Southwestern Historical Quarterly* vol. 91, no. 4 (April 1988).

Green, Stanley C. *The Mexican Republic: The First Decade, 1823–1832.* Pittsburgh: University of Pittsburgh Press, 1987.

Green, William E. "Remembering the Alamo." *American Heritage* vol. 37, no. 4 (June/July 1986).

Greer, Mary Autry. "Sketch of Father's Life." Transcript of a letter, re: Micajah Autry, n.d. In the Micajah Autry File, Defenders Collection, the Daughters of the Republic of Texas History Research Library, San Antonio.

Gregory, Jack, and Rennard Strickland. *Sam Houston with the Cherokees, 1829–33.* Austin: University of Texas Press, 1967.

Groneman, Bill. "Crockett's Last Stand." *Alamo Lore and Myth Organization* vol. 4, no. 4 (December 1982).

Guerra, Mary Ann Noonan. *The Alamo.* San Antonio: Alamo Press, 1983.

———. *Alamo Heroes.* San Antonio: Accurate Lithograph and Printing Company, 1981.

———. *The Missions of San Antonio.* San Antonio: Alamo Press, 1982.

Habig, Marion A. *The Alamo Chain of Missions: A History of San Antonio.* Chicago: Franciscan Herald Press, 1968.

———. *The Alamo Mission: San Antonio de Valero, 1718–1793.* Chicago: Franciscan Herald Press, 1968.

Hale, Charles A. *Mexican Liberalism in the Age of Mora, 1821–53.* New Haven: Yale University Press, 1968.

Haley, James L. *Texas: An Album of History.* Garden City, N.Y.: Doubleday & Company, 1985.

Hamill, Hugh M., Jr., ed. *Dictatorship in Spanish America.* New York: Alfred A. Knopf, 1966.

————. *The Hidalgo Revolt: Prelude to Mexican Independence*. Gainesville: University of Florida Press, 1966.

Hardin, Stephen L. "J. C. Neill: The Forgotten Alamo Commander." Paper presented at the Alamo Symposium, San Antonio, March 5, 1989.

————. "A Volley from the Darkness: Sources Regarding the Death of William Barret Travis." *The Alamo Journal* no. 59 (December 1987).

Haring, C. H. *The Spanish Empire in America*. San Diego: Harcourt Brace Jovanovich, Publishers, 1975.

Harris, Helen Willits. "Almonte's Inspection of Texas in 1834." *Southwestern Historical Quarterly* vol. 41, no. 3 (January 1938).

Hauck, Richard B. *Crockett: A Bio-Bibliography*. Westport, Conn.: Greenwood Press, 1982.

Haythornthwaite, Philip. *The Alamo and the War of Texan Independence 1835–36*. London: Osprey Publishing, 1986.

————. "Notes on Moses Rose." Two Letters to Kevin Young, February 2 and 19, 1983. In the Moses Rose File, Defenders Collection, the Daughters of the Republic of Texas History Research Library, San Antonio.

Heale, M. J. "The Role of the Frontier in Jacksonian Politics: David Crockett and the Myth of the Self-Made Man." *The Western Historical Quarterly* vol. 4, no. 4 (October 1973).

Hennessy, Alistair. *The Frontier in Latin American History*. Albuquerque: University of New Mexico Press, 1978.

Henson, Margaret Swett. *Anglo-American Women in Texas, 1820–1850*. Boston: American Press, 1982.

————. *Juan Davis Bradburn: A Reappraisal of the Mexican Commander of Anahuac*. College Station: Texas A&M University Press, 1982.

Hill, Jim Dan. *The Texas Navy: In Forgotten Battles and Shirtsleeve Diplomacy*. Austin: State House Press, 1987.

Hofschroer, Peter. "Flintlocks in Battle." *Military Illustrated* vol. 1, no. 1 (June/July 1986).

Hogan, William R. *The Texas Republic: A Social and Economic History*. Norman: University of Oklahoma Press, 1946.

Holman, David. *Buckskin and Homespun: Frontier Texas Clothing, 1820–1870*. Austin: Wind River Press, 1979.

Holtman, Robert B. *The Napoleonic Revolution*. Philadelphia, J. B. Lippincott Company, 1967.

Horsman, Reginald. *Race and Manifest Destiny: The Origins of American Racial Anglo-Saxonism*. Cambridge: Harvard University Press, 1981.

Houstoun, M. C. *Texas and the Gulf of Mexico: Yachting in the New World*. Philadelphia: G. B. Zieber and Company, 1845.

Humphreys, R. A., and John Lynch. *The Origins of the Latin American Revolutions, 1808–1826*. New York: Alfred A. Knopf, 1965.

Huson, Hobart. "A New Approach to the Teaching of Texas History in Our

Schools and Colleges." *Los Bexarenos Newsletter* vol. 1, no. 1 (February 1985).

Huston, Cleburne. *Deaf Smith: Incredible Texas Spy.* Waco: Texian Press, 1973.

Hutton, Paul Andrew. "Davy Crockett, Still King of the Wild Frontier." *Texas Monthly* (November 1986).

Ivey, James E. "Construction Methods Used at the Alamo." *Alamo Lore and Myth Organization* vol. 4, no. 2 (June 1982).

―――. "The Losoyas and the Texas Revolution." *Alamo Lore and Myth Organization* vol. 4, no. 1 (March 1982).

―――. "Mission to Fortress: The Defenses of the Alamo." Unpublished ms. Copy in DRTL.

―――. "The Problem of the Two Guerreros." *Alamo Lore and Myth Organization* vol. 4, no. 1 (March 1982).

―――. "South Gate and Its Defenses." *Alamo Lore and Myth Organization* vol. 3, no. 4 (December 1981).

―――. "Southwest and Northwest Wall Gun Emplacements." *Alamo Lore and Myth Organization* vol. 3, no. 3 (September 1981).

James, Marquis. *The Raven: A Biography of Sam Houston.* St. Simon, Ga.: Mockingbird Books, 1981.

Jameson, John Franklin. *Privateering and Piracy in the Colonial Period: Illustrative Documents.* New York: Macmillan Publishing Company, 1923.

Jarratt, Rie. *Gutierrez de Lara: Mexican-Texan, The Story of a Creole Hero.* Austin: Creole Texana, 1949.

Jenkins, John H. *Basic Texas Books: An Annotated Bibliography of Selected Works for a Research Library.* Austin: Jenkins Publishing Company, 1983.

Johnson, William Weber. *Heroic Mexico: The Violent Emergence of a Modern Nation.* Garden City, N.Y.: Doubleday & Company, 1968.

Jones, Oakah L., Jr. *Santa Anna.* New York: Twayne Publishers, 1968.

Kellman, Steven G. "Louis (Moses) Rose: Coward?" *Alamo Lore and Myth Organization* vol. 4, no. 3 (September 1982).

―――. "The Yellow Rose of Texas." *Journal of American Culture* vol. 5, no. 2 (Summer 1982).

Kelly, Isabel Truesdell. *Folk Practices in North Mexico.* Austin: University of Texas Press, 1965.

Kemp, Louis Wiltz. *The Signers of the Texas Declaration of Independence.* Houston: Anson Jones Press, 1944.

Kiev, Ari. *Curanderismo: Mexican-American Folk Psychiatry.* New York: Free Press, 1968.

Kilgore, Dan. *How Did Davy Die?* College Station: Texas A&M University Press, 1978.

King, Richard. *Susanna Dickinson, Messenger of the Alamo.* Austin: Shoal Creek Publishers, 1976.

Koury, Michael J. *Arms for Texas: A Study of the Weapons of the Republic of Texas.* Fort Collins: Old Army Press, 1973.

————. "Cannon for Texas: Artillery in the Revolution and the Republic." *Military History of Texas and the Southwest* vol. 10, no. 2 (1972).

Labadie, Joseph H., comp. *La Villita Earthworks: A Preliminary Report of Investigations of Mexican Siege Works at the Battle of the Alamo.* San Antonio: Center for Archaeological Research, University of Texas, 1986.

Lang, James. *Conquest and Commerce: Spain and England in the Americas.* New York: Academic Press, 1975.

Lanier, Sidney. *San Antonio de Béxar.* San Antonio: Bainbridge and Corner, 1980.

Lewis, Mrs. Clifford. "Notes on William Irvine Lewis." In the William Lewis File, the Daughters of the Republic of Texas History Research Library, San Antonio.

Lindsay, Merrill. *The Kentucky Rifle.* Arma Press and the Historical Society of York County, 1972.

Linenthal, Edward Tabor. "A Reservoir of Spiritual Power: Patriotic Faith at the Alamo in the Twentieth Century." *Southwestern Historical Quarterly* vol. 91, no. 4 (April 1988).

Link, Arthur S., et al. *The American People: A History.* Vol. 1. Arlington Heights, Ill.: AHM Publishing Company, 1981.

Lockhart, James, and Stuart B. Schwartz. *Early Latin America.* Cambridge: Cambridge University Press, 1983.

Lofaro, Michael A. *Davy Crockett: The Man, The Legend, The Legacy, 1786–1986.* Knoxville: University of Tennessee Press, 1985.

Looscan, Adele B. "Micajah Autry, A Soldier of the Alamo." *Texas Historical Association Quarterly* vol. 14 (1911).

Lopez, Antonio. *Santa Anna: Revolution and Republic.* Dallas: American Guild Press, 1957.

Lord, Walter. "Myths and Realities of the Alamo." In *The Republic of Texas,* edited by Stephen B. Oates. Palo Alto: American West Publishing Company, 1968.

————. *A Time to Stand.* New York: Pocket Books, 1963.

Lozano, Ruben Rendon. *Viva Tejas: The Story of the Tejanos, The Mexican-Born Patriots of the Texas Revolution.* San Antonio: Alamo Press, 1985.

Lynch, John. *The Spanish American Revolutions, 1808–1826.* New York: W. W. Norton and Company, 1973.

McAlister, Lyle N. *The 'Fuero Militar' in New Spain, 1764–1800.* Gainesville: University of Florida Press, 1957.

McDonald, Archie P. "Anglo vs. Spaniard: Early Conflict." *Military History of Texas and the Southwest* vol. 16, no. 1.

————. *Travis.* Austin: Jenkins Publishing Company, 1976.

McDowell, Catherine, comp. *A Guide to the Texana Holdings of the Texas*

History Library of the Daughters of the Republic of Texas. San Antonio: DRTL Library, 1978.

Mahon, John K. *History of the Militia and the National Guard.* New York: Macmillan Publishing Company, 1983.

Markham, Felix. *Napoleon and the Awakening of Europe.* New York: Collier Books, 1972.

Martin, James C., and Robert Sidney Martin. *Maps of Texas and the Southwest, 1513–1900.* Albuquerque: University of New Mexico Press, 1984.

Meinig, D. W. *Imperial Texas: An Interpretive Essay in Cultural Geography.* Austin: University of Texas Press, 1969.

"Men of the Alamo: Thomas R. Miller." *Seguín Enterprise* (August 4, 11, and 25, 1960).

Merk, Frederick. *History of the Westward Movement.* New York: Alfred A. Knopf, 1978.

————. *Manifest Destiny and Mission in American History: A Reinterpretation.* New York: Alfred A. Knopf, 1963.

Meyers, L. F., ed. *History, Battles and Fall of the Alamo.* San Antonio, 1896.

Meyers, Marvin. *The Jacksonian Persuasion: Politics and Beliefs.* New York: Vintage Books, 1957.

Miller, Robert Ryal. *Mexico: A History.* Norman: University of Oklahoma Press, 1986.

Miller, Thomas E. "Living in the Shadow of the Alamo: The Story of Charles Edward Travis." *Baylor University Report* vol. 11, no. 10 (March 1983).

Mixon, Ruby. "William Barret Travis: His Life and Letters." Master's thesis, University of Texas, 1930.

Moorehead, Max L. *The Presidio: Bastion of the Spanish Borderlands.* Norman: University of Oklahoma Press, 1975.

Morey, Elizabeth May. "Attitude of the Citizens of San Fernando Toward Independence Movements in New Spain, 1811–1813." Master's thesis, University of Texas, 1930.

Morphis, J. M. *History of Texas from Its Discovery and Settlement.* New York: United States Publishing Company, 1875.

Morton, Ohland. *Teran and Texas: A Chapter in Texas-Mexican Relations.* Austin: Texas State Historical Association, 1948.

Muir, Andrew Forest. "Tories in Texas, 1836." *Military History of Texas and the Southwest* vol. 4, no. 2 (Summer 1964).

Myers, John Myers. *The Alamo.* New York: E. P. Dutton and Company, 1973.

Nance, Joseph Milton. *After San Jacinto: The Texas-Mexican Frontier, 1836–1841.* Austin: University of Texas Press, 1963.

Nastair, Abraham P. *Borderland in Retreat: From Spanish Louisiana to the Far Southwest.* Albuquerque: University of New Mexico Press, 1976.

Nevin, David. *The Texans.* New York: Time-Life Books, 1975.

Nevins, Allan, and Henry Steele Commager. *A Pocket History of the United States*. New York: Pocket Books, 1981.

Newell, Chester. *History of the Revolution in Texas*. New York: Arno Press, 1973.

Nixon, Pat Ireland. *A Century of Medicine in San Antonio: The Story of Medicine in Bexar County, Texas*. San Antonio: privately published, 1936.

———. *The Medical Story of Early Texas: 1528–1853*. San Antonio: Mollie Bennett Lupe Memorial Fund, 1946.

Oakes, James. *The Ruling Race: A History of American Slaveholders*. New York: Alfred A. Knopf, 1982.

Oates, Stephen B., ed. *The Republic of Texas*. Palo Alto: American West Publishing Company and Texas State Historical Association, 1968.

O'Connor, Kathryn Stoner. *The Presidio La Bahia del Espiritu Santu de Zuniga, 1721–1846*. Austin: Von Boeckmann-Jones, 1984.

Osterweis, Rollin G. *Romanticism and Nationalism in the Old South*. Gloucester: Peter Smith, 1964.

Paredes, Raymund. "The Origins of Anti-Mexican Sentiment in the United States." *New Directions in Chicano Scholarship* vol. 6 (1977).

Paulding, James Kirke. *The Dutchman's Fireside*. New York: University Publishing Company, 1900.

———. *The Lion of the West*. Edited by James M. Tidwell. Stanford: Stanford University Press, 1954.

———. *Westward Ho! A Tale*. New York: Harper and Brothers, 1845.

Paz, Octavio. *The Labyrinth of Solitude*. Translated by Lysander Kemp, Yara Milos, and Rachel Phillips Belash. New York: Grove Press, 1985.

Pessen, Edward. *Jacksonian America: Society, Personality, and Politics*. Homewood, Ill.: Dorsey Press, 1978.

Pletcher, David M. *The Diplomacy of Annexation: Texas, Oregon and the Mexican War*. Columbia: University of Missouri Press, 1973.

Pohl, James W., and Stephen L. Hardin. "The Military History of the Texas Revolution: An Overview." *Southwestern Historical Quarterly* vol. 89, no. 3 (January 1986).

Pool, William C. *A Historical Atlas of Texas*. Austin: Encino Press, 1975.

Potter, Reuben M. *The Fall of the Alamo: A Reminiscence of the Revolution of Texas*. Edited by Charles Grosvenor. Hillsdale, N.J.: Otterden Press, 1977.

Presley, James. "Santa Anna in Texas: A Mexican Viewpoint." *Southwestern Historical Quarterly* vol. 62, no. 4 (April 1959).

Prucha, Francis Paul. *The Sword of the Republic: The United States Army on the Frontier, 1783–1846*. London: Macmillan Company, 1969.

Raat, W. Dirk, ed. *Mexico: From Independence to Revolution*. Lincoln and London: University of Nebraska Press, 1982.

Reapproaching the Texas Revolution: The Alamo Myth. A four-cassette set of tapes of a symposium, held in November 1985, at the DeGolyer Library, Southern Methodist University, Dallas, Texas.

Reed, Nelson. *The Caste War of Yucatan.* Stanford: Stanford University Press, 1964.

Remini, Robert V. *Andrew Jackson.* New York: Harper & Row, 1966.

———. "Texas Must Be Ours." *American Heritage* vol. 37, no. 2 (February/ March 1986).

Riding, Alan. *Distant Neighbors: A Portrait of the Mexicans.* New York: Alfred A. Knopf, 1985.

Rives, George Lockhart. *The United States and Mexico, 1821–1848.* 2 vols. New York: Charles Scribner's Sons, 1913.

Robbins, Roy M. *Our Landed Heritage: The Public Domain, 1776–1936.* Gloucester: Peter Smith, 1960.

Rohrbough, Malcolm J. *The Land Office Business: The Settlement and Administration of American Public Lands, 1789–1837.* New York: Oxford University Press, 1968.

Rorabaugh, W. J. *The Alcoholic Republic: An American Tradition.* New York: Oxford University Press, 1979.

Rosenberg, Charles. *The Cholera Years: The United States in 1832, 1849, and 1866.* Chicago: University of Chicago Press, 1962.

Rosenthal, Philip. "Notes on Anthony Wolfe." Two Letters dated December 19, 1982 and February 10, 1989. In the Anthony Wolfe File, Defenders Collection, the Daughters of the Republic of Texas History Research Library, San Antonio.

———, and Bill Groneman. *Roll Call at the Alamo.* Fort Collins: Old Army Press, 1985.

Rydjord, John. *Foreign Interest in the Independence of New Spain: An Introduction to the War for Independence.* Durham: Duke University Press, 1935.

Sánchez Lamego, Miguel A. "The Battle of Zacatecas." *Texana* vol. 7, no. 3 (1969).

———. *The Siege and Taking of the Alamo.* Translated by Consuelo Velasco. With comments by J. Hefter. Santa Fe: Blue Feather Press, 1968.

———. *El Soldado Mexicano, 1837–1847: The Mexican Soldier.* Mexico City: Editions Nieto-Brown-Hefter, 1958.

———. *Treinta Contra Cuatrocientos.* Mexico City: Editorial Militar Mexicana, 1966.

Santos, Richard G. *Santa Anna's Campaign Against Texas, 1835–1836.* Salisbury, N.C.: Documentary Publications, ca. 1968.

Scarborough, Jewel Davis. "The Georgia Battalion in the Texas Revolution: A Critical Study." *Southwestern Historical Quarterly* vol. 63, no. 4 (April 1960).

Schlesinger, Arthur M., Jr. *The Age of Jackson.* Boston: Little, Brown and Company, 1945.

Schmidt, Henry C. *The Roots of Lo Mexicano: Self and Society in Mexican Thought, 1900–1934*. College Station: Texas A&M University Press, 1978.

Schmitz, Joseph W. *Texas Culture: In the Days of the Republic, 1836–1846*. San Antonio: Naylor Printing Company, 1960.

Schoelwer, Susan Prendergast, with Tom W. Glaser. *Alamo Images: Changing Perceptions of a Texas Experience*. Dallas: DeGolyer Library and Southern Methodist Mexican Press, 1985.

―――. "The Artist's Alamo: A Reappraisal of Pictorial Evidence, 1836–1850." *Southwestern Historical Quarterly* vol. 91, no. 4 (April 1836).

Schwarz, Ted. *Forgotten Battlefield of the First Texan Revolution: The Battle of Medina, August 18, 1813*. Edited by Robert Thonhoff. Austin: Eakin Press, 1985.

Scott, Sir Walter. *Ivanhoe*. New York: Scholastic Book Services, 1960.

―――. *Waverly*. New York: Leavitt & Allen, 1900.

Sears, Edward S. "The Low Down on Jim Bowie." In *From Hell to Breakfast*, edited by Mody C. Boatright and Donald Day. Dallas: Southern Methodist University Press, 1944.

Shackford, James Atkins. *David Crockett: The Man and the Legend*. Chapel Hill: University of North Carolina Press, 1986.

Sibley, Marilyn McAdams. "The Burial Place of the Alamo Heroes." *Southwestern Historical Quarterly* vol. 70, no. 2 (October 1966).

―――. *Texas Republic: A Political History, 1836–1845*. Austin: University of Texas Press, 1956.

―――. *Travelers in Texas: 1761–1860*. Austin: University of Texas Press, 1967.

Siegel, Stanley. *A Political History of the Texas Republic*. Austin: University of Texas Press, 1956.

Singletary, Otis A. *The Mexican War*. Chicago: University of Chicago Press, 1960.

Slotkin, Richard. *The Fatal Environment: The Myth of the Frontier in the Age of Industrialization, 1800–1890*. New York: Atheneum, 1985.

―――. *Regeneration Through Violence: The Mythology of the American Frontier, 1600–1860*. Middletown, Conn.: Wesleyan University Press, 1973.

Smith, Justin H. *The Annexation of Texas*. New York: Barnes and Noble, 1941.

Smith, Ruby Cumby. "James W. Fannin, Jr., in the Texas Revolution." *Southwestern Historical Quarterly* vol. 23, nos. 2 and 3 (1919).

Soto, Miguel. "Juan N. Almonte Versus Texas: Two Moves Against Texas Independence." Paper presented at the The Alamo Revisited: An Interpretation of the Independence of Texas, a symposium sponsored by Universidad Nacional Autonoma de Mexico, San Antonio, February 7, 1986.

Sowell, A. J. *Early Settlers and Indian Fighters*. Austin: Ben C. Jones, 1900.

―――. *Rangers and Pioneers of Texas*. San Antonio: Shepard Brothers, 1884.

Spurlin, Charles. "American Attitudes in the Mexican-American War." *Military History of Texas and the Southwest* vol. 12, no. 2.

———. "Camp Life of Texas Volunteers in the Mexican War." *Military History of Texas and the Southwest* vol. 15, no. 4.

Steinfeldt, Cecilia. *San Antonio Was: Seen Through a Magic Lantern.* San Antonio: San Antonio Museum Association, 1978.

Stenberg, Richard R. "Jackson, Anthony Butler, and Texas." *Southwestern Social Science Quarterly* vol. 13, no. 3 (December 1932).

———. "Jackson's Neches Claims, 1829–1836." *Southwestern Historical Quarterly* vol. 39, no. 4 (April 1936).

———. "The Texas Schemes of Jackson and Houston, 1829–1836." *Southwestern Social Science Quarterly* vol. 15, no. 3 (December 1934).

Streeter, Thomas W. *Bibliography of Texas, 1795–1845.* Woodbridge, Conn.: Research Publications, 1983.

Strong, Bernice. "Notes on James Bowie's Alleged Children." Letter to L. Tuffly Ellis, June 14, 1984. The Daughters of the Republic of Texas History Research Library, San Antonio.

Stuck, Walter G. *Jose Francisco Ruiz.* San Antonio: Witte Memorial Museum, 1943.

Teer, L. P. "Was There a Coward at the Alamo?" *Frontier Times* vol. 39, no. 6 (October/November 1965).

Thonhoff, Robert H. *The Texas Connection with the American Revolution.* Burnett, Tex.: Eakin Press, 1981.

Thorpe, Raymond W. *Bowie Knife.* Albuquerque: University of New Mexico Press, 1948.

Tijerina, Andrew Anthony. "Tejanos and Texas: The Native Mexicans of Texas, 1820–1850." Ph.D. diss. University of Texas at Austin, 1977.

Timmons, Walter H. *The Anglo-American Advance into Texas, 1810–1830.* Boston: American Press, 1981.

———. *Morelos, Priest, Soldier, Statesman of Mexico.* El Paso: Texas Western Press, 1963.

———. *Tadeo Ortiz: Mexican Colonizer and Reformer.* El Paso: Texas Western Press, 1974.

Tinkle, Lon. *13 Days to Glory.* College Station: Texas A&M University Press, 1985.

Tolbert, Frank X. *The Day of San Jacinto.* New York: McGraw-Hill, 1959.

Toor, Frances. *A Treasury of Mexican Folkways.* New York: Bonanza Books, 1985.

Trotter, Robert T. *Curanderismo, Mexican-American Folk Healing.* Athens: University of Georgia Press, 1981.

Turner, Frederick C. *The Dynamic of Mexican Nationalism.* Chapel Hill: University of North Carolina Press, 1968.

Turner, Martha Anne. *The Life and Times of Jane Long.* Waco: Texian Press, 1969.

———. *William Barret Travis: His Sword and His Pen.* Waco: Texian Press, 1972.

Vigness, David M. *The Revolutionary Decades, 1810–1836.* Austin: Steck-Vaughn Company, 1965.

———. *Spanish Texas, 1519–1810.* Boston: American Press, 1983.

Von Schmidt, Eric. "The Alamo Remembered—From a Painter's Point of View." *Smithsonian* vol. 16, no. 12 (March 1986).

Voss, Frederick S. "The Likenesses of Davy Crockett." *Southwestern Historical Quarterly* vol. 91, no. 4 (April 1986).

Wagner, Patrick J. "Come and Take It Comes Home." *Alamo Lore and Myth Organization* vol. 4, no. 1 (March 1982).

Ward, Forrest E. "Pre-Revolutionary Activity in Brazoria County." *Southwestern Historical Quarterly* vol. 64, no. 2 (October 1960).

Ward, John William. *Andrew Jackson: Symbol for an Age.* New York: Oxford University Press, 1981.

Warren, Harris Gaylord. *The Sword Was Their Passport.* Baton Rouge: Louisiana State University Press, 1943.

Webb, Walter Prescott, ed. *The Handbook of Texas.* 2 vols. Austin: Texas State Historical Association, 1952.

Weber, David J. *The Extranjeros.* Santa Fe: Stagecoach Press, 1967.

———. *The Mexican Frontier, 1821–1846: The American Southwest under Mexico.* Albuquerque: University of New Mexico Press, 1982.

———, ed. *New Spain's Far Northern Frontier: Essays on Spain in the American West, 1540–1821.* Albuquerque: University of New Mexico Press, 1979.

Weinberg, Albert Katz. *Manifest Destiny: A Study of Nationalistic Expansion.* Gloucester: Peter Smith, 1948.

Welter, Rush. *The Mind of America.* New York: Columbia University Press, 1975.

Weniger, Del. *The Explorers' Texas.* Austin: Eakin Press, 1984.

Wharton, Clarence Ray. *El Presidente: A Sketch of the Life of General Santa Anna.* Austin: Gammel's Book Store, 1926.

White, Grace. *Abel Morgan.* San Antonio, 1972.

Wilbur, C. Keith. *Revolutionary Medicine: 1700–1800.* Chester, Conn.: Globe Pequot Press, 1980.

Williams, Amelia W. "A Critical Study of the Siege of the Alamo and of the Personnel of Its Defenders." *Southwestern Historical Quarterly* vol. 36, no. 3 (April 1933) and vol. 37, no. 4 (January 1934).

———. "Notes on Alamo Survivors." *Southwestern Historical Quarterly* vol. 49, no. 4 (April 1946).

Williams, Lawrence D., Jr. *Deaf Smith*. San Antonio, 1964.

Williams, Robert H., Jr. "Travis—A Potential Sam Houston." *Southwestern Historical Quarterly* vol. 40, no. 2 (October 1936).

Wiltshire, Susan Ford. "Sam Houston and the *Iliad*." In *Houston and Crockett: Heroes of Tennessee and Texas, An Anthology,* edited by Herbert L. Harper. Nashville: Tennessee Historical Commission, 1986.

Winston, James E. "Kentucky and the Independence of Texas." *Southwestern Historical Quarterly* vol. 16, no. 1 (July 1912).

———. "Mississippi and the Independence of Texas." *Southwestern Historical Quarterly* vol. 21, no. 1 (July 1917).

———. "New York and the Independence of Texas." *Southwestern Historical Quarterly* vol. 18, no. 4 (April 1915).

———. "Pennsylvania and the Independence of Texas." *Southwestern Historical Quarterly* vol. 17, no. 3 (January 1914).

———. "Virginia and the Independence of Texas." *Southwestern Historical Quarterly* vol. 16, no. 3 (January 1913).

Wood, David Eason. "Economic Development of Texas, 1820–1860." Master's thesis, Sam Houston State Teachers College, 1940.

Wooten, Dudley G. *A Comprehensive History of Texas, 1685–1897.* 2 vols. Dallas: Scarff, 1898.

Worrell, Estelle Ansley. *Early American Costume*. Harrisburg: Stackpole Books, 1975.

Yoakum, H. *History of Texas from Its First Settlement In 1685 to Its Annexation to the United States in 1846.* 2 vols. New York: Redfield, 1856.

Young, Kevin Russell. "A Family of Rebels: Some Notes on the Kin of James Butler Bonham." Unpublished. In the James Bonham File, Defenders Collection, the Daughters of the Republic of Texas History Research Library, San Antonio.

———. "Major Babbitt and the Alamo 'Hump.' " *Military Images* vol. 6 (July/August 1984).

———. *Notes and Related Correspondence Covering the United States Army Quartermasters' Occupation of the Alamo, 1846–1854.* San Antonio, 1984.

———. "Notes on Moses Rose." Letter to Philip Haythornthwaite and Tom Devoe, n.d. In the Moses Rose File, Defenders Collection, the Daughters of the Republic of Texas History Research Library, San Antonio.

———. *Texas Forgotten Heroes*. Goliad, Tex.: Goliad County Historical Commission, 1986.

Zavala, Adina de. *History and Legends of the Alamo and Other Missions in and Around San Antonio*. San Antonio: privately printed, 1917.

INDEX